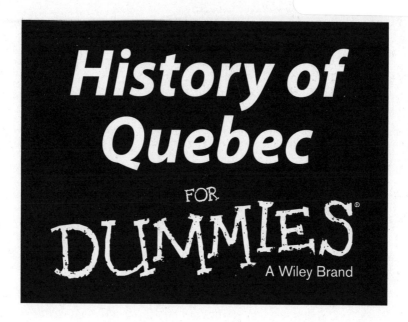

History of Quebec

FOR DUMMIES®

A Wiley Brand

by Éric Bédard, PhD

Foreword by Jacques Lacoursière

FOR DUMMIES®
A Wiley Brand

History of Quebec For Dummies®

Published by
John Wiley & Sons Canada, Ltd.
6045 Freemont Blvd.
Mississauga, Ontario, L5R 4J3

www.wiley.com

For general information on John Wiley & Sons Canada, Ltd., including all books published by John Wiley & Sons, Inc., please contact our Customer Care Department within the Canada at 800-567-4797, outside Canada at 416-646-7992, or fax 416-236-4448. For technical support, please visit www.wiley.com/techsupport.

Wiley publishes in a variety of print and electronic formats and by print-on-demand. Some material included with standard print versions of this book may not be included in e-books or in print-on-demand. If this book refers to media such as a CD or DVD that is not included in the version you purchased, you may download this material at http://booksupport.wiley.com. For more information about Wiley products, visit www.wiley.com.

Library and Archives Canada Cataloguing in Publication

Bédard, Éric, 1969

    History of Quebec for dummies / Éric Bédard.

Includes index.

Translation of: L'histoire du Québec pour les nuls.

Also issued in electronic format.

ISBN 978-1-118-44055-1

    1. Québec (Province) History. I. Title.

FC2911.B4313 2013   971.4   C2013-900799-7

ISBN 978-1-118-44055-1 (pbk); ISBN 978-1-118-43976-0 (ebk); ISBN 978-1-118-43974-6 (ebk); ISBN 978-1-118-43975-3 (ebk)

Manufactured in the United States of America

1 2 3 4 5 RRD 18 17 16 15 14 13

Contents at a Glance

Foreword...*xiii*

Introduction *1*

Part I: New France (1524–1754).............................. 7
Chapter 1: Looking for China — and Finding Quebec! (1524–1610)............................9
Chapter 2: Founding a Colony (1611–1660)...25
Chapter 3: Exploring a Continent (1661–1701)..41
Chapter 4: A French Province (1701–1754) 55

Part II: Conquered but Still Alive (1754–1867) 71
Chapter 5: The Coming of the English (1754–1763) 73
Chapter 6: The American Temptation (1763–1790)..85
Chapter 7: The Birth of Lower Canada and the Parti Canadien (1791–1822) 97
Chapter 8: From the Repression of the Patriotes
   to the Act of Union (1823–1840) 111
Chapter 9: Responsible Government and Religious Awakening (1840–1860)........125
Chapter 10: Confederation (1860–1867)...137

Part III: Survival (1867–1939).............................. 149
Chapter 11: "Riel, Our Brother, Is Dead" (1867–1896)......................................151
Chapter 12: Conscription (1897–1928)...163
Chapter 13: The Depression (1929–1938) 175

Part IV: The Quiet Reconquest (1939–1967) 189
Chapter 14: War (1939–1944) 191
Chapter 15: Le Chef (1944–1959) 203
Chapter 16: The "Quiet Revolution" (1959–1962)..217
Chapter 17: The Reforms Continue (1963–1967) 231

Part V: Province or Country? (1967 to Today) 247

Chapter 18: Revolt (1967–1972) 249
Chapter 19: The Opening of James Bay and the Election
  of the Parti Québécois (1973–1979) 263
Chapter 20: Federalism: A Risk Worth Taking (1980–1987) 279
Chapter 21: Almost a Country (1987–1995) 295
Chapter 22: Balanced Budget and Reasonable Accommodation (1996–2012) 311

Part VI: The Part of Tens 327

Chapter 23: Ten Mythical Personalities 329
Chapter 24: Ten Quebec Symbols 337
Chapter 25: Ten Quebec Landmarks 345

Index 353

Table of Contents

Foreword..*xiii*

Introduction 1
About This Book 2
What You're Not to Read 2
Foolish Assumptions..2
How This Book Is Organized 3
Part I: New France (1524–1754)...3
Part II: Conquered but Still Alive (1754–1867)...........................3
Part III: Survival (1867–1939) 4
Part IV: The Quiet Reconquest (1939–1967)..............................4
Part V: Province or Country? (1967 to Today)............................5
Part VI: The Part of Tens...5
Icons Used in This Book 5
Where to Go from Here 6

Part 1: New France (1524–1754) 7

Chapter 1: Looking for China — and Finding Quebec! (1524–1610) . . .9
Setting Out to Conquer the West...9
Why the Europeans wanted to explore......................................10
Who went where 10
What they found when they arrived: An inhabited New World.....11
France gets into the race 14
Moving toward the Founding of Quebec 18
Focusing on the fur trade..18
Meeting Samuel de Champlain: A true visionary 19
Founding Quebec 21
Consolidating an alliance 23

Chapter 2: Founding a Colony (1611–1660)..25
Hesitant Beginnings...25
Moving into action 25
Luring settlers 28
A New Impetus 31
The Company of One Hundred Associates.................................31
The mystics' adventure 34
The Iroquois threat...36

Chapter 3: Exploring a Continent (1661–1701) **41**

The Decisive Move Forward 41
L'État, c'est moi! (The state, it is I!) 42
A big push 44
Toward the Great Peace of 1701 48
French America 49
War and peace 51

Chapter 4: A French Province (1701–1754) **55**

The Weakening of New France 55
Clashes between England and France 56
The Treaty of Utrecht 58
An Ancien Régime Society 59
A diverse population 60
A struggling economy 63
Day-to-day beliefs 66
War again 68

Part II: Conquered but Still Alive (1754–1867) **71**

Chapter 5: The Coming of the English (1754–1763) **73**

Identifying the Appeal of New France for the English 73
The determination of the Anglo-Americans 74
The English go all out 75
English Conquest, or French Abandonment? 78
The siege of Quebec and the battle of the Plains of Abraham . . . 78
The surrender of Montreal 81
The 1763 Treaty of Paris 82

Chapter 6: The American Temptation (1763–1790) **85**

To Assimilate or to Woo? 86
The Royal Proclamation 86
The Quebec Act 89
The American Revolution 91
The Americans turn angry 91
The American invasion 93
The arrival of the Loyalists 96

Chapter 7: The Birth of Lower Canada
and the Parti Canadien (1791–1822) **97**

Setting Up a Government with the Constitutional Act 98
Their own parliament 98
Language: A hot topic 99

Dampening the Mood of Optimism with War and New Leadership......102
The shadow of the French Revolution.............................102
The emergence of the Parti Canadien.............................104
The crisis of 1810...105
Seeing the British Empire at War and at Peace....................107
A second American invasion......................................107
Pax Britannica...108

**Chapter 8: From the Repression of the Patriotes
to the Act of Union (1823–1840)** **111**

Louis-Joseph Papineau,
Republican Leader..111
The Old World and the New World................................112
Papineau, man of destiny.......................................112
The quarrel over government finances
and the 1832 election...114
A delicate situation...115
The 92 Resolutions and the Russell Resolutions..................116
The Parti Canadien's grievances................................116
Hostility to reform..117
The reaction in London...118
The Patriotes' Defeat and Its Consequences 119
Popular assemblies...119
Brawls and battles...121
The Act of Union of 1840.......................................123

**Chapter 9: Responsible Government and
Religious Awakening (1840–1860)** **125**

Louis-Hippolyte LaFontaine, Reformer...........................125
Avoiding the fate of the Acadians..............................126
Presenting a manifesto to the voters of Terrebonne 126
Discovering the great reform government of 1848................129
A Religious Revival..131
Signs of awakening...131
Ignace Bourget's program.......................................133
Heaven is blue, hell is red!...................................134

Chapter 10: Confederation (1860–1867)......................**137**

Falling Apart in the Province of Canada........................137
Political instability..138
Having to fend for themselves 139
The economy hits a roadblock 140
A Solution: Confederation 142
A draft constitution 142
Supporters and adversaries 145
The British North America Act 147

Part III: Survival (1867–1939) 149

Chapter 11: "Riel, Our Brother, Is Dead" (1867–1896) 151
The Church Grabs Hold of Education.. 152
   Chauveau: Premier by default 152
   The Catholic Program 153
Fighting for Autonomy 155
   Influence peddling — and moderation............................. 155
   The rise of the Liberals 156
Fighting for an Economic Leg to Stand On................................ 158
   Quebec embarks on industrialization 158
   Taking hold of the economy, but how?............................ 161

Chapter 12: Conscription (1897–1928).........................163
Opposing Imperialism... 163
   Laurier's compromises 164
   Henri Bourassa and the nationalist movement............... 165
   The conscription crisis 167
Prosperity through Foreign Capital 170
   Triumph of the free market 170
   The emergence of a modern Quebec state...................... 173

Chapter 13: The Depression (1929–1938) 175
The Effects of the Stock Market Crash...................................... 175
   The defects of the liberal economy................................. 176
   Immediate government reactions..................................... 177
   Whose fault is it?.. 179
The Union Nationale.. 181
   The opposition gets organized 181
   A new regime is installed 184

Part IV: The Quiet Reconquest (1939–1967) 189

Chapter 14: War (1939–1944)..................................191
The Shadow of Conscription... 191
   The election of 1939... 192
   General mobilization 193
   The 1942 vote 195
Godbout the Reformer.. 197
   Women get the vote!... 198
   Compulsory education.. 199
   Economic achievements and federal incursions 200

Chapter 15: Le Chef (1944–1959). **203**

Defending the Established Order 203
    A regime in control 204
    The cold war era 205
    The miners of Asbestos 208
Striving for Autonomy and Development.................................209
    Income tax 209
    Developing Quebec...212
Seeing Impatience Grow 213
    Exasperated moralists...213
    Divided nationalists 214
    The Liberals...215

Chapter 16: The "Quiet Revolution" (1959–1962) **217**

Regime Change...218
    Mourning and succession..218
    A Liberal victory 219
Equal Opportunity...221
    Emphasizing the state over the church 222
    Educating the masses...223
    Healthcare for all 226
Masters in Our Own House 227
    Breaking through the glass ceiling 227
    Completing the nationalization of hydroelectricity 228

Chapter 17: The Reforms Continue (1963–1967) **231**

Fighting Social Exclusion 232
    Women's rights 232
    The very poor...233
    The Caisse de Dépôt et Placement 234
Fighting for the Independence of Quebec 235
    Special status...235
    Birth of the independence movement.................................238
Seeing the Union Nationale Back in Power 240
    Choosing continuity 241
    Equality or independence..243

Part V: Province or Country? (1967 to Today) ***247***

Chapter 18: Revolt (1967–1972). **249**

The Founding of the Parti Québécois 250
    Sovereignty-association 250
    The Saint-Léonard crisis 252

Violence and Radicalization 256
    The October Crisis...256
    Social radicalization 259

Chapter 19: The Opening of James Bay and the Election of the Parti Québécois (1973–1979) 263

From Robert Bourassa to René Lévesque 264
    The James Bay development...264
    French: Quebec's official language 266
The Election of the Parti Québécois 268
    A new step-by-step strategy 269
    The first sovereignist government 271
    The charter of the French language 273
    A blizzard of reforms 276

Chapter 20: Federalism: A Risk Worth Taking (1980–1987)........279

The Parti Québécois's Ordeal 280
    The defeat of the "yes" side..280
    Repatriation of the Canadian constitution 283
Recovery from Recession and Political Impasse.............................286
    Confrontation and cooperation 286
    A changing of the guard in Ottawa and Quebec 289
    The Meech Lake Accord 291

Chapter 21: Almost a Country (1987–1995) 295

Canada in Crisis 295
    A looming failure...296
    Repairing the damage..301
The Second Quebec Sovereignty Referendum 304
    Creation of the camp for change 304
    1995, when everything seemed possible 307

Chapter 22: Balanced Budget and Reasonable Accommodation (1996–2012) 311

The Bouchard Years 311
    The return of "good government" 312
    The constitution: A lull followed by an impasse........................314
Quebec in Search of Itself..317
    Which way for the Quebec model?..318
    The crisis of reasonable accommodation 322
    Right, left, right, left 325
    A woman premier...326

Part VI: The Part of Tens 327

Chapter 23: Ten Mythical Personalities......................329
Maurice Richard and the Riot of 1955.......................................329
Louis Cyr: Strong Man...330
Albani: The Great Singer...330
Céline Dion: International Star...331
Leonard Cohen: The Soothing Voice..332
Émile Nelligan: The Accursed Poet...333
Michel Tremblay: Putting "Joual" on Stage...............................333
Gratien Gélinas...334
Olivier Guimond: A True Comedian 335
Guy Laliberté: A Clown in Space...336

Chapter 24: Ten Quebec Symbols 337
Saint-Jean-Baptiste Day: French Canadian or Québécois Celebration?....337
"Gens du pays": The Unofficial Anthem......................................338
L'homme rapaillé: "I Have Never Traveled Anywhere
    but to You, My Country"...339
The Plouffe Family: A True Québécois Saga................................339
Swearing in Quebec: A Throwback to an Earlier Era? 340
The Arrow Sash: Patriote Symbol...341
Square Dancing: "And Swing Your Partner!".............................342
The Sugar Shack: An Indigenous Heritage.................................342
The Bombardier Ski-Doo...343
The Montreal Canadiens: A Hockey Dynasty.............................344

Chapter 25: Ten Quebec Landmarks 345
The Plains of Abraham and the Battle of Memory 345
Mount Royal: An Extinct Volcano? 346
The Saguenay Fjord and Its "Incredible Depth" 346
Sainte-Anne-de-Beaupré: Sanctuary for the Faithful 347
Île d'Orléans: Birthplace of French America..............................348
The Magdalen Islands: Acadian Refuge after the Deportation 348
The Quebec Citadel: Remains of a Fortified City.......................349
Percé Rock: Gateway to the St. Lawrence 349
Wendake: Last "Reserve" of the Hurons....................................350
Manic-5: The Pride of a Conquering People 351

Index 353

Foreword

*H*istorian Éric Bédard is an academic who knows how to make his subject accessible to everyone, an ability he demonstrates in *History of Quebec For Dummies*. By telling the story chronologically rather than using a thematic approach, he allows readers to "see" the evolution of Quebec, from the French regime to the present. All aspects of Quebec's history are covered. Intended for a mass audience, the book aims for a better understanding of this part of the country that is always in search of itself and that, one day, through experience, will no doubt find its place in the world.

No one who has read *History of Quebec For Dummies* will be able to plead ignorance of the history of this Canadian province, which Canadian Prime Minister Louis Stephen Saint-Laurent described as similar to other provinces. "They say," he declared in September 1954, "that the province of Quebec is not a province like the others. I do not share this opinion." Needless to say, Premier Maurice Duplessis of Quebec did not agree with this statement.

The way Éric Bédard has divided Quebec history into periods will surprise those who are used to thinking of the 1960s and the election of the Liberals under Jean Lesage as the beginning of what is called the "Quiet Revolution." Instead, the author highlights the coming to power of Adélard Godbout, the Liberal premier who held office during World War II and whose achievements, although more or less forgotten today, were notable. The innovative nature of this interpretation is expressed in the title of this part of the book, "The Quiet Reconquest." I agree with Éric Bédard on this point — and, indeed, on his interpretation of Quebec's past as a whole. In my view, as in Bédard's, the stage was set for rapid change to take place starting in 1960. Otherwise, the changes that Quebec would both enact and witness cannot be understood. In the traditional interpretation, it seems that everything changed overnight and Quebec suddenly entered into a new mode of civilization: Education took on a new face and the Catholic religion lost its importance. But these profound changes were in the making for a long time.

The book does not seek to present a sanitized history. You can see that especially in Part V, which asks the question "Province or country?" Here Bédard sets aside his political orientation, knowing full well that historians who openly take a position on the future of Quebec in their work will see their writings discredited. A historian is a prophet — but a prophet who looks to the past! Bédard has taken the wise precaution of avoiding prognostication on the future of Quebec.

Part VI focuses primarily on Quebec's cultural life. Too often in a work of this kind, this aspect is skimmed over or even ignored. But not in *History of Quebec For Dummies.* Bédard looks at a variety of aspects of Quebec culture — including Michel Tremblay's play *Les belles-sœurs,* which caused a scandal in Quebec in the late 1960s, and which continues to resonate with audiences, as the success of its 2012 revival in Paris demonstrates.

Few historians in recent years have ventured to write a comprehensive overview of the history of Quebec. Éric Bédard should be commended for having undertaken this task. He was certainly well prepared to do it. His presence in the media — television, radio, and newspapers — has made him a first-class communicator. You can read his *History of Quebec For Dummies* without running to the dictionary. The absence of footnotes makes the narrative easier to understand — everything is in the text. It follows the usual formula for history books in this series. The text is interspersed with inserts devoted to anecdotes and other specific points. Summaries further enhance the reader's understanding of events.

Congratulations to historian Éric Bédard for bringing Quebec's past to life, a colorful past where hope and despair followed each other in rapid succession. Quebec's motto is *"Je me souviens"* ("I remember"). Reading *History of Quebec For Dummies,* you will find out why it is important to remember, and just what is it that you are remembering.

— Jacques Lacoursière

Historian and member of the Royal Society of Canada

Introduction

"*M*on pays ce n'est pas un pays, c'est l'hiver!*" ("My country is not a country, it's winter"), sang the poet Gilles Vigneault.

Yes, Quebec is winter, snow, cold, piercing January winds. It's the majestic St. Lawrence River and its many tributaries, crisscrossing the American continent. It's the vast forests, the countless lakes, the beautiful countryside of Témiscamingue, Charlevoix, the North Shore, and the Gaspé Peninsula.

It's also Quebec City, the *vieille capitale,* perched above the river on Cap Diamant, its face turned to the shores of Europe. And, of course, Montreal, Quebec's inventive, creative metropolis, the leading French city of the New World, a meeting place and a crossroads of cultures, the nerve center of a young nation.

But most of all, Quebec is a people — brave, stubborn, and determined. A people that, from its first days in the New World, had to be strong-willed, hardy, and courageous to face the rigors of the Quebec winter, clear the land by moonlight, raise large families, explore a vast continent, survive Iroquois attacks and the hostility of the American colonies, and later withstand the greed of wealthy merchants and the turmoils of the Industrial Revolution and the Depression of the 1930s.

This great adventure is the story that's told in the pages that follow. It's a story of resistance and affirmation, marked by resilience and yet haunted by the frustration of having to start over. The story of a people that came through trials and tribulations and overcame dejection and resignation. The story of a dream, the dream of French America, and of the crucible of the British Conquest. Most of all, it's the story of a long and patient reconquest through which Quebecers took back their territory, their economy, and their political life.

Quebec's motto is *"Je me souviens"* ("I remember"). Unfortunately, too many Quebecers seem to look at their past as a demoralizing *"Grande noirceur"* ("great darkness") that holds little of interest for the present and the future. Nothing could be further from the truth. Quebec history is rich, fascinating, and often inspiring, filled with surprising turns and larger-than-life personalities.

This is the story that will unfold as you read this book.

About This Book

In this book, I follow the thread of Quebec's development, identifying the turning points and explaining the underlying forces at work. I tell the story in strict chronological order and provide profiles of the most important personalities. The history of Quebec was made by men and women, people whose ideas were shaped by their time. Did these people, with their passions and their dreams, sometimes make mistakes? Maybe. But my goal is to avoid being too cynical or making hasty moral judgments; instead, I try to understand their actions and explain their decisions.

The history of Quebec is one piece of the history of the world. Its key moments can be explained only in relation to the great discoveries of the 16th century, the Catholic Counterreformation of the 17th century, the geopolitical tensions of the 18th century, the Industrial Revolution of the 19th century, and the world wars of the 20th century, along with the development of the welfare state in the West and the decolonization movement of the 1960s. You can't understand what was happening in Quebec without keeping an eye out for major events taking place in France, Britain, the United States, and other parts of the world.

What You're Not to Read

You can safely skip anything marked by a Technical Stuff icon. (For more on icons, see "Icons Used in This Book," later in this Introduction.)

You can also skip *sidebars,* which are the gray boxes of text. The information in sidebars is interesting, but not absolutely critical to your understanding of the topic at hand.

Foolish Assumptions

I don't make a tremendous amount of assumptions about you, the reader of this book, but I do make a few:

- ✔ You aren't a historical researcher. You're just someone with an interest in the history of Quebec.
- ✔ You may have grown up in Quebec but feel you have a poor knowledge of its history, either because you've forgotten large chunks of what you learned in high school or because you never learned it in the first place.

    ✔ You may have recently moved to Quebec, and you're looking for a better understanding of your new home.

    ✔ You may be traveling to Quebec and want to know the history of what you'll see when you get there.

How This Book Is Organized

History of Quebec For Dummies is divided into seven parts, comprising 25 chapters. Here's an overview of what each part covers.

Part I: New France (1524–1754)

In the earliest part of its history, Quebec was called New France. The young colony sometimes inspired extravagant dreams — dreams of a French and Catholic America. The impressive figures who walked across the stage of New France gave flesh to those dreams: Samuel de Champlain, Marie Guyart, Paul de Chomedey de Maisonneuve, Jeanne Mance, Pierre Le Moyne d'Iberville. In Part I, I explain why France wanted to explore the New World in the 16th century. Before the arrival of the French, what is now Quebec was inhabited by Aboriginal peoples, either nomadic or semi-sedentary. A number of these peoples made alliances with the first French settlers who founded the towns of Quebec and Montreal. I introduce the most important explorers, describe the institutions of New France, and seek to understand why this vast colony was so sparsely populated.

Part II: Conquered but Still Alive (1754–1867)

The Anglo-American colonies had larger populations than New France, and they looked covetously at the Mississippi Valley and France's possessions in North America. In Part II, I recount the main events of the war in which British and American armies conquered New France. After the conquest, the Canadiens of the St. Lawrence Valley were confined to a small reserve called the "Province of Quebec." A few years later, the American colonies, now in revolt against Britain, again cast their eyes on this territory. After the American War of Independence, Quebec became host to the "Loyalists," immigrants from the south who wanted to remain faithful to the British crown and demanded real British institutions, which came into being in 1791. But the domination of these institutions by English merchants was a source of discontent among the French-speaking majority, which established a party that rebelled against the British metropolis in 1837–1838. Repression of these rebellions was followed by the Act of Union and a major religious revival in the mid-19th century.

Part III: Survival (1867–1939)

In 1867, Quebec became a Canadian province. Why did Quebecers agree to this new confederation? What would be the powers of the new province of Quebec? What would be the place of francophones in the new country called Canada? In Part III, I answer these complex questions as simply as possible.

A fundamental event in bringing to light the place of francophones in Canada was the hanging of the Métis leader Louis Riel in 1885. Two important political figures, Honoré Mercier and Wilfrid Laurier, came to power as a result of this event. This was also the period of the Industrial Revolution, which for French Canadians was a time of economic inferiority and large-scale emigration to the United States. This economic inferiority was accentuated by the Depression of the 1930s. While the Quebec government made efforts to bring the Depression to an end, reform movements brought a new party into being.

Part IV: The Quiet Reconquest (1939–1967)

The reform program instituted by the government of Adélard Godbout (1940–1944) and postwar prosperity helped Quebecers regain their confidence and emerge from the long period when their main focus was survival. However, in 1944, they elected a conservative government headed by Maurice Duplessis. Returned to power repeatedly, Duplessis ruled Quebec with an iron hand, fiercely resisted federal intrusion into provincial fields of jurisdiction, brutally repressed strikes, and praised the virtues of rural, traditional Quebec. The election of the *"équipe du tonnerre"* ("hell of a team") in June 1960 was a turning point. A new political generation gave Quebec a healthcare system that provided free medical care and an education system that better prepared Quebecers to meet the challenges of postindustrial society. Above all, it endowed Quebec with a modern state that would make it possible for the French-speaking majority to catch up economically.

Part V: Province or Country? (1967 to Today)

The late 20th century was completely dominated by the debate over Quebec's political status. Some people demanded a thorough reform of Canadian federalism leading to Quebec's recognition as an "associated state" or a "distinct society." Others, who sometimes compared Quebec with Algeria, Cuba, or Vietnam, dreamed of building a sovereign, independent country. A series of political movements and parties took up the cause of Quebec independence. Among these was the Parti Québécois, which came to power in 1976 and held an initial referendum in May 1980, in which Quebecers rejected "sovereignty association." In the wake of the referendum, negotiations began in an effort to achieve greater recognition and respect for Quebecers within Canada. This constitutional saga culminated in the failure of the Meech Lake Accord in June 1990. With English Canadians having rejected Quebec's minimum demands, Quebecers founded a new federal party, the Bloc Québécois, and once again elected the Parti Québécois to form the Quebec government in 1994. The new Parti Québécois government called a second referendum for October 30, 1995, which the No side won by a razor-thin margin. This close call sent a shockwave through the rest of Canada. The question remains unresolved.

Part VI: The Part of Tens

In Part VI, we look in turn at ten personalities, ten symbols, and ten landmarks, all of them expressive of the history of Quebec. Quebec comes alive through some of the dimensions of its popular heroes, its culture, and its geography. Why do Quebecers swear the way they do? What's the origin of the arrow sash? When did Percé Rock lose its second arch? Where did the first inhabitants of the Magdalen Islands come from? And what about Louis Cyr, Rocket Richard, and Leonard Cohen? These sketches, brief though they are, cast light on additional layers of Quebec history.

Icons Used in This Book

Throughout the book, icons appear in the margins. Each icon helps you see at a glance what kind of information is presented in the passage beside it. Using the icons, you can focus on the kind of material you're especially interested in or come back to a point you're looking for. Here's what the icons in this book mean:

The broad sweep of history is peppered with seemingly insignificant incidents and idiosyncrasies that reveal something about a person, event, or phenomenon. Anecdotes remind us that this is "human" history!

Paragraphs marked by this icon are moments that imprinted themselves in Quebecers' consciousness. Those who were there have never forgotten these moments. In the history of any society, key dates are hooks that give us entry points into the flow of time.

This icon marks places where I focus on one of the many personalities who have left their mark on Quebec. What were their family origins and social background? What ideas did they hold dear? What motivated their political and social actions?

This icon points out an event or element in Quebec history that is especially important and should be remembered.

This icon marks information that's interesting, but not essential to your understanding of the subject at hand.

Where to Go from Here

If you want a full picture of the history of Quebec, you can always start at the very beginning and read through to the end. But you can dip into whichever parts interest you most. Use the Table of Contents and Index to find the subjects that fascinate you. Or just open the book at random and start reading. You're sure to find fascinating stories of impressive men and women who made Quebec what it is today.

Want to read further about Quebec? Head to www.dummies.com/go/ historyofquebecfd where I list a number of other resources you can dive into, including a chronology of important events and a map of the province.

Part I
New France
(1524–1754)

The 5th Wave   By Rich Tennant

1534–Jacques Cartier discovers Canada and starts fur trading with the Iroquois indians.

Winter, 1535–Sadly, Cartier's men never made contact with the other tribe who traded in space heaters.

In this part . . .

A painful birth and difficult beginnings. . . . France got off to a late start in exploring the New World. Like the other European powers, it initially sought a route to Asia. After some hesitation, Quebec was chosen as the capital of New France. This early settlement was established by Samuel de Champlain, who forged links of trust and friendship with the Montagnais, Algonquians, and Hurons. But it wasn't until the time of Louis XIV, his minister Jean-Baptiste Colbert, and the intendant Jean Talon that the colony truly began to develop.

In the late 17th century, a new people made its appearance. These "Canadiens" never gave up on their homeland, despite repeated attacks by the Iroquois and the growing appetite of the Anglo-American colonies. In addition to clearing new land, they explored the Great Lakes, paddled down the Mississippi, founded Louisiana, and went as far west as the Rockies.

Chapter 1

Looking for China — and Finding Quebec! (1524–1610)

. . . .

In This Chapter

▶ Exploring the New World

▶ Looking at the role of the French in founding Quebec

. . . .

T he New World nation of Quebec was founded by adventurers, missionaries, and women and men who wanted to improve their lot and dreamed of a better world. When they crossed the ocean in the 15th and 16th centuries, Europe was experiencing an unprecedented period of growth. Portugal, Spain, and England were seeking new routes to China. Taking advantage of new scientific discoveries, sailors set out to sea, crossed the Atlantic, discovered America, and founded colonies.

France, 16th-century Europe's leader in wealth and population, made the first move to colonize Quebec. In this chapter, I fill you in on when and why French leaders decided to set out for the New World, the circumstances that fed their curiosity about these vast western lands, and the ambitions that drove the French state. I also explain what the early explorers discovered (hint: they weren't the first people there) and what kind of relationship developed between the French and the indigenous peoples. Finally, I tell you why the French decided to settle in the St. Lawrence Valley and found Quebec.

Setting Out to Conquer the West

In the 16th century, all western European powers were curious about the New World. This desire to travel and look beyond their shores took shape in the context of the Renaissance, an extraordinary and unprecedented period of artistic and intellectual growth and economic and political upheaval.

The Vikings: First explorers to the party

Well before the 16th century, the Vikings had explored the shores of the American continent. This great nation of conquering mariners originated in Scandinavia. They established settlements in Greenland that lasted three centuries, founding villages and erecting a bishop's palace. Greenland was not very far from the shores of Newfoundland, and Vikings settled there around the year 1000 A.D. Their presence lasted several centuries, but they had completely abandoned Newfoundland by the time a later generation of Europeans decided to set out.

Why the Europeans wanted to explore

A combination of factors explains western Europeans' sudden desire to explore a vast world:

✔ **The fall of Constantinople:** Constantinople, the capital of the Eastern Roman Empire, was the gateway to Asia for Europeans. Caravans brought back silks, precious gems, and spices (which were used to preserve staple foods). Constantinople fell to the Turks in 1453, which spelled trouble for the Europeans: The gateway to Asia was now closed. To import these riches from the Orient again, new routes had to be explored to avoid Arab and Muslim peoples who were hostile to Christian Europe, and for good reason: Christians had repeatedly invaded their part of the world during the bloody Crusades of the Middle Ages.

✔ **The search for gold:** In the 15th century, a number of European cities experienced rapid growth. Paris, Naples, Venice, and Florence each had more than 100,000 inhabitants. With the economy flourishing, gold coins were increasingly required for commerce. Suppliers in North Africa and the Middle East wanted to be paid in hard cash. The problem: Gold mines supplying Europeans were running out. For growth to continue, new deposits had to be found, and the New World was a place to look.

Who went where

To find a new way of reaching Asia or to venture into distant lands to discover gold, technical innovation was vital. People needed more sophisticated methods of navigation, and they had to have faster and better ships that could accommodate large crews and heavy loads of food.

The Renaissance atmosphere prevailing in Europe gave rise not only to lively discussions among scholars but also to a variety of innovations that were useful to the great adventurers. They could now set out to sea for months at a time. No ambition was too great for the intrepid sailors, mostly of Italian origin, who staffed these ships. The race to Asia could begin!

Portugal finds a route around Africa

The Portuguese were the first to undertake this bold odyssey. Led by Henry the Navigator, the Portuguese discovered the Azores and explored the coast of Africa. In 1488, they rounded the Cape of Good Hope, opening the route to India. Ten years later, Vasco de Gama reached the Indian subcontinent.

Spain discovers America

These Portuguese successes led Spain, Portugal's great neighbor and competitor, to follow suit. With the southern route already explored, the Italian navigator Christopher Columbus urged Spain to finance a westward expedition — a truly bold venture because the route was completely unknown.

But circumstances favored Columbus. In 1492, the Spanish monarchs defeated the Arabs and achieved full political union. On October 12 of that year, Columbus reached unknown territory. He was not in Asia, however, but in America. The Spaniards settled in and were soon exploiting the new continent's gold.

English incursions farther north

These impressive Spanish conquests stirred envy in other countries. England also had ambitions of finding new ways to Asia, but by a northerly route. On May 2, 1497, Giovanni Caboto (called John Cabot by the English) left the port of Bristol. On June 24, he reached the shores of Newfoundland, planted an English flag, and took possession. He, too, thought he had arrived in Asia. He returned the following year but soon became disenchanted: These new lands offered plenty of fish and furs but very little gold or other precious metals.

What they found when they arrived: An inhabited New World

Neither Spain nor England discovered a route to Asia. Between the Orient of their dreams and Old Europe lay a New World inhabited by a variety of unknown peoples.

The origins of "Homo americanus"

The earliest inhabitants of the New World were members of the species *Homo sapiens sapiens*. These bipeds were capable of producing tools and had a good knowledge of flora. Their presence in America resulted from two waves of immigration: They came from Asia across the Bering Strait or by sea along the west coast of the American continent in small boats, arriving about 15,000 years ago (or as long as 30,000 years ago, by some accounts) and settling mostly in South America. These migrants belonged to tribes that hunted herds of mammoths and buffalo.

About 5,000 years ago, a second wave of migrants followed the same route but settled in the northwest. This second wave arrived at the end of a long ice age estimated to have begun about 100,000 years earlier. For thousands of years, Quebec, along with the entire northeast of the continent, was covered with a thick layer of ice. With the ice receding, living in the more northerly regions was possible.

Number and diversity

At the time the first Europeans arrived, the American continent may have been inhabited by about 80 million people, most of whom lived in the south. The indigenous population of North America is thought to have been somewhere between 4 million and 9 million; of these, 500,000 to 2 million lived in Canada.

The first Europeans to arrive were immediately struck by the cultural diversity of the peoples they encountered. Most had their own languages, ancestral customs, and spiritual beliefs. Some nomadic people lived from hunting, fishing, and gathering. Subsistence for these people was easy in the summer but more difficult in the winter. Others were partly sedentary, combining cultivation of the soil with nomadic subsistence activities and living in large settlements. Rivalries for control of a resource or a territory often erupted between indigenous peoples. Wars sometimes set them violently against one another well before the Europeans arrived.

Although their customs were very different from those of the Europeans and their means of fighting were less sophisticated, they were neither bloodthirsty barbarians nor noble savages motivated solely by higher thoughts. The passions that moved them were similar to those of the Europeans.

Culture shock

The encounter between the Europeans and *First Nations* (the various indigenous people in Canada) produced a real shock, for both sides. To begin with, the Europeans came bearing illnesses that wiped out huge numbers of indigenous people, because they lacked the protective immunity to fight these diseases. The Europeans suffered less from bacteriological shock, but many died in adapting to the new continent, especially in the winter months.

The shock was also cultural. The Montagnais of northern Quebec thought the first ships were floating islands, saw their sails as strange clouds, and believed the first cannon shots were horrible thunderclaps. They were fascinated by the hairiness of the Europeans, as well as by the wine they drank while eating, which they initially thought was blood.

This culture shock also affected the Europeans, who saw more relaxed social and sexual customs among the indigenous peoples and a more liberal way of raising children. They also discovered a number of new products: tobacco, maple sap, canoes, and snowshoes.

The three indigenous groups in Quebec

When the Europeans arrived, three main indigenous groups shared the territory of Quebec. Each of them was subdivided into tribes and occupied a specific part of the territory. These three groups were as follows:

✔ **The Algonquians:** Made up of nomadic tribes, the Algonquian peoples were divided as follows: the Montagnais (or Innu) roamed along the north shore of the St. Lawrence as far as the St. Maurice River; the Cree lived south of James Bay; the Maliseet lived along the St. John River; the Odawa inhabited the Témiscamingue region and the area north of Lake Huron; the Algonquians proper covered an area along the north shore of the Ottawa and St. Lawrence rivers extending from the Témiscamingue region to west of the St. Maurice. Other Algonquian tribal groups lived outside Quebec's current boundaries (such as the Mi'kmaq of the maritime provinces and the Ojibwa of Lake Superior). The French generally maintained good relations with these peoples.

✔ **The Iroquoians:** When Jacques Cartier arrived from France in 1535, Iroquoian tribes were settled at Stadacona (in what is now Quebec City) and Hochelaga (Montreal). In the latter part of the 16th century, the Iroquoian tribes abandoned these posts and settled farther south and west. When the French returned early in the 17th century, the Iroquoians had disappeared. Consisting mostly of semi-sedentary tribes, this major Aboriginal family included the Iroquois, divided into the Five Nations of the Iroquois Confederacy: Mohawks, Oneidas, Onondagas, Cayugas, and Senecas. They lived in the areas around Lake Ontario and Lake Erie. The Hurons of the Great Lakes, with whom the French established close relations, were also part of the broader Iroquoian cultural family, as were the Pétuns and the Neutral, even though the Iroquois regarded them all as irreconcilable enemies.

✔ **The Inuit (or Eskimos):** Completely isolated from the two other Aboriginal families in Quebec and from the early French colonists, the Inuit (or Eskimos) lived in Labrador and the far north.

Finally, the Europeans brought firearms with them. These weapons transformed relationships and led to new wars. Even though the balance of power clearly favored the colonists from Old Europe, both First Nations and Europeans were transformed by this encounter. Confrontation with indigenous peoples was sometimes brutal. To establish their culture and religion, the Spanish massacred entire populations or reduced them to slavery. In comparison, the French, perhaps because they were fewer in number, adopted a more open attitude.

France gets into the race

Compared to Portugal and Spain, 16th-century France did not seem to be in any great hurry to find a new route to Asia. This was because its attention was turned more toward Italy and the Mediterranean, which remained the great trade crossroads of Europe. The Spanish conquest and the achievement of Magellan's crew in circling the entire world in three years (1519–1522), discovering a passage between South America and Antarctica along the way, finally persuaded France to get into the race.

Verrazzano's exploration

Financed by bankers in Lyon and backed by King Francis I, the Florentine sailor Giovanni da Verrazzano explored the Atlantic coast of North America in 1524. When he began his trip, the shores of South America, the Caribbean, Florida, and Newfoundland had been mapped. But the central part of North America's Atlantic coast remained unknown. During his two-month expedition aboard the *Dauphine,* Verrazzano tried to find a route leading to "Cathay," another name for China. Such a discovery would leapfrog what Magellan had found, enabling France to get back on top.

After reaching North Carolina in March, he headed north along the coast, setting foot on the continent several times. The land he discovered seemed to him "the most pleasant and the most favorable there could be for any type of crop." He met indigenous peoples, regarding some of them as courteous and polite but others as barbaric and hostile. In political and economic terms, Verrazzano's expedition was a failure. However, thanks to him, Europeans learned, as Verrazzano himself wrote, "this land or New World . . . forms an entity. It is not attached to Asia or to Africa. . . . This continent thus seems to be enclosed between the eastern sea and the western sea."

Jacques Cartier arrives in Gaspé

This conviction on Verrazzano's part did not convince everyone. The hope of finding a route to Asia persisted, and the riches of the new continent stirred greed. The French king chose Jacques Cartier, a sailor from Saint-Malo, near the boundary between the French provinces of Brittany and Normandy, to lead a new expedition. Cartier's mission was "to discover certain islands where it is said that we may find a large quantity of gold and other rich things."

On April 20, 1534, he left the port of Saint-Malo. It was a modest expedition, with just two ships and 60 men. After a rapid crossing, Cartier arrived in Newfoundland, followed the Strait of Belle Isle, and sailed down the west coast of Newfoundland. He then explored the Gulf of St. Lawrence and the Baie des Chaleurs, where he met Aboriginals from the Mi'kmaq tribe. After following the Gaspé peninsula to where the town of Gaspé now lies, he came across other Aboriginals of the Iroquoian family.

"Long live the King of France"

The people Cartier encountered were from Stadacona (in present-day Quebec City) and were there to fish for mackerel. The contact went fairly well. Cartier saw them as true "savages." In his diary, he wrote, "They have only small skins as clothing, which they use to cover the indecent parts of the body. . . . Their heads are completely shaved. . . . They eat flesh nearly raw."

On July 24, Cartier erected a cross "30 feet high" on which was written "Long live the King of France," a gesture the Iroquoians did not much appreciate. Using facial expressions, they indicated that these lands belonged to them and that they saw the erection of this cross as improper. As explorers of that era often did, Cartier kidnapped two Aboriginals, the sons of the chief with whom he had established ties during his brief stay in Gaspé. On July 25, Cartier's crew continued on its course, going around Anticosti Island, following part of the north shore of the Gulf of St. Lawrence, and returning to France, circumventing the shores of Newfoundland.

The results of this initial expedition by Cartier were rather meager: no route to Asia, no discovery of gold. The longstanding claim that Jacques Cartier "discovered" Canada in 1534 is probably exaggerated. Cartier clearly planted a cross and took symbolic possession of a territory, but he did not found a colony.

The "Kingdom of Saguenay"

The next year, Cartier set out again. The two captive Aboriginals, presented to the king, held out the prospect of magnificent discoveries. A majestic river, they said, would lead to the village of Stadacona. Cartier was overjoyed: What if this were a new route to Asia? The two young Iroquois claimed that there was a fabulous place overflowing with wealth: the "Kingdom of Saguenay." No more was needed to whet the curiosity of the French.

On July 26, 1535, the three ships of Jacques Cartier's second expedition reached Blanc-Sablon, at the eastern edge of what is now Quebec's North Shore. After sailing into the Gulf of St. Lawrence, Cartier's men approached Île d'Orléans and Stadacona. The two Aboriginals, by now dressed European-style and speaking French fairly well, were returned to their community. Cartier met Donnacona, their chief, who tried to dissuade him from continuing farther south. But the sailor from Saint-Malo had other ideas in mind. His goal was to reach Hochelaga, in present-day Montreal, to seek a new route to Asia.

On the evening of October 3, Cartier saw the fortified settlement at the foot of a small hill, which he named "Mount Royal." Approximately 1,000 Aboriginals lived there in about 50 long, spacious houses. The contact was warm. They exchanged presents. Cartier climbed Mount Royal on foot. He admired the mountain ranges in the distance and saw that the river turned into rapids, later called the Lachine Rapids. Cartier believed this river route could lead to the Kingdom of Saguenay. On October 5, he returned to Stadacona, where relations with Chief Donnacona had deteriorated. The chief had advised Cartier against going to Hochelaga, perhaps because he wished to maintain a privileged connection with the French sailor.

The scourge of scurvy

For the first time, Frenchmen decided to spend the winter in the St. Lawrence Valley, a decision some of them would later regret. Ill prepared for the rigors of the climate, many sailors suffered from scurvy, a disease resulting from a vitamin C deficiency. The Europeans ravaged by this illness lost their teeth and their strength. Twenty-five of the 110 men in Cartier's crew succumbed to it, but the ordeal did not discourage Cartier. He insisted on discovering the Kingdom of Saguenay, but he lacked men and food to continue his mission. To learn more about this mysterious kingdom, he brought Donnacona and two of his sons to France — without, of course, seeking their approval. None of them would see their homeland again.

Conscript prisoners

Jacques Cartier's tales captivated King Francis I, who had visions of securing the wealth of Saguenay for his kingdom, but it would be some time before a new expedition set out. Cartier earned some promotions but was soon out-flanked by a nobleman, Jean-François de La Roque, Seigneur de Roberval. Appointed "lieutenant general of Canada," Roberval was placed in charge of an important mission. He was not only to explore or exploit a territory but also to found a true colony and convert the indigenous peoples to the Christian faith.

Origin of the words *Canada* and *Quebec*

The first occurrences of the word *kanata* appear in Jacques Cartier's accounts of his travels. The kidnapped Aboriginals spoke to him of the "kanata" road, meaning "cluster of huts." The kanata road was the one that led to the interior of the continent and to a village. But the word stuck, and *Canada* came to designate the lands over which Donnacona reigned and to which the majestic river led. Later, French administrators used the name *Canada* to refer to the inhabited territories of the St. Lawrence Valley. Part of New France in the mid-18th century, Canada was separate from Acadia and Louisiana.

In the original writings of the explorers, Quebec was written *Kebec*. This Algonquian word means "the place where the river narrows." If you had sailed upriver from the Gulf of St. Lawrence, you would find that the two banks were closest together at Quebec City. The explorers naturally came to use the word *Kebec* to designate what would become the capital of New France.

Though Cartier did not lead this third expedition, he was nevertheless part of it. He left France before Roberval, on May 25, 1541, at the head of five vessels. The two men had trouble persuading other Frenchmen to embark with them. Lacking volunteers, they conscripted criminals. Two months later, Cartier arrived in Stadacona with his crew alone. Roberval had been delayed.

"As false as Canadian diamonds"

When Cartier arrived in Stadacona, the Aboriginals received news of Donnacona, who had died around 1539. Relations with the Aboriginals were tense, so much so that Cartier decided to settle upriver in a spot he named "Charlesbourg-Royal." Members of his crew thought they had discovered diamonds and gold there, finds that appealed to Cartier's greed. In a hurry to show these diamonds to the royal court, he prepared a hasty return.

On June 7, 1542, he met up with Roberval in St. John's, Newfoundland. The lieutenant general of Canada was obviously counting on the pilot from Saint-Malo to guide him. But in the middle of the night, Cartier left him in the lurch and returned to France. Sadly, what he thought were diamonds were merely quartz pebbles and iron pyrite ("fool's gold"), giving rise to the long-used expression "as false as Canadian diamonds."

Cartier's trans-Atlantic career came to an abrupt end. What he had learned by exploring the St. Lawrence would serve later sailors who ventured into the same waters, but his quick return to France was his undoing. No further expedition would be entrusted to him. With nobody to guide him, Roberval stumbled blindly into a continent he scarcely knew. In the spring of 1543, he decided to go back to France. The founding of a French colony in the St. Lawrence Valley was put off indefinitely.

Moving toward the Founding of Quebec

It would be a good half-century before France again considered establishing itself in North America. There were efforts to set up colonies in Brazil and Florida between 1555 and 1565, but these failed as abysmally as had the first attempt in the St. Lawrence Valley. In the second half of the 16th century, France was torn by internal struggles. From 1562 to 1598, a series of religious wars considerably weakened royal authority. Violent conflicts caused the death of two to four million French people. This was a time for consolidation of the kingdom, not imperial expansion. Henry IV's accession to the throne in 1589 provided a way out of the crisis. In 1598, with his Edict of Nantes, the Huguenot who had converted to Catholicism allowed Protestants freedom of conscience, enabling France to achieve a degree of peace.

Focusing on the fur trade

Though the French state may have neglected the Gulf of St. Lawrence and the shores of Newfoundland, fishermen and merchants did not. Jacques Cartier's travels were known to ship owners in Normandy and Brittany, and they fully intended to exploit the wealth of these distant lands. Sailors from northwestern France soon encountered Basque and Spanish vessels pursuing the same commercial goals.

From cod to beaver

The ship owners' primary interest lay in fishing. The shores of Newfoundland teemed with cod. Between 1550 and 1580, French cod fishermen from Saint-Malo, Dieppe, Rouen, and Bordeaux brought back sizable cargoes of fish. At a time when many practicing Christians were forbidden from eating meat on Friday, fish provided essential protein. Though this trade may have been less lucrative than dealing in gold, precious gems, or spices, it was profitable enough to be worth pursuing for several decades.

Around 1580, a new trade was added to fishing: the fur trade. From the 1550s on, cod fishermen brought back furs from America in addition to their cargoes of fish. The supply of beaver pelts came from exchanging goods with the indigenous peoples. Much in demand in European high society, these pelts found ready buyers — fur hats were in vogue.

During the 1570s, furs from America benefited from a tense political situation in Europe. Access to furs from Russia, the traditional supplier of this luxury good, was made difficult by blockades in the Baltic Sea. Norman and Breton merchants sensed that this would be a good business for them, and they began to focus on the fur trade in the early 1580s. Basques also got into the game. In the Gulf of St. Lawrence, competition became fierce. The European market soon became flooded with American furs, and the price collapsed as a result. Customers were obviously not complaining, but the ship owners demanded government intervention to regulate the trade.

An early public-private partnership

In 1587, open war broke out between fur traders. Ships were burned in the St. Lawrence River. The following year, King Henry III of France innovated by awarding a fur trade and mining monopoly in the St. Lawrence Valley to Jacques Noël, a nephew of Jacques Cartier, for a 12-year period. Labor was also guaranteed — the king allowed him to select "60 persons, either men or women, each year in our prisons." In exchange for this monopoly, Noël and his associate agreed to build the structures needed to operate his business. This privilege came as a shock to the Breton traders. In their eyes, Noël had neither the talent nor the knowledge to run a monopoly of this kind. They all but accused him of being an impostor. On May 5, 1588, Henry III yielded to their arguments and restored free trade in the St. Lawrence Valley.

This sort of about-face would recur several times. Other monopolies would be granted and then withdrawn. Until 1627, France proved very hesitant. On rare occasions, it aspired to found a real colony in North America and extend its influence over the New World. But most of the time, resources failed to follow. Lacking political ambition, France turned to monopolies, which it awarded to a series of resourceful and adventurous merchants whose primary ambition was something other than founding a colony. Driven mostly by material interests, these merchants sought above all to run their businesses. For a long time, French policy looked very much like what we now call PPPs (public-private partnerships): The government awards privileges to an individual or company. In return, it expects this individual or company to look after public responsibilities: building bridges and other infrastructure, transporting and helping with the upkeep of colonists, and so on.

Meeting Samuel de Champlain: A true visionary

Fortunately, the vision and unshakable convictions of an exceptional individual, Samuel de Champlain, made up for this hesitant and haphazard French policy. Had it not been for this remarkable person, Quebec would not have been founded.

An illegitimate son of Henry IV?

It was only very recently, in April 2012, that Samuel de Champlain's baptismal certificate was discovered. Baptized as a Protestant in La Rochelle on August 13, 1574, he later converted to Catholicism. Champlain grew up in Brouage, a small port city in the French province of Saintonge, in rather modest circumstances.

In early adulthood, he seemed to have had privileged access to King Henry IV. Starting in the summer of 1601, the king awarded him an annual pension — a very rare favor. Some researchers say this privileged link could have been due to a filial relationship: Samuel de Champlain may have been one of Henry IV's many illegitimate sons.

The king's openness to human diversity, his genuine tolerance of varied beliefs, and his skill in conciliation and compromise appear to have left a deep impression on the young Champlain. His talents as a draughtsman and cartographer may be what first drew attention to him. He was also a highly experienced sailor who crossed the Atlantic at least 27 times between 1599 and 1633. In the many writings he left, he showed great curiosity about the flora and the peoples he discovered. From the time of his earliest voyages, he was convinced that riches abounded in this New World land. But to grow and prosper, he said, this young colony would need settlers. If it remained a mere trading post, the colony would have no future. It was vital for a population to take root there.

Renewed colonial ambitions

Henry IV, who had great ambitions for his kingdom, revived the project of colonizing North America. Several attempts were made. In 1598, about 40 beggars, vagabonds, and prisoners were sent to Sable Island, off the coast of present-day Nova Scotia. Left to their own devices, they revolted and killed one another. By 1603, only 11 of them were still alive.

In 1600, a merchant to whom the king had just awarded a monopoly organized an expedition to Tadoussac, a small post at the mouth of the Saguenay River, a fur-trade crossroads already well known to sailors. The small dwelling built there was not suited to the climate. During the winter of 1600–1601, a number of Frenchmen gave up the ghost in Tadoussac.

Champlain was not involved in these expeditions. From 1599 to 1601, he explored Spanish colonies in South America, where he was shocked by the treatment inflicted on indigenous peoples. In 1603, a new expedition was mounted by Commander Aymar de Chaste, the new holder of the fur-pelt monopoly in the St. Lawrence. Champlain learned of the existence of this mission and found a way of joining it — as a simple observer (though everyone knew he had the king's ear). The crew set sail in March. The purpose was less to establish a colony than to reconnoiter the area and establish links with the indigenous peoples.

"Smoking up" in Tadoussac

On May 26, 1603, the French landed at Tadoussac. Montagnais from various tribes were there, along with Algonquians living farther south. The encounter went quite well. There was a reason for the Algonquians' good humor: Some of them were fresh from a stirring victory against their Iroquois enemies. The French noticed about 100 scalps dripping with blood.

The presence of Montagnais interpreters who had spent some time in France facilitated communication. The tales they told of their time in Europe caught the attention of the other Montagnais. The representatives from the Old World were then welcomed as prestigious guests! The grand chief who was there said he favored the establishment of the French on the territory, but on condition that they fight the Iroquois enemy.

A great feast followed these warm exchanges. Champlain ate moose for the first time: Its flesh, he noted, tasted like beef. Once the meal was over, chants and dances delighted the Frenchmen. "All the women and girls began to remove their skin robes and became totally naked, showing their natural state," Champlain noted. He was impressed by the beauty of these "well rounded" Montagnais women! "All these peoples," he wrote, "have well-proportioned bodies, with no deformities." The gathering was a real success. It sealed a basic alliance that would enable the French to establish roots in the St. Lawrence Valley. In a ceremony typical of major festivities among Aboriginal peoples, they smoked tobacco, a sign of the respectful relations between the early French and the natives of the St. Lawrence Valley. These relationships of trust would enable the French to explore the interior of the continent and confront the harsh winters as they set out to discover heretofore unknown rivers, lakes, and regions.

Champlain used this visit to explore the Saguenay River. He was impressed by the depth of its fjord and by the white beluga whales that came to the surface. Along the river, he saw only mountains and forests. There was no site that seemed suitable for colonization. He decided to sail up the St. Lawrence and check places explored by Jacques Cartier 60 years earlier. On June 22, he cast anchor at the former village of Stadacona, which was now uninhabited. Champlain continued inland, crossing the mouth of the St. Maurice and reaching Montreal Island, where the village of Hochelaga had also disappeared.

Founding Quebec

Back in France, Champlain published the account of his journey to Tadoussac. The gathering with indigenous people fascinated readers hungry for exotic tales. But even with the encouraging prospects he described, and despite fur traders' expeditions, the French did not settle in the St. Lawrence Valley until 1608. After Aymar de Chaste died suddenly, the monopoly was awarded to Pierre Dugua de Mons, a Protestant from Saintonge whom Champlain knew well. Dugua de Mons chose the Atlantic coast over the St. Lawrence Valley. Being easier to reach, it seemed to be a region better suited for trading and for establishing a settlement. Therefore, with the king's agreement, Dugua de Mons set his sights on Acadia. Champlain complied with this decision, but the experiences of Sainte-Croix Island (during the winter of 1604–1605) and Port-Royal (1605–1607) were inconclusive in the short term.

Chaotic beginnings

These disappointing results left Henry IV impatient and gave ammunition to competitors of Dugua de Mons. In 1608, the king renewed his monopoly, but for only one year. With some effort, Champlain persuaded Dugua de Mons to return to the St. Lawrence Valley. In April 1608, the *Lévrier* and the *Don-de-Dieu,* under the command of François Gravé du Pont and Champlain, left the port of Honfleur. Thus far, France's attempts at colonization in North America had all met with failure. This was a last-chance mission — it was make it or break it.

The arrival at Tadoussac on June 3 did not bode well. Basques were trading furs there, openly contravening the monopoly awarded by the French king. When Gravé du Pont ordered them to cease their activities, the Basques fired on the French. Champlain, a skilled negotiator, intervened, and both parties agreed to settle the matter in France.

On July 3, the crew arrived at Quebec. At the foot of a rocky cape, along the shores of the St. Lawrence, Champlain had his "habitation" built. The two-story structure served as a workshop, a warehouse, a dwelling, and even a temporary fortress. But why did he favor this site over others? There were essentially two reasons:

- ✔ **It was an ideal site for defense.** Quebec provides plenty of advantages in military terms. This is where the banks of the St. Lawrence are closest to each other. The rocky cape, later named Cape Diamond, provides an excellent view of the river, making it easier to see the enemy and prepare accordingly.

- ✔ **It was a trade crossroads.** Deeper into the interior of the continent than Tadoussac, Quebec was closer to sources of fur supply. A number of tribes friendly to the French crossed paths there.

A foiled plot

François Gravé du Pont and Samuel de Champlain brought a number of indentured workers with them. Among them were carpenters, blacksmiths, and a surgeon, but there were no women or clerics. As soon as they arrived there was plenty to do, and the men set to work.

Locksmith Jean Duval had other ideas, however. A schemer, Duval persuaded three other men to assassinate Champlain, take control of the new colony, and establish an alliance with the Basques. A few days before the planned attack, one of the conspirators broke down and told the whole story. His former accomplices were taken into custody, along with the initiator of this mini–coup d'état. A trial was held, the first in the history of Quebec. The four men were sentenced to death, but Duval's three comrades were sent back to France. Duval himself "was hanged and strangled in the said Quebec," Champlain reported, "and his head was placed at the end of a spike to be planted in our fort's most prominent place."

Consolidating an alliance

To secure what was intended to be a permanent presence in Quebec, links with the indigenous peoples of the St. Lawrence Valley had to be strengthened. The safety of the few Frenchmen there was at stake. The strongest ties are often created in adversity, and Champlain renewed his 1603 promise to fight the Iroquois enemy at the earliest opportunity.

In the summer of 1609, the French moved into action. On June 28, they left Quebec with their allies, headed for Iroquois country. "I resolved to go and fulfill my promise," Champlain wrote, "and I embarked with the savages in their canoes, taking with me two men of good will." A few days later, after going up the Richelieu River, they reached the large lake that the founder of Quebec named after himself. This was the first time Frenchmen had explored this area. The expedition enabled Champlain to observe indigenous beliefs and ways of waging war. One thing that really struck him was the great importance indigenous people attached to premonitions in their dreams — they kept asking him what his own dreams foretold.

On the morning of July 30, the confrontation took place at Ticonderoga, at the narrow passage between Lake Champlain and Lake George. The fight pitted the allies of the French (Hurons, Algonquians, and Montagnais) against 200 Iroquois from the Mohawk tribe. Hidden behind his companions and armed with a *harquebus* (an early type of portable gun), Champlain awaited a signal before advancing. Then "our men began calling to me loudly, splitting in two to open the way to me, and I stood at the head, marching 20 paces forward until I was some 30 paces from the enemy. Once they saw me, they halted while contemplating me, and I them." The bearded European, dressed in a coat of armor that glinted in the sun, took the Mohawks by surprise. Champlain aimed at two of their chiefs, killing them with a single shot. Two Frenchmen flanking him on either side immediately opened fire. These murderous thunderclaps threw the Iroquois off stride, and they beat a hasty retreat. The courage shown by Champlain and his strategic use of firearms impressed his indigenous allies. The French demonstrated, above all, that they could keep their word.

Aboriginal torture

Returning from this initial victorious campaign against the Iroquois, the French learned of the treatment that First Nations people could inflict on their enemies. The founder of Quebec was horrified by the tortures and acts of cruelty casually meted out to the dozen captured prisoners.

After celebrating their victory, they turned to the captives as if it were a familiar ritual. They burned them with firebrands, tore out their fingernails, poured boiling water on their heads, and pierced their arms near the wrist. After killing one of the prisoners, they opened his belly, threw his entrails into the lake, and cut his heart into pieces that the other prisoners were forced to eat. "This is how these peoples behave," stated Champlain, deeply shocked by what he saw. "It would be better for them to die fighting . . . than to fall into the hands of their enemies."

This violence helped the warriors exorcise the fears they felt during combat. When Champlain or other Europeans argued that these treatments were inhumane, the Aboriginals responded that if the situation were reversed, their enemies would treat them the same way.

On June 19, 1610, a new confrontation with the Mohawks at Sorel also resulted in a victory for the French and their allies. For several years to come, these two victories would cool the Iroquois's ardor for invading the St. Lawrence Valley. In two years, Champlain had accomplished a great deal. Quebec was founded, the First Nations alliance was consolidated, and the St. Lawrence Valley was secured. These were all conditions that would favor the fur trade and colonization of the territory.

Unfortunately for Champlain, a shadow was cast on these fine projects by the assassination of Henry IV on May 14, 1610. Before his death, the king had taken the fur monopoly away from Dugua de Mons.

Would everything have to start again from square one?

Chapter 2

Founding a Colony (1611–1660)

. . . .

In This Chapter

▶ Seeing how Champlain got people to move to New France

▶ Recognizing the impact of Cardinal Richelieu

. . . .

After the death of Henry IV, the 9-year-old *dauphin* (heir apparent), Louis XIII, was not ready to govern in his own right. Queen Marie de Médicis, who had scant interest in America, assumed the regency. This meant that, overnight, Champlain lost privileged access to royal power. If he wanted to pursue his grand enterprise, he'd have to be clever and find new allies.

In 1611, free competition, open to all traders, prevailed in the St. Lawrence Valley. Quebec remained a modest fur-trading post in the hands of private interests. The winter of 1608–1609 decimated the group of Frenchmen living there. By 1611, only 17 men — and no women — inhabited Quebec. Apart from some summer gardening, no agriculture was practiced. Vision and conviction were needed to imagine that a real colony was in the process of emerging. Luckily, Samuel de Champlain had no shortage of these qualities!

Hesitant Beginnings

Until the mid-1620s, the fate of New France was highly uncertain. Champlain made many trips backs and forth between France and the young colony to seek support and attract settlers. The political officials in charge of the colony were inconsistent. French policy was hesitant and uncertain. Champlain was most often left to his own devices.

Moving into action

Samuel de Champlain was an effective and determined propagandist who didn't allow himself to be defeated. He lobbied forcefully, building new relationships in Paris and continuing to boast about the wealth to be discovered in New France. He also deepened his relationships with First Nations allies.

ANECDOTE

Hélène Boullé, age 12: An "arranged" marriage?

On December 30, 1610, in Paris, Samuel de Champlain married Hélène Boullé, the daughter of Nicolas Boullé, financial clerk to the king and an upstanding Parisian bourgeois. At the time of the wedding, the bride was just 12 years old! Champlain was 38. In the marriage contract, it was stated that Hélène Boullé would go to live with her husband later, at age 14.

All signs point to this being an arranged marriage. Champlain was not so much marrying a woman as connecting himself to a highly influential family. In addition to finding a backer for the colony in the royal family, he also had to forge ties with the administrators of the court. Even in the most intimate aspects of his life, Champlain thought only about New France.

A small island facing Montreal, Île Sainte-Hélène, may have been named in honor of his young wife. Evidence indicates, however, that the couple's marital life was not a happy one. The life and manners of Hélène Boullé were entirely Parisian. She agreed to live in New France for only four years (from 1620 through 1624). After her stay in America, she left her husband and devoted herself to pious works.

Throughout the 17th century, it was not uncommon to see older men marrying young girls. Such unions were authorized because women were, for a long time, far less numerous than men in the colony.

Finding a powerful sponsor

In 1611, the must urgent (and most difficult) task was to find new support in the king's court. Champlain thought he had found the ideal sponsor in Charles de Bourbon, the Count of Soissons, governor of Normandy, and a member of the royal family. Charles showed some interest, but he died suddenly, barely a month after being appointed.

Champlain soon turned to another blood prince: the energetic and impetuous Henri de Bourbon, Prince of Condé, a first cousin of the king. This future "viceroy" of New France was not lacking in flair. As soon as he was appointed, he renewed Champlain's position. Unfortunately, Henri de Bourbon quickly became an embarrassment: In the autumn of 1615, he was sent to prison for openly confronting his cousin, the king, who was planning to marry a Spaniard. Henri de Bourbon was held in prison for three years and obviously a little preoccupied by that fact, so he didn't devote much time to New France. Neither he nor his successors assumed the political leadership Champlain was hoping for.

Even while he was busy in Paris, Champlain did not neglect maintaining links with the Aboriginal allies who continued to supply France with furs. They had trouble following French policy in the St. Lawrence. After the death of Henry IV, the French government alternated between allowing free competition and awarding monopolies. In this context, whom could the Aboriginals trust? Champlain, who claimed to represent France? Or traders, who sought only short-term profit? This inconsistency weakened the alliance. Champlain persuaded the authorities to clarify matters. Starting in 1613, the fur trade was again regulated by a policy of monopolies. No more anarchy or unbridled competition. A single group of merchants, designated by the court, would from that point forward be in charge of purchasing pelts.

A winter in Huronia

With help from his Aboriginal allies, Champlain continued to explore the interior of the continent. In 1613, he went up the Ottawa River for the first time. The Ottawa was a route to the Great Lakes region, long called the *Pays d'en haut* (upcountry). Most Hurons lived in this area, between what we now call Lake Huron and Lake Ontario. Huronia was home to some 20,000 to 30,000 people, split into several tribes, living in some 20 villages with an average population of about 1,500 each. A semi-sedentary people, they grew corn and bartered with the surrounding nations, as well as with the French. The *Pays d'en haut* would long remain the hub of the fur trade. The 17th-century Hurons were seen by other indigenous peoples as intermediaries who bartered and sold.

In 1615, Champlain decided to venture into Huronia for the first time. When he arrived, the Hurons were planning to attack the Iroquois tribes. Faithful to his commitment, Champlain and his men took part in the expeditions. A confrontation occurred near present-day Syracuse, New York. The Franco-Huron attack did not go as planned. Two arrows struck Champlain — one in the wrist, the other in the knee. Along with the other wounded men, he was carried by the Hurons in a kind of basket. The basket was very uncomfortable, the trip was long, and the suffering was unbearable. Champlain was forced to spend the winter in the *Pays d'en haut,* living for several months among the friendly Hurons.

He was amazed at the freedom of their sexual mores (he refused the sexual advances of a young woman!) and impressed with their farming techniques and food conservation methods. However, as a European convinced of the superiority of his civilization, Champlain deplored the absence of legal frameworks and the lack of parental authority over children. Overall, he must have found life among them pleasant — he wrote, "all these people are of jovial humor."

Étienne Brûlé and the importance of interpreters

To deal with First Nations and trade in furs, you had to speak their language. The French were initially so few in number and so heavily dependent on the alliance with indigenous peoples that they weren't able to impose their own language. To communicate, they had to rely on the aid of interpreters, a function handled mostly by other Frenchmen. In Champlain's time, the most famous of them was Étienne Brûlé.

Born around 1592 and arriving in Quebec probably in 1608, Brûlé lived among the Algonquians for nearly a year. Brûlé learned their language, became familiar with their customs, and helped write a dictionary. Sadly, he left no written trace of his time with them. Champlain took a liking to this young man. Brûlé may later have returned to France and married.

In any case, Champlain found him among the Hurons in 1615. Historians are perplexed by Brûlé's oral tales of his adventures, spiced with improbable discoveries and fanciful scenes of torture. Nevertheless, he is thought to have been the first European to explore Lake Superior.

Brûlé was a free spirit who adopted the Aboriginals' sexual mores and refused to submit to orders. Accused of treason after serving the English, he went to live among the Hurons and appears to have been murdered around 1632. He is still regarded with fascination today, largely because he was a person in between, a bridge between cultures, an apostle before his time of ideas like *métissage* (crossbreeding) and hybridity.

Luring settlers

Working in Paris and in the *Pays d'en haut* to safeguard the colony, Champlain was more concerned with Quebec's survival than with its development. But to provide more solid foundations for this precarious undertaking, he needed to attract French colonists who would settle in North America.

The Récollets' program

To help him in this task, Champlain relied on religious figures who saw New France as a promising mission territory. In May 1615, four clerics of the Récollet order arrived in Tadoussac. One of them left to live among the Hurons; the others built a small church and celebrated their first masses. They were soon convinced that only French settlers, modeling a pious life, could convert the "savages" to the Christian faith. According to these Récollet fathers, it was not possible to become a good Christian without having previously become "civilized" in the European manner. Indigenous people could adhere to the new creed being urged on them only by settling on a piece of land and raising a family.

This way of seeing things wasn't universal. The traders didn't share this great spiritual design. Instead, they feared that if First Nations people cast aside their traditional way of life, they would be less useful to the fur trade.

Other wealth to exploit

The clerics' arguments were not the only ones advanced in favor of settlement. Other arguments were of a more economic nature. To persuade Paris to support New France, Champlain drew up an impressive inventory of the colony's wealth, which wasn't limited to furs. The memorandum he produced in the winter of 1617–1618 renamed Quebec "Ludovica," in honor of King Louis.

Among the sources of wealth found in the colony were the following:

- ✔ **Fishing:** Champlain estimated that 800 to 1,000 ships came each year to fish for cod in the Gulf of St. Lawrence and off the Newfoundland coast. He was also convinced that other fish such as salmon, herring, sturgeon, and trout could form the basis of a lucrative trade.

- ✔ **Forestry:** The St. Lawrence Valley was rich in hardwood forests. There were large quantities of oak, a highly sought-after wood for building warships.

- ✔ **Agriculture:** Champlain boasted of the fertility and quality of the land. He said it could be used to grew hemp, wheat, and even grapes. Livestock could also flourish on these lands, providing plenty of leather.

- ✔ **Mining:** Gold and diamonds were nowhere to be found, but there were deposits of iron and copper, both highly useful for the economy.

Champlain was filled with optimism. He asserted that these sources of wealth could bring the royal treasury up to six million livres a year, an impressive figure. To exploit them, French know-how was essential, just as settlers were essential to provide a stable and competent workforce.

The livre was the currency of France until 1795.

Louis Hébert, the first settler

The people who had lived in Quebec since 1608 were not settlers so much as workers bound by contracts for a specific length of time. Most of them returned home after a few years. Louis Hébert and his family were different. Born in 1575, Hébert, the son of a doctor who moved in Paris's best social circles, dreamed of settling in America. After an unpromising initial experience in Acadia, he was persuaded by Champlain to sell everything he owned in France and settle in Quebec. On March 11, 1617, he left Honfleur with his wife, Marie Rollet, along with his three children and his brother-in-law. The crossing was very difficult, with their ship tossed about near ice floes. Hébert's wife was so convinced the crew would end up in "the bellies of fish" that she asked to receive the last rites. But they arrived safe and sound! Hébert signed a two-year contract and brought with him a few seeds to cultivate the land. After the two years were over, he decided to stay, and he became a key figure in the young colony.

The beginnings of the seigneurial system

In 1623, the viceroy of New France gave Louis Hébert a concession on the heights of Quebec, in the heart of the present-day old city. The awarding of this noble fief was a form of recognition for services rendered to the colony. Starting in 1627, these fiefs were called *seigneuries*.

In 1663, New France had 68 seigneuries, mostly grouped around Quebec, Trois-Rivières, and Montreal. Until the Conquest of 1760, seigneuries were the favored mode of land concession by *Ancien Régime* France.

Seen from above, most seigneuries resembled long rectangles stretching from the shores of the river. The seigneur had a large area of land but was required to grant censives to newly arrived settlers. After 1711, this duty became a formal obligation.

These lands were provided free of charge, on condition that the habitants farm the land and fulfill duties to the seigneur (annual rent and chores, a portion of harvests, and so on). The seigneur also had responsibilities to his censitaires. In particular, he had to ensure their protection and put a mill at their disposal.

This *Ancien Régime* form of ownership was fundamentally unequal. In a conflict between a seigneur and a censitaire, the law generally came down in favor of the seigneur. That said, New France's seigneurs, at least in the early days of colonization, were very different from the great French aristocrats, who were often indifferent to the hardships of the people under them. They came from modest backgrounds and lived among the habitants, sharing their insecurities. Some historians have claimed that the early seigneurs in New France served, in effect, as "colonization agents."

Divergent views

Champlain welcomed settlers like Louis Hébert, as did the Récollets. But settling in New France meant agreeing to engage in labor. This was no place for slackers! What were needed were women and men with no fear of work, not tourists looking for something exotic. In 1621, Champlain expelled two households that, he said, were only "having a good time, hunting, fishing, sleeping, and getting drunk."

A group of cousins from Caen to whom the fur trade monopoly was granted in 1620 agreed to cover the costs of transporting, feeding, and lodging new families. But the Récollets felt they weren't doing enough. They appear to have found all sorts of excuses for failing to meet their colonization commitments. The problem was, these merchants saw colonization as a costly undertaking that often cut into their slim profits. If it were up to them, New France would remain a trading post. These divergent views would soon be brought up in the king's court. A political decision was required.

A New Impetus

Louis XIII began to govern on his own in 1617. His reign would be dominated by Cardinal Richelieu, a larger-than-life figure who, starting in 1624, would hold a position equivalent to prime minister. For France to regain its greatness, as Richelieu saw things, it would have to develop its empire and fight "reformed" Christians, the Protestant Huguenots, who were dividing the kingdom. In 1627, Richelieu ordered the siege of La Rochelle, the last great Huguenot bastion in France. The era of religious tolerance established by King Henry IV was now over. The views of Cardinal Richelieu converged with those of the mystics who dreamed of building a Christian New World. Wanting to give concrete form to their religious faith, these nuns and holy men, supported by generous sponsors, went out to convert pagans in New France and many other parts of the world.

The Company of One Hundred Associates

France couldn't regain its imperial grandeur without the proper means and resources. Once in power, Cardinal Richelieu set out to find these resources. After consulting some people — and shutting out others — he moved into action.

Finally some support

On April 29, 1627, Richelieu signed a deed establishing a large company owned by about 100 associates. The official name of the new entity was the *Compagnie de la Nouvelle-France* (Company of New France). Heading it was a committee equivalent to a board of directors. To direct operations and implement the cardinal's policies, there was an *intendant,* who handled day-to-day decisions. The company's mission was to "populate the said country with Catholic natives of France who, through their example, would dispose these [Aboriginal] nations toward the Christian religion and civil life, even establishing royal authority there." The company would also "draw from the newly discovered said lands advantages in trade for the use of the king's subjects." This amounted to colonizing New France and exploiting its wealth.

Richelieu set ambitious goals: The company would be required to find 200 to 300 people each year to cross the Atlantic. The aim was to attract 4,000 settlers to New France. Each new arrival would be lodged, fed, and maintained for three years, after which he could settle on a piece of land that would be provided free of charge. The company's charter included extensive religious conditions. It would have to provide land and cover the subsistence costs of clergy settling in the colony. Only Catholics would be allowed to settle there — a serious error, in the view of some historians. By excluding the Protestant minority, Richelieu deprived the colony of a large and dynamic group that could have played a decisive role. In return, the Company of One Hundred Associates obtained a monopoly on all trade conducted in the colony, with the exception of fishing. The area covered was huge — it stretched from the Arctic Circle to Florida.

Off to a fast start

Faithful to its commitment, the company contracted four ships packed with more than 400 settlers. The convoy also carried foodstuffs, tools for clearing land, and seeds of all sorts. This was certainly the most ambitious expedition since New France's earliest days — and the most expensive. For the ships to leave Dieppe in April 1628, the associates had to bleed their new company dry.

The timing was unfortunate, however. In reaction to the siege of La Rochelle, King Charles I of England had just declared war on France. Informed by Huguenot spies that Richelieu was organizing a major expedition to New France, the English monarch called on the services of Scottish privateers, the Kirke brothers. Their mission was to intercept the French ships and capture the young colony.

Champlain capitulates

In July 1628, the privateers intercepted an initial French ship. The invaders took Tadoussac and, guided by Montagnais who had changed sides, they went upriver as far as Cap Tourmente. After passing themselves off as representatives of the One Hundred Associates, they destroyed the few farm dwellings located there, slaughtered the livestock, and took prisoners.

On July 10, Champlain was handed a letter from the Kirke brothers informing him that their mission was to take New France. They promised to respect the clergy and the honor of the women. Champlain replied that he had enough rations to await reinforcements. In reality, he and his men were driven almost to starvation. Every pea was counted. Something unprecedented occurred: Frenchmen traded beaver pelts to their Aboriginal allies for eels.

The Kirke brothers knew Champlain was bluffing. Rather than attack Quebec, they preferred to have the French give up on their own. But their patience, and that of Charles I, was limited. The winter of 1628–1629 was long and harsh. The few dozen settlers in Quebec seemed to have no future. On July 19, 1629, with the Kirke brothers unaware that peace had been reestablished between France and England, a new letter handed to Champlain demanded immediate capitulation. Three English vessels were moored facing Quebec.

Left to his own devices and short of rations, Champlain gave up. On July 20, 150 English soldiers took possession of the Quebec post. The next day, the English flag was flying. Most of the French, including Champlain, returned to France via London.

Starting again from scratch

The interception of the convoy in 1628 and the capture of Quebec hobbled the beginnings of the Company of One Hundred Associates. But back in France, Champlain did not despair. He published *Voyages en Nouvelle-France*, a large book summing up his experiences and reminding readers of the colony's vast potential.

After long and laborious negotiations, England finally handed New France back to France on March 29, 1632, under the Treaty of Saint-Germain-en-Laye. On July 13, the Kirke brothers, feeling bitter, abandoned Quebec, taking with them a final shipment of beaver pelts, their fourth since they arrived in the colony. They failed to found a "New England" in the St. Lawrence Valley, but they did manage to pocket significant gains!

To restart development of the French colony in North America, Richelieu appointed Champlain as governor and agreed to have subcontractors back the efforts of the Company of One Hundred Associates. They had to start again almost from scratch. This took a huge effort: The Quebec post was a field of ruins.

"We will be just one people"

Champlain's crossing in the spring of 1633 was his last one. He died two years later, on December 25, 1635. His final years in New France were a busy time. He founded a new post at Trois-Rivières in 1634 and made sure arriving settlers had everything they needed to get off to a good start. He worked relentlessly with help from Aboriginal allies, with whom he renewed contact on his return in May 1633. During a discussion with Montagnais representatives, he explained that the Quebec fort would have to be rebuilt. "When this big house is ready," he said, "our boys will marry your daughters, and we will be just one people."

The "boys" Champlain was talking about finally began to arrive in 1634. Among them was Robert Giffard, who came from the Perche region south of Normandy. This master surgeon, employed by the company, had spent a winter in New France in the mid-1620s — enough to dream of returning and settling there for good. In January 1634, the One Hundred Associates awarded him the seigneury of Beauport. Giffard set out immediately to recruit settlers. In June, thanks to his efforts, 48 people landed in Quebec.

Giffard recruited other people from Perche in the following years. The convoys of 1635 and 1636 brought more indentured workers. Their motivations were many and varied: Some dreamed of having access to a piece of land, the most precious possession at the time. Others saw an opportunity to have their mastery of a trade recognized. (After six years practicing a trade in New France, an indentured worker could demand the title of "master" in France, enabling him to open a shop in a city.) These new arrivals came especially from Normandy, Île-de-France, and west-central France (Saintonge and Poitou). In 1634, about 400 French people were living in the St. Lawrence Valley. Weddings were celebrated and baptisms were recorded. From 1627 to 1663, a population of pioneers established roots in New France. A people was in the process of taking shape.

The mystics' adventure

Richelieu's grand plan, the self-interested calculations of some merchants, and recruitment efforts by some seigneurs are only part of the explanation for the surge in population. An old French adage says that faith can sometimes raise mountains. Nothing was truer in the 17th century, when religious belief was a basic motive for action among many French people and other Europeans. In reaction to the advances of Protestantism, the Roman Catholic Church also introduced reforms. It wasn't enough to besiege La Rochelle, starve Huguenots, and fight the Protestant evil militarily. For the church to win and retain the adherence of the faithful, priests needed more guidance, elites needed more education, and the more zealous religious orders had to be encouraged. Many of these orders spread the message of Christ through their work with children, the ill, and the poor, firming up the faith of doubters and converting pagans around the world. For Catholic reformers, New France clearly constituted a formidable challenge!

Jesuits on a mission

Among the religious institutions established during the Catholic Counter-Reformation was the Society of Jesus, the Jesuits. Founded in 1540 by Ignatius of Loyola and Pope Paul III, the Jesuit order was devoted to apostolic work and the training of elites. Reporting directly to the pope, the Jesuits had access to circles of power. Richelieu, for example, attached great importance to what they said, including their views on New France. North America had long interested the Jesuits. In 1612, some of them traveled to Port-Royal. After devising a catechism intended for indigenous peoples, they returned to France.

To support the evangelical work of the Récollets, who had arrived in 1615, three Jesuit priests — Charles Lalemant, Ennemond Massé, and Jean de Brébeuf — landed in New France on June 15, 1625. On arriving, they sought the services of interpreters so that they could enter into contact with allied First Nations. Father Brébeuf spent his first winter among the Montagnais and later spent time with the Hurons. A large tract of land in the heart of Quebec given to the Jesuits in 1626 showed their already sizable influence. In 1632, the Jesuits were chosen over the Récollets and the Capuchins to evangelize New France and bring First Nations into European life. Three years later, thanks to a philanthropist's gift, they founded a seminary in Quebec. Their greatest contribution to the discovery and development of New France lay in their writings. Over a 40-year period (1632–1672), in their *Relations,* the Jesuits recounted what they saw and experienced. These writings, a unique record of the mores of indigenous peoples and daily life in New France, aroused great interest in well-informed circles. Some people of faith even found in them the inspiration needed to set off and conquer the New World.

The Société Notre-Dame de Montréal

Reading the *Relations* also inspired others to act. In 1639, Jérôme Le Royer de la Dauversière, a tax collector living in modest circumstances; Father Jean-Jacques Olier, founder of the Sulpicians; and several backers founded the Société Notre-Dame "for the conversion of the Savages of New France." The goals set by this society were strictly spiritual. The aims were to establish an agricultural colony, found a seminary, train missionaries, and convert indigenous people.

The following year, the group acquired the island of Mont-Royal. Their project was supported by the Jesuits and received Richelieu's blessing. The group recruited Paul de Chomedey de Maisonneuve and Jeanne Mance to implement their plan. Maisonneuve was a career military officer who was strongly attracted to the venture's spiritual dimension. Austere and courageous, he would draw no personal benefit from his participation. Jeanne Mance, a layperson who was close to the Jesuit Charles Lalemant, came from a bourgeois background that was filled with piety. A philanthropist entrusted her with control of a substantial sum to be used for building a hospital.

A "foolish venture"

The first expedition financed by the Société Notre-Dame de Montréal set out from the port of La Rochelle on May 9, 1641. It consisted of two ships with some 40 devout women and men aboard. This first group of "Montréaliste" recruits received a chilly reception from Governor Montmagny in Quebec. This was a "foolish venture," he said! Montreal Island was too exposed to Iroquois attacks. Settling there was far too dangerous. Rather than going to Montreal, Montmagny suggested, why not simply settle on Île d'Orléans, much closer to Quebec? Maisonneuve's reply left no doubt as to his determination: "Sir, what you say to me would be good if I had been sent to deliberate and choose a site. But since it has been determined by the company that sent me that I would go Montreal, . . . you will approve, that I will go there to start a colony, even if all the trees on the island were to turn into as many Iroquois!"

After spending a winter in Quebec, the Montréalistes set out in the spring and took possession of Montreal Island on May 17, 1642. In August, reinforcements arrived from Europe: 12 new colonists would contribute to the Société Notre-Dame's civilizing dream. A stockade that could house up to 70 people was soon set up. The early months went by happily. But then hard reality caught up. On June 9, 1643, Iroquois from the Mohawk tribe attacked five young Frenchmen working on building a frame. According to the *Relations* of 1643, three of them were struck down and scalped. The governor's dire prediction seemed to be coming true.

Marie Guyart and the arrival of the Ursulines

Among the assiduous readers of the *Relations* was Marie Guyart, also known as Marie de l'Incarnation (1599–1672). This widow felt the call of God at an early age but waited until her son turned 12 before devoting herself to religion. When the time came, she left her son behind and entered the Ursuline order, founded in 1530 and dedicated to the contemplative life and the education of young girls. Following a dream in which she saw herself in "a large and vast country, full of mountains and valleys," as she wrote in her autobiography, she decided to go and live in New France. On May 4, 1639, she left the port of Dieppe. She would never again set foot in her French homeland.

Other mystics accompanied her — some of them Ursulines, but also nursing sisters who founded Hôtel-Dieu hospital in Quebec and laypeople such as Madeleine de la Peltrie, another reader of the *Relations* who helped found several of Quebec's central institutions. On July 27, these people of faith were greeted in Quebec by Charles Huault de Montmagny, the governor who had succeeded Champlain.

Marie Guyart chose to devote herself to the mission of converting and educating young Aboriginals. By her own admission, her success was limited. "For every hundred girls who passed through our hands, scarcely one did we civilize," she wrote. "We find docility and spirit in them, but when we least expect it, they climb over our fence, like squirrels, and run off into the woods with family members, where they find greater pleasure than in all the amenities of our French houses." She left many letters that give us a better understanding of indigenous languages and spirituality.

The correspondence of this courageous and enterprising woman with her son, whom she would never see again, inspired others to enter religious life. Cited as a "mistress of spiritual life," she was beatified by Pope John Paul II on June 22, 1980.

The Iroquois threat

The French who settled in the colony were convinced of their civilization's moral superiority, but with a few rare exceptions they didn't aspire to exterminate the indigenous communities surrounding them. Even if they had had the will to do this, they wouldn't have had the power or the means. Confrontations with the Iroquois, which began in earnest in the 1640s after a long period of calm, resulted from fierce competition between First Nations aiming to take control of the fur trade. This struggle involved the French as allies of the Hurons, Algonquians, and Montagnais.

The Communauté des Habitants

These tensions among indigenous people directly affected the fur trade. Attacked by their Iroquois enemies in the mid-1630s, Hurons from the Pays d'en haut, who were the main fur suppliers, sent smaller shipments. This was bad for business. Already highly indebted, the Company of One Hundred Associates had little choice but to operate through intermediaries who would share the financial risks of a trade that fluctuated with intertribal wars. Also, the Montréalistes wanted the colony's inhabitants to have greater control of the fur trade. They had their contacts in the king's court through the Compagnie du Saint-Sacrement, a powerful Catholic society with an extensive network.

The growing Iroquois threat in the 1640s and pressures from the Montréalistes accounted for the creation of the Communauté des Habitants in 1645. The French associates remained the masters of New France in such things as administering justice, land concessions, and the choice of governor, but they agreed to yield the fur trade and the heavy responsibility of settlement to an entity consisting of people who actually lived in the colony. In 1647, the Communauté des Habitants was headed by the governors of Quebec and Montreal, the Jesuit superior, and representatives elected by a significant portion of the populace. Working in this way, the new entity empowered the settlers and helped create a sense of belonging to the colony.

The eclipse of a people

During the first great Iroquois war, from 1647 to 1653, settlers in the St. Lawrence Valley had to close ranks. The Mohawks and their allies launched an unprecedented offensive against their Huron enemies. They had a major advantage: firearms, supplied by the Dutch. The French had always refused to trade guns for furs, and the Hurons paid the price for this policy: The lightning attacks of 1648 and 1649 were devastating. Thousands of Huron warriors were killed or reduced to slavery. Their frightened communities fled west or sought refuge in Quebec. Their stories spread quickly and sowed terror. Terrible epidemics contributed to the sudden destruction of Huronia, as did the presence of the Jesuit missionaries, who created a rift in Huron society between a traditionalist camp that favored peace with the Iroquois and converts who continued to support the alliance with the French. Fathers Brébeuf and Lalemant were captured, tortured, and killed. Some Hurons regarded them as responsible for their misfortunes. The missionaries may have caused the Hurons to lose confidence in their traditions.

The settlers under threat

This powerful Iroquois offensive reached into the St. Lawrence Valley. Pumped up by their relatively easy victories against the Hurons, the Iroquois increased the number of raids and proved to be quite aggressive. The settlers clearing land on Montreal Island were ordered to take refuge inside the Ville-Marie fort. In March 1651, about 50 Iroquois arrived in Montreal. Hidden around the fort, they patiently awaited their victims. On May 6, they seriously wounded a settler and captured his wife, whom they burned alive after cutting off her breasts. In July the Montréalistes, led by the courageous Lambert Closse, drove back the Iroquois who were planning to attack the hospital founded by Jeanne Mance. The small post at Trois-Rivières also suffered a number of attacks during this period. The Iroquois usually arrived by canoe in complete silence. Using harquebuses and tomahawks, they killed Frenchmen who were out hunting game. On June 6, 1651, Pierre Boucher, in charge of the Trois-Rivières post, was ordered to create small companies of militia. This was a first.

Saving Montreal

In 1650, the fate of New France hung in the balance. "This place would be an earthly paradise for the Savages and for the French were it not for the Iroquois terror that arises almost continuously and makes this place almost uninhabitable," state the *Relations* of 1651. As Marie de l'Incarnation wrote to her son, the settlers seemed to have only two options: "Either die or return to France." With no army to protect them, the fur trade was interrupted and agriculture became impossible.

Despite the strength of their convictions, the highly exposed Montréalistes had to face facts: Without reinforcements, their cause was lost. For the first time, Maisonneuve showed signs of being discouraged. To save Montreal, Jeanne Mance agreed to divert a significant amount of money intended for construction of the Hôtel-Dieu hospital. This enabled Maisonneuve to return to France and offer reasonable conditions to about 100 men who would come to cultivate the land and defend the Montreal post. This group of recruits, which included people who practiced various trades and came from every region of France, arrived in 1653. Among the recruits was Marguerite Bourgeoys, the founder of the Congrégation de Notre-Dame, devoted to the education of girls and Aboriginal women. Without these people, Montreal would've been finished.

A disaster barely averted

After a few years of calm, hostilities began again. In October 1657, the Mohawks resumed their surprise attacks and gratuitous violence. Even with two fortified houses built in 1658 and the arrival of about 100 settlers and nursing sisters in 1659, Montreal could not long resist a large-scale Iroquois attack. There were rumors that the Iroquois were getting ready to launch an offensive in the spring of 1660. At this moment, a controversial figure in Quebec history stepped onto the stage: Dollard des Ormeaux was a bachelor who was born in 1635 and arrived in the colony in 1658. Some portray him as a vulgar fur trader; others see him as a genuine hero who sacrificed his life to save his people. For some, he was a greedy upstart; for others, a holy martyr.

Whatever Dollard des Ormeaux's true motives may have been, we do know that with 16 other young men he organized an expedition to Long Sault on the Ottawa River. Was he out to intercept a shipment of furs, or did he intend to halt the Iroquois offensive? It's hard to say. He and his men set out on April 20, 1660, and arrived during the night of May 1. They took a position high up in a small fort that had been abandoned by the Algonquians. Soon after they arrived, about 250 Iroquois launched two attacks, which the Montréalistes and their Huron allies brilliantly drove back. A few days later, nearly 500 Iroquois came to reinforce the initial contingent. Fighting lasted for five days. On May 12, the battle ended with all the Frenchmen massacred.

What has remained in Quebec's collective memory of this episode is that the "sacrifice" of Dollard des Ormeaux and his companions may have deterred the Iroquois from undertaking their major offensive. After all, the Iroquois supposedly told themselves, if a handful of settlers could hold out for such a long time against a great army, what would happen when they attacked Montreal or Quebec?

In the short term, the Montréalistes were saved. But sooner or later, France would have to find a more effective way of protecting its colony from the continuing attacks.

Monseigneur de Laval bans the booze trade

On June 16, 1659, François de Laval arrived in Quebec with the title of "apostolic vicar." He was appointed directly by Rome and not by the archbishop of Rouen, who regarded New France as part of his diocese. These jurisdictional disputes didn't prevent this quasi-bishop from assuming his seat and establishing his magisterium. A true product of the Counter-Reformation, the 36-year-old cleric sought — often to the point of intransigence — to have the church's powers respected. Some priests and members of religious orders rejoiced at the arrival of a prelate who could exercise real authority, but others found him inflexible, authoritarian, and too jealous of the privileges of his rank.

One of his first decisions was to excommunicate those who engaged in the liquor trade with the Aboriginal peoples. Prior to his arrival, other leaders of the colony, including Champlain, had prohibited merchants from bartering furs for alcohol. This trade appears to have been introduced during the period of English occupation (1629–1632).

From the time they discovered liquor, Aboriginal people would consume it in large quantities, not because they enjoyed the taste but because of the intoxication that alcohol provided. Many found that a state of drunkenness enabled them to communicate with higher powers, awakening them to the world of dreams and reveries, to which they attached great importance. In the eyes of the missionaries, intoxication led to a loosening of morals and got in the way of evangelization.

The merchants and the governor saw the excommunication decreed by Monseigneur de Laval as excessive. To validate his position, the apostolic vicar obtained a learned opinion from theologians at the Sorbonne, as well as support from the king himself. The decisive event that ended up convincing some of the more recalcitrant merchants was the great earthquake of February 5, 1663, felt throughout northeastern North America. No deaths were recorded, but some people got the scare of their lives. For the clergy, the cause was obvious: The earthquake was a sign of divine anger. For a time, this put a stop to the liquor trade!

Chapter 3

Exploring a Continent (1661–1701)

● ●

In This Chapter

▶ Appreciating the vision of Louis XIV, Jean-Baptiste Colbert, and Jean Talon

▶ Waging a new war against the Iroquois — and the English

● ●

The 1660s were economic hard times for New France, caused primarily by fear. The 3,000 habitants were people of character, but they had no military training and they had to defend themselves as best they could against the Iroquois who lay low, awaited their prey, and attacked without warning. In August 1661, the arrival as governor of Baron Pierre Du Bois d'Avaugour, a career military officer, probably reassured the habitants. Alas, the new governor brought only about 100 men with him — clearly not enough to impose peace.

Many people felt that all was lost. And yet, a turnaround was in the offing. In France at that time, a kind of renaissance was occurring, led by an enthusiastic young king who aimed to instill new energy in his kingdom. He was guided by top officials in his circle such as Jean-Baptiste Colbert, who worked to rationalize the administration, rebuild the economy, and consolidate the empire. With the very dedicated Jean Talon as intendant of the colony, New France would benefit from this constructive energy. New settlers arrived from France in fairly large numbers. A battle-tested army neutralized the power of the Iroquois warriors for some time. Meanwhile, explorers fought over Hudson Bay, discovered the Mississippi, founded Louisiana, and laid the foundations of a great French America.

The Decisive Move Forward

In 1661, France was in a better position to hear the distress signals coming from the inhabitants of its distant North American colony. There were a number of reasons for this: The kingdom had achieved a measure of internal peace. For nearly 20 years, France had been torn by revolts. Some of these were led by ambitious princes, others by local officials who felt their constituents were overtaxed and denounced excessive concentration of power. But in the late 1650s, order was reestablished. On the external front, France was at peace with Spain, a key neighbor and competitor with which it signed the Treaty of the Pyrenees in 1659. The most important date, however, was March 9, 1661, the day Cardinal Jules Mazarin died. With the blessing of Anne of Austria, Louis XIII's queen consort who had assumed the regency after her husband's death in 1643, Mazarin had governed France for 18 years.

L'État, c'est moi! (The state, it is I!)

On August 26, 1660, Louis XIII's successor made a triumphal entry into Paris with his wife, Marie-Thérèse. The royal couple took their places. The Sun King's seat was covered with gold brocade. This was unimaginable splendor! A long procession, taking four hours, paid tribute to the monarch and ended with the traditional release of doves. With these pompous *Ancien Régime* (Old Regime) rituals, the young king took symbolic possession of the capital. His natural flair and youth stirred great hope. Could he bring new vigor to this old country?

The Sun King takes power

With Mazarin dead, young Louis XIV could both reign and govern. Early in his reign, an ambassador in Paris drew this portrait of him:

> He is of vigorous complexion, of great height, and of majestic aspect; his face is both open and imposing, his manner courteous and serious; he is of cheerful temperament but by no means of excessive liveliness, for he also conveys melancholy, giving him a level-headed air.

The young man liked hunting, war, and great celebrations. He worked tirelessly, reading the thick dossiers given him by his advisors and preparing detailed sets of instructions.

Louis XIV wasn't just a ceremonial king who represents the kingdom but makes no decisions of his own. Though he had influential ministers, no prime minister resolved sensitive matters in his place. His regime was considered an absolute monarchy, and Louis XIV was the sole master. No opposition force or elected chamber could stand in his way or challenge his decisions.

But he was in no way a capricious tyrant who arbitrarily terrorized defenseless subjects. Convinced of the greatness of France, then the dominant power on the international scene, the Sun King respected inherited tradition, watched over his subjects like a good father, and felt a concern for everything related to his kingdom, including New France — at least early in his reign.

The mercantilism of Jean-Baptiste Colbert

Jean-Baptiste Colbert (1619–1683) was one of Louis XIV's top officials. Discovered by Mazarin, he was appointed intendant of finance and minister of the navy. In Colbert's view, France's power depended not only on its army, but also, and especially, on its industrial production. To dominate Europe and the world, it had to export its manufactured products and import as little as possible. Colbert's aim was to avoid depending on foreign products and to seek economic self-sufficiency in all areas. To implement this economic strategy, prosperous and dynamic colonies would be needed.

Colbert's action plan was quite simple: The colonies would have to generate commodities lacking in France, and they would have to consume French products. This economic doctrine had a name — mercantilism — and Colbert applied it more methodically than his predecessors had. To play a central and useful role, the colonies would have to devote themselves to productive activities that would enable the kingdom to grow and prosper.

In 1661, Louis XIV and Colbert were determined to act to promote their colonies. This was precisely what one of them, New France, wanted! That year, the colony's leaders moved heaven and earth to get the royal authorities more involved.

Pierre Boucher's persuasive arguments

As soon as he arrived in the colony, Governor Du Bois d'Avaugour inspected the Trois-Rivières and Montreal posts, which were the most exposed to Iroquois attacks. His verdict was a bombshell: France must immediately send "powerful support." To overcome the Iroquois "rabble," he said, at least 3,000 soldiers would be needed. With the aim of persuading the king and his court to move forward, the governor delegated Pierre Boucher, a former official of the Trois-Rivières post, to go to France.

Only 12 when he arrived in New France with his family, Boucher had come to know the colony like the back of his hand. At an early age, he left on a mission with the Jesuits to learn Aboriginal languages and be an interpreter. After a first marriage to a Huron woman who died in childbirth, he later married Jeanne Crevier, settled in Trois-Rivières, and courageously confronted the Iroquois.

Early in 1662, Boucher had a personal audience with the king and a long talk with Colbert. They listened attentively to his description of New France. As he would later write in his *Histoire véritable et naturelle . . . de la Nouvelle-France (True and Natural History of New France)*, the Iroquois threat had to be eliminated very quickly. "It is not possible to go hunting or fishing for fear of being killed or captured by those rascals," he wrote. Boucher was convinced that the colony could finally prosper once it was rid of this threat.

New France "is a good country" where one can find "much of what one may desire," he said, adding that "the land is very good and highly productive, and is not at all ungrateful. . . . The country is covered with fine, thick forests, inhabited by numerous animals of varied species."

But exploiting this wealth and contributing in this way to the greatness of France would require ensuring peace and security for its people. The message was very clearly received.

It should be noted that Boucher was far from alone in conveying a message of this kind to the authorities. The Jesuit lobby also became involved, as did Monseigneur de Laval.

A big push

In the following months and years, the government of Louis XIV launched an ambitious program of administrative reforms and sent 1,200 soldiers, as well as several hundred *filles du roy* (literally, "daughters of the king") to provide wives for the settlers. Never before had so much effort been expended to get New France up and running.

A royal colony

In New France and other colonies, the king and his government established a new system of political and administrative control. The Company of One Hundred Associates was handed over to the king; the businessmen involved were to receive compensation, but at a much later date. For the first time, the colony didn't come under a company but under royal authority, as if it were a province of the kingdom.

Starting in 1663, the new power structure was as follows:

- **Governor:** The king's personal representative, the governor was drawn from the French aristocracy. He was in charge of the army and external relations with surrounding colonies, as well as handling connections with the Aboriginal nations.

- **Intendant:** Unlike the king's power, the governor's powers were limited by the prerogatives of the intendant, a new position in New France. As the colony's top civil servant, he led the internal administration and received orders from the minister of the navy. The intendant appointed judges, planned budgets, and coordinated land distribution.

- **Sovereign Council:** The governor and the intendant sat on the Sovereign Council, a new body. The Sovereign Council served as the final court of appeal and was a forum for deliberation. It also included the titular bishop and a group of local councilors, varying in number over time.

The colony's inhabitants could, like those in France, make representations to the Sovereign Council, but this system of colonial government was not in any way democratic. Nor did the king and his minister of the navy, concerned with preserving government authority over all parts of the kingdom, necessarily mind if the governor and the intendant occasionally fought over jurisdictional issues. Divide and conquer!

These new institutions were modeled on those established in the French provinces in the preceding years. Typical of the *Ancien Régime,* they were intended to rationalize and centralize administration.

Reinforcements at last!

While it was reforming the colony's institutions, the French government decided to eliminate the Iroquois threat. The king assigned this mission to a loyal and trusted person: Sieur Prouville de Tracy. The 63-year-old career military officer was sent to different parts of the empire to reestablish royal authority. After a mission in the Caribbean, he landed in Quebec on June 30, 1665. Companies of the Carignan-Salières Regiment arrived at the same time. This contingent consisted of 1,200 soldiers who set out to conquer the Iroquois territories further south.

You can imagine the relief felt by the few thousand settlers — reinforcements at last! Marie Guyart, who had fallen into despair a few years earlier, suddenly turned optimistic at the sight of these soldiers. "Tracy," she wrote to her son, "has produced wonders in the Islands of America, leading everyone to obey the King; we hope he will do no less in all the nations of Canada."

Tracy's mission was far from a walk in the park. He had to not only defend the inhabitants, but also launch an offensive. The five Iroquois nations soon learned of his arrival. They also found out that the French were building three forts in strategic places, near water, which would make surprise attacks more difficult. Instead of starting a war that they knew they would lose, four Iroquois nations gave up and signed a peace treaty in December 1665. Only the Mohawks held out.

On January 9, 1666, Tracy left Quebec with more than 500 soldiers. Overconfident in his capacities, he defied the cold and headed into unfamiliar forests without guides. He and his army got lost, food began to run out, and men died of cold. Never again would a French officer launch an attack in midwinter.

The following autumn, Tracy set out on a new offensive. His army of 1,200 men included soldiers, settlers, and Aboriginal people. After reaching Mohawk country, he ordered several villages burned. Unable to fight back and short of food, the Mohawks were forced to make peace. In July 1667, an agreement was reached. For the inhabitants of New France, it was the beginning of a peaceful interval that would last 15 years.

We need "women to marry," and soon!

After peace was achieved, hundreds of French soldiers were urged to settle in the colony. Seigneuries were offered to officers of the regiment. Many soldiers settled on land held by their former captains. Other men also agreed to take up the challenge of New France. The journeys of these hundreds of laborers were financed by the French West India Company, which had held a monopoly of trade in all French possessions since 1664.

Whether former soldiers or new indentured workers, these young, vigorous men soon noticed the scarcity of women. Women born in the colony were often married at age 12. Winter nights in New France were long, and without women, they were also boring. Authorities in France were made aware of the situation and arranged for the arrival of women to marry, also known as *filles du roy*. This type of immigration started in the late 1650s, but it didn't gain momentum until about 1663.

Between 1663 and 1673, 770 of these women arrived in New France, representing 8 percent of all immigrants who settled in the colony in the 17th century. Their average age was 24, and they were mostly orphans from the most deprived sectors of French society. Contrary to a long-held belief, however, they were not prostitutes.

In order for these women to adapt to the country without too much difficulty, and in order for them to find husbands quickly, the intendant Jean Talon recommended to Colbert that the women recruited "be in no way disagreeable on the outside" and that they "be healthy and strong for work in the countryside." The great majority of them married quickly — some very quickly. Of course, they had plenty of men to choose from! A man who wanted a satisfactory outcome from this mix-and-match had every interest in offering something besides fine words. A cleared plot of land and a spacious cabin were often suitable assets. In a matter of months, sometimes weeks, these *filles du roy* found husbands, settled on a piece of land, and became pregnant. Between 1664 and 1702, they gave birth to 4,459 babies!

Jean Talon's ambitious program

Jean Talon (1626–1694) was the first real intendant of New France. He held his position in the colony for a combined total of only five years (1665–1668 and 1670–1672), but he left a lasting mark. As a senior official serving the French government, Talon first worked in the army and then in the region of Hainaut in northern France. He was a bachelor who was fully devoted to his work, and was both a highly talented organizer and a visionary. He didn't just draw up fine plans for the future; he administered a policy, launched projects, and inspired people to do more than they thought they could.

The language of New France

The French of the *Ancien Régime* spoke numerous dialects. The French spoken in Île-de-France, the area around Paris, did not become standard until the 19th century, with the development of a widespread school system. People who arrived in New France starting in the late 17th century were struck by the quality of the French language spoken by the inhabitants, despite their varied regional origins.

In all likelihood, the *filles du roy* contributed heavily to this linguistic unity. Nearly 85 percent of them spoke — or at least could get by in — French. Some 265 of the 770 *filles du roy* came directly from Paris. Even though many of the soldiers and laborers were from rural areas, a number of them had had to transit through cities before settling in the colony. Most of these men formed part of a mobile and urban France where speaking French was essential for finding work.

In the 17th century, the inhabitants of New France were not considered to have an "accent." Their language was the French spoken in Paris and in the king's court. It was only starting in the 19th century that travelers from France found the Quebec accent strange or provincial.

The 17th-century settlers brought with them words, expressions, and a vocabulary associated with their region or trade. Some of these words and expressions are still commonly used by people in Quebec but are regarded as archaic by their French cousins. Examples include *s'abrier* (to cover up), *c'est de valeur* (what a pity), *il mouille* (it's raining), *traîner* (to wander or roam), and *être allège* (to move unburdened).

With his boundless energy, Talon used every means at his disposal in his efforts to diversify the economy of New France. Like Colbert, he regarded the economy as a key source of greatness and power. Within a few years, the colony began producing more wheat and vegetables, growing hemp and hops, manufacturing shoes, and weaving wool.

Producing was one thing; selling was another. The local market was too small, and shipping to France or the Caribbean too expensive, for this production to pay its way. Shipyards were set up and small boats were built, along with a large ship for the king. These initiatives were bold, but production costs were too high for this strategy to be viable.

The result: Merchants maintained their concentration on furs. But there was a problem: Beavers providing quality pelts were receding further and further from the St. Lawrence Valley. Getting these pelts would require going deeper into the continent and building new alliances with Aboriginal tribes.

From French settlers to Canadiens

The word *Canadien* first appeared in the writings of Jacques Cartier. The sailor from Saint-Malo used this term to designate the Iroquois of Stadacona. This word returned in the writings of Champlain, but it now referred to the Aboriginal peoples of the St. Lawrence Valley, along with the Mi'kmaqs.

The first settlers to establish roots in the colony early in the 17th century were described by the authorities as *habitants* or *François.* It was not until after 1670 that the word *Canadien* came to designate those who were neither native people nor French people just passing through. A Canadien was someone born in the colony who regarded it as his country and New France as his primary homeland and place of belonging.

It was in the last third of the 17th century that French authorities began regarding Canadiens as forming a distinct people with their own character and their own way of seeing things. The correspondence of governors with ministers of the navy is filled with accounts such as those of the Marquis de Denonville. "The Canadiens," Denonville wrote to his superior in November 1685, "are all big, well built, and well set on their legs, accustomed by necessity to living with little, sturdy and vigorous, but very willful and frivolous, and prone to debauchery. They have spirit and vivacity." What truly astonished French observers was the Canadiens' spirit of independence. Pierre-François-Xavier de Charlevoix, a Jesuit traveler and historian, noted that "from birth, they breathe an air of freedom, making them very pleasant in the business of life!"

A pro-birth policy

In addition to putting great effort into diversifying the economy, Talon pressed for large-scale immigration. But Colbert feared depopulating France. Talon's ambitions were constantly held back by the government. New France was already falling well behind the English colonies in population. Census figures from 1666 show that, not counting soldiers, the colony's population barely exceeded 4,200. Even with the arrival of the *filles du roy,* Talon found that retaining soldiers and indentured workers was nowhere near enough to solve the population problem. Pro-birth measures — encouraging early marriages and promoting large families — had to be adopted. Allowances were granted to families with ten or more children. Bonuses were provided to men who married before age 20 and to women who said "I do" before age 16. Free education was promised to the 26th child! (Yes, the 26th child.)

Toward the Great Peace of 1701

Following Jean Talon's departure, the royal court began to lose interest in New France. The war against Holland (1672–1679) took up the king's attention, and Colbert reduced supplies. The colony would have to look after its own defense and handle its own efforts to attract new settlers. Meanwhile, the British Empire in America was expanding, developing its trade, and increasing its population. New France again was left to its own devices. But instead of becoming bitter, its leaders moved into action, pushing the boundaries of the colony ever further, laying the foundations for a great French America, and signing a peace treaty with the Iroquois.

French America

North America in the second half of the 17th century was still a place where explorers were inspired by the quest for wealth and glory. The interior of the continent remained almost unknown. Some sought new routes to the west, where the finest furs could be found; others strove to find a passage to the south; the greatest dreamers were still hoping to find a route that would finally lead to China.

As with all great figures who inspire others, these explorers' flaws were often an extension of their virtues: They were brave to the point of temerity, determined to the point of obstinacy, and sure of themselves to the point of vanity. They served the king while they sought to make their own fortunes.

What about the cost of their missions? That was the least of their concerns! But for all that, their exploits were extraordinary.

Were Radisson and des Groseilliers turncoats?

Médard Chouart des Groseilliers (1618–1696) and Pierre-Esprit Radisson (1640–1710) were quick in making their mark as explorers. Des Groseilliers arrived in the colony around 1641 and went to Huronia with the Jesuit mission. Radisson landed in New France at an early age and settled in Trois-Rivières. As a teenager, he was taken prisoner by the Iroquois, who adopted him and taught him their language. After he escaped, Radisson linked up with des Groseilliers, his brother-in-law.

For a year (1659–1660), at a time when tensions with the Iroquois were acute, the two men undertook a great journey of exploration that brought them to the western edge of Lake Superior. They brought back a magnificent shipment of furs from their expedition. On their return, they expected to be congratulated and rewarded. Instead, the governor imposed a fine on them and had their convoy seized. The king's representative accused them of conducting this trip without his permission. The two men were so outraged that they offered their services to the English and founded a company, the Hudson's Bay Company. From 1670 to 1675, they ran trading posts in the heart of the Hudson Bay region. Their business thrived. They also developed an excellent knowledge of this northern area.

With this expertise, they decided in 1675 to return to France and serve their country again. But Colbert mistrusted them, as did Governor Frontenac of New France, who refused to back development of a new French company. In response, des Groseilliers left the trade and Radisson went back to England. He easily took back the Hudson's Bay Company posts lost to the French. In 1687, he was even naturalized as an Englishman. Radisson and des Groseilliers — *coureurs de bois* (literally, "runners of the woods"), explorers, and adventurers — owed much of their fortune to their knowledge of Aboriginal cultures. They enabled England to establish a northern foothold; the encirclement effect this created was a great source of worry to the authorities in New France until 1713.

Cavelier de La Salle, the murdered hero

While the north and the west may have been interesting, New France's real fascination was with the south. Young Louis Jolliet, accompanied by Father Jacques Marquette, became the first Canadian navigator to explore the Mississippi, from 1672 to 1674. Although the Aboriginal tribes he met along the river told him of the existence of a great sea further south (the Gulf of Mexico), the cautious Jolliet preferred to turn back.

Later, Robert Cavelier de La Salle (1643–1687) continued along the Mississippi right to its mouth. La Salle was a defrocked Jesuit who had always had a taste for adventure. His superiors in the Society of Jesus found him unstable, emotional, prone to anger, and impetuous. This young man from a great bourgeois family had numerous contacts. One of his brothers was a Sulpician (a priest from the Society of Saint-Sulpice) living in Montreal. Arriving in New France in 1667, Cavelier de La Salle was soon made seigneur of "Lachine" — a portentous name, given his great ambition of discovering a route to the Far East. He was convinced he could do this if he could make it to the southern sea, but he had no experience in navigation and no knowledge of Aboriginal cultures.

After a few disastrous expeditions, Cavelier de La Salle finally managed to make it down the Mississippi to the Gulf of Mexico on April 6, 1682. Three days later, he took possession of the territory in the name of the king and founded Louisiana in a solemn ceremony.

If his story had ended there, it would have been wonderful and glorious. But sadly, the explorer met a tragic end. Intoxicated by his discovery, Cavelier de La Salle had struggled to persuade the king and his court to finance an ambitious expedition that would make it possible to establish posts in Louisiana. To do this, however, the Mississippi Delta would have to be found by way of the Gulf of Mexico. Cavelier de La Salle left in July 1684 but would never succeed in finding the mouth of the river. He had brought his crew much too far west. Determined to make his mission succeed at any cost, he and his crew set out on foot. For three years they sought the elusive river. The terrible conditions fostered disillusionment and despair and were not conducive to the finer traits of human nature. As the months went by, La Salle's authority eroded. The more aggressive crew members found a solution: assassination. On March 19, 1687, he was assassinated with a bullet to his head. His body was stripped naked and abandoned deep in the heart of Texas, near where the city of Houston now stands.

D'Iberville the conqueror!

On March 2, 1699, Pierre Le Moyne d'Iberville (1661–1706) finally discovered the mouth of the Mississippi. For this exploit, he was named a Chevalier de Saint-Louis, the kingdom's highest military honor, issued for the first time to a Canadien. Louis XIV made no mistake in entrusting the perilous mission of restarting the colonization of Louisiana to this authentic hero of the seas. He was a son of Charles Le Moyne, a courageous Montréaliste, a prosperous merchant, the seigneur of Châteauguay, and someone with a good knowledge of Aboriginal cultures. D'Iberville first made his mark in 1686 during an expedition to James Bay. His leadership qualities were obvious to everyone, and his reflexes as a warrior were impressive. After taking back the main posts along Hudson Bay from the English, he undertook an expedition against Newfoundland, leading 125 Canadiens. In the course of four months in the summer of 1696, he conquered all the English posts along the Newfoundland shore: 1,830 Englishmen were taken prisoner, 200 were killed, and 371 enemy boats were burned — a stunning success!

In Louisiana, d'Iberville erected forts and founded Biloxi (now in the state of Mississippi) and Mobile (now in Alabama). The great navigator was absolutely convinced of the strategic importance of the new colony. As he wrote in a prophetic memorandum dated 1699,

> If France fails to seize this part of America, the most beautiful part, to have a colony strong enough to resist the English colony further east, . . . the English colony, becoming quite substantial, will grow to the point that, in less than 100 years, it will be strong enough to seize all of America and to drive out all other nations.

Before he died under mysterious circumstances in Havana, where he is buried, d'Iberville prepared a great expedition against the British Empire's main coastal cities in North America. In his eyes, to survive and develop, New France would have to halt the expansion of these competing colonies at any cost.

War and peace

In 1685, when Jacques-René de Brisay, the Marquis de Denonville, became governor of New France, his main concern was the Iroquois threat. For several years, English fur traders in New York State had been trying to persuade the Iroquois to deal with them. The Iroquois were tempted to give in to their flattery.

Well established in the Great Lakes area thanks to Fort Cataraqui, the construction of which began in 1673, the French controlled the western fur trade. In March 1684, the Iroquois intercepted a major fur shipment. Governor La Barre responded by sending an army of 1,600 men to harass them. But he was a poor strategist. Once there, he dithered for many weeks, hesitating to launch an attack against the Iroquois villages. Meanwhile, food supplies ran short, and his soldiers complained of famine. After a semblance of negotiations, the governor recalled the troops. Nothing was settled.

A preventive attack

Urged on by the English, the Iroquois attacked Aboriginal allies of the French further west with impunity, harming the fur trade. For it to flourish once again, Denonville believed it was vital to launch a preventive attack. He also envisaged an offensive against New York, where the authorities were supplying enemy tribes with weapons. The king prohibited him from going ahead with this project. In November 1686, the government of Louis XIV signed a treaty of neutrality with England concerning American issues.

After assembling his troops at Fort Cataraqui, the governor set off to attack the Senecas, the targeted Iroquois nation. Following an easy victory on July 13, 1687, Denonville ordered his men to slaughter livestock, burn harvests, and destroy four villages. A witness, Baron de La Hontan, wrote, "We spent five or six days cutting down the corn with our swords." Having set out to fight the Iroquois, the French and Canadian troops satisfied themselves with starving an entire people for the coming winter.

This scorched-earth policy seemed, in the short term, to provide the hoped-for results. In addition to taking possession of the territory, New France achieved a degree of peace and quiet, and its commercial activities resumed.

The horrible Lachine massacre

After a year of calm, the political climate changed beyond recognition. On May 7, 1689, England under William III, a new Protestant king, joined the League of Augsburg and declared war on France. Neutrality in America was over. A few weeks later, the five Iroquois nations met in Albany, New York, and vowed not only to take revenge following the preventive attack of 1687 but also to fight alongside the English against France.

On the night of August 4–5, 1689, nearly 1,500 Iroquois warriors crossed the St. Lawrence at Lake St. Louis, its widest point in the Montreal area. On the opposite shore, the inhabitants of the hamlet of Lachine were sleeping peacefully. Because of torrential rain, they didn't hear the enemy prowling around their homes. At daybreak, the attack was launched. It was terrible and pitiless. After killing the men, who were valiantly defending their homes and families, the Iroquois burned the farms. The prisoners were tortured, with the bellies of pregnant women cut open and tiny children skewered, roasted, and eaten.

In the following days and weeks, the Iroquois "did everything that rage could inspire in a fierce nation that felt outraged," Baron de La Hontan wrote. Governor Frontenac, who had just replaced the Marquis de Denonville as head of the colony, got his fill of frightening tales from that night of horror. "It would be hard to convey to you," he wrote to his minister, "the general consternation I found among all the people and the despondence among the troops." All told, 200 people were massacred, and 125 were taken prisoner.

Escalation

Such butchery could not go unanswered. Like Denonville, Frontenac envisaged an attack on New York, but he lacked the troops needed for an operation of that scope. However, he still wanted to attack the English, who supplied the weapons. Three surprise raids were planned in February 1690 against villages in New England. The most spectacular attack was the one on Schenectady, a fortified village in New York colony. On the evening of February 28, the French and Canadian attackers, backed by their Aboriginal allies, took the villagers by surprise. Those who resisted were killed, and fire spread everywhere. The assailants perpetrated a massacre equivalent to the one in Lachine; 60 inhabitants were slaughtered and 25 were taken prisoner — another very sad episode.

The English colonists obviously were not going to sit idly by. Because they were not the direct cause of the Lachine massacre, they felt they had been attacked unjustly. With their Iroquois allies, they intended to strike a fatal blow against New France as soon as possible. Two army corps were mobilized. The first one was to attack Montreal by an inland route, while the second was to take Quebec via the Gulf of St. Lawrence. This pincer strategy would require Frontenac to divide his troops and fight on two fronts. But in war, as in life, things rarely happen as planned.

The fighters headed for Montreal were soon stopped by a smallpox epidemic. About 300 of the 1,500 Iroquois gathered at Lake Champlain died of the disease. Troop morale took a hit, and General John Winthrop preferred to abandon the campaign. Meanwhile, the fleet led by William Phips left the port of Boston and easily took Port-Royal in the middle of May. On October 10, Governor Frontenac learned that the enemy troops were approaching Tadoussac. He decided to concentrate all his forces in Quebec.

"From the mouths of my cannon"

New France was far from being out of danger; indeed, the situation was grave. The bishop, Monseigneur de Saint-Vallier, published a pastoral letter in which he urged all the colony's inhabitants to fight these "enemies, not only of us, the French, but also of our faith and our holy religion." On October 16, the 34 ships in the Anglo-American fleet and their 2,000 men faced Quebec. The next day, Phips sent an emissary bearing a white flag.

Blindfolded, the man was brought to the Château Saint-Louis, the governor's official residence. His message was clear: To avoid a bloodbath, the French had to give up the city. Phips gave Frontenac one hour to capitulate. The old governor's response was immediate and spirited:

> I will not make you wait that long. . . . I have no reply to give your general other than from the mouths of my cannon and muskets; may he learn that this is not the way a summons is sent to a man like me.

Phips's attack, which began the next day, was a fiasco. His cannon did not reach the interior of the city, and his men were easily pushed back by the Canadian militiamen at Beauport. Fearing that he could be locked in by ice, he threw in the towel and left the area. Phips lost hundreds of men. Following the departure of the English, the Quebec church was named Notre-Dame-de-la-Victoire.

The decline of the Iroquois

Phips's defeat was an ill omen for the Iroquois, who relied on their alliance with the English to counteract the French hold on the fur trade. In the 1690s, the Iroquois confederacy's power to strike hard was in steady decline. War and illness decimated its troops, and some Iroquois defected, adopting the Christian faith and living in Jesuit villages in New France. In ten years, the number of Iroquois fighters fell from 2,550 to 1,230. An Iroquois chief told English representatives in 1694, "The fat is melting away from our flesh and spilling onto our neighbors, who are growing fatter and living in ease while we become thin."

An expedition against the Iroquois in August 1696, led by an aging Frontenac carried on a chair through the forests, was emblematic of the Five Nations' disarray. They showed no resistance. These difficulties also created political divisions among the Iroquois. Some wanted to keep fighting, while others wanted to begin peace negotiations with the French. The Five Nations chiefs gradually leaned toward this second option.

Peace to men of good will

On August 4, 1701, some 40 Aboriginal nations gathered in Montreal. On that day, their representatives signed the Treaty of Montreal. People in Montreal would remember this ceremony for a long time. All told, nearly 1,300 Aboriginal people lived for three weeks in this small town of about 2,600 inhabitants. The ceremony took place at the same time as the annual fur fair. To keep things from getting out of hand, the authorities banned the sale of alcohol.

The dignitaries were received with great pomp by Governor Louis-Hector de Callière, who gave an important speech:

> Today I am ratifying the peace we have made. . . . I am again taking all your axes and all your other instruments of war, which I am placing with mine in a pit so deep that nobody will be able to take them back and disturb the tranquility I am reestablishing among my children.

This peace, assuring France of domination in the west, meant that the Iroquois and the Aboriginal peoples of the *Pays d'en haut* would stop making war, and all could go freely after furs and move around undisturbed. The Iroquois also agreed to remain neutral in case of conflict between France and England. After the document was signed, the peace pipe was smoked.

A chapter in the history of New France was now closed.

Chapter 4

A French Province (1701–1754)

In This Chapter

▶ Seeing another attempt by the British to take Quebec

▶ Discovering daily life in New France

*T*he Great Peace of Montreal marked the end of hostilities with the Iroquois. Unfortunately, this did not mean an end to threats to New France. As Pierre Le Moyne d'Iberville had predicted in his memorandum (see Chapter 3), the expanding British colonies coveted the vast territories explored and conquered by the French Empire. After a few clashes and an attempted invasion, the Treaty of Utrecht (1713) ushered in an era of relative peace and harmony.

For 30 years, New France developed. Its population grew, its social structure became more complex, and its economy diversified. Daily life took shape, marked by a set of beliefs and customs. But even though they were part of an empire that had global reach, the people of the St. Lawrence Valley lived on borrowed time — because they were growing in the shadow of a constellation of Anglo-American colonies that planned to occupy the entire American continent.

The Weakening of New France

New France's relations with the British colonies depended directly on France's policy toward England. New France couldn't attack its neighbors if France was at peace with England. And the British colonies couldn't take Quebec or invade Acadia unless England had declared war on France.

From 1702 to 1713, the two countries confronted each other in the War of the Spanish Succession. In October 1700, King Charles II of Spain, who had no heir, bequeathed his kingdom and empire to the Duke of Anjou. The problem: The duke belonged to France's ruling Bourbon family. England and other powers feared that the king of Spain's designation of a Bourbon successor would allow France to dominate Europe and the world. Seeking to ensure a better balance of power on the continent, England signed a pact with the Netherlands; Denmark and the German principalities soon joined in.

One of England's concerns was America. If France were to control the Spanish colonies in South America, it could easily block expansion of the English colonies in North America . . . and, in particular, hinder their trade.

Clashes between England and France

Once the war between England and France was officially declared, the Anglo-American colonies had a green light. They could mobilize troops and organize a major offensive.

Guerrilla warfare in New England

The leaders of New France were well aware that their colony's situation was precarious. Governor Vaudreuil, who came to office in 1703, adopted a simple strategy: On the one hand, maintain good relations with the Iroquois and ensure that they remained neutral; on the other, support France's Abenaki allies in New England, who were at war with the English.

In 1703 and 1704, the French organized a series of surprise raids on small towns on the American east coast. In August 1703, the town of Wells, Maine, suffered a surprise attack by French Canadians and Abenaki. Nearly 300 people were captured. A few months later, in February 1704, another contingent attacked Deerfield, a village in Massachusetts not far from Boston. Nearly 20 houses were sacked, 150 people were captured, and 7 others died in combat. In August 1704, the Abenaki, with strong support from the French, attacked Groton, another village not far from Boston.

Among those brought as prisoners to Montreal was young Matthias Farnsworth, 14, who was working in the fields at the time he was captured. Held as a slave, and later a domestic servant, Farnsworth francized his name and became the ancestor of all the Phaneufs of Quebec.

We must invade!

These surprise attacks terrorized New England. The colonies' leaders sent a diplomatic mission to New France, but the talks had no concrete results. However, the American delegates did take advantage of being in New France and spied on the St. Lawrence Valley.

In the English colonies and London, the voices advocating an invasion of Canada were getting louder. In *Magnalia Christi Americana,* published in London in 1702, one writer argued that Canada constituted "the main source of New England's problems." New England couldn't hope to expand and prosper without envisioning the conquest of the neighboring colony. The same year, the governor of New York claimed that this conquest would be easy, as long as the necessary resources were committed to the task.

In 1708, an American soldier, Colonel Samuel Vetch, sent a memorandum to London bringing together a series of arguments in favor of invading New France. He wrote,

> To the extent that they are aware of the value of the British kingdom in America, from the point of view of both its power and its trading ability, all thoughtful minds can only be astonished to see a nation as great at sea, as strong in number, and also as wisely jealous of its trade suffer so patiently while troublesome neighbors like the French settle peacefully beside her, and especially while, with a weak and dispersed population, they surround and compress the entire British Empire on the continent between themselves and the sea.

At the earliest possible moment, the colonel insisted, England must take Quebec and get rid of this irksome neighbor.

London's big push

To the great satisfaction of the people of New England, London decided to proceed. In Europe, France's armies were in retreat. The British government now believed the time had come to deliver a major blow in America. They assigned huge resources — 14 warships, 80 guns, and more than 5,000 sailors — to Admiral Hovenden Walker. The American colonies also helped finance the expedition and provide the muscle.

In 1710, the Anglo-Americans easily took Port-Royal, but they put off the invasion of the St. Lawrence Valley until the following year. As in 1690, the strategy was to put New France in a vise. An army would take Montreal from the south, and another, larger one would come up the St. Lawrence and attack Quebec. But, as in 1690, the operations didn't go as planned.

An expedition that fell — into the water

During the summer and fall of 1711, all of New France was busy preparing for an attack. Vaudreuil erected entrenchments and ordered women, children, and the elderly to take refuge in the surrounding area. Canadian militiamen were mobilized. An army of 2,600 men, led by General William Nicholson, went up the Hudson River, ready to invade Montreal Island once Walker's vessels berthed in Quebec. But weeks passed and no signal was given. On October 7, the *Héros,* a French ship, anchored in Quebec. The captain confirmed that he hadn't seen any English ships. Vaudreuil immediately decided to withdraw his troops to the region of Montreal. Soon the governor learned that Nicholson's men had turned back and returned to Albany. But where were Walker's vessels? What happened?

Walker's fleet had suffered a terrible catastrophe: Late in the night of September 2, near Anticosti Island, Walker was awakened by men who believed they had seen the north bank of the St. Lawrence. Orders were given to change direction and go back upriver. However the navigators had very little knowledge of the river, and the conditions were terrible — the fog was very thick, and there were high winds. At dawn on September 3, the water calmed. Walker went on deck and found that misfortune had struck his powerful armada. Several of his large ships had hit the reef of Île aux Œufs, east of the North Shore. Nearly 1,000 members of his crew were drowned. Others who survived fell victim to the icy waters and died from cold. The days that followed were spent helping survivors and patching up damaged vessels. Completing the mission was impossible; the conquest of Quebec was put on hold. Walker's career was over. England would never again entrust him with a mission.

When the residents of Quebec heard the news, they renamed Notre-Dame-de-la-Victoire (Our Lady of Victory) church "Notre-Dame-des-Victoires" (Our Lady of Victories)! But they didn't maintain their mocking tone for long. Instead, the people of New France breathed a huge sigh of relief.

The Treaty of Utrecht

A few months later, a long period of negotiations involving France, Britain, and their respective allies began in Utrecht, Netherlands. Louis XIV's enemies gradually became resigned to the idea that a Bourbon would reign in Spain. They expected, however, that the Sun King would make significant concessions. Unfortunately for the Canadiens, the vast territory of New France would serve as Louis's bargaining chip.

Large concessions in America

The Treaty of Utrecht, signed on April 16, 1713, officially ended the War of the Spanish Succession. The clauses that relate directly to New France gave the advantage to Britain:

- **Hudson Bay to the English:** "All lands, seas, sea-coasts, rivers, and places" that depend on the Hudson Bay, as well as all the "buildings" and "fortresses" of this northern region were transferred to the English. The Hudson's Bay Company now had a safe territory in the western part of the continent in which to seek its pelts. The trappers of the St. Lawrence Valley would have a fierce competitor to deal with.

- **Acadia to the English:** In 1710, the British had captured Port-Royal, which they had renamed Annapolis Royal. With the Treaty of Utrecht, they could now stay and make this place a permanent home. Acadia was confirmed as a British possession. From this point on, it bore the name "Nova Scotia."

- **Newfoundland to the English:** Article 13 of the Treaty stipulated that the island of Newfoundland and adjacent islands will "belong of right wholly to Britain." France surrendered all claims to this huge island. Pierre Le Moyne d'Iberville's triumph was now a thing of the past.

✔ **Cape Breton to the French:** Even if the French made major concessions along the east coast, they wanted to keep the island of Cape Breton, which they quickly renamed "Île Royale." Having a presence in the Atlantic satisfied several objectives:

- France wanted to offer the Acadians a safe haven.

- For security reasons, France planned to maintain a gateway to the Gulf of St. Lawrence.

- France would have access to a seaport open year-round.

All these concessions threw a significant shadow over the future of New France. The treaty showed clearly that this colony was not a priority for the French. It could even be said that the final transfer of the colony to Britain through the Treaty of Paris in 1763 was foreshadowed in the Treaty of Utrecht.

New France besieged

But let's not get ahead of ourselves. In 1713, New France was still part of France. The colony was more exposed than before, so France undertook a major effort to fortify it, as if the colony was suddenly under siege. An imposing fortress was built on Île Royale, at the recently founded town of Louisbourg. Construction of a very expensive fortress began in 1717. Attempts were made to bring in settlers to Louisbourg, although not without difficulty. French people who had settled in Newfoundland migrated there, but very few Acadians left their homes.

Nevertheless, by 1740 the population of Louisbourg was close to 4,000. With warehouses being built up, the town became the hub of a large triangular trade that connected the St. Lawrence Valley with the West Indies. Most of its people were indentured workers, merchants, and soldiers. At times, the authorities found it difficult to maintain order. Alcohol and smuggling proved more attractive to some soldiers than defending New France. In 1744, a mutiny caused considerable chaos.

Other forts were erected as well. Starting in 1716, a stone wall was built around Montreal. Four years later, work began on fortifications in Quebec. Special attention was also paid to the Great Lakes and Lake Champlain. Fort Niagara was built between Lake Ontario and Lake Erie. Others would follow. The forts built along the Richelieu River were also strengthened.

An Ancien Régime Society

Although the people of New France felt that the colony rested on fragile foundations, to say the least, they were not paralyzed by this sense. The peace that prevailed between 1713 and 1744 promoted the colony's development.

Its institutions, the way it was organized, and the mentality of its inhabitants were largely those of a society belonging to the French *Ancien Régime* (Old Regime).

A diverse population

Up until the Conquest, New France continued to welcome immigrants. The population was not made up of a single group but comprised people from different backgrounds and social orders.

Some basic data

The latest demographic research indicates that about 30,000 French people set out on the great voyage to New France before 1760. Of this number, 27,000 arrived alive. The journey was often difficult — some ships didn't make it, and hygienic conditions onboard were often deplorable. All in all, of the 27,000 immigrants, 14,000, or a little more than half, settled in New France.

Is that a lot or a little? It all depends on your perspective. Obviously, compared to the British colonies, it's very little. However, compare New France to the other French colonies in America, in the Caribbean, and the picture is different.

Retention of French immigrants was higher in the north than in the south. In New France, the vast majority of newcomers were either soldiers or indentured workers. Before crossing the Atlantic, the indentured workers had signed a contract providing for a predetermined stay. Most of them saw it as a temporary contract, not a permanent move. The fact that more than half of them nevertheless stayed on shows that New France had a real power of attraction. For many people under the *Ancien Régime,* the possibility of acquiring land and having property to pass on to one's descendants would be a major factor in the decision to found a family. And land was something that New France had in abundance.

Although immigrants didn't pour in the way they had when Jean Talon was intendant, immigration continued in the 18th century. Between 1714 and 1754, approximately 4,500 immigrants settled in New France. They included indentured workers and soldiers stationed in the colony, but most of them, it appears, were unsavory characters, including hundreds of salt smugglers who sold salt illegally in France. France wanted to get rid of these smugglers, and the colony accepted them without complaint because once they were in New France, most of them mended their ways and were on their best behavior. New France in the 18th century also received some *libertines* (sons of good French families who were considered immoral and whose sexual mores often led to scandal). It was believed that a spell in New France would set them straight. The bishop obviously didn't view their arrival favorably.

Population growth in the St. Lawrence Valley under the *Ancien Régime*

Census techniques under the *Ancien Régime* were less sophisticated than today. Nevertheless, the French government periodically wanted to know how many people were living in the colonies. Here are the figures found in documents of the time, revised by demographers with expertise in these issues.

Year	Population
1640	400
1653	1,500
1661	2,500
1666	4,219 (2,657 in the region of Quebec; 602 in Trois-Rivières; 760 in Montreal)

Year	Population
1673	6,705
1681	10,077
1692	13,041
1706	18,842
1718	25,971
1727	34,355
1737	45,108
1750	58,100

When the small number of immigrants is taken into account, population growth was fairly rapid. The population effectively doubled every 25 years. However, these numbers were no match for those of the British colonies. In 1700, there were already 275,000 people in the British colonies, and 50 years later there were 1.2 million. The gap appeared insurmountable.

The few immigrants didn't outpace the natural growth of the population. The birth rate in New France was higher than that of other pre-industrial societies. Did the inhabitants of the colony have especially active libidos? Hard to say. The main explanation lies in the phenomenon of early marriage. Land was easily accessible, and a person could quickly settle down and start a family. By mid-adolescence, a woman would typically have her first child. Life was also healthier than in France. Famines were rare, firewood was easier to find, and hunting was open to all, so the infant mortality rate was lower than in France.

From France and elsewhere

The vast majority of immigrants who settled in the St. Lawrence Valley before 1760 were of French origin. It would be wrong, however, to think that the population was ethnically homogeneous. In addition to French, the population included

- ✔ **Prisoners from New England:** Victims of surprise raids, about 1,000 prisoners from New England lived and sometimes settled in the St. Lawrence Valley before 1760.

- ✔ **Black slaves:** Before 1760, about 455 blacks lived in New France. These were slaves purchased by seigneurs, clergy, and merchants. Their status was set out in the Code Noir adopted by Louis XIV's France in 1685. The economy didn't lend itself to having slaves, which is why there weren't more of them.

- ✔ **Aboriginals:** Two classes of Aboriginals were part of the population:

  - **Domiciled:** These Aboriginals lived in villages run by Jesuits. So, there were, for example, Hurons in Jeune-Lorette, near Quebec; Abenaki in Saint-François and Bécancour, near Trois-Rivières; and Iroquois settled in Sault-Saint-Louis and Lac des Deux Montagnes, in the Montreal area.

  - **Slaves:** Before 1760, approximately 1,500 Aboriginals had slave status. Like the blacks, they were domestics or agricultural workers.

  Whether domiciled or slaves, Aboriginals didn't assimilate into the French society of the *Ancien Régime,* despite many efforts by the authorities. Attached to their customs and their history, the vast majority retained their distinct identity.

Because they wanted the population to increase faster, Champlain and Richelieu would've liked to have seen more Frenchmen marrying First Nations women. They entertained no prejudice against this particular type of union. In the early 18th century, however, the colonial authorities changed their tune completely. In 1709, the governor and intendant wrote to the minister,

> Bad blood should never be mixed with good; the experience we have had in this country, that all the Frenchmen who married Indian women have become libertines, lazy, or totally irresponsible and accountable to no one . . . must keep us from allowing such marriages.

Between 1644 and 1760, there were, at most, 180 mixed marriages.

Social mobility and the glass ceiling

Under the French *Ancien Régime,* the society was made up of three groups: the nobility, the clergy, and the third estate. On rare occasions, France summoned the "Estates General," which brought these three sectors together for an update on the status of the kingdom and authorization to raise new taxes. In the fall of 1672, Governor Frontenac gathered representatives of the colony in a similar fashion, but Louis XIV's minister Colbert disapproved of the initiative. The exercise would never be repeated.

It should be noted that social divisions were much less rigid than in France. The social configuration of the *Ancien Régime* was more evident in the cities of New France, which accounted for about 20 percent of the population. In rural areas, however, New France was clearly America. A hard-working and courageous settler with a basic level of social skills could obtain a seigneury or become a prosperous fur trader. As in all colonial societies, however, the most prestigious positions — those of governor, intendant, and bishop, for example — were reserved for people from the mother country.

In 1725, France refused to appoint a Canadian governor. Paris feared losing control. The one exception — and the one that proves the rule — was the appointment of the Canadien Pierre Rigaud de Vaudreuil in 1755 as governor of New France.

A struggling economy

During the long period of peace following the Treaty of Utrecht, New France's authorities encouraged economic diversification. Despite many obstacles, some initiatives bore fruit.

Impediments

To develop businesses and prosper, dynamic entrepreneurs must be able to rely on certain minimum conditions. In New France, these conditions were seriously deficient. Why? There are at least five possible explanations:

- **A shortage of artisans and laborers:** Industries require a skilled workforce, with qualified workers, in order to develop. And qualified workers were sorely lacking in New France from the mid-17th century on. Even though wages were higher than in France and it was possible to become a "master" faster than you could in France, very few artisans and skilled workers immigrated in the 18th century. The intendants regularly called for more, but their appeals yielded very few results.

- **An unstable currency:** To allow for trade and the exchange of goods, an economy needs a functioning currency. Until the 18th century, this currency consisted of coins. After the long reign of Louis XIV, marked by costly wars, these coins were in short supply. Influenced by the Scotsman John Law, France began to issue paper money, redeemable for coins as needed. To stimulate lending, New France issued this paper money several times. But the system was not yet perfected. The money's actual value fluctuated according to circumstances, which created a lot of uncertainty — not suitable for promoting economic activity.

- **A kingdom of monopolies:** Fur remained a mainstay of New France's economy in the 18th century. Between 1670 and 1760, in Montreal alone, 13,055 contracts were signed with traders heading west to obtain furs. But no matter how many *coureurs de bois* or trappers there were, they could sell only to one customer when they returned. The fur trade was, therefore, strictly regulated by the government of France. From 1700 to 1706, the monopoly was awarded to the *Compagnie de la Colonie,* managed by Canadian interests. The company went bankrupt, but other companies took over. This monopoly structure meant that the sector was not competitive, and it gave rise to smuggling. To get the best price, many Canadian trappers sold their furs to English merchants.

✔ **Lack of roads:** The primary obstacle to trade was a river that was frozen six months a year. This was a significant impediment that the British colonies didn't face, because their ports were open year-round. This major problem was compounded by the difficulties of travel within the colony. Until the early 18th century, people relied on river routes, but this wasn't always convenient. Finally, between 1706 and 1737, a road known as the *chemin du roy* was built on the north shore, allowing the journey between Quebec and Montreal to be completed in four days. It was the first real road in the colony — and it would be the only one for a long time.

✔ **Corruption:** Under the French *Ancien Régime*, the line between the public interest of the state and the private interest of its leaders was not always clear. Governor Frontenac, flat broke when he arrived, clearly took advantage of his position to pocket huge profits from the fur trade. During the period covered by this chapter, Michel Bégon, intendant from 1711 to 1726, also abused his office. And then there was the intendant Bigot (see Chapter 5).

The fact that some economic activity took place in New France in the face of these multiple barriers to trade is almost a miracle. Despite these obstacles, and despite several poor harvests caused by the whims of Mother Nature, agricultural production in the colony improved during the 1720s and 1730s.

Wheat supplants fur

In 1714, nothing yet suggested such progress. Vaudreuil and Bégon wrote to their minister, "There is every reason to fear that most of the land will never be cultivated." Bread was scarce and expensive. Inhabitants of the Quebec region complained about this publicly.

Who was to blame? As far as the authorities were concerned, the only culprits were the settlers themselves, whom they regarded as poor farmers, too lazy to innovate. But this accusation was clearly unjust. Could anyone really blame the inhabitants for practicing subsistence agriculture? What was the incentive to produce a surplus if there was no market?

Over the years, market conditions changed. The population of the West Indies, made up primarily of slaves, kept growing. St. Lawrence Valley farmers found an active market there for the wheat they produced. This proved a great incentive to develop more intensive cultivation. Between 1721 and 1734, the area of cropland tripled and annual wheat production in bushels per capita doubled. Canadian production passed through Louisbourg, which allowed the wheat trade to be carried on throughout the year. Starting in 1736, wheat exports surpassed even fur exports in value.

PORTRAIT

The conquest of the west

After Joliet, La Salle, and Le Moyne d'Iberville, Pierre Gaultier de La Vérendrye (1685–1749) was certainly one of the most impressive explorers in the history of New France.

La Vérendrye was the grandson of Pierre Boucher and the son of René Gaultier, a soldier of the Carignan-Salières regiment who became seigneur and governor of Trois-Rivières. He originally seemed headed for a military career. He took part in the raid against Deerfield in 1704, enlisted in the French army in Europe, and was seriously wounded in combat during the War of the Spanish Succession. After his return to New France, he married and began clearing a piece of land — a quiet, settled, and apparently uneventful life.

And yet new horizons emerged for him starting in 1730. That year, he went to Lake Superior where he was appointed commander of a fort. Like Cartier, Champlain, and La Salle, he dreamed of discovering the fabled western sea. Through contacts he developed with First Nations, he heard of rivers and lakes that would lead him there. The authorities of New France and the minister of the navy gave him permission to explore these new areas. Between 1731 and 1741, he founded at least six forts.

To finance his expeditions, La Vérendrye worked with fur traders. His mission became blurred. Should he devote himself to exploration or simply bringing in furs? Like previous explorers, he also had to deal with various First Nations at war with one another. One of his sons was killed by Sioux warriors on June 6, 1736.

His greatest exploit was to travel all the way to Lake Winnipeg by canoe. In January 1743, one of his sons went as far as the Rockies via a tributary of the Saskatchewan River. The routes explored by La Vérendrye and his sons became familiar to the *coureurs de bois* of the St. Lawrence Valley, who spent months in the west searching for furs and, while there, also found women. The coming together of these adventurers and First Nations women gave birth, a century later, to the Métis nation.

Wood and iron

"France will perish for lack of wood," Colbert declared one day. Lack of wood is a serious handicap for a country that wants to build ships, establish a navy, and develop maritime trade. The forests of New France were full of oak, cherry, spruce, and elm. The idea of exploiting this wealth, championed by the intendant Jean Talon, resurfaced in the 18th century.

First, Louis XV's minister Maurepas agreed that France would import masts for its galleys, but these were expensive to transport and of poor quality. He then agreed to import planks along with resin and tar. A proposed shipyard was also discussed. Maurepas agreed in principle, but on the condition that Canada would produce all the parts necessary to build warships. After many discussions, construction was finally begun on the *Canada,* a 500-ton store ship, in June 1742. In the years that followed, several warships were also built: the *Caribou,* followed by the *Castor* and the *Carcajou.*

To build these boats, iron was also needed, and New France had plenty. In 1736, construction began on the Saint-Maurice Forges. Two years later, the first blast furnace became operational. It produced parts for high-quality ships and guns.

Unfortunately, neither of these two industries thrived. In both cases, production costs were way too high. Skilled workers were recruited from France and demanded high wages. Canadian vessels were poorly received because the wood wasn't quite right. As for the Saint-Maurice Forges, the French state poured in large amounts of money but didn't make a profit. The trading partners to whom the government granted the iron-mining monopoly died prematurely or became insolvent.

Day-to-day beliefs

Every era has its beliefs and customs, conditioned by religious institutions and their representatives, and by ideas that are in the air and are held to be true. The people of New France didn't escape this conditioning from the *Ancien Régime.*

Was New France a theocracy?

The idea of separating church and state was inconceivable under the *Ancien Régime.* The two institutions had to work hand in hand — the king was both a spiritual leader and a political leader. Nevertheless, even if religious devotees and mystics played a very important role in the development of the colony, New France was never a *theocracy* (a society subject to the church). The power of the church and its most influential orders (Jesuits, Récollets, and Sulpicians) were limited by that of the state, which was jealous of the church's privileges.

Initially, Bishop Laval wanted to report directly to Rome and become a figure superior to the governor in the hierarchy, but the king opposed this. After receiving his title of bishop, he was forced to take an oath of loyalty to the king on April 23, 1675. Political authorities consistently favored decentralization of the church. They approved the establishment of *fabriques,* or lay boards, where simple parishioners oversaw the administration of parish property. They also urged Laval's successor to solidify the position of priests. Once appointed, priests couldn't be removed by the bishop, even if he wanted them gone.

In 1756, New France had 44 parishes, led by Canadian priests trained at the Séminaire de Québec, the only institution in the colony that provided "classical" training. The priests were rooted in their community and respected by the people. But the priesthood was not the most popular career. In the 18th century, even priests were lacking in New France.

Fear of hell

Religion connects and unites. It brought the inhabitants of New France together every Sunday and at the most fundamental and important moments in people's lives: birth, marriage, and death. The God of the people of New France, however, was nothing like the friendly and benevolent bearded God of today. He was a vengeful God who inspired fear. As soon as a person took his last breath, God started counting the person's "sins," those moral faults committed during a lifetime. Those who had never repented of their sins would burn in hell for eternity. In the eyes of the clergy, earthquakes and crop failures were punishments inflicted by God.

The religion of the *Ancien Régime* was filled with duties. To avoid the wrath of God, the people of New France performed demanding and often humiliating rituals. They had to forgo meat on Fridays and during Lent, which precedes the Easter celebration. To demonstrate their piety, some married women refused to have sex with their husbands on days of "penance." The faithful also had to confess their sins, a practice that discouraged many from committing them. Women were required to follow a fairly strict dress code.

Resigned to disease

Far from the major intellectual and scientific centers of Europe, the inhabitants of New France greeted death with resignation. Its timing was chosen by God. Death was an integral part of their everyday lives. Although a small number of people reached their 60s, life expectancy barely exceeded 40. Disease, too, was greeted with resignation. Tumors, diarrhea, and dysentery were common, and people often died of them. Obviously, medical treatments were not what they are now. But the causes of these diseases are striking to a reader today.

Hygiene conditions were terrible. In the popular imagination, dirt was not only inevitable but a virtue! *Ancien Régime* proverbs testify to this: "If you want to grow old, do not remove the oil from your skin," "Dirt nourishes hair," and "Those who bathe do not live long." Many men also felt that smelling bad would attract more women. As some said, "The more the buck stinks, the more the goat likes him!"

Epidemics often spread at lightning speed. It was not surprising: The sewers were open and the water was often contaminated. The food didn't provide all the vitamins people needed, especially in winter. Despite their resignation, people turned to all sorts of bizarre practices, ointments, and products that had supposed healing properties. So, to cure a toothache, people were told to cut their nails on Monday; for a cough, drinking one's urine could help; to combat rheumatism, applying a smoked herring to the painful spot was recommended; and so forth. In some cases, people turned to particular saints, who it was believed could help cure certain diseases. The official church rejected these superstitions, which fell within the realm of magical thinking.

War again

In March 1744, a new conflict broke out between France and Britain. The War of the Austrian Succession lasted four years. Just as had happened with the king of Spain a few decades earlier, the emperor of Austria died on October 20, 1740, leaving no male heir. His daughter Maria Theresa was the designated successor, but rival powers challenged her legitimacy. France decided to ally with Frederick II of Prussia, who coveted some pieces of the Austrian Empire. The first Franco-Prussian victories dragged England into the fray. This European war again gave the green light to the Anglo-American colonies.

"As stupid as peace"

When war was declared, it was the French who first launched raids against British positions in the former Acadia. The governor of Louisbourg wanted to retake Port-Royal, but the Acadians preferred to remain neutral. A few months later, it was the New England colonies' turn to organize a major expedition against Louisbourg and its fortress, which the French believed to be impregnable. The New Englanders mobilized impressive resources. The expedition arrived off Île Royale on May 11, 1745. A delegation of New Englanders tried to convince the governor to abandon his post, but he refused.

For 47 days, the New Englanders incessantly shelled the French town. On June 27, the French surrendered. The French minister of the navy organized a counterattack the following year, but adversity and bad luck conspired against the expedition. In 1748, the European powers signed the Treaty of Aix-la-Chapelle. In exchange for a possession in India, Britain agreed to give Louisbourg back to the French. New Englanders were furious. All that for nothing? In France, many thought that Louis XV hadn't been able to take a strong stand in the negotiations. "As stupid as peace" was a disparaging phrase that made the rounds.

The La Galissonnière memorandum

La Galissonnière, governor of New France in the late 1740s, tried to persuade the French government to boost development of the colony. In a memorandum dated December 1750, he acknowledged that such an effort would require large investments: "It cannot be denied that this colony has always been an expense for France, and that will likely continue to be the case for some time to come, but at the same time it is the strongest bulwark we have to oppose English ambitions." He proposed building a series of forts in highly strategic areas, a recommendation that would be followed to a degree in the years to come.

But would this be enough to contain Anglo-American ambitions?

Resigned to bad husbands

Choosing a good husband was an important matter for women in New France. Under the *Ancien Régime,* sex before marriage was strictly prohibited. That's why premarital pregnancies were rare (only 8 percent in the early 18th century). For both men and women, pregnancy before marriage was very risky. A man who ducked out of it could be dragged to court and charged with "kidnapping for seduction." To avoid marriage, he would have to prove to the judge that the pregnant woman did not comport herself properly and was not worthy to be his future wife. Hence, a woman with child would have to have the man charged to preserve her honor. Otherwise, she risked being seen as "loose."

For young couples, courtships were very short. The interested young man would be invited to the home of the coveted young woman. Often, he hardly saw her and didn't converse with her. By about the fourth visit, he would be expected to clearly indicate to her father his intention to marry the young woman. "One must discuss marriage or discontinue any exchange," said the Baron de La Hontan. "Otherwise, scandal will follow, as it must." Most men sought robust, well-padded women. Those with delicate or skinny frames didn't garner much interest — they might have difficulty managing the heavy farm work required. Curves were synonymous with health.

Although it was common for neighbors to marry, marriages weren't forced — the woman's consent was essential. This was fortunate, because once the couple was married, it was almost impossible to get out of it. According to the Coutume de Paris, the legal system that governed marriage at the time, the husband became the head of the family and his wife was subservient. The wife lost her legal autonomy. "When the cock has crowed, the hen should be silent," went the saying. Of course, within the intimacy of families, many women gave their opinions and participated in decisions. But in the public square, they had no rights of citizenship.

What happened when a woman ended up with a man who was idle, depraved, or violent? Did she have any recourse? According to the church, she had to resign herself to her situation. This is at least what Antoine Déat, the pastor of Notre-Dame de Montréal parish, preached in a sermon in 1751. When dealing with abusive husbands, he counseled wives to keep it a "big secret." Rather than condemn their husbands' violence, they must "resort to gentleness and patience." He recommended, "Stop being an imperious woman, and your husband may be less prone to losing his temper."

Part II
Conquered but Still Alive (1754–1867)

The 5th Wave   By Rich Tennant

1791 THE BRITISH INVADE QUEBEC

2013 THE INVASION CONTINUES

In this part . . .

Here, I explain why New France fell into the hands of the English during the Seven Years' War. I also show you how, in this new hostile empire, the ancestors of today's Québécois resisted attempts at assimilation, turned their backs on the American Revolution, and benefited from new parliamentary institutions. Then I look into what the rebellions of 1837 really meant and what happened as a result of the Patriotes' failure in Lower Canada, as well as the religious awakening of the 1840s and the origins of Canadian confederation. This period of little more than a hundred years was filled with twists and turns!

Chapter 5

The Coming of the English (1754–1763)

In This Chapter

▶ Seeing how the English had their way in New France

▶ Considering whether France abandoned New France or England won it

*I*n this chapter, I give you a closer look at events in New France, across North America, and in Europe during this short period, because the stakes were enormous — the future of France and Britain as civilizations.

From 1754 to 1763, the France of King Louis XV and the Britain of King George II (succeeded by George III in 1760) clashed on numerous battlefields around the world. France was the era's leading power, but Britain had a powerful navy and wanted to dominate the world. The domination of Anglo-Saxon culture in Quebec today originated in this war of the mid-18th century.

Also at stake was the destiny of a people. In 1754, the Canadiens in the St. Lawrence Valley were still French subjects. But by 1763, they had become part of an empire that was foreign to them and hostile to their culture, their laws, their traditions, and above all, their religion. The Canadiens, recently formed and newly self-aware, would soon face the tragic possibility of their own disappearance.

Identifying the Appeal of New France for the English

In the mid-18th century, New France was impressively large. Its immense territory extended from the Gulf of St. Lawrence through the Great Lakes and the Ohio Valley to the mouth of the Mississippi River.

This continent-sized colony was very sparsely populated, however, with barely 70,000 inhabitants — a few more if you include the settlers who were beginning to take root in Louisiana. Most of them lived in the St. Lawrence Valley. The vast colony was part of the reality that the Canadiens, a people of peasants and *coureurs de bois,* had to reckon with. They learned many things from the Aboriginal people, including elements of the art of war — ambushes and surprise attacks that could create panic among adversaries who often outnumbered them.

These adversaries were the Anglo-Americans — 1.5 million people living in their 13 prosperous colonies to the south, clustered mainly along the Atlantic coast. New York City alone had a population of 50,000, six times as large as Quebec's. Founded by religious dissidents in the 17th century, these colonies had a great deal of autonomy. Nearly all had parliaments and local militias. Visionaries such as Benjamin Franklin sought to unite the 13 colonies and turn them into one great nation, but in the mid-18th century this project got a cool reception, with each colony looking out for itself.

Given this population imbalance between Franco-Canadiens and Anglo-Americans, there was reason to believe that the end of New France was imminent. But in fact, nothing had been decided. To win this wager, the British would have to mobilize their best men and invest huge sums of money.

The determination of the Anglo-Americans

Acadia was ceded to the English in 1713 under the Treaty of Utrecht (see Chapter 4). Soon afterward, they founded a new colony, Nova Scotia. To limit English influence in the area, the French built the fortress of Louisbourg on Île Royale, as well as Forts Saint-Jean, Beauséjour, and Gaspareaux at the eastern edge of their mainland empire. Other Americans coveted lands further west. Virginians and Pennsylvanians wanted to settle in the Ohio Valley, but the French and Canadiens blocked their way. In 1753 alone, they erected Forts Presqu'île, Le Bœuf, and Machault near Lake Erie, in the heart of the area in question. In the east and west alike, the Anglo-Americans felt themselves encircled or their development blocked. Despite difficulties in establishing a common strategy, they were in a hurry to drive out their adversaries.

George Washington's early days

In 1754, the French completed Fort Duquesne, at the site of present-day Pittsburgh. Virginians saw this as pure provocation! George Washington, a 22-year-old lieutenant colonel at the outset of a brilliant military and political career that would culminate in his becoming the first president of the United States, was sent to the site, heading a force of about 120 Virginia militiamen. The French quickly responded by sending about 30 men, including Joseph Coulon de Villiers de Jumonville. He went to meet the Virginia militiamen and ordered them to leave the "lands of the King's Domain."

As he read his summons, de Jumonville was attacked by an indigenous ally of the Virginians, who split his skull with a tomahawk. This horrid scene was followed by a bloody confrontation, in which Washington's men were victorious. One month later, a force of 500 Canadian militiamen and indigenous allies, led by de Jumonville's brother, counterattacked and won an easy victory. Fort Necessity, built by the Virginians near Fort Duquesne, was demolished. This episode set off open hostilities. The Franco-Canadiens were shocked by the brutal attack perpetrated against one of their own, while the Anglo-Americans felt a threat at their doorstep.

The Great Disturbance

This confrontation stiffened the resolve of the Anglo-Americans in Nova Scotia, who deeply mistrusted the Acadians. To keep their lands and their religion, these Catholics of French descent had agreed to remain neutral in case of conflict between Britain and France. On June 16–17, 1755, the Anglo-Americans easily took Forts Beauséjour and Gaspareaux, a first step in breaking the encirclement on the eastern front. After this raid, the conquerors demanded that the Acadians abandon their neutrality and serve the British Empire. The penalty for refusal would be prison. Nevertheless, faithful to their traditions and themselves, the Acadians refused.

This heroic refusal to submit would have its price: deportation, known to generations of Acadians as *le Grand Dérangement* (the Great Disturbance). Because of their simple desire to remain neutral, all Acadians were now considered rebels. Their mere presence in Nova Scotia would paralyze the progress of colonization, the Anglo-Americans said.

The British decided to expel an entire population from its lands and ship them as far away as possible. During the summer and fall of 1755, men, women, and children were herded like cattle and scattered through the American colonies south of Massachusetts. More than 7,000 people (out of about 12,000) were victims of this sad exercise in ethnic cleansing. Some died of starvation, while others returned to settle on lands in present-day New Brunswick, where a portion of the Acadian people was reconstituted in the 19th century. Others took refuge in the St. Lawrence Valley and let the Canadiens know what had happened.

The English go all out

To be rid of New France, the Americans needed help from their mother country. Up until 1756, fighting was limited to American territory. But in Europe, war clouds were gathering over France and Britain.

On July 8, 1755, the two mother countries officially broke off relations. This decision came after an English admiral sank two French warships, the *Alcide* and the *Lys,* off the coast of Newfoundland. In the following months, the British boarded several French vessels.

England officially declared war on France on May 18, 1756. England wasn't alone in the field, however. Its alliance with Prussia meant that it had substantial support on the European continent, allowing it to focus on its colonies and its navy. France, meanwhile, was allied with Austria, its hereditary enemy. This pact, which required the mother country to focus most of its forces on the European continent, did not bode well for New France.

Pitt in power

On May 19, 1756, the French won a stunning victory on the island of Minorca, a strategic English possession in the heart of the Mediterranean. Admiral John Byng was held responsible for this humiliation and was shot by firing squad the following year.

Meanwhile, the defeat produced a great political upheaval in London. King George II and his Parliament sought a savior who could put the kingdom back on the road to victory. They felt they had found him in William Pitt, a passionate orator who was unusual among British politicians in that he was not a courtier — indeed, he was one of the first whose power base was public opinion rather than intrigues in the royal court. A member of a faction called the Patriots, he believed that wars led by the country's militias rather than by foreign mercenaries would forge the national spirit. Above all, he considered Britain's true destiny to be on the seas and in the colonies rather than in Europe. In his view, America, rather than the battlefields of Europe, was where the English could defeat their old French enemy.

The arrival of Montcalm

It would take time for Pitt's strategy to produce its first results. In 1756, France entrusted the command of its army in New France to Louis-Joseph de Montcalm. At age 44, he was an experienced military officer who had several major campaigns under his belt along with France's highest military honor, the Cross of Saint-Louis. He also had an extraordinary group of young subordinates. His second-in-command, the Chevalier de Lévis, a future marshal, was an intrepid and courageous commander, as well as a true diplomat. His aide-de-camp, Louis-Antoine de Bougainville, was already a recognized scientist who would leave valuable accounts of his world travels to posterity.

A peculiar army

Montcalm led what was, to say the least, a colorful army. First, there were battalions from the regular army, formed by about 8,500 career soldiers who arrived from France. Next were local soldiers from the *compagnies franches de la marine*. Finally, there were 15,000 Canadien militiamen, ill equipped but courageous. As for the Aboriginal allies, Montcalm was unsure what to do with them. He saw little of value in Canadian and Aboriginal methods of warfare. On this issue, and many others, he was not on the same wavelength as Governor Vaudreuil, a Canadien by birth, who was officially in charge of New France's defense. The tension between the two men would hinder operations.

Montcalm's troops soon won significant victories, indicating that New France's fate had not yet been sealed.

Victory at Fort William Henry (1757)

In the summer of 1757, Montcalm gathered 8,000 men, including 1,800 Aboriginal allies, and attacked Fort William Henry, an English fort at the southern end of Lac Saint-Sacrement (now Lake George), less than 100 kilometers (62 miles) north of Albany. After two ultimatums and intensive artillery fire, the Anglo-American forces agreed to surrender on August 9. The Anglo-Americans' honor was saved, and Montcalm had the enemy belligerents and their families escorted to another fort. But things went badly wrong. Along the way, a number of prisoners were attacked, and some were massacred by Aboriginal allies, some of whom were drunk. This failure to respect the protocol of war greatly shocked American public opinion.

The victory of Carillon (1758)

The Anglo-Americans' response was dramatic. They tried to open a southern route along Lake Champlain and the Richelieu River to bring their troops to the outskirts of Montreal. Their first target was Fort Carillon. A huge contingent of American militiamen and English soldiers was mobilized to take the French fort — nearly 15,000 men all told, led by Major General James Abercromby. To deal with this contingent, the French and Canadiens had only 3,500 men. This force subjected Abercromby's troops to heavy fire. Victory was won on July 8. The Anglo-Americans suffered enormous losses. The French forts in the south held up. The English did not give up the idea of taking Montreal from the south, but all eyes now turned to the east.

Women who refused to eat horsemeat!

In the winter of 1757–1758, famine swept New France as a result of poor summer harvests along with unexpected population growth caused by the arrival of soldiers and 2,000 Acadian refugees. In addition, men of fighting age had less time to devote to their land, and shipments from France were often intercepted by the English. Also, the intendant, François Bigot, already suspected of corruption, may have hidden food supplies to push up prices and pocket a tidy profit.

When winter arrived, bread was rationed and wheat was replaced by rice. Worse yet, beef consumption was prohibited. To put food on the table, there remained cod, pork — or horsemeat. In December 1757, women came out to demonstrate. In his *Journal de campagne,* the Chevalier de Lévis even spoke of a "riot." They were demanding larger portions of bread and were refusing, for religious reasons, to eat horse — a "friend of man," they said. Governor Vaudreuil did not flinch. He even threatened to put the women in jail if they ever challenged his orders again.

But resistance did not come only from women. A few days later, soldiers refused to eat horsemeat. Vaudreuil threatened to hang soldiers who defied his authority. Lévis asked the soldiers to show understanding. Meanwhile, as hundreds of Acadians died of hunger, Intendant Bigot held large banquets where nothing was lacking.

The capture of Louisbourg

The other route for attacking New France lay along the St. Lawrence. But to get there, the English first had to topple the town and fortress of Louisbourg. They committed themselves to this goal with all the means at their disposal, bringing 24 warships, 18 frigates, and 16,000 men to take Île Royale. The landing took place on June 8, 1758. They quickly encircled the citadel and pounded it relentlessly. The besieged forces, far fewer in number and with no reinforcements, capitulated on July 26. Among the officers who stood out during this attack was the young James Wolfe, whose ardor and combativeness were noteworthy. He was entrusted with the mission of taking Quebec.

English Conquest, or French Abandonment?

The capture of Louisbourg by the English, coming on top of the victory of their Prussian ally at Rossbach in Saxony on November 5, 1757, made up for their many defeats in America. These gains consolidated Pitt's power and legitimized his strategy. The prime minister's gaze remained fixed on America. His plan was simple: to invade New France from the south and the northeast. This pincer strategy was well known to the French and Canadiens, who, in the spring of 1759, concentrated most of their forces in Quebec.

The siege of Quebec and the battle of the Plains of Abraham

The English did not skimp on resources to take Quebec. This time, nearly 40,000 men were mobilized: sailors, soldiers from the regular army, and American militiamen who dreamed of taking revenge. Thirty-two-year-old General James Wolfe also wished to settle the matter of the Canadiens: "I own it would give me pleasure to see the Canadian vermin sacked and pillaged and justly repaid their unheard-of cruelty," he wrote to a correspondent in the spring of 1759. Ships of the English navy left the port of Halifax bound for Quebec on May 5, 1759. Two weeks later, residents of Le Bic in the Lower St. Lawrence saw the first English vessels. Fires were lighted all along the St. Lawrence to let villages further south know that enemies were arriving. Governor Vaudreuil ordered the villages evacuated and all militiamen mobilized.

Wolfe is foiled

General Wolfe's troops settled in across from Quebec in late June. His plan was to take Quebec from the Beauport shore, but Montcalm's troops, working day and night, erected fortifications, which forced him to abandon the landing.

Protected by an impressive rocky bluff, the capital of New France was very hard to approach. Wolfe attempted a diversion and found a way to distribute a manifesto to the inhabitants, promising them his protection and assuring them that they could enjoy the use of their property without fearing any disturbance. But his words failed to sway the Canadiens, whose unity held firm. Nearly 15,000 militiamen aged 16 to 60 responded to an appeal from their company. When English sailors or soldiers came too close to shore or ventured onto land, Wolfe complained, "Old people 70 years of age, and boys of 15, fire on our detachments and kill or wound our men from the edges of the woods."

Quebec comes under cannon attack

Unable to rally the Canadiens, the English general placed troops at Pointe-Lévy, on the south shore of the St. Lawrence River, less than one kilometer (⅔ mile) from the capital. On July 12, the bombardment of Quebec began in earnest. Most of the cannonballs reached the Upper Town, but nobody was killed. Nearly every night the bombardment resumed. On July 16 and July 23, incendiary bombs wreaked havoc. In September, the beautiful cathedral lay in ruins, and more than 530 houses had been ravaged or burned. Reports indicate that more than 13,000 cannonballs pounded the city during the summer — even today, Quebec City residents will occasionally discover them buried in the ground. Targeting civilian populations was not common in that era. The aim of the bombardment was largely psychological.

Failed landings

On July 31, Wolfe attempted an initial landing further east, toward the Montmorency River. A large English warship pounded the coast for many hours. Between five and six o'clock in the afternoon, nearly 2,000 English and American soldiers set foot there and launched a disorganized assault on the French and Canadian troops. The discipline of the men led by Lévis and a heavy storm got the better of the enemy, who suffered serious losses and beat a retreat. A few days later, English troops attempted another landing further west, near the small village of Neuville. This time it was Bougainville who succeeded in repulsing the enemy.

The politics of rage

Wolfe's men found these two setbacks hard to swallow. Unable to confront military forces, they decided to attack civilian populations living peacefully along both shores of the St. Lawrence. On August 9, a group of Americans landed at Baie-Saint-Paul and burned about 40 houses. The next day, English soldiers set fire to the villages of Saint-Antoine, Sainte-Croix, and Saint-Nicolas, further south. On August 19, the inhabitants of Portneuf and Deschambault fell victim to looting and pillaging. The following week, a bloody confrontation occurred in Saint-Joachim, a short distance east of Quebec. Village priest René Portneuf and other inhabitants resisted the Rangers courageously. Those captured were scalped, tortured, and killed. On August 31, some 1,200 men left Pointe-Lévy on a mission to set fire to every village on the south shore between Kamouraska and Quebec.

Going for broke

As summer waned, Quebec still wasn't in English hands. The citadel held out. Struck by a heavy fever in late August, Wolfe was showing signs of discouragement. Montcalm's troops didn't flinch. They awaited winter, which would be their best ally in these circumstances.

But the young English general had other ideas. He decided his troops would land in an unexpected place, Anse au Foulon. Located just southwest of the capital, this cove was kept under watch night and day. After they landed, the troops would have to climb a rampart more than 50 meters (164 feet) high, lugging their weapons and equipment. Wolfe wanted to take the enemy by surprise. His general staff thought that this decision was nothing short of suicidal. Until the day before the landing, which took place on the night of September 12–13, they tried to dissuade the young general, but they weren't successful.

The fateful battle

On the morning of September 13, 1759, a French sentry posted at Anse au Foulon saw movement on the river. A voice answered him in excellent French. The sentry was deceived, and the English troops, with their heavy equipment, laboriously reached the plateau of the Plains of Abraham, just west of the capital. In a decision that would be criticized, Montcalm, taken by surprise, engaged the English in combat. At about 10 o'clock, the two armies stood face to face. Wolfe let the French and Canadiens approach and take scattered shots at the English. Then his voice rang out: "Fire!" The first English salvo created a shock wave. "Brutal fire at very short range," one witness wrote, "the most amazing I have ever seen." More deadly salvoes followed. The French and Canadian troops retreated and took refuge behind the city walls. The total number of casualties was under 1,000. Both generals were mortally wounded.

Montcalm's errors

Historians have discussed extensively the French general's decision to engage in combat against the English. His critics accused him of having joined the battle too soon. He should have stayed behind the walls in Quebec and awaited reinforcements from Bougainville and Lévis. Bougainville's troops, posted in Neuville, could have taken Wolfe's troops from behind. Lévis had been sent to Montreal in August with several battalions that could have made the difference.

Another error he was blamed for was to have brought Canadian militiamen into his regular army. After the initial English salvo, they sank to the ground and ran to hide instead of continuing their advance in a tight phalanx. This failing by the Canadiens, who had not been trained as professional soldiers, led to the belief that the French troops had been completely decimated. Hence, the psychological impact of the first salvo.

Montcalm's defenders say he had no choice but to engage in combat. This attack by Wolfe could be seen as a diversion to facilitate the landing of English troops in Beauport. A quick preventive victory against the English on the Plains of Abraham would have undermined their morale.

The surrender of Quebec

On the night of September 13–14, the French troops left Quebec and set up camp further west, along the Jacques-Cartier River. Their aim was to retake the capital as soon as possible, before winter. But the Canadian militiamen and soldiers inside the city walls were unaware of this and feared a long siege. With the risk of food supplies running short, Jean-Baptiste-Nicolas-Roch de Ramezay, the commander of the Quebec garrison, received a request from the leading figures in the city, who feared the fury of the enemy soldiers. "There is no shame in giving in when there is no chance of winning," they wrote. Talks began on September 17. The next day, a surrender was signed, and English troops came inside the city walls. The Union Jack was quickly hoisted in the most visible spot.

The reaction in American cities and in London was ecstatic. For the English, Wolfe became the prime symbol of courage and patriotism.

The surrender of Montreal

The fall of the capital to the English and Americans did not mean the end of New France. The cities of Trois-Rivières and Montreal remained under French control. Some people were overcome by despair, but others still believed victory was possible and planned a response.

Lévis in command

Among the latter was the Chevalier de Lévis who, after Montcalm's death, inherited the command of French troops in America. His great obsession was to retake Quebec quickly. Aware that the morale of his troops was very low, he saw a recapture of Quebec as a way of lifting spirits and inducing discouraged Canadian militiamen to return to service. He also urged his officers to show more consideration toward the Canadiens. "You know that we are accused of having acted too severely toward them," he wrote. "It is essential to treat them well and for them to live in harmony with our troops."

The victory of Sainte-Foy

This strategy soon produced results at the Battle of Sainte-Foy. Lévis waited for the ice to melt in April before recapturing Quebec. All available men, both regular troops and the militia, were mobilized. Although the British had more powerful artillery, ground maneuvers by Lévis's troops and his men's courage made the difference. The English had no choice but to retreat behind the city walls. Quebec was again besieged, this time by French and Canadian forces.

Before launching a final assault against the city, Lévis chose to await reinforcements from France. In the days and weeks following the Battle of Sainte-Foy, he and his men kept their eyes focused on the river, hoping to see ships flying the French flag. The reinforcements never arrived. Worse yet, on May 15, it was English ships that sailed up the St. Lawrence. Lévis wrote to the intendant, François Bigot, "I fear that France has abandoned us." The next day, the siege was lifted and the troops headed toward Montreal.

Montreal falls

Not without reason, the English felt victory was at hand. All their North American armies converged on Montreal. In the meantime, the main French forts around the Great Lakes to the west and around Lake Champlain and along the Richelieu River to the south had fallen to Anglo-American forces. The way was clear for the Anglo-American forces led by Generals Jeffery Amherst, William Haviland, and James Murray. Unlike Quebec's inhabitants, people in Montreal had no natural barrier to protect them. The level-headed Governor Vaudreuil saw no alternative but to surrender. Negotiations began, and an initial document was placed on the table. But discussions stalled over the issue of the honors of war generally granted by conquerors to the conquered. Because the English refused these honors to the French, Lévis rejected the treaty of surrender. With great flair, he chose to burn his flags rather than hand them to the enemy.

The document of surrender

On September 8, 1760, Vaudreuil signed the final document of surrender. A Canadien by birth, the governor thought first and foremost of his compatriots, who would have to cope with the aftermath of this defeat. The document contained 55 articles. The British were magnanimous, given the circumstances, or they were simply pragmatic. They knew they couldn't restrain an entire people by force. The surrender, therefore, established the following:

- ✔ **Freedom of religion:** The Canadiens would not be forced to give up their Catholic faith.

- ✔ **Respect for property rights:** The Canadiens and their religious congregations retained their property.

- ✔ **No Frenchman or Canadien who had fought was be taken prisoner and sent to England or to a British colony:** Those who had fought retained freedom of movement. They could stay behind or they could leave for France unmolested, on condition that they play no further role in the war then underway.

The 1763 Treaty of Paris

The English and Americans had achieved major military victories in the New World, but the fate of New France was not yet completely sealed. The war between Britain and France was continuing in Europe and elsewhere. Peace talks began with the fall of Quebec, but a new alliance between France and Spain, initialed on August 15, 1761, led the French to believe they could negotiate better terms. This Pacte de Famille (family pact, an allusion to the Bourbon family, which reigned in both France and Spain) prolonged the conflict.

Military occupation

With the French and British armies fighting on other battlefields, the St. Lawrence Valley was placed under military occupation. In Quebec, Montreal, and Trois-Rivières, three administrations headed by military officers were established in anticipation of the final outcome. Through General Amherst, the officers received clear instructions from King George III himself to

> "prevent any soldier, sailor or another from insulting the French inhabitants who are now subjects of the same Prince, forbidding anyone to offend them by reminding them in a less than generous manner of this inferiority to which the fate of war has reduced them, or by making insulting remarks about their language, their clothing, their fashions, their customs and their country."

Despite these polite remarks, many members of the Canadian elite decided to leave occupied New France. These 4,000 Canadiens were civil servants, military officers, and merchants. Though departures had begun before the surrender of Montreal, the pace quickened in 1760. Most returned to France, but some settled in French Guiana (in South America) or elsewhere in the French Empire.

Among the Canadiens who stayed, there was no hint of rebellion. Instead, they were relieved that the war had finally ended. Some held a grudge against France for suspending the payment of bills of exchange in October 1759. Rather than divert precious gems to the colony, France had issued paper money that inhabitants of the colony could convert to coins as required. The French decision to suspend conversion pushed a number of people into bankruptcy. Others were quite happy to see the colony rid of François Bigot, the intendant accused of embezzlement, who had returned to France.

Bigot, a scapegoat?

The loss of Canada did not go unnoticed in France. The government, led by the Duc de Choiseul, sought someone to blame. In 1761, Bigot was sent to the Bastille, the political prison of France's *Ancien Régime*. There began what in Paris was called the "Canada affair," a huge trial that captured public attention for two years. Bigot and his accomplices were accused of having "abused the name and authority of His Majesty" and of having stashed away a "considerable fortune based on public misfortune." In a brief more than 1,000 pages long, Bigot denied all the charges against him, but a guilty verdict was rendered on November 14, 1763. After wavering between hanging and beheading, the authorities finally chose to ban him for life from the kingdom. Bigot fought to restore his reputation until his death in 1778.

Voltaire and the "acres of snow"

Philosopher of the Enlightenment, defender of freedom of conscience, friend and advisor to kings, and great admirer of British institutions, Voltaire (1694–1778) opposed the Seven Years' War. He found it absurd for France to go into debt to send troops to America with the aim of holding onto New France.

In 1758, he published *Candide,* in which one of the characters exclaims: "You know that these two nations [France and England] are at war over a few acres of snow *[quelques arpents de neige]* somewhere around Canada and that they are spending on this fine war more than all of Canada is worth." The expression *quelques arpents de neige* became etched in memory.

The following year, Voltaire created a scandal by holding an event celebrating the fall of Quebec. On September 6, 1762, he urged Choiseul to abandon his colony: "I like peace more than I like Canada, and I believe France can be happy without Quebec." His main argument was that Canada was proving expensive and giving almost nothing in return. In his *Précis du siècle de Louis XV,* he saw a muddle: "If one-tenth of the money engulfed by that colony had been used to clear our uncultivated lands in France, it would have brought a considerable benefit, but it was decided to support Canada, and 100 years of effort along with all the money poured in were lost, with no benefit in return."

But Canada's destiny was not to be decided by one man, as influential as he may have been! With the fall of Quebec, the French government may already have decided to give up New France to the English — mostly for economic reasons and because this was required in the interests of its foreign policy in the short and medium term. Two centuries later, a French president would attempt to pay Louis XV's debt!

The end of New France

On February 10, 1763, France and Britain signed the Treaty of Paris. Article 4 dealt specifically with Canada and New France. In the eastern part of the continent, France gave up all claims to Nova Scotia (Acadia) and yielded Île Royale (renamed Cape Breton). Canada and the entire west of the continent were also yielded to the British, who became the masters of North America. As regards the Canadiens themselves, article 4 stated that they could keep their religion and leave the colony within 18 months of the treaty being signed. Nothing was said about language. French was the international language of that era, spoken by members of the European elite.

In North America, the French retained only the islands of Saint-Pierre and Miquelon, fishing stations off the Newfoundland coast. England had conquered Guadeloupe, Martinique, and other Caribbean islands during the war. They were returned to France, which also kept Saint-Domingue (present-day Haiti), a sugar-producing slave colony.

Chapter 6

The American Temptation (1763–1790)

In This Chapter

▶ Shaping the new colony's institutions

▶ Considering the consequences of the American Revolution

*O*n June 20, 1763, a great celebration was held in Paris. The mood of the revelers was relief: Peace had finally returned! The loss of New France seemed already to have been forgotten. The Duc de Choiseul, who headed Louis XV's government, believed the British had inherited a poisoned chalice. "There will be nothing other than revolution in America, which will occur but of which we are unlikely to see any trace here, putting England in a weakened condition under which she will no longer be cause for fear in Europe," he wrote in a memorandum to the king in 1765. In other words, "perfidious Albion" (as the French sometimes referred to England) had clearly won a great victory in North America, but it was hardly on the verge of world domination. The "American revolution" he spoke of would come sooner than expected. George III's kingdom may have emerged victorious from the Seven Years' War, but its coffers were empty, and expectations among Americans were very high.

The British faced an equally difficult task in the former New France. Although they were few in number, the English merchants who settled in the St. Lawrence Valley demanded British institutions. Their hopes were soon dashed. The first governors of the Quebec colony quickly saw that assimilation of this people of French descent and Catholic faith would take much longer than expected. It should be noted that the Quebec experience was something new for the British. For the first time in its history, the British Empire had to deal with a Western people whose religion and language were foreign to them — a people, moreover, from a powerful kingdom that England had been fighting since the Middle Ages. Through a curious turn of events, this same people could become a major ally for Britain, which faced a challenge in its colonies to the south.

To Assimilate or to Woo?

After France and England signed the Treaty of Paris, the task of shaping the new colony's institutions remained. The English government asked the Board of Trade in London, whose members habitually advised the government on major policies related to trade and the colonies, to develop its thinking on this issue.

The Royal Proclamation

On October 7, 1763, a Royal Proclamation set out the rules for administering the former French colony. A month later, Governor James Murray received his instructions. The key elements were as follows:

- **A new name, the Province of Quebec:** Previously, Quebec was the name of only a city. Starting in 1763, the name *Quebec* designated not just the capital but also a territory and a group of people, those living in the St. Lawrence Valley. It would be another two centuries before its inhabitants thought of themselves primarily as "Québécois."

- **A much smaller territory:** The era of a continent-sized colony was clearly over. The Province of Quebec was limited to the St. Lawrence Valley and its surroundings. The Abitibi region, much of Témiscamingue, Labrador, Anticosti Island off the Gaspé coast, and the far north were not part of it. Nor were the Great Lakes or the Ohio Valley. Much coveted by the Americans, the Ohio Valley had come under British trusteeship and was the site of an intensely competitive fur trade.

- **Catholicism under surveillance:** The Treaty of Paris guaranteed that the Catholics of New France could retain their religion "as far as the laws of Great Britain permit" — an ambiguous phrase given that, at the time, Britain didn't allow the Roman Catholic Church to participate in the religious affairs of the empire. In its instructions to Murray, the government indicated that he would have to respect Catholics' freedom of worship but admit no "Ecclesiastical Jurisdiction of the See of Rome." The governor was also ordered to facilitate establishment of the Church of England so that "the said inhabitants may by degrees be induced to embrace the Protestant religion."

- **Authoritarian government:** The people of New France had no house of assembly. The governor and his intendant, aided by a sovereign council, made all major decisions. At that time, most British colonies had elected assemblies, usually formed by a small landowning elite. Only a chamber of that type had the power to levy taxes. In the eyes of the English leaders, granting a representative institution to this recently conquered people was premature, with inhabitants of French descent certain to obtain a majority. Therefore, the governor was given full powers, including the power to establish an English system of justice.

The early days of the press

At the time of New France, no printing presses or newspapers existed. All books, periodicals, and newspapers were imported from France. Thomas Gilmore and William Brown, two young printers from Philadelphia, sensed a business opportunity. After receiving formal support from Governor Murray, the two men bought a press in London and set up shop on Saint-Louis Street in Quebec City.

The first issue of *La Gazette de Québec,* the very first newspaper to be published in the colony, appeared on June 21, 1764. This bilingual publication (which also went by the name *The Quebec Gazette*) informed its readers of what was happening in the world and in the colony. Starting in October 1764, the governor required all priests to subscribe to it, because all laws and decrees were published in it. Circulation was low (about 150 copies), and the number of readers was limited. But its content was transmitted through public readings, and copies were passed from one person to another.

On June 3, 1778, another newspaper saw the light of day: *La Gazette du commerce et littéraire, pour la ville et district de Montréal.* The founders were Fleury Mesplet and Valentin Jautard, two freethinkers influenced by Enlightenment ideas. Mesplet, of French descent, met Benjamin Franklin in London and emigrated to the United States in 1774. But this French-language weekly was published for only a year. After criticizing decisions by Governor Haldimand and spending time in prison, Mesplet launched *La Gazette de Montréal (The Montreal Gazette)* on August 25, 1785. This bilingual newspaper was more reserved in its stance toward the administration but continued to take liberal positions, inspired by the spirit of the Enlightenment. Around 1810, *The Gazette* became the newspaper of the English-speaking minority.

The Test Oath

What the English government sought was, initially, the gradual conversion of the colony's Catholics to Protestantism and, in the longer term, outright assimilation of the Canadiens to English culture. Faithful to his government's intentions, Governor Murray ruled in 1764 that anyone who wanted to work in the colonial administration would be required to take the Test Oath. To obtain an official position or responsibility, it was necessary to swear an oath renouncing the cult of the saints, the power of the pope, and the authority of the Church of Rome. For Catholics, this meant renouncing their religion, something unthinkable at the time! The Test Oath, thus, effectively excluded all Catholics from public service. This measure obviously delighted recently arrived British Protestants, as well as the few French-speaking Protestants living in the colony who, although tolerated prior to the Conquest, could not obtain official positions.

English justice

On September 17, 1764, by decree, Governor Murray established new judicial institutions for both criminal and civil matters. In particular, this involved the introduction of *habeas corpus,* the principle under which anyone deprived of liberty has to be given a fair trial and formally convicted by a recognized court. The new subjects accepted this principle, as well as the English practice of trial by jury.

However, they deplored the confusion caused by Murray's decree regarding the local administration of justice. Militia captains, who under the French regime enforced the customary law of Paris, were suddenly replaced by justices of the peace who didn't speak a word of French — and who enforced civil law that the inhabitants did not understand. A hybrid system of justice soon developed, and French civil law continued to be used. In July 1766, the governor made some concessions. Civil cases involving French speakers would be tried by French speakers, he ruled, and that was that! But this was just a temporary solution — the legal framework was still not settled.

A new bishop? Not that simple

To be consistent with its Test Oath, the English government ought normally to have put off appointing a bishop until later. But the priests in the 113 parishes needed a superior, and the English authorities were seeking loyal allies who could be counted on to be obedient. The last bishop, Henri-Marie Dubreil de Pontbriand, who died in July 1760, had asked the faithful to take an oath to the new king, George III, and to avoid proselytization. The ideal replacement for de Pontbriand, in Governor Murray's eyes, was Jean-Olivier Briand, whom he preferred to Étienne Montgolfier, the Sulpician superior in Montreal elected by the colony's canons. Briand was officially ordained in March 1766. But although he was a staunch ally of the English Crown, the Catholic Church remained in a precarious state. Briand was appointed only after months of hesitation, and neither his succession nor the future of his church in North America seemed assured.

The Scots of the North West Company

Most of the early English-speaking settlers in the colony were of Scottish descent. An initial cohort blended in with the French-Canadian majority, while another group developed its own identity and became quite prosperous.

In 1763, General Murray acquired several seigneuries that had been abandoned by their title holders who chose to return to France. He gave willing officers the chance to settle on these vast plots of land, located in the magnificent Charlevoix region. Between 150 and 300 Scotsmen involved in the siege of Quebec in 1759 accepted this offer. One of them, Hugh Blackburn, married Geneviève Gagnon in 1776 and had 13 children. Some of his descendants, all French-speaking, settled in the Saguenay–Lac-Saint-Jean region.

Around 1780, Simon McTavish, James McGill, Alexander Mackenzie, and a few others, all fur traders of Scottish descent, formed the North West Company, based in Montreal. The company soon came to dominate this key sector. In the 1780s alone, they shipped more than 100,000 beaver pelts abroad and provided fierce competition for the Hudson's Bay Company, owned by English interests. In 1785, proud of their success, they founded the Beaver Club. One membership requirement was to have spent at least one winter tracking down beaver deep in the interior of the continent. Another was to drink plenty of alcohol. Beaver Club meetings gave rise to memorable drinking sessions!

Unhappy British merchants

In 1766, about 500 of the Province of Quebec's inhabitants were of British origin. They formed what soon became known in the colony as the "British Party." Most of them were merchants, and they weren't happy with the decisions of Governor Murray, whom they regarded as favoring the "French Party." The colony still had no house of assembly, in which only "real" British subjects would be represented. Also, French civil law still applied and — the height of stupidity, in their eyes — a bishop had just been appointed.

Governor Murray had a high opinion of the Empire's new subjects, as correspondence with his superiors indicates. The Canadiens, he said, formed "perhaps the bravest and best race upon the globe" who could "in a very short time become the most faithful and useful set of men in this American Empire." Just as he held the Canadiens in high esteem, he showed aristocratic disdain for the English merchants newly arrived in the colony. Exasperated by these men, whom he described as "adventurers of mean education" or even as "rapacious fanatics," he took no account of their views and acted as he saw fit.

The pragmatic Carleton

Murray's indifference to the merchants' grievances cost him his position. The merchants succeeded in having the governor recalled. Sadly for them, his replacement would follow a similar line. Guy Carleton was also a military officer. He had taken part in the siege of Louisbourg and the Battle of the Plains of Abraham, where he suffered a head wound. This appointment caused some surprise, for it was the first time he was asked to head a civilian government in peacetime. He arrived in the colony on December 23, 1766, and soon showed great independence of spirit and judgment, refusing to join any particular camp.

A little under a year after he arrived, it became clear to him that assimilation would not occur any time soon. In a letter to his superiors, dated November 25, 1767, he showed great clarity. His Majesty's Canadien subjects, Carleton stated, far outnumbered the newer arrivals, and this numerical superiority was unlikely to diminish in the future. His letter noted that the colony's climate was "inhospitable," making it harder to attract new settlers, and that the Canadiens had a very high birth rate. (The Catholic Church would later refer to this as "the revenge of the cradle.") The Canadian race, he wrote, had roots so vigorous and prolific that it would end up populating the country to a point where any new element transplanted in Canada would be completely overwhelmed, except in the cities of Quebec and Montreal. The future would prove him right.

The Quebec Act

The English government's initial plan to acculturate this new population was going nowhere. But the plan may have worked. The hypothesis of massive immigration was not totally off the mark. Between 1764 and 1776, more than 125,000 people left the British Isles to settle in North America. If one-quarter or one-third of them had chosen the St. Lawrence Valley, the history of the Province of Quebec would have been totally different. But as Governor Carleton soon noticed, this was not the case. Another course of action would be required.

The Canadiens' petition

The Canadiens were by no means passive subjects. They were quick to demand a change of direction by the new authorities. Because there was no large-scale immigration from Britain, recognizing the right of the new French-speaking subjects to retain their language, their civil law, and their religion would be necessary. In the early days of the English regime, 95 Canadiens signed a petition demanding respect for their institutions. Nine years later, in 1773, a group of 75 Canadiens sent a memorandum to London. Their list of grievances was forthright. Both groups swore loyalty to the English Crown. Their demands, they insisted, were aimed only at obtaining the most basic justice and harmony between subjects in the colony.

Recognition of a distinct society

On June 22, 1774, after a long process of consultation, King George III gave royal assent to the Quebec Act. Rather than assimilate the Canadiens, the British government chose (at least in the short term) to accommodate them by agreeing to most of the grievances in their 1773 memorandum:

- ✔ **An expanded territory:** The map of the Province of Quebec was completely redrawn. To the St. Lawrence Valley were added areas including Labrador, the Great Lakes region, and the Ohio Valley. It almost looked as if the territory of the former New France was being reinstated!

- ✔ **Abolition of the Test Oath:** Under the Quebec Act, Catholics no longer had to renounce their faith to obtain official positions. A simple oath of allegiance would be required, but it would no longer contain religious references. Canadiens could gain access to a new body, the Legislative Council, that would advise the lieutenant governor.

- ✔ **The Catholic Church gets its tithe and its bishop:** To ensure its survival, the Catholic Church had to rely on tithes. This tax paid by the faithful again became compulsory and was recognized by the English authorities. In the appointment of the bishop, a clever ploy was found. Instead of having a bishop named by Rome or by a foreign ecclesiastical chapter, the bishop of Quebec would himself designate a younger coadjutor, or second-in-command, who would succeed him on his death. This let London save face and guaranteed a future for the Catholic Church in North America.

- ✔ **The retention of French civil law:** The Quebec Act was very clear on the subject of laws: "All His Majesty's Canadian subjects . . . many hold and enjoy their property and possessions, together with all customs and usages relative thereto, and all other their civil rights. . . . In all matters of controversy, relative to property and civil rights, resort shall be had to the laws of Canada as the rule for the decision of the same." The seigneurial system was thus maintained; the seigneurs would remember this generosity.

Broadly inspired by the thinking of Guy Carleton, the Quebec Act did not go unchallenged. A member of Parliament in London, Edmund Burke, believed that this legislation, allowing the subjects of a British colony to have recourse to French law, risked "destroying our English liberties" — a point of view shared by the English merchants in the colony, who felt they had been completely abandoned by their mother country.

The American Revolution

The Quebec Act appeared to demonstrate an open attitude on the part of Britain toward its subjects of French descent and Catholic religion. But to explain the true intentions that lay behind this apparent generosity, I need to go back a few steps and place the Quebec Act in a much broader context. In 1774, the British Empire was on the verge of collapse. A majority of Americans, unhappy with their mother country's policies, were seriously considering a unilateral declaration of independence. The Quebec Act could be seen as a way of buying peace at low cost and wooing a people who may be needed in the future. The leadership in London had to focus on American rebels who dared to challenge its decisions and confront its authority.

The Americans turn angry

In the aftermath of the Seven Years' War, the British government adopted an imperialist policy in violation of the tradition of colonial autonomy. Guided by its own interests, Britain disappointed American expectations and abused its power.

The western boundary blocked

Some Americans had taken up arms against New France because they coveted lands further west, particularly in the Ohio Valley. In 1763, London decided to ban settlement west of the Appalachian Mountains, reserving these fine lands for the Crown. The aim was to maintain fur-rich territories for private companies and to reward indigenous allies who had fought with the English during the war. The English authorities also feared that development of the west would turn chaotic. This decision enraged Americans from Pennsylvania and Virginia, as well as frontiersmen who dreamed of adventure and hoped to get rich quick. It held back the development of the American colonies at a time when tens of thousands of immigrants were arriving in the aftermath of the war.

Taxes, taxes, taxes

The English had not skimped on resources in conquering New France. The British government was heavily in debt after the Seven Years' War. In 1763, as soon as the conflict with France was over, indigenous tribes led by a chief named Pontiac attacked several American colonies. Maryland, Virginia, and Pennsylvania suffered more than 2,000 casualties. The British government then decided to station 10,000 regular army troops on American soil. The upkeep of these troops was expensive, however.

In London, people felt that the Americans should do their part. In this context, the British government imposed a series of new taxes on the Americans: in 1764, a tax on sugar and certain luxury products; in 1765, a heavy tax on paper used for political purposes (the Stamp Act); in 1767, a series of taxes on other products, including tea. These taxes were seen as an affront. The tax on paper caused great harm to newspaper printers and reduced freedom of expression. Americans felt that only their state assemblies could levy taxes. On the basis of the principle of no taxation without representation, they argued that only their elected representatives had the authority to impose taxes.

Things heat up in Boston

To challenge these taxes, American intellectuals wrote treatises, elected officials went before the courts, and ordinary citizens boycotted English products. A climate of confrontation was developing in several colonies, and tempers began to flare.

On March 5, 1770, an altercation between an English army detachment and a group of demonstrators turned violent, with several American deaths. The Boston Massacre increased the pressure on London. The following month, it suspended its unpopular taxes, except for the tax on tea. The tea tax, though mostly symbolic, led to a dramatic event: the Boston Tea Party. On the night of December 16, 1773, a small group of American Patriots from Boston, wearing indigenous disguises, boarded three British vessels and threw 343 crates of tea into the harbor. This act of defiance provoked the anger of the English authorities.

Five "Intolerable Acts"

In the eyes of the English, this went too far. George III and his government were convinced that only a show of force would make the Americans listen to reason. In the winter and spring of 1774, London adopted a series of harsh laws:

- The port of Boston would be closed until the dumped tea was paid for and the people showed remorse.
- Massachusetts residents lost the right to choose their government.
- English soldiers or civil servants posted in the colonies would no longer be tried in American courts.
- English troops could be lodged in people's homes at the people's expense.

Not without reason, the Americans denounced these abuses of power, describing them as "Intolerable Acts" that went against the most basic English freedoms.

But the worst of all these laws, some people said, was the Quebec Act, which again blocked Americans from the western part of the continent and granted undue privileges to the Catholics of French descent whom they had fought a few years earlier. A young Patriot named Alexander Hamilton, who later helped lay the intellectual foundations for the American republic, saw the "Canada affair" as even more serious than the Boston Tea Party. Some Americans felt that Britain, by giving the Canadiens all they asked for, was trying to hold back American development. A relationship of trust was broken.

The American invasion

Delegates from the 13 American colonies soon met and drafted a response to the Intolerable Acts. On September 5, 1774, the First Continental Congress gathered in Philadelphia. The delegates were far from agreement on a number of points. The "Loyalists" were very attached to British institutions and balked at endorsing a definitive break with the mother country. The "Patriots," however, believed that the independence of the American colonies was preordained, not only because England had abused its authority but also because the Americans had to break with obsolete and corrupt monarchical institutions. These Patriots envisioned adopting a republican constitution under which Americans could aspire to happiness and could live more freely.

Defeating the British army was no simple matter, however. The Americans hurriedly formed an army, led by George Washington. In their quest for victory, every option was placed on the table, including trying to persuade the Canadiens to fight alongside the Americans.

Appeals to the Canadiens

On October 26, 1774, delegates to the Congress agreed to launch an appeal to the Canadiens. In their densely written document, the American delegates argued that the Canadiens should be wary of the concessions granted by the English Crown in the Quebec Act. These changes were granted arbitrarily and could be revoked at the stroke of a pen. If the Canadiens joined the American colonies, the delegates promised, they could maintain their civil law and their religion, and also enjoy true freedom of the press, a more equitable system of justice, and a house of assembly. It took some time to translate this appeal and send it to Quebec.

Two additional appeals to the Canadiens were written by Americans, one by the Massachusetts delegates (February 21, 1775) and the other by the Second Continental Congress (May 27, 1775). The Congress's letter appealed to the pride of the Americans' northern neighbors: "We can never believe that the present race of Canadians are so degenerated as to possess neither the spirit, the gallantry, nor the courage of their ancestors."

At the same time as they tried to lure Canadiens with arguments, the Americans were devising invasion plans. A spy came to size up the mood in the colony. The arrival of troops was imminent.

"Don't listen to the rebels"

Among the first people to react officially to calls for sedition against the British was Bishop Jean-Oliver Briand. On May 22, 1775, he issued a stark pastoral letter. Supporting the Americans was out of the question: "A band of subjects revolting against the legitimate sovereign, who is also ours, has of late burst into this province . . . with a view to dragging you into their revolt." It would be a serious error to go along with "their pernicious design," considering the "recent favors" granted by "His Very Gracious Majesty, King George III" in the Quebec Act. The bishop reminded Canadiens that they had sworn allegiance to the king and that forsaking this allegiance would mean failing in one of their most sacred duties. But above all, the prelate insisted, disobeying the authorities would be a very serious matter: "Do not listen to the rebels who seek to make you unfortunate and to stifle in your hearts the feeling of submission to your legitimate superiors engraved by education and religion."

Montreal occupied, Quebec besieged

In late June 1775, the American Congress officially issued an order. Two contingents of soldiers would invade the northern colony. The first contingent of 2,000 men, led by General Richard Montgomery, set out to take Montreal. They came down the Richelieu River and, with some difficulty, took Fort Saint-Jean and Fort Chambly. This forced the "Redcoats," as the British troops were called, to retreat to Sorel. On November 13, the Americans entered Montreal. They promised the inhabitants that they could keep their properties and that none of them would be required to take up arms.

After the occupation of Montreal was established, Montgomery's men headed down the St. Lawrence and lent a hand to the second American contingent, which had reached the gates of Quebec City via the Chaudière River. Posted at Pointe-Lévy, the 1,000 men led by Benedict Arnold had besieged the city since November 8. On December 31, the Americans launched an attack on Quebec City. But it failed, and the Americans gave up. By June 1776, Quebec was British again.

A harsh winter, the spread of a smallpox epidemic, and serious supply problems were the causes of the American defeat. The arrival of substantial British reinforcements, consisting mostly of German mercenaries, also weighed in the balance, as did the apparent indifference of the colony's inhabitants to the American cause. Though Washington's army may have recruited a few hundred Canadiens, most of the populace didn't budge. Was this out of obedience to the bishop's letter? Were they generally happy with the Quebec Act? Or did they simply not care? It's hard to know. But one thing was certain: The Canadiens resisted the American temptation.

Did France consider retaking Canada?

This defeat did not keep the Americans from pursuing their struggle. On July 4, 1776, they formally declared their independence from Britain. But the former mother country was not about to be pushed aside. The following month, British armies took New York. Fierce battles broke out, and the American Patriots were still far from winning the fight. On October 17, 1777, they won a major victory at Saratoga. On February 6, 1778, the French entered the fray and signed a military alliance with the Americans — a significant source of support that could well make the difference!

During the negotiations leading to this alliance, the Americans tried to discern French intentions. Was France, under Louis XV, seeking to reconquer Canada and rectify certain clauses in the 1763 Treaty of Paris? The British spread this rumor in the 13 American colonies in 1775. Charles Gravier, Comte de Vergennes, the French foreign minister at the time, was very clear on this issue. On August 7, 1775, he wrote to his ambassador in London, "As for the specter raised before the Americans in our regard, it does not take even mediocre ability to imagine ways of reassuring this people, so jealous of its freedom and independence; the council of the king of England is making a grave error *if it persuades itself that we regret losing Canada as much as it may repent for having acquired it.*" Article 6 of the 1778 treaty was quite explicit: There was no thought of retaking Bermuda "or any part of the continent in northern America" that was conceded to the British in 1763. As the French saw it, harming their old enemy was one thing; reconquering Canada was quite another.

Pierre du Calvet's crusade

In June 1778, a new governor arrived in Quebec. Sir Frederick Haldimand, of Swiss descent, spoke excellent French. As a mercenary, he had early on attracted the attention of his superiors. After playing a role in several major North American battles in the Seven Years' War, he became "governor in chief for the Province of Quebec" at a crucial time. With the American colonies headed toward independence, it was essential to hold onto Britain's northern colonies. A tough approach was needed. Any sympathy for republican ideas would be harshly repressed.

Pierre du Calvet knew something of this. Born in France in 1735, he emigrated to New France in 1758. His import-export business made him a prosperous merchant. A favorite of Murray and Carleton, he was appointed a justice of the peace. But on September 27, 1780, the tide of fortune turned. He was accused of conspiring with the American enemy and would spend two years and seven months behind bars, without even a trial. Incriminating letters sent to the American Congress were invoked by the colony's attorney general. Proclaiming his innocence, he published *Appel à la justice de l'État (A Call for State Justice)* in July 1784, accusing Haldimand of violating the most basic British freedoms, habeas corpus in particular. Drowned in a shipwreck in 1786, Pierre du Calvet could not pursue the legal action he planned to launch against the governor. But his book bore witness to the climate of suspicion then prevailing in the colony.

For French-speaking people in North America, this was a fateful decision. They now knew for certain that they would have to fend for themselves to ensure the survival of their culture.

The arrival of the Loyalists

Aided by their alliance with the French, the Americans triumphed. On September 3, 1783, their representatives signed the Treaty of Paris. This was a victory for the Patriots and republicans. But there were about 500,000 American Loyalists, and many of them had great difficulty accepting this outcome. About 50,000 decided to go into exile. They felt an attachment to the Crown and British institutions, and many saw themselves as authentic "English patriots."

Where they went

The natural impulse for thousands of Loyalists was to seek refuge in the north. The city of Halifax, founded in 1749, welcomed several hundred of them, as did Prince Edward Island and Newfoundland. The 7,000 Loyalists who settled in Quebec were a source of special concern for the British authorities, who didn't want them to be too close to their former country and, at the same time, sought to prevent their blending into the majority French Catholic population. This explains why 6,000 Loyalists settled west of the Ottawa River, north of Lake Ontario. About 500 more settled in the Gaspé peninsula on the Atlantic coast, between Douglastown and New Carlisle. However, this initial wave of Loyalist refugees was denied access to the fine lands of the Eastern Townships — something that would be granted later.

What they expected

The English merchants welcomed these new arrivals with open arms. Finally they had reinforcements! The Loyalists expected to be greeted with respect by the British authorities. After all, they'd remained loyal to the Crown. From the time they arrived, they believed this loyalty would be recognized and rewarded. Land was granted to them, and the authorities promised them true English institutions. But they had very traditional ideas about such institutions. There were not many reformers among them, and even fewer "democrats" — a term associated at the time with anarchy and disorder.

But how would they regard the Canadiens? And what powers would they be willing to concede to their new compatriots?

Chapter 7

The Birth of Lower Canada and the Parti Canadien (1791–1822)

In This Chapter

▶ Adopting the Constitutional Act

▶ Putting the kibosh on the optimism of the time

▶ Surviving a new U.S. invasion

*A*merican independence and the immigration of Loyalists forced Britain to rethink the organization and functioning of its North American colonies. In 1784, a petition by nearly 2,300 inhabitants of the Province of Quebec reached London. It attacked the Quebec Act of 1774 as "inadequate" and "the Cause of much Confusion in our Laws." It called for the establishment of a "House of Representatives," but only if this was "Composed of Your Majesty's Old and New Subjects" alike. There was no question of excluding Catholic Canadiens. This petition was signed by 855 Quebecers of British Isles origin and 1,436 Canadiens who came from an emerging social class consisting of lawyers, doctors, and businessmen. The seigneurs, who were well represented in the council that assisted the governor, had no quarrel with the Quebec Act.

London acknowledged the petition, but had no intention of authorizing institutions that would give too much power to the people. A number of British politicians had been stung by the American War of Independence and the democratic spirit of the "Patriot" leaders. When he met the first American ambassador in June 1785, King George III was clear. "I will be very frank with you," he said. "I was the last to consent to the Separation, but the Separation having been made and having become inevitable . . . I would be the first to meet the Friendship of the United States as an independent Power." The British authorities might be prepared to concede a house of assembly, but there was no question of letting the settlers believe they would be the only masters of the ship. After all, an empire is an empire!

Setting Up a Government with the Constitutional Act

After considering several scenarios, including uniting all its North American colonies in a confederation (an idea that would resurface later), the British government finally adopted the Constitutional Act. Officially proclaimed on December 26, 1791, this act brought with it substantial and lasting change.

Their own parliament

For the first time in their history, the inhabitants of the St. Lawrence Valley could elect representatives to a parliament. Canadiens, who made up the majority, now had a place to voice their ideas and beliefs. With the laws they adopted, they could put their own stamp on the direction of their community.

Splitting the colony in two: Upper Canada and Lower Canada

The British government aimed both to satisfy the Loyalists who had fled the new American republic and convince the Canadiens of the superiority of British institutions. But to get satisfactory results, according to the influential British intellectual and member of Parliament Edmund Burke, uniting the old and new subjects in a single colony was unwise. The Canadiens had their own language, laws, and customs, so London should give them their own colony, even if this would make a small British minority unhappy.

Convinced by this argument, the British government created two new colonies, geographically separate and with different legal systems. Located west of the Ottawa River and on the north shore of the Great Lakes, the colony of Upper Canada constituted the historic heart of today's Ontario. Thousands of Loyalists had already settled there in 1791. The other colony, which included the southern portion of what is now Quebec, was called Lower Canada. This was the new name assigned to the former Province of Quebec. In 1791, it had a population of about 150,000.

Voting for its own laws — under the supervision of the governor

The Constitutional Act extended the more liberal provisions of the Quebec Act. There was no question of reducing the rights of the Catholic clergy, or of going back on recognition of the seigneurial system and French civil law. Anxious to find a balance between the power of the king, large landowners (the aristocracy), and the people, the 1791 act placed at the head of the colony a governor who represented the British Crown and gave assent to the colony's laws. No legislation could take effect without the governor's consent — and that of London, because the English Parliament reserved the right to disallow any law that was not to its liking.

But it was not the governor's responsibility to determine the legislative agenda. This was the job of the Executive Council and especially of two legislative bodies, one of which was completely new:

✔ **A Legislative Assembly composed of elected representatives:** The inhabitants of Lower Canada could now elect 50 members of the Legislative Assembly. Most men were eligible to vote. To qualify one had to be at least 21 years old, never have been found guilty of "Treason or Felony," be a "Subject of His Majesty," and pay rent or own a small property. Women, Jews, and Aboriginals were not explicitly excluded from the electorate. The Assembly could initiate bills and pass them — along with those that came from the Executive Council — by majority vote. But before being submitted to the governor, they had to be reviewed and approved by another legislative body.

✔ **A Legislative Council composed of members appointed by the governor:** Equivalent to what we now call the Senate or upper chamber, the Legislative Council was made up of at least 15 people appointed for life by the governor. In fact, this body had existed since 1774. Initially, several Canadian seigneurs were appointed. The institution quickly became the stamping ground of the English bourgeoisie, which used its powers to thwart certain projects supported by the Canadian majority or to impose its own agenda.

After laws were ratified by the governor, they still had to be implemented. This was the task of the Executive Council. Unlike today's cabinet, its members were selected and appointed by the governor, not chosen from the majority in the elected Assembly.

Receiving an enthusiastic response

Although the powers of the Legislative Assembly were quite limited, the elites of the new Lower Canada celebrated the adoption of the Constitutional Act with great pomp. Feasts and banquets were organized — a new era was beginning! In his personal diary, the sculptor François Baillairgé wrote that "1792 is the first year of freedom in this country." On January 14, 1792, other enthusiasts founded a "constitutional club" in Quebec. Its members' stated goal was to deepen their knowledge of the "British Constitution" and to encourage economic development in the colony. They would study the great English philosophers of law and parliamentarianism to better adapt to the new institutions they had inherited.

Language: A hot topic

The first election campaign in the history of Quebec began in May 1792, as candidates vied to win the confidence of voters. All tactics, including intimidation, appear to have been allowed. In the May 17 edition of *The Quebec Gazette,* a "Notice to Canadiens" attributed to Pierre-Amable de Bonne denounced the "concerted coalition" of "English traders" that threatened "our happiness and the security of our properties." Naturally, those targeted were quick to condemn these remarks as "defamatory." A campaign leaflet of one of the named candidates described the British merchant as the best friend of the farmer whose hard work he rewards.

Choosing a speaker of the Assembly

The confrontations of the campaign offered a taste of what awaited the winning candidates. The position of member of the Assembly came with no compensation, so only a tiny elite could afford the luxury of engaging in politics. Of the 50 elected, 30 were successful businessmen and half had seigneuries. The British minority, overrepresented in relation to its proportion of the population, demonstrated ethnic solidarity in winning a third of the seats in the new Assembly.

On December 18, 1792, members gathered in the chapel of the bishop's palace in Quebec City. In this improvised parliamentary chamber, they would designate the speaker who would preside over the work of the Assembly — an important function, because the speaker also acted as representative of the Assembly to the governor. The English members proposed three candidates for the post, while the Canadiens rallied around the candidacy of Jean-Antoine Panet. Panet prevailed — an outcome that enraged some of the English-speaking members because of Panet's limited proficiency in English, which Assembly member John Richardson described as the "language of the Empire." On December 20, the speaker-elect delivered his speech in French — a first.

Deciding on a language for the Assembly

French was the language of European cultural and political elites in the 18th century. Its prestige undoubtedly worked in the favor of the Canadiens when it came time to decide on the language to be used in the Assembly. In January 1793, an initial debate raged on this sensitive issue. In John Richardson's view, the question should not even have arisen: "Being governed by laws made in the English language is a birthright of every British subject, and no power on earth, except the Parliament of Great Britain, can remove this privilege." Assembly member Philippe de Rocheblave did not agree. If it imposed English by force, Britain would only intensify "national bias" and "chicanery," he said. Gabriel Elzéar Taschereau also denounced Richardson's arguments, which he said "would keep us in bondage." Rather than extol the language of their ancestors or appeal to national feeling, French-speaking members called for caution and compromise — an approach that prevailed. Assembly members agreed that all bills would be presented in both languages, but the English version would take precedence when it came to criminal law, while French would take precedence on issues involving civil law.

In this way, French-Canadian members of the Lower Canadian Assembly made parliamentary institutions their own, in their mother tongue. They quickly established clear rules, including setting the quorum at 34. In this way, French-Canadian members were able to prevent the minority from passing laws without their consent. From the outset, the members also agreed that all matters involving government finances would have to be approved by the Assembly (an issue that would come back to haunt political discussions later on). The remainder of the legislative agenda was not very developed in the early years.

The school system gets off to a slow start

In the first half of the 19th century, the development of the public school system in Quebec suffered several failures. Three groups had widely divergent views on the issue.

The powerful minority of English-speaking merchants dreamed of a network of Protestant schools supported by the colony. In 1801, the merchants had the idea of developing a royal institution that would establish a network of primary schools. The Catholic Church denounced the plan, going so far as to urge its followers to boycott the new schools.

In 1824, the Assembly of Lower Canada passed the *Loi des Écoles de Fabriques* (Parish Schools Act), which suited the church much better. The *fabriques* managed the tithes — taxes levied by the church to administer parish budgets, covering such items as the church building, the rectory, and good works. Each *fabrique* was managed by a lay churchwarden, with assistance from the priest who oversaw the operations. The 1824 legislation allowed for the possibility that the *fabriques* would be able to establish schools if they wanted to. But this new system didn't work.

In 1829, the Parti Canadien obtained passage of another schools act, the *Loi des Écoles de Syndics,* which gave authority to local notables and the state. This did not please the church, but it did lead to positive results — at least until the English-speaking minority blocked the budgets allocated by the Assembly to this public network just before the 1837 rebellion.

A noteworthy figure from that era who was dedicated to the cause of education was Joseph-François Perrault (1753–1844). Adventurer, politician, and translator of a classic work on parliamentary practice that appeared in 1803, Perrault devoted the latter part of his life to education. Along with other leaders, he founded the Education Society of the District of Quebec in 1821.

The main characteristic of Perrault's educational program was that it was aimed not at the elites but at the people. Unlike many church people of that time, Perrault didn't believe that poverty was inevitable. Through instruction, all people could become better farmers or improve their lot, but this would happen only if school was free for the poor.

In Perrault's view, schools must transmit moral principles, often inspired by religion. But he didn't want churches to have control over the school system. He felt it was first and foremost parents' obligation to see to the religious education of their children, outside of school hours — a very avant-garde point of view!

Dampening the Mood of Optimism with War and New Leadership

Despite these sometimes bitter debates about language, it was an optimistic time. Many people felt that they were participating in an age of political progress. This momentum would be dampened, however, by a new war between France and Great Britain and the arrival of an uncompromising governor.

The shadow of the French Revolution

Support for the United States had cost France dearly. To levy new taxes, King Louis XVI convened the Estates-General in 1789. However, things didn't go as planned. Representatives of the Third Estate (those who were neither nobles nor clergy) quickly defined themselves as the only legitimate voice of the nation. On July 14, protestors stormed the Bastille prison and killed its governor. On August 4, members of the new "National Assembly" abolished the privileges of the nobility. On August 26, they adopted the Declaration of the Rights of Man and of the Citizen. After attempting to flee his country, Louis XVI was finally ready to agree to a new constitution on September 14, 1791. The new regime, a constitutional monarchy, resembled the one prevailing in Britain.

An ode to the revolution

Overall, these early events that shook France were viewed positively by the press and enlightened Lower Canadians. On January 28, 1790, *The Gazette* published an "Ode to the Revolution," very much inspired by the spirit of the Enlightenment. Many compared this revolution to the one that transformed England in 1688, as if the French were finally coming close to the great English model. As for the new constitution of 1791, it was hailed by *The Quebec Gazette,* which saw in it a "sublime mix of the philosophical spirit of the 18th century and the energy of the ancient Romans."

War and terror

But the tide turned quickly. Under the new regime, the church and its priests were subject to the ideas of the revolution. Priests who refused to swear allegiance to the new regime were sentenced to be deported. The pope was outraged, and Louis XVI refused to support the Assembly's decision. Starting in the summer of 1792, a wave of radicalization swept everything in its path. The royal family was imprisoned; the king was executed on January 21, 1793; and the queen was guillotined in October of the same year. After declaring war on several European monarchies — including England on February 1, 1793 — France became a revolutionary republic. The more moderate leaders were executed, and the counterrevolutionaries from the Vendée were exterminated. This "terror" was orchestrated by Robespierre, the new strongman of the regime.

Most members of the elite in Lower Canada immediately denounced the radicalization in France. In April 1793, members of the Assembly passed a motion deploring the declaration of war against Great Britain and unambiguously condemning the execution of Louis XVI — which the resolution described as "the most terrible crime and the most disgraceful for society." On May 7, Judge William Smith said that the conquest of Canada had been an act of providence, because it had saved the new subjects from the horrors of the revolution.

From the free French to their brothers in Canada

The climate of suspicion in Lower Canada was fed by the ambassador of revolutionary France to the United States, Edmond-Charles Genêt, who published an address to the Canadiens in June 1793:

> Everything around you invites you to freedom. The country you live in was conquered by your fathers. It owes its prosperity only to their efforts and yours. This land belongs to you. It should be independent. Break then with a government that has become the bitterest enemy of the freedom of the people.

On his own initiative, the ambassador envisioned a potential invasion of Canada. Some Canadiens were in fact willing to take up arms. Among them was the young Henri Mézière, overcome by the "love of freedom," as he wrote to his parents, and burning to leave for France to fight alongside the revolutionaries. But republicans like him were few and far between in Lower Canada.

ANECDOTE

A spy in the colony?

With France and England at war again, loyalists seized the opportunity to launch a hunt for liberal sympathizers and insist on unwavering loyalty to the British Crown. In May 1797, all French nationals were ordered to leave the colony, and French-Canadian Assembly members, caught up in the fear of subversion, agreed to suspend habeas corpus.

On the evening of May 10, 1797, David McLane, an American native of Providence, the capital of Rhode Island, was arrested. He told anyone who would listen that he planned to recruit about 15 people to prepare a surprise attack on the Quebec garrison. The goal was no less than to incite a revolution in Canada with the help of France! The trial lasted only a few days. The authorities believed that they were holding a spy, and they wanted to set an example. The sentence meted out to McLane was chilling: He would be hanged and drawn.

The execution took place on July 21. He was hanged in the public square in Quebec City. After butchering the accused, the executioner burned his bowels — a scene of carnage that sowed fear in the public. In all likelihood, David McLane was more a pathological liar than an authentic spy. He probably needed a good psychologist more than anything else.

A providential conquest?

After the fall of Robespierre in July 1794, the terror faded but the war continued. The young general Napoleon Bonaparte won spectacular victories on behalf of the republic. But he suffered a major defeat at Aboukir Bay in Egypt on August 1, 1798. Part of the French fleet was sunk by British sailors under the command of Admiral Nelson. This defeat suffered by revolutionary France offered the bishop of Quebec the opportunity he had been seeking to respond to the events in France. On January 10, 1799, Joseph-Octave Plessis violently condemned the philosophical basis of the revolution, which he charged had brought about impiety, disorder, and war. In his eyes, the British conquest had allowed the Canadiens to escape this calamity and enjoy healthier and stronger institutions (criminal law, freedom of religion, and so on) than those introduced by the revolutionaries. The conclusion of his speech put his loyalty on an exalted plane. Plessis believed that Nelson's victory had been brought about by divine providence: "Let us celebrate this glorious event. Anything that weakens France helps to draw it further away from us. All that takes it further away ensures our lives, our freedom, our peace, our properties, our worship, our happiness."

The emergence of the Parti Canadien

The war between Britain and France had a positive impact on the economy of Lower Canada. The timber trade was booming. This prosperity strengthened the position of a business class made up primarily of English speakers. This ruling class happily welcomed the arrival of a second wave of Loyalist immigrants from the United States, most of whom settled in the Eastern Townships. Between 1791 and 1812, the English-speaking population increased from 10,000 to 30,000. This minority believed in free enterprise and trade.

In January 1805, the group launched a newspaper, *The Quebec Mercury*. Its editors accused the Canadian majority of wallowing in ignorance and being lazy, apathetic, and indifferent to progress. The tone became particularly aggressive when the Assembly decided to tax trade rather than land to finance the construction of new prisons. The merchants alleged that such a tax would slow commerce, and they fought the Assembly's plan in vain. The defeat embittered many of them.

Pierre Bédard's struggle

These repeated accusations against the Canadian majority shocked Assembly member Pierre Bédard. This son of a baker from Charlesbourg studied at the Séminaire de Québec before becoming a lawyer. Elected in 1792, with no special talent as an orator, he stood out because of his encyclopedic mind. Passionate about science and philosophy, he contributed to founding the Library of Parliament in 1802, which was soon well stocked with reference books. He also developed a very thorough knowledge of English law. His admiration for British institutions was sincere — in fact, it was precisely on the basis of British constitutionalism that he attacked the pretensions and prejudices of the English-speaking minority. His loyalty to the Crown was beyond question.

But although Bédard did not show any sympathy for the American republic and had no particular enthusiasm for Napoleonic ambitions, he did claim for himself and his people the same freedoms granted to subjects of British origin. This was the position of the "Parti Canadien," of which he became a leading figure.

The reform program of the Parti Canadien

In response to the *Mercury*'s attacks, Pierre Bédard founded *Le Canadien,* a newspaper that appeared for the first time on November 22, 1806. Its program included the following ideas:

- ✔ **The sanctity of freedom of the press:** One of the most important English freedoms was the freedom to express oneself without risk on matters relating to the colony's government.

- ✔ **Equality before the law:** Whether French or English, subjects of the colony should be equal before the law and enjoy the same freedoms.

    In defending this principle of equality before the low, Bédard and his followers didn't have Native Americans or Jews in mind. In 1807, they even objected to the election of Ezekiel Hart. Until 1832, at least in Lower-Canada (see Chapter 8), no Jew could run for office in the British Empire. In truth, they mainly wanted to remove an ally of the English-speaking minority.

- ✔ **Independence for the Assembly:** To ensure the smooth functioning of the Assembly, Bédard felt that the members should receive compensation, the speaker should have a salary, and officers of the colony (judges or officials appointed by the governor) should be excluded. Such measures would prevent the concentration of power and better reflect the will of voters.

- ✔ **Better control of expenditures by the Assembly:** According to Bédard, it was up to the elected members of the Assembly to control the colony's administrative costs, including the expenses involved in allowing the governor to operate. In the English system, only elected officials were empowered to levy taxes. Logically, the Parti Canadien argued that ministers responsible for implementing laws that had budgetary implications should answer for their actions before the House. In the early 19th century, this understanding of "ministerial responsibility" was cutting edge.

The crisis of 1810

Despite the moderation of the proposed reforms, some people were outraged. In a letter to the speaker of the Assembly dated June 6, 1808, the secretary to the governor described *Le Canadien* as a "seditious and defamatory publication" whose mission was to "antagonize people and create a spirit of discord and animosity."

Craig, the "little king"

This sentiment was echoed by James Craig, governor of Lower Canada from 1807 to 1811. Born in 1748, this career soldier was a hardliner with little taste for compromise. In this time of war against Napoleon, he was suspicious of everything French. For their part, the Canadiens picked up on the nickname given to him in the army, "little king Craig." Angered by the material printed in *Le Canadien,* Craig was easily persuaded by his most rigid advisers that the Constitutional Act should be suspended and Upper Canada and Lower Canada united. The merchants were convinced that only such drastic measures would improve east–west trade and reduce the Canadiens to minority status for good.

But the Canadiens saw things differently. In 1808, they elected a majority of members from Pierre Bédard's party. When they arrived in the House, the policies they supported were generally those outlined in *Le Canadien,* including a law prohibiting judges from standing as candidates in elections. Craig saw this law almost as an affront and called a new election, which was held in the fall of 1809. He had bad luck, however: Voters reelected the same members.

Le Canadien shut down, Bédard imprisoned

Although London urged him to be more conciliatory, Craig wouldn't budge. The governor wanted a new majority. So, he decided to postpone the session that had just begun and dissolve the Assembly. Craig believed that such action was necessary to curb the "development of democratic influence." On March 17, he took things a step further and ordered the seizure of *Le Canadien* and the arrest of the printer Charles Lefrançois. Two days later, Pierre Bédard, François Blanchet, and Jean-Thomas Taschereau were arrested and imprisoned. The three members of the Parti Canadien were accused of "traitorous practices." On March 21, a proclamation from the governor was printed and distributed throughout the territory. Craig described the arrested leaders as malicious and wicked people.

The church in hot water

Bishop Joseph-Octave Plessis didn't like the Parti Canadien's agenda, which tended "to destroy every principle of subordination," as he wrote to a correspondent in December 1809. But that wasn't quite the same thing as openly supporting the policy of Governor Craig. The bishop feared that Craig's changes would work to the disadvantage of the church, as the majority of his flock supported the Parti Canadien. He nevertheless agreed to have the priests read the governor's proclamation and continued to preach "respect and submission." In the election of 1810, he even encouraged voters to vote against the candidates from Pierre Bédard's party. Plessis came to regret this direct intervention because voters, once again, did as they pleased. Bédard's victory was complete. Even though he was behind bars, he was reelected, as was François Blanchet.

In light of the lack of evidence against them, Craig eventually had to release Taschereau and Blanchet. With heavy hearts, the two Assembly members paid a large fine and signed a declaration in which they acknowledged their "crimes" and asked for pardon. Pierre Bédard, however, refused to sign anything and demanded a trial complete with due process of law. His stubborn resistance meant that he was deprived of his liberty for 391 days. His family was likewise deprived of an income, forcing his wife to rent their home to strangers.

Seeing the British Empire at War and at Peace

The British government didn't approve of the conduct of its representative in Lower Canada. The repeated dissolutions slowed legislative work and plunged the colony into confrontation. All this came at a bad time — the mother country needed resources from its colonies.

Since 1806, Napoleon's France had maintained a continental blockade, forcing England to look to North America for supplies of timber and wheat. Because England was also in the midst of its "industrial revolution," the first of its kind in the world, and London had become a huge manufacturing center, Britain was reliant on stable and prosperous colonies.

Craig was disavowed, recalled to London, and replaced by George Prevost. This military man of Swiss origin was a shrewd diplomat and spoke excellent French.

A second American invasion

The dominant event of the new governor's term of office was a new invasion. During the war between France and England, the United States tried to remain neutral. Merchants, however, needed access to the vast European market. In June 1807, a British ship intercepted an American frigate, ostensibly to look for deserters but in reality to discourage Americans from trading with the French. More such incidents occurred, some of which led to casualties; these incidents harmed business and increased tension between the United States and Britain. In retaliation, the young republic issued an embargo on imports of European goods. Some of the U.S. political elite felt it necessary to go further and declare war on Britain. This is what President James Madison did in June 1812. The target? The two Canadas to the north.

Upper Canada: The main battlefield

In 1812, the American republic was a rising power. Its population had reached 7.5 million, and it had an army of about 12,000 men. Its leaders were betting that Britain would attach more importance to the war against Napoleon than to its colonies in North America, which had a population of barely 500,000. From the beginning of the conflict, the United States attacked the towns and shorelines of Upper Canada, which were much more accessible than the Maritimes and Lower Canada. In the months following the declaration of war, almost all attacks on Upper Canada were repulsed by the colony's soldiers, militia, and Aboriginal allies. In the young colony, these victories strengthened the feeling of belonging to a distinct national community.

The Voltigeurs: Canadian fighters to rescue the Empire

Pierre Bédard and most of the leaders of the Parti Canadien at the time had a negative view of the American republic. From 1806 to 1810, *Le Canadien* denounced "Yankee" greed and lack of interest in things of the spirit. This anti-Americanism, in addition to the attractive pay the army was offering, probably explains why it wasn't hard to recruit Canadian volunteers into a light infantry unit dubbed "Les Voltigeurs."

Charles-Michel de Salaberry, one of the few Canadian officers in the British army, was named to head this unit. Born in 1778 to a society family with ties to the English aristocracy, Salaberry enlisted in the army when he was only 14 years old. He served first in the Caribbean, and then in Ireland and the Netherlands. Promoted to lieutenant colonel, he was the obvious choice as leader of the Voltigeurs.

The new unit was mobilized quickly. In November 1812, it held off the Americans at Lacolle. To stop British reinforcements from coming to Upper Canada, the Americans planned to occupy Montreal. On October 21, 1813, 3,000 U.S. troops crossed the border and came up the Châteauguay River toward Montreal. A fierce battle ensued on October 26 in the vicinity of Allan's Corner, lasting four hours. Even though he led a group of only 29 officers and 481 soldiers, Salaberry gave the impression of commanding a much larger army. To conceal the real strength of his forces, he built a mound at the river bend. The 2,000 American soldiers under the command of Wade Hampton beat a hasty retreat and abandoned the plan to occupy Montreal. For this brilliant victory, Salaberry received a commemorative medal. Many generations of French Canadiens evoked his memory to show their loyalty to the Crown. The war ended in a stalemate in 1814.

Pax Britannica

The French defeat at Waterloo on June 18, 1815, marked the end of Napoleon's reign. For the British, the French emperor had been the last obstacle on the road to world domination. Their merchant navy was the largest and their economy the most dynamic in the world. They used steam before anyone else, which accelerated transport of their manufactured goods around the world. This economic strength was coupled with political power. Britain may have lost its American colonies, but it controlled key sites in the

Mediterranean and was well established in North America and the Far East (Australia, New Zealand, and Singapore in 1819, and Hong Kong in 1842). While staying away from conflict in Europe, it pursued an effective diplomatic strategy that ensured the maintenance of a balance of power.

Agricultural crisis (despite the Corn Laws)

In 1815, London adopted the Corn Laws, which guaranteed a preferential tariff to colonial wheat and other grains. This mostly benefited the farmers of Upper Canada, whose population grew from 75,000 in 1812 to 1.4 million in 1860. This wheat-driven prosperity explains the initiative to build a major canal on the St. Lawrence, begun in 1820. That year, Lower Canada had 420,000 inhabitants, of whom 80,000 were British. Instead of benefiting from the preferential tariff, farmers in Lower Canada experienced serious difficulties.

The causes of this crisis, which began in 1815, were multiple. Soil exhaustion played a role, as it did in the decline of agriculture in the northeastern United States. Lack of interest by Canadian farmers in new techniques and the seeming impossibility of breaking into the English market were other factors.

The model that predominated in Lower Canada was subsistence agriculture, not more intensive production. But subsistence agriculture was quickly reaching its limit as free land in the seigneuries became increasingly rare. The seigneurial zone produced little surplus and yet gradually was becoming overcrowded — a combination that certainly did not bode well.

The powerful bourgeoisie

During this period, the powerful English bourgeoisie continued on its upward path, thanks in great measure to the timber trade. To finance its activities, it founded the Bank of Montreal in 1817 and the Quebec Bank the following year. In 1822, the Montreal Board of Trade brought together the English merchants who really counted — men like John Molson, Sr. (1763–1836), who founded the brewery that bore his name in 1785 and launched the first steamboat to run between Quebec and Montreal in 1809. His son, John, Jr. (1787–1860), continued his father's activities and also founded a bank. Other prominent merchants of John Molson, Jr.'s generation were John Redpath (1796–1869), who was involved in the construction of canals and public buildings and also known for his sugar refinery, and William Price (1789–1867) of Quebec City. Price was another extremely successful and influential entrepreneur and a major exporter of squared timber to the British navy, who, during the 1840s, controlled nearly 20,000 square kilometers (7,722 square miles) of forest reserves in the Saguenay–Lac-Saint-Jean region. All these men, at one time or another, dabbled in politics and protected their interests.

The union plan

In 1822, this bourgeoisie was exasperated by some of the Assembly's decisions. French-Canadian Assembly members wanted to maintain an autonomous tariff policy in their colony, while their counterparts in Upper Canada sought harmonization. In addition, the French-Canadian members continued to demand greater control of government finances. In this strained atmosphere, a proposal to unite Upper and Lower Canada was presented to the English Parliament. Without any consultation with the people of Lower Canada, the bill was brought forward in secret by British MP Edward Ellice, the seigneur of Beauharnois and spokesperson for the merchants of Lower Canada. Governor Craig's old project was rising from the ashes. As always, the objectives were commercial as much as political. The goal was to remove the artificial boundary between Upper and Lower Canada to accelerate east–west trade and marginalize the French Catholic population.

But rumors of the plan made their way to Quebec City, causing an unprecedented backlash, not only from the Parti Canadien but also from the entire French-Canadian population of Lower Canada. A petition was drawn up to denounce the bill on grounds that it would establish a preference in favor of the minority that would be "humiliating to the inhabitants of this province," contrary to their "rights as British Subjects," and dangerous to their interests. The petition was signed by 60,000 Lower Canadians. In the face of this outcry, the British government retreated.

The union plan aroused suspicion in a new generation of Parti Canadien members, and one of their leaders went to London to persuade the British government to reverse its position.

This rising star was named Louis-Joseph Papineau.

Chapter 8

From the Repression of the Patriotes to the Act of Union (1823–1840)

In This Chapter

▶ Looking at the role of Louis-Joseph Papineau

▶ Zeroing in on reactions from the English-speaking minority and from London

▶ Paying attention to the Patriotes' failure and its consequences

*I*nspired by liberal and anticolonial movements in Europe and the Americas, the Parti Canadien, led by Louis-Joseph Papineau, called for more justice and democracy. However, its 92 resolutions were rejected by London, leading to armed clashes in 1837 and 1838. The military defeat of the Patriotes was followed by a period of repression. The British government's special envoy, Lord Durham, then proposed the union of Upper Canada and Lower Canada, which he believed would lead to the assimilation of the French Canadians. His proposal was implemented in part. In 1840, the British government passed the Act of Union and created a new colony: the Province of Canada.

Louis-Joseph Papineau, Republican Leader

Pierre Bédard died in 1829, but for several years, a new generation had been emerging within the Parti Canadien. New blood and new ideas were needed to confront the political challenges facing the colony. Louis-Joseph Papineau had these in ample measure.

The Old World and the New World

These new ideas resonated in a very specific international context. Everywhere, people were seeking to overthrow the old order. On everyone's lips, a single word: *freedom!*

The rights of Europeans

The rebellions of 1837–1838 in Lower Canada were not an isolated uprising. They were part of a much broader movement throughout the West. In France, the revolution of July 1830 put an end to the old authoritarian Bourbon dynasty, which had ruled since the fall of Napoleon in 1815. In England, a new "radical" party that denounced the inequalities between rich and poor forced the adoption of significant democratic reforms — including the Reform Bill of 1832, which gave a greater number of people in Britain the right to vote. In Ireland, the great Daniel O'Connell campaigned courageously for Catholic emancipation.

Winds of change in the Americas

The Americas, too, were experiencing the winds of change. As the United States continued to grow and prosper, it became a model for people who dreamed of a more egalitarian and democratic world. Meanwhile, the Latin American nations were freed one by one from their former colonial masters. Argentina declared its independence in 1816, and Chile did the same just two years later. Colombia, inspired by the great Simón Bolivar, became an independent republic in 1819, as did Mexico in 1821. The following year, it was Brazil's turn to separate from Portugal. North and South American elites alike were convinced that the New World offered the most promising future for men and women of goodwill.

Papineau, man of destiny

The inhabitants of Lower Canada witnessed all these changes and wanted to take part in the century's forward movement. These events that shook the world were reported and discussed in the local newspapers.

Son of a good family

Louis-Joseph Papineau (1786–1871) was exceptionally well informed about what was happening elsewhere. Originally from Montreal, the son of a good family, he was a very cultured man and keenly aware of the politics of the day. He was also an impressive orator whose speeches, interspersed with quotations from classical authors, captivated audiences in the Legislative Assembly and at major public gatherings. A lawyer, he was elected to the Assembly for the first time in 1808. In 1815, at 29, he was appointed speaker of the Assembly by his fellow members — at the time the most prestigious position after the governor. He officially became the head of the Parti Canadien in 1817. That same year he became a true seigneur when he bought the Petite-Nation seigneury in the Ottawa Valley from his father. Three years later, he married the daughter of an Assembly member, Julie Bruneau, an intelligent woman who was as well informed as he was and with whom he had a very rich correspondence.

The republican political leader was so respected and admired for his culture and intelligence that his name lives on in a well-known phrase frequently used by Quebecers. When an idea is simple and easy, people say that "it does not take a Papineau brain" to understand it!

The shock of London's misery

Although Louis-Joseph Papineau had the refined upbringing of a gentleman, he espoused the cause of the people. Until his trip to London in 1823, he vigorously supported the British institutions that he thought offered the best guarantees of stability and order while allowing the people to elect their representatives.

His trip to the British capital, however, gave him a much different, more realistic view of Great Britain. Papineau was shocked by the poverty he saw there. He gradually concluded that there was something corrupt and decadent about the Old World of Europe. To improve the political institutions of Lower Canada and increase the power of the people, he felt it was better to take inspiration from the experiences of the New World.

A caste of aristocrats

America, Papineau insisted, was not destined to have a hereditary aristocracy that lived at the expense of the people. People of the New World must be free and equal. He lamented that in Lower Canada a small elite continued to behave like a caste of aristocrats. Composed mainly of English merchants recently arrived in the colony, this elite group controlled key political institutions of the colony, such as the Executive Council and the Legislative Council. It also speculated on the lands of the Eastern Townships, where many Canadiens wanted to settle and start a family. According to Papineau, this privileged elite stood in the way of people's aspirations by blocking important bills emanating from the Legislative Assembly, through which the French majority in Lower Canada had a voice.

The emancipation of the Jews

Papineau didn't just speak on behalf of people of French origin. The French-Canadian leader demanded more justice for all citizens of the colony, whatever their background. On March 19, 1832, at his party's initiative, important legislation was adopted providing that "persons professing the Jewish religion" who lived in the colony and were born British subjects could now have "all the rights and privileges of the other Subjects of His Majesty." This emancipation of the Jews was a first in the British Empire.

The quarrel over government finances and the 1832 election

A large part of the population supported the Parti Canadien's grievances, including the question of the Assembly's control of government finances. At issue were the sums the elected members allocated to the governor for the administration of the colony.

In 1828, a petition signed by 87,000 residents of Lower Canada was sent to London. It cited the following:

- ✔ **An autocratic governor:** The petition complained about the behavior of Governor Dalhousie, who wanted to retain sole control over management of the budgets allocated by the Legislative Assembly.

- ✔ **Incompetent officials:** The petitioners also decried the negligence of officials, who often couldn't speak a word of French but still received large salaries from the colony's coffers.

- ✔ **Over-representation of English-speaking people in the Legislative Council:** Not only were English-speaking people over-represented in the Legislative Council, but some of them were downright dishonest, taking advantage of their positions for their personal benefit.

- ✔ **The electoral map:** The petition criticized the outrageous way in which the colony was divided into constituencies to the advantage of the English-speaking minority.

- ✔ **The real power:** Above all, the petitioners insisted on the Legislative Assembly's power over the budget. No longer would taxes taken from the people benefit a few privileged merchants from the elite. The case of Councilor John Caldwell, who in 1823 had misappropriated £96,000 for his personal use, was very much in the petitioners' mind. They were united in wanting their elected representatives to exercise real control over the sums that were allocated to the governor.

A delicate situation

For the British government, the situation was delicate. It was hard for the government to be opposed to the old principle of "no taxation without representation," which the Parti Canadien, increasingly influenced by the rhetoric of the American Revolution, invoked. This desire to better control the colony's expenses also gave rise to a new strategy in which the Assembly made use of its powers. To put pressure on the governor, the Assembly periodically refused to vote for funding. In this way, Papineau hoped to force the hand of the representatives of the British Crown and bring about beneficial institutional reforms.

Mounting tension

This quarrel over government finances increased tension in the colony. Shortly after his arrival in 1830, Governor Aylmer tried to find a solution. He proposed distinguishing between the fixed costs of administration (for example, paying the salaries of colonial officials) and other expenses devoted to more specific projects. The elected Assembly would have no control over the first category of expenses — the "civil list," which would have represented less than 20 percent of the overall budget — but it would have full control over the second category.

Aylmer went even further. In 1832, he suggested to Papineau and John Neilson, the Parti Canadien's lieutenant in the Quebec City region, that they join the Executive Council — in other words, that they become ministers of the Crown. He further proposed the appointment of more French-speaking people to the Legislative Council.

Riot in Montreal: Three dead

Papineau and Neilson, perhaps influenced by the arrival of more intransigent young Assembly members elected in 1830, considered these proposals insufficient. They issued their refusal in 1832, a year marked by a spectacular riot during a by-election in the west end of Montreal. The by-election pitted Stanley Bagg, who favored the positions of the English elite, against Daniel Tracey, a Lower Canadian of Irish descent and an unreserved supporter of Louis-Joseph Papineau's party. Tracey's positions were shared by Edmund O'Callaghan, another Lower Canadian of Irish origin, who would succeed Tracey as editor of the newspaper *The Vindicator*.

When the voting period of several days ended on May 21, Tracey had a slight lead. Some goons from his opponent's side intimidated voters, and a violent confrontation between supporters of the two sides broke out. The Riot Act was invoked and the British army intervened and opened fire. In the end, three people who had nothing to do with the clashes, all of them French, were killed. An inquiry ordered by Governor Aylmer supported the army, while two investigations commissioned by the Legislative Assembly accused the forces of law and order of having abused their power. The whole affair added fuel to the fire.

The cholera epidemic and the opening of Grosse Île

Another defining event in Lower Canada in 1832 was the cholera epidemic that began to spread in June of that year. Carried by European immigrants who were arriving in ever greater numbers, the epidemic wreaked havoc in the cities of Quebec and Montreal. In 1831, when the colony's authorities learned about the spread of this terrible disease that killed its victims in less than 24 hours, they set up public health facilities on Grosse Île near Quebec City. All European immigrants were required to undergo a medical examination. Those who were sick and ships carrying the disease were rigorously disinfected. However, these measures did not curb the disease, which came from Asia and about which almost nothing was known at the time.

Several years later, Grosse Île would receive shiploads of Irish fleeing the famine that plagued the country from 1845 to 1849. Hungry and sick, more than 5,000 Irish would be buried there, making Grosse Île an important memorial site for the Irish nation. Many Irish children lost their parents in the tragic crossing of the Atlantic. With the help of the Catholic Church, acting as a humanitarian organization, many of them were adopted by French-Canadian families. In most cases, these children retained their original names — O'Neil, Ryan, Johnson, Burns — and their descendants would build modern Quebec.

The 92 Resolutions and the Russell Resolutions

Political tensions in Lower Canada were exacerbated by the economic downturn of the 1830s. Harvests were poor, seigneurial land was scarce or farmed by the seigneurs themselves, and land in the Eastern Townships was too expensive for young Canadiens. In 1837, the United States underwent a major financial crisis. In 1833, Lower Canada's Legislative Assembly refused to vote the governor's budgetary allocation. From April 1833 to January 1834, the Parti Canadien organized popular assemblies in a number of constituencies. The atmosphere was not conducive to finding practical solutions to overcome the crisis: The tone was confrontational and the rhetoric vindictive. A wind of change was blowing across Lower Canada. The quarrel over government finances couldn't continue indefinitely; it was time to make a decisive move and propose clear changes to London.

The Parti Canadien's grievances

Louis-Joseph Papineau took on this task, assisted by the young Assembly member Augustin-Norbert Morin. Together, they wrote a document containing 92 resolutions that encompassed the list of grievances at that time.

This explosive 80 page-plus document, the great charter of the Parti Canadien, was passed by the Legislative Assembly on February 21, 1834. Among the most important ideas its authors put forward were the following:

- ✔ **They confirmed that the inhabitants of Lower Canada remained loyal to the British Crown.** The proposed reforms were not aimed at independence or secession. Above all, the inhabitants of Lower Canada wanted to be considered true British subjects and not second-class citizens because of their French origin.

- ✔ **They demanded that members of the Legislative Council no longer be appointed by the governor but rather be elected by the people.** Lower Canada was a land of liberty, so it didn't have an aristocracy.

- ✔ **They sought to make the Executive Council more responsible for its actions to Parliament and not just to the Crown, represented in the colony by the governor.** To implement laws and enact important measures, the Executive Council should always enjoy the trust of the people's representatives.

- ✔ **The "resolutionaries" called for the Assembly to have full control over expenditures in the colony as well as the granting of land.**

- ✔ **The authors made it clear that if the mother country was to reject all these grievances, the "resolutionaries" could turn to other viable and promising political models existing on the American continent, such as the one chosen by the United States.**

This list of grievances was adopted after a long debate in the Assembly: 56 members voted in favor; 23, against. Papineau's new strategy didn't gain unanimous approval. A number of Assembly members from Quebec City considered the document too radical and feared a brutal confrontation with the British army, the most powerful in the world at the time. An overwhelming majority of the electorate, however, sided with Papineau. Elections in the fall of 1834 gave the Parti Canadien a resounding victory, with 77 of the 88 seats.

Hostility to reform

After the quarrel over government finances, adoption of the 92 resolutions and the Parti Canadien's triumph once again increased tensions. Thanks to its presence on the Legislative and Executive councils, the powerful minority of English merchants had a veto over all laws passed by the popularly elected Assembly. It established several associations that were clearly hostile to the reforms proposed by the Parti Canadien.

Intolerant merchants

Peter McGill, George Moffatt, and a number of others operating in the timber, banking, transportation, and alcohol sectors were among the major merchants who financed these associations. This minority claimed to be "loyal" to the true principles of British constitutionalism. Its ideas were expressed through the Montreal *Gazette* and the *Herald,* a newspaper edited by Adam Thom that regularly published racist comments directed against the Canadiens.

This intolerance also characterized the thinking of members of the Doric Club, a semi-clandestine organization that threatened to resort to arms if the views of the Parti Canadien prevailed. Their public declaration of March 22, 1836, stated, "If we are deserted by the British government and the British people, rather than submit to the degradation of being subject of a French-Canadian republic, we are determined by our own right arms to work out our deliverance."

A divided Assembly

The 92 resolutions were sent to London, and on June 12–13, 1834, Augustin-Norbert Morin presented them to a House of Commons special committee. Taken aback by this list of grievances, the British government appointed Lord Gosford, a new governor, who took office in 1835. Mandated to report on the situation in Lower Canada, the Crown's representative did not have an easy job. The views of the majority and the minority were so far apart that compromise seemed impossible. Even the Parti Canadien's members were divided on how to proceed.

Some, like the journalist Étienne Parent of *Le Canadien,* believed in letting things play out and allowing the new governor to do his job, while others, including Papineau himself, felt that they must continue to exercise strong pressure by voting only a portion of the funds requested by the colonial administration. The English merchants were wary of the governor, who had ordered that the British Rifle Corps, a militia hostile to the Parti Canadien, be dissolved on January 15, 1836. They were far from convinced that London would side with them.

The reaction in London

The report Gosford submitted on March 2, 1837, showed some openness to the claims of the Parti Canadien. But in the end, the British government opted for a hardline approach.

On March 6, 1837, the minister John Russell presented ten resolutions to the House of Commons, intended to end the crisis in Lower Canada. Russell's resolutions represented a flat refusal of the Parti Canadien's demands, and the English merchants were relieved:

  ✔ **There would be no question of electing members to the Legislative Council.** According to the minister, that would exclude inhabitants of British origin.

> ✔ **Likewise, there was no question of making the government responsible to the Assembly.** Such a reform, the minister argued, would distort the functioning of Great Britain's monarchical institutions.

> ✔ **The British government refused to give the Assembly complete control over budgets and expenditures.** Henceforth, the governor would have the power to draw the money he needed from the colony's treasury, which would put an abrupt end to the quarrel over finances and take away the Parti Canadien's leverage.

This decision came as a great shock to the people of Lower Canada. Even *Le Canadien,* a newspaper known for his moderate stance, saw it as an "act of aggression" that, in effect, broke the "social contract" that bound the colony to the English homeland. In the minds of many, the die was now cast.

The Patriotes' Defeat and Its Consequences

The Russell resolutions plunged Lower Canada into a climate of confrontation. Each side prepared its defenses and bided its time. The summer and fall of 1837 promised to be hot.

Popular assemblies

Before proceeding, both sides needed to mobilize and discuss the way forward. This is what both the "Patriotes" and the "Loyalists" did at large public meetings held in communities from La Malbaie east of Quebec City to Vaudreuil outside Montreal, from Sainte-Scholastique northwest of Montreal to Saint-Hyacinthe in the east. No significant region was left out. Throughout 1837, these meetings attracted nearly 50,000 people, just under 10 percent of the entire population of the colony.

Resisting a tyrannical power

The first meeting organized by the Parti Canadien was held in Saint-Ours, a village in the Richelieu Valley. Participants proclaimed that the Russell resolutions had the effect of depriving the people of "any guarantee of liberty and good government for the future of this province." They agreed that the inhabitants of Lower Canada had to resist a "tyrannical power."

Inspired by the American revolutionary experience, the Patriotes of Saint-Ours passed a resolution that proposed a boycott of tea, tobacco, wine, and rum imported from England and suggested making smuggled products legal. In the following weeks, the Patriotes of Lower Canada extended the boycott to clothing and urged people to use locally produced fabrics. Another resolution evoked the heroic figure of Louis-Joseph Papineau, Lower Canada's Daniel O'Connell: "To more effectively bring about the regeneration of this country, we should follow the example of Ireland and rally everyone around one man."

The revolutionary solution

During the summer of 1837, all eyes were on the leader of the Parti Canadien. Accompanied by young Assembly members such as Louis-Hippolyte LaFontaine and Augustin-Norbert Morin, as well as more experienced leaders like Wolfred Nelson and Edmund O'Callaghan, he traveled throughout Lower Canada delivering speeches. He addressed a meeting in Saint-Laurent in Montreal on May 15, and another one at Sainte-Scholastique two weeks later. These were the long speeches of a revolutionary leader who denounced the subjection of Lower Canada to an empire that was foreign to the ideas of the New World.

Papineau shouted out to the crowd in Saint-Laurent:

> The European colonial system must be reformed and recast, or misery, paralysis of the mind and of industry, hatred, and strife will be such a natural and constant result that all colonies will have the most urgent reasons to advance the time of their separation. When you say colony, you are saying plunder and insolence among those who govern, humiliation and scarcity among the governed. . . . The government of English nobles will hate you forever; we must respond in kind. It hates you because it loves despotism, while you love liberty.

In every speech, Papineau reminded listeners of the grievances outlined by his party, denounced the often treacherous actions of the rulers and "parasites" who surrounded them, explained the impasse resulting from the Russell resolutions, and praised republican institutions that preferred talent over money.

Authorities fear the worst

These speeches and some more radical resolutions that attacked the seigneurs and even the church led authorities to fear the worst. On June 15, Governor Gosford banned public meetings. His proclamation was not respected by the Parti Canadien. The Loyalists also held public meetings. Gathered in Rawdon on June 29 and Montreal on July 6, they condemned any "disobedience to the law," which could only lead to "dismemberment of the Empire."

The church preaches submission

A few months later, it was the Catholic Church's turn to condemn what the Patriote leaders were saying. Jean-Jacques Lartigue, the first bishop of Montreal, invited the faithful to submit to the authorities and turn away from calls for revolution and confrontation that, in his view, could only lead to a civil war. This call for submission was directly inspired by an *encyclical* (letter) of Pope Gregory XVI, who in August 1832 had condemned the liberal ideas that inspired the Irish and Polish liberation movements. Not all members of the lower clergy followed the bishop's approach, however. Some, such as Étienne Chartier, curé of Saint-Benoît, did not hesitate to support the Parti Canadien cause.

Disagreement on strategy

Between August 18 and 26, 1837, the Assembly had to decide whether to allocate the funds needed for the proper functioning of the colony. Within the Parti Canadien, two camps emerged:

- ✔ The moderates, inspired by the journalist Étienne Parent, felt it best to lower the pressure and adopt the budget. Without clear and unequivocal support from the United States, they argued, the Patriote movement was in danger of hitting a wall.

- ✔ The more radical faction, among them Papineau, believed that the time for compromise had passed; now was the time to mobilize.

As a result, the budget was not adopted and Gosford decided to dissolve the Assembly, a crucial decision that deprived the Parti Canadien of its primary platform.

Going all out

On October 23 and 24, Loyalists met in Montreal while Patriotes met in Saint-Charles. The Loyalists repeated their grievances against the Parti Canadien and portrayed Papineau as a dangerous demagogue inspired by the most damaging ideas of French republicanism.

The Patriotes proudly waved banners with the slogans "INDEPENDENCE," "Canadiens die but do not know how to surrender," and "Liberty, we will win or die for it!" One banner proclaimed the dream of greater solidarity with the English reformers in the neighboring colony: "Our friends in Upper Canada: Our strength is in our unity." Speaker after speaker mounted the podium. Each declared that he was ready for the greatest sacrifice "to wrest the soil upon which we were born out of vile slavery." The address adopted looked very much like a declaration of independence.

Brawls and battles

The die was now cast. The political phase was over; the military phase had begun. The Patriotes had a great orator in Papineau, but they had no real military leaders. The merchants, on the other hand, were supported by the imperial army and by well-equipped militias determined to put an end to the matter.

Confrontation on St. James Street

On November 6, supporters of the two camps clashed on St. James Street in Montreal. That day, following a peaceful political assembly, members of the Fils de la Liberté were attacked by members of the Doric Club. The Doric Club members were soon joined by supporters who, in a moment of rage, attacked Papineau's house, vandalized the offices of *The Vindicator,* and smashed windows at the bookstore owed by Édouard-Raymond Fabre, known for his sympathy with the Patriote cause. The house of Robert Nelson, another Parti Canadien leader, was also damaged by angry protesters who resented the idea that an English-speaking person could support Papineau's cause. During the days that followed, Gosford dismissed all judges suspected of being pro–Parti Canadien and appointed Loyalists in their place.

A price on Papineau's head

In the following days, Sir John Colborne, commander of the British forces in Lower Canada, decided to go on the offensive and attack the Canadian rebels at Saint-Charles in the Richelieu Valley. He had 1,700 regular army soldiers at his disposal along with hundreds of volunteer militiamen, often less experienced but more determined to crush the enemy.

On November 23, in a clash that lasted nearly six hours, a contingent of Colborne's troops was beaten by 1,500 men under Wolfred Nelson at Saint-Denis. Two days later, British troops defeated the Patriotes at Saint-Charles. Desperate times called for desperate measures: Governor Gosford issued arrest warrants for the main leaders of the Parti Canadien. A £4,000 reward was promised to anyone who would bring in Papineau. Martial law was declared, making it unnecessary to obtain warrants to put people in jail.

Saint-Benoît in ashes

Having settled matters in the Richelieu Valley, Colborne turned his attention to the Deux-Montagnes region, on the north shore of the St. Lawrence west of Montreal. On December 14, a violent confrontation took place in Saint-Eustache, where nearly 200 Patriotes were holed up in a church. To combatants who feared for their lives, the Patriote leader Jean-Olivier Chénier counseled, "Stay calm, some will fall, and you will take their guns."

But this determination was not enough: The British troops, led personally by Colborne, were more numerous and much better armed. After four hours of fighting, 70 Patriotes had fallen in battle and 118 others had been taken prisoner. Proud of their victory, the militia burned 60 buildings, confiscated papers that could incriminate other Patriotes, and stole the spoils that lay on the ground. The next day, the village of Saint-Benoît, which surrendered without resistance, was reduced to ashes.

The fatal blow

During these weeks of clashes, several Parti Canadien leaders took refuge in the United States, including Louis-Joseph Papineau, who tried in vain to convince the U.S. government to support the Parti Canadien's cause. It was because of this lack of support that he refused to take part in the second insurrection of November 1838. At Lacolle and Odelltown, two villages close to the U.S. border, the Patriotes' attempt to avenge the previous year's defeat was crushed by local militias loyal to the British Crown. This second insurrection dealt a fatal blow to the Canadiens' movement.

The moving testament of Chevalier de Lorimier

In the weeks following the second rebellion, 855 people were arrested, 108 were charged with high treason, 58 were deported to Australia, and 12 were hanged in the Pied-du-Courant prison in Montreal. Chevalier de Lorimier, one of those on death row, left a haunting political testament, written on the eve of his execution, which took place on February 15, 1839:

> Despite so much misfortune, my heart still remains strong and full of hope for the future, that my friends and my children will see better days; they will be free. I feel certain of this; my conscience, which is at peace, assures me of it. . . . Long live liberty, long live independence!

At the end of 1839, one of the darkest years in the history of Quebec, some people felt crushed. The Assembly had been suspended, the merchant minority was in power, and Papineau had taken refuge in France and would not return until 1845.

The Act of Union of 1840

The British government sought a lasting solution to the instability not only in Lower Canada but also in the neighboring colony of Upper Canada, itself torn by a political crisis that pitted loyalists against reformers.

Lower Canada's declaration of independence

On February 28, 1838, Robert Nelson, self-proclaimed leader of the provisional government, read a unilateral declaration of independence for Lower Canada. Containing 18 articles. It promised a democratically run republic, the right to vote for all men 21 years and older, separation of church and state, public education for all, an independent press, abolition of the seigneurial system, and abolition of the death penalty except in cases of murder. Article 3 provided a new form of treatment for the "savages." In the Republic of Lower Canada, Aboriginal people would enjoy the same rights as those of European descent. The new republic would be bilingual, as English and French would be "used in all public affairs." The statement ended with a promise of sacrifice: "We, by these present, solemnly pledge to one another our lives and our fortunes, and our most sacred honor." As the Patriotes would be crushed in November 1838, this declaration would never come into effect, but the dream of a free republic would be kept alive.

The British government appointed Lord Durham to report on the situation in the two colonies. He had a liberal view of the world and was close to the top of British reformers. The moderates in the Parti Canadien expected a lot from him. The British envoy arrived in Quebec on May 27, 1838, and left that fall, after meeting reformers in Upper Canada and representatives of the English minority in Lower Canada. Assisted by a battery of experts, he filed his report to the minister of the colonies on February 4, 1839.

His analysis was mixed. He agreed with the reformers of Upper Canada but had absolutely no sympathy for the principles upheld by the Parti Canadien. In Lower Canada, he wrote, "I expected to find a conflict between the government and the people; I found instead two nations warring in the bosom of a single state; I found a struggle, not of principles, but of races." People "without history or literature," according to Lord Durham, the French-speaking people of Lower Canada needed to be assimilated into British culture to become genuine British subjects.

To break the impasse in the two colonies, he proposed two solutions:

- ✔ **The union of Upper and Lower Canada into one colony:** This proposal was clearly aimed at the assimilation of the French Canadians, in the relatively near future.

- ✔ **The granting of responsible government:** In order to govern, the Executive Council of the new colony should have the confidence not only of the representative of the British Crown but also of the elected representatives of the people in the Legislative Assembly.

On July 23, 1840, the Act of Union received royal assent. The act provided for the following:

- ✔ **The union of Upper and Lower Canada into one colony, which was now called the Province of Canada:** The official language of the new colony would be English.

- ✔ **Equal representation for the east and west sections:** This equality disadvantaged the former Lower Canada, whose the population was considerably greater than that of the former Upper Canada.

- ✔ **Consolidating the funds of the two former colonies into a single budget:** Again, this provision disadvantaged inhabitants of Lower Canada, who would absorb the heavy debts of the neighboring colony.

- ✔ **Prohibition of the French language:** The only recognized language of the Province of Canada would be English.

There was no question in 1840 of granting responsible government to the inhabitants of a colony. The Province of Canada would be headed by a governor appointed by London.

This situation would change a few years later, following a surprising alliance that Lord Durham did not foresee.

Chapter 9

Responsible Government and Religious Awakening (1840–1860)

• •

In This Chapter

▶ Looking at LaFontaine's winning of responsible government

▶ Seeing signs of religious awakening

• •

*W*ith the failure of the Parti Canadien, a new strategy was put in place. After the confrontation on the battlefield, a more modest reform of British institutions was the goal. Louis-Hippolyte LaFontaine's party hoped that this reform would allow French Canadians' ancestral culture to be preserved. At its heart was responsible government, which they won in 1848.

While these political changes were taking place, Quebec underwent a genuine religious awakening in the mid-19th century. This awakening took several forms and led to an increase in the Catholic Church's power and influence. Monseigneur Ignace Bourget, Montreal's second bishop, was highly energetic in imposing his particular conception of religion, implacably hostile to the ideals of freedom that held many minds in their grip at the time.

Louis-Hippolyte LaFontaine, Reformer

Louis-Hippolyte LaFontaine (1807–1864), the son of a humble carpenter from Boucherville on the south shore of the St. Lawrence opposite Montreal, was a Montreal lawyer first elected to the Assembly in 1830. Regarded as a brilliant recruit for the Parti Canadien, he soon gained a reputation as a radical. This label arose from a pamphlet he put out in 1834, fiercely attacking two Canadiens who had supported Papineau's cause but accepted appointments from the colonial governor as ministers of the Crown. In addition to denouncing these turncoats, LaFontaine vigorously supported free institutions and left open the option of armed confrontation in case Britain refused the Parti Canadien's demands.

During the mass meetings in the summer of 1837, LaFontaine accompanied Papineau almost everywhere he went and, during the short August 1837 session of the Legislative Assembly, he took a hard line against the colonial administration. Like other Patriote militants, he and his wife, Adèle, wore *étoffe du pays,* the homespun cloth of Quebec. A journalist who made fun of Adèle's "shepherdess's trappings" was the recipient of a solid punch in the face from LaFontaine himself. The fiery legislator gave as good as he got!

Avoiding the fate of the Acadians

LaFontaine broke with Papineau in November 1837, just a few days before the initial clashes with Sir John Colborne's armies. Like the journalist Étienne Parent of *Le Canadien,* LaFontaine believed that this sort of direct confrontation could lead to the Canadiens' disappearance as a nationality. He feared his people could suffer the fate meted out to the Acadians. With catastrophe looming, he tried to persuade the governor to call the legislature into session to find a political solution to the crisis.

While Papineau sought support in the United States, LaFontaine headed to London and tried to reason with British members of Parliament. But he couldn't escape his radical past and was viewed with suspicion. Several months after his return from Europe, he was imprisoned for a few weeks. From his dungeon, LaFontaine devised a new strategy seeking to preserve what he saw as essential.

Presenting a manifesto to the voters of Terrebonne

After the Act of Union was decreed by London, an election was called in the eastern and western sections of the new Province of Canada to choose the colony's representatives. A number of Quebec candidates promised that, if elected, they would fight the Act of Union, adopted without the people's consent. But LaFontaine saw things differently. He presented his new strategy in a manifesto published on August 25, 1840.

No question of giving up

According to the 33-year-old LaFontaine, looking backward would be counterproductive. French Canadians must resign themselves to union, he said, even if it was imposed by force. This meant taking part in the political life of the new colony — but not to the extent of humiliating themselves and going back on all their principles! The inhabitants of the new colony were living in America. They had become accustomed to social equality and would never agree to be led by a minority of privileged men who scorned the people.

So, what could be done? Given the situation, how could arbitrary rule be prevented? How could the legislature's powers be increased? The answer was simple, LaFontaine said:

> ✔ **No government positions should be accepted until London recognized "ministerial responsibility."** Instead of government ministers being chosen arbitrarily from among friends of the regime, the colonial governor should appoint members of the party winning a majority of seats in the election. These ministers, LaFontaine believed, would personify the true aspirations of the people and would have full legitimacy in launching reforms and making appointments. Without this "ministerial responsibility," political tensions would grow, and British constitutionalism would lose all credibility.

> ✔ **An alliance should also be formed with reformers in Upper Canada who, like those in Lower Canada, had fought to obtain greater justice and democracy.** Based on common principles of action, a pact of this sort would bring victory for the principles being put forward by liberal thinkers in Britain.

Elected by Anglo-Protestants

LaFontaine presented clear ideas inspired by the best thinking that was emerging from England. His next task — and it wasn't an easy one — was getting elected in the vote set for February 1841. His recent enemies, with assistance from the governor, set up the polling place for his Terrebonne riding in a village hostile to the reform leader. Voters favorable to LaFontaine in some cases had to go up to 20 kilometers (12 miles) to exercise their voting rights. Once there, they were intimidated by thugs.

LaFontaine withdrew from the race, but he had other ways of making himself heard. His opening to the Upper Canadian reformers soon produced results. Robert Baldwin, his new ally, agreed to give up a seat for him, so that a by-election was held a few months later. LaFontaine, a Catholic of French descent, was elected in York by an Anglo-Protestant majority — this was unheard of! In 1844, the mirror image occurred in the Rimouski riding, where Baldwin was elected. This exchange of friendly services marked the start of real collaboration between Canada's English- and French-speaking elites. Celebrated by some, denounced by others, the reform alliance brought the colony into a new political era.

"I owe it to myself" to speak French

When LaFontaine took his seat in the colonial parliament for the first time in September 1842, he knew that his mother tongue was no longer recognized. French was banned, a forbidden language, even though French speakers formed a majority of the population of the Province of Canada — as they would continue to do until around 1850.

The *guerre des éteignoirs*

In 1841, it was agreed that the eastern and western sections of the colony would have different school administrations. But that did not resolve the issue of educational financing. Some of the funding came from government, but this was far from sufficient. The proposed solution was a school tax, to be levied by the municipalities and later by school boards. Jean-Baptiste Meilleur, the first superintendent of public instruction, could sense that this tax was unpopular. So, in 1845, he suggested that it should be voluntary and that property owners should pay according to their means. Many property owners balked, feeling that they were already taxed heavily enough by priests or seigneurs. Some didn't care about education because their children were no longer of school age or had to work the land. The voluntary tax was a failure.

In 1846, a compulsory tax was imposed. This measure was considered too coercive, and it raised the ire of some inhabitants. But the political, clerical, and intellectual elites formed a bloc supporting it, condemning this *guerre des éteignoirs* (war of the extinguishers) led by opponents of enlightenment through education, seen as vital to achieving prosperity and national revival. The "extinguishers" used all sorts of means to express their case. Many simply refused to pay the tax, while others heckled the school trustees, and a few went so far as to set fire to their schools!

The problem came down to confidence more than anything else. At that time, the educational system was disorganized, and the teachers were poorly trained. Many people were reassured when school inspectors were appointed, and order was gradually brought into the system during the 1850s.

KEY DATE

His mother tongue's forbidden status did not stop LaFontaine from rising in the House on September 13, 1842, and making his maiden speech in French. Before a stunned audience of English-speaking members, he said:

> Although I may be as familiar with the English language as with the French language, I would nevertheless make my maiden speech in the language of my French-Canadian compatriots, if only to issue a solemn protest against the cruel injustice of that part of the Act of Union that seeks to forbid the mother tongue of half the population of Canada. I owe this to my compatriots; I owe it to myself.

Governor Charles Bagot, who was open to reform ideas, arrived in the colony in 1842 and appointed LaFontaine and Baldwin as ministers. But this first government produced scarcely any results. Bagot died prematurely in May 1843 and was replaced by Charles Metcalfe, whose highly authoritarian conception of power led LaFontaine and Baldwin to resign. In 1845, efforts were made to persuade LaFontaine to join the government, but because he knew it would not have much leeway, he refused. His time would come three years later.

Discovering the great reform government of 1848

Starting in 1848, the inhabitants of the Province of Canada had effective control over their local affairs. Their government, formed by the majority party, could now initiate substantial reforms and launch major projects without constantly being blocked by the governor and his clique. Responsible government meant that the Crown's representative could no longer identify himself with a party or take stands in elections. He also lost the power to appoint civil servants or sit in the cabinet. This institutional reform was implemented by Lord Elgin, the governor who had arrived in January 1847. Implementing instructions from his home government, the British envoy called on LaFontaine and Baldwin to form a government after they won the general election.

London takes a step back

Responsible government in Canada was won in a context of political change in England in the mid-1840s. Many people wanted to loosen ties with the colonies. Some argued that the colonies were an expensive burden and should be taking greater care of their own needs; others promoted trade liberalization. For these "free traders," it was no longer worth giving preference to products from the colonies, especially if they cost more! In 1846, the British government decided to buy wheat at the best price on the market. This measure shocked many merchants in the Province of Canada, who had enjoyed favored access to the British market. Quite simply, they felt they had been abandoned by their mother country.

Enough is enough!

These same merchants saw the granting of responsible government as another affront by the mother country. How could England allow a man like LaFontaine — a Catholic from a conquered people — to exercise power in a British colony? This was beyond comprehension! As if that weren't enough, one of the first measures adopted by the new government was to allow the use of French in the legislature. Worse yet, the reform cabinet planned to indemnify inhabitants of Lower Canada whose property had been ransacked or destroyed outright in the often harsh repression during the troubles of 1837–1838. A comparable payment had been offered in 1841 to the inhabitants of Upper Canada. The new cabinet saw this not as rewarding rebels but as righting a wrong. For the more radical among the English-speaking minority — the Orangemen, as they were called — this was going too far!

Women lose their voting rights

One of the reforms adopted by the LaFontaine-Baldwin government in 1849 involved changes to the elections act, including alteration of the election period. Since the Constitutional Act had come into force, elections had continued as long as voters showed up at the polling place. The election period could go on for many days and could end in a brawl, especially if results were close. The secret ballot wasn't introduced until 1875, so vote counting took place in public. Partisans in each camp were easy to identify. Thugs would sometimes intimidate their adversaries and keep them from getting to the polling station. Under electoral reform, polling stations would be open for only two days. Another new feature was that all voters had to be registered on lists before exercising their voting rights.

To vote, you had to be a property owner and at least 21 years old. These qualifications didn't necessarily exclude women. From 1792 to 1849, in the Montreal district alone, 857 women, representing 2 percent of the electorate, exercised their voting rights (74 percent of them were widows, and 60 percent were French-speaking). In 1827, petitioners complained of a returning officer in Quebec City's Upper Town denying two widows who were entitled to vote their right to cast their ballot. "The petitioners are not aware that there is any imperfection in women's minds placing them below men on the intellectual scale," the petition read.

The reform of 1849 specified that women, even if they were property owners, could no longer vote. This stirred no public debate — as if 19th-century politicians took it for granted that women were confined to the domestic sphere or were indifferent to political issues! When the issue resurfaced in 1874, a journalist wrote in the November 20 issue of *La Minerve* that allowing women to vote would be "the final utopia proposed for the adoption of human stupidity [that] should occur only after the abolition of property and the proclamation of communism, with the family abolished and communism relieving parents of the care and raising of their children. Women would then have time to deal with politics!"

Parliament set on fire

On April 25, 1849, Montreal was the capital of the Province of Canada. (Because agreement couldn't be reached on a site, the colony's capital rotated every four years.) On that day, more than a thousand demonstrators gathered outside the Parliament building at the opening of the session. Lord Elgin, who had just addressed the members, was heckled by angry protesters who decided to take Parliament by storm. The members were hunted down, the building was ransacked, and the thousands of books and documents in the library were burned — the memory of an entire era up in smoke! Alas, the protesters' fury did not end there. LaFontaine was chased all the way to his house and threatened with death. The security forces scarcely managed to contain the anger of the enraged mob, protecting the reform leader's home in this dire situation. LaFontaine and his wife barely escaped retribution. But this intimidation failed to impress him. The indemnity bill was approved.

The end of the seigneurial system

The reformers adopted major pieces of legislation during the 1850s, notably bringing about decentralization of the justice system and creation of the first three teachers' colleges. The most important reform, brought in by LaFontaine's successors after he retired from political life in 1851, was abolition of the seigneurial system. Starting in 1854, land could be sold freely, as property. The seigneurs were compensated fairly for their losses. This structural change occurred without a revolt or a bloodbath.

A Religious Revival

The middle of the 19th century was marked by sharp tensions between French and English speakers. The arrival of large numbers of immigrants from the British Isles tended to heighten this antagonism. Irish Catholics and Protestants brought their clan wars with them. The Catholics accused the English of starving their people, while the Protestants feared world domination by Catholics. This did little to build harmony between French and English speakers in Quebec!

Meanwhile, in addition to these ethnic and political tensions and effects of the failure of the 1837–1838 rebellions, other crises — less visible but still significant — generated plenty of anxiety, especially among the young.

Signs of awakening

Since 1815, grain production had been falling, and wheat exports kept declining. Agriculture was in a rut, with each farm harvesting barely enough to feed the family. Young people in the 1830s and 1840s looked for other opportunities. The land in the old seigneurial area along the St. Lawrence was almost all occupied, while land in the Eastern Townships was more or less accessible but subject to speculation by greedy merchants and foreigners. As a result, many French Canadians decided to settle in cities, especially Quebec City and Montreal (both majority English speaking in the mid-19th century), or left for the United States to build new lives. In 1849, a special committee of the Legislative Assembly published an initial report on the emigration of French Canadians. This concern was just beginning.

A search for meaning

The political tensions, economic difficulties, and lack of opportunity for many young people explain the religious revival of the 1840s. During these years of uncertainty, a large number of people sought meaning in their own lives and the life of their country. They were looking for something solid to believe in and clear answers that would enable them to face the harshness of life.

Some felt that society could only achieve renewal and a fresh start through a moral revival. This was fertile ground for the church, whose representatives showed an ability to respond effectively to this spiritual thirst.

A preacher draws crowds

Among the signs of this spiritual quest was the triumphal tour of a preacher from France, Monseigneur de Forbin-Janson. This native of Provence and former bishop of Nancy gave his first sermon in Quebec City on September 6, 1840, a few weeks after the Act of Union was adopted. Forbin-Janson was a powerful, theatrical orator accustomed to large crowds. The world he described was dualistic: On one side were the sins of revolutionaries, who believed they could reinvent everything without help from God. On the other side were the believers, who continued to work within the church, preaching the example of a healthy life inspired by the life of Christ. On one side lay disorder, anarchy, and democracy; on the other, divine authority, monarchy, and promises of a better life. As Forbin-Janson attacked the sins of the French Revolution, French Canadians recalled the painful failure of the rebellions.

Forbin-Janson's tour of Quebec drew large and enthusiastic crowds. Word spread from one parish to the next. Nobody wanted to miss this impressive show. In Trois-Rivières and Sainte-Marie-de-Beauce, nearly 10,000 people came to hear him. At Christmastime in 1840, 25,000 people gathered at Mont Saint-Hilaire to plant a huge 20-meter (66-foot) cross. Similar enthusiasm erupted several years later during a tour by Charles Chiniquy, another gifted preacher. The French-Canadian clergy nurtured this fervor, holding processions and retreats. Many people came out of these great gatherings transformed, seeking to prolong their spiritual experience.

A call from God

The most pious parishioners felt a call from God and decided to enter the priesthood or a religious order. Careers in the church hadn't been very popular in the early 19th century, and Quebec hadn't had enough priests to serve all its parishes for years. This situation changed radically starting in the 1840s.

The sudden rise of vocations was unmistakable, among both men and women. And it would continue! Quebec became a very clerical society. In a generation immersed in religious revival, French Canadians — especially those from modest backgrounds — were tempted by the exciting career opportunities the church offered. A vocation meant a life that would be different from the one their parents had known: free education, and jobs in many religious orders as teachers or social workers among the destitute. Many women found that a religious vocation was a way to escape misery and live an autonomous life. A well-maintained religious house or a fine rectory next to a church was more luxurious than the average home in that era, and looking forward to a settled and comfortable life in one of these establishments was far from disagreeable! The religious vocation had its advantages.

Among laypeople, the religious revival of the 1840s manifested itself in several ways. Before leaving for the hereafter, the dying were less likely to refuse absolution. Every Sunday, the faithful took communion in growing numbers. Crosses were erected at village entrances and volunteer associations were founded, mostly to fight the vice of *intemperance* (excessive drinking of alcohol). The Catholic Church was growing more powerful and influential than ever before, and its power rested primarily on its popular base of believers who agreed to be involved in the causes it favored. Without their spiritual needs, the Catholic hierarchy would've gotten nowhere.

Ignace Bourget's program

Ignace Bourget (1799–1885) channeled this religious fervor with great energy and effectiveness. Born in Lauzon, Bourget did his classical studies at the Petit Séminaire de Québec. He was ordained a priest at age 23 and became secretary to Jean-Jacques Lartigue, an influential figure known for his hostility to liberal and democratic ideas (the same could be said of the Church of Rome as a whole). In 1840, Bourget succeeded Lartigue and became the second bishop of Montreal, a position he held until 1877.

An outstanding organizer and a man who knew how to wield power, Ignace Bourget was convinced that the pope was infallible and that the church was a bulwark against the excesses of modernity. He had a profound impact on the Montreal community and on the Catholics of his time. Attentive to what was going on around him and quick to nip the first feeble efforts at Protestant proselytizing in the bud, Bourget felt that his people had emerged from the rebellions in an unsettled state and sought to offer them a new mission, more in keeping with his spiritual conception of the world.

Recruiting priests and nuns in France

As soon as he became bishop, Bourget started a newspaper, *Les Mélanges Religieux,* which would be the voice of the Catholic hierarchy. In the summer of 1841, he went to Europe and met the leaders of large religious orders. His goal was to persuade them to send members of their orders to French America. Bourget was looking for priests and nuns who would found institutions to guide the faithful. His trip produced substantial results.

Oblates of Mary Immaculate arrived in September 1841. They held retreats in parishes, settled in Longueuil, and then established themselves in Ottawa — called Bytown at the time — where they founded a university that exists to this day. The Jesuits returned to Quebec in 1842. Though very active in the era of New France, this order was banned by the French government in 1764 and then suppressed by the pope in 1773. The colony's last Jesuit had died in 1800.

Bourget wanted the Jesuits, now restored, to devote themselves to educating the elites, something they excelled at. In particular, they founded Sainte-Marie and Brébeuf colleges in Montreal, institutions that went on to educate many key figures in the history of Quebec. The Sisters of the Sacred Heart sent representatives in 1842, followed by the Sisters of the Good Shepherd in 1844. The Sacred Heart sisters devoted themselves to training nuns, while the Good Shepherd sisters mostly looked after orphans.

Exceptional women

The bishop of Montreal also supported the initiatives of Quebec laypeople. In 1848, he took part in the founding of the Saint-Vincent-de-Paul Society, an institution created in France to help the destitute. This faith-inspired devotion was also manifest among exceptional French-Canadian women who, with support from Bishop Bourget, founded major institutions.

These women included Émilie Gamelin (Sisters of Providence), Eulalie Durocher (Sisters of the Holy Names of Jesus and Mary), Rosalie Jetté (Sisters of Mercy), and Marie-Anne Blondin (Sisters of Saint Anne). These women gave the best of themselves to teaching, as well as to the care of the developmentally delayed, unwed mothers, and other outcasts. Thanks to these women, an entire support and solidarity network was established. Because government wasn't directly involved in social matters at the time, this network survived with the help of charitable donations and the devotion of people who walked the talk.

Heaven is blue, hell is red!

Though he supported ministerial responsibility, Ignace Bourget condemned more radical liberalism or anything that could take the form of revolution. In 1848, France and the rest of Europe went through political upheavals, a period referred to as the "Spring of Nations." In France, the regime of Louis-Philippe d'Orléans collapsed, and a revolution led to the Second Republic. This development had a significant impact on Quebec, inspiring the former Patriote leader, Louis-Joseph Papineau.

Papineau advocates annexation to the United States

Back from exile in 1845, Papineau resumed the fight he had helped lead in 1837 and denounced LaFontaine's policy of reform. His main criticism was that the union of the two Canadas wasn't democratic because Quebec didn't have enough representatives in the legislature. He called for breaking all links that united the colony with England.

His speeches didn't go unnoticed. A number of young people at the Institut Canadien, a discussion forum founded in December 1844 to promote enlightened debate, supported Papineau. In July 1847, these young people launched *L'Avenir,* a newspaper that clearly drew its inspiration from the French liberalism that lay behind the revolutionary ideas of 1848. Papineau and his supporters took their activism to great lengths. In 1849, they signed a manifesto advocating nothing less than annexation of the Province of Canada to the United States.

A fruitful alliance

Ignace Bourget deeply mistrusted these ideas. His condemnation took a political turn in January 1849, when he published a pastoral letter calling for respect for the "legitimately constituted authorities" and denouncing "seditious speeches." Bourget was obviously targeting Papineau and his supporters, who were in the process of forming a political party. The church and supporters of LaFontaine slyly stigmatized this new party by associating it with the *rouges* (reds) in France who had just been involved in revolution — a way of sowing fear in the population. The party of LaFontaine and his successors gradually came to be identified with the *bleus* (blues) who would slowly evolve into the Conservative Party. The alliance between the church and the *bleus* was powerful and long lasting. To persuade the faithful to vote the right way, clerics often repeated that heaven is blue and hell is red!

The European doctrine that led Bourget to take a position against liberal ideas and the party that upheld them was known as *ultramontanism*. Adherents saw true authority as coming from God, represented on Earth by the pope in Rome, the great capital of the Catholic world, which Bourget visited seven times. In 1870, church authorities declared the pope "infallible." Guided by the Holy Spirit, he could never be wrong or in error. When required to choose between government and church, the faithful were always to obey their religious leader. For ultramontanes, the spiritual took precedence over the temporal. Religion could not be a private, personal matter. It had to inspire every law and guide each believer on a daily basis. This movement was encouraged by Pope Pius IX, who headed the church from 1846 to 1878. I'm not going too far when I describe Bourget's devotion to Pius IX as a cult. In 1864, the sovereign pontiff drew up a "Syllabus of Errors" of modernity, a landmark document symbolizing the church's fight against democracy, socialism, and all the new ideas of the age.

Censoring "evil books"

The 1850s were marked by confrontations between Bourget's church and the more radical liberals. The bishop of Montreal denounced the "evil books" found at the Institut Canadien, which he said spread ideas that went "against faith and morals." To counteract these so-called subversive ideas, he founded the Œuvre des Bons Livres in 1845 and, nine years later, the Union Catholique, a cultural institution that respected the religious orthodoxy of the Montreal prelate and was meant to compete with the Institut Canadien.

Liberals refused to be cowed and forcefully denounced this church interference. But their voices were scarcely heard. This was the beginning of church censorship of books and ideas, which would weigh heavily on Quebec for generations. But it didn't stop more resourceful people from procuring the books banned by the church. (After all, breaking the rules is part of youth, isn't it?)

Was Bourget infallible?

Not everyone was willing to go along with Bourget's obstinacy. When he refused religious burials to freethinkers, many Catholics thought he was being overzealous. Some conservative politicians were wary of him and weren't willing to entrust the education system to the church. His superiors objected to the opening of a Catholic university in Montreal, a project that had always been close to Bourget's heart. Laval University in Quebec City, founded in 1852, opened a small branch in Montreal in 1878.

Even at the Holy See, there was some mistrust toward Bourget. The French Sulpicians, who maintained a large presence in Montreal, had certain privileges and didn't appreciate the changes the bishop introduced. The same was true of the Irish Catholics, who succeeded in persuading Rome to found an English-speaking parish in the heart of the city. The impressive Mary Queen of the World Cathedral that Bourget arranged to have built on what is now René-Lévesque Boulevard in Montreal may well have been inspired by St. Peter's Basilica in Rome, but the bishop of Montreal was not infallible!

Emotional reunions

During the summer of 1855, the French flag fluttered almost everywhere along the St. Lawrence Valley to welcome the crew led by Commander Paul-Henry de Belvèze as they headed upriver aboard *La Capricieuse*. This was the first time since the Conquest that a French warship had visited France's former North American colony. The official aim of the visit was to develop commercial ties with the Province of Canada, with a view to opening the Canadian market to French products. There was absolutely no question of recapturing the colony lost during the Seven Years' War. In 1855, France (under Napoleon III) and England (under Queen Victoria) had become allies and were fighting side by side against Russia in Crimea. That same year, on a visit to Paris, Joseph-Guillaume Barthe, an active member of the Institut Canadien, published *Le Canada reconquis par la France (Canada Reconquered by France)*. His book drew little attention.

Though not many French Canadians dreamed of being re-conquered by France, Commander Belvèze received a very warm welcome. A grand ball was held in Quebec City. A Monument to the Brave was unveiled in his presence in honor of the French and English soldiers who had died in the Battle of the Plains of Abraham. The French representative was invited to give many speeches, though he was careful to avoid nurturing national antagonisms. The departure of *La Capricieuse* saddened the romantic poet Octave Crémazie, who was inspired to write this poem: "Adieu noble flag! Will we see you again? . . . Ah! As you depart, at least allow us some hope / So that we can, O Frenchmen! sing of your return." In 1859, France sent its first consul to Quebec.

Chapter 10

Confederation (1860–1867)

. . . .

In This Chapter

▶ Seeing how the Province of Canada was being torn apart

▶ Coming up with a confederation

. . . .

A s they entered the 1860s, the leaders of the Province of Canada were very pessimistic. Political instability and the American threat required some hard thinking about grouping the British North American colonies in a new federal political system.

In Quebec, this plan had staunch supporters and fierce opponents. Supporters saw it as a terrific opportunity to develop a great country in which French Canadians could play a leading role. Opponents feared political marginalization, or even assimilation.

Fundamental issues regarding Quebec's future played out during this time.

Falling Apart in the Province of Canada

In 1860, the Province of Canada was being torn apart from the inside and threatened from the outside. Its political leaders were having a hard time developing a program for governing that could win the support of a majority of its elected legislators. Worse yet, many people were demanding major reforms. They felt poorly represented by the colony's institutions.

This instability could not have come at a worse time, with Britain distancing itself from the colonies. The Empire was providing less and less protection of its colonies' borders, and its bankers were not keen on financing Canada's railways. Without railways, there could be no modern economic development, and without an army, the Province of Canada risked being invaded by American troops. Things were looking grave. What could be done?

Political instability

After responsible government was granted, people soon recognized that administering the Province of Canada was not child's play. Forming a government became a real headache! From 1854 to 1864, the Legislative Assembly created and then defeated nine governments. The members could not agree on a common program. Why? There were three reasons. I cover each reason in the following sections.

Two sections, two administrations

The first problem was that each section was administered differently. The western part — what is now Ontario — was English-speaking and Protestant. The Protestants were divided into competing churches, which is why many of them demanded government neutrality in matters of religion. The eastern part — today's Quebec — was primarily French-speaking, and the Catholic Church played a key role there, with church and state working closely together. Each section of Canada had its own school system and its own particular laws and customs. Once in government, the leaders of each section made their own appointments and practiced their own patronage. And there was absolutely no question of one section sticking its nose into the other section's affairs!

The headache of political parties

A second problem was a change in how political parties acted in the 1850s and 1860s. Although the Conservatives in Ontario agreed to share power with French Canadians, many continued to mistrust them and dreamed of building a great British nationality in America — Anglican in religion and English in language.

This mistrust was shared by the Ontario Liberals under George Brown, a leader who was gradually gaining ground in the western section. Unlike his predecessor, Robert Baldwin, Brown was strongly biased against Catholics, whom he suspected of seeking to dominate the world. This mistrust made it difficult to collaborate with Liberals in the eastern section who, while opposing the ultramontane thinking of Ignace Bourget, could not make a clean break with the Catholic Church. LaFontaine's successors, more conservative in their views, could not ally themselves with Brown either. Because they opposed annexation to the United States, they naturally turned to the western Conservatives, who were attached to the imperial connection. But collaboration between these two political tendencies was not a natural fit.

Long live "rep by pop"!

Finally, immigration and demography were favoring the western Anglo-Protestants. Around 1850, the western section passed the eastern section in population. The Act of Union of 1840 called for each section to have an equal number of representatives. But George Brown soon made parliamentary

representation by population (so-called "rep by pop") his party's great rallying cry. He fought for each section to have a number of members reflecting
the actual population. He even made this a condition for joining the government. The problem was that a majority of French Canadians fiercely opposed
"rep by pop," fearing that, once in the majority, the Anglo-Protestants would
meddle in their business.

Having to fend for themselves

For Britain, the price of granting responsible government to the Province
of Canada was disengagement from its colony. In some British circles, the
very idea of empire no longer had the same level of support it once had.
The colonies wanted more freedom and autonomy? Well, let them look after
themselves! Let them take care of financing an army on their soil and building
railways. Although easy to understand, this disengagement came at a very
bad time for the people of the Province of Canada.

Rumors of American invasion

From 1861 to 1865, the United States was torn by a civil war between the
slave-owning South and the abolitionist North. During this fratricidal confrontation, the southern states formed an independent nation that received
support from English elites. This support caused great irritation in the North.
On November 8, 1861, the northerners intercepted a British vessel and found
southern partisans aboard. Tensions reached new heights. The northerners,
led by President Abraham Lincoln, envisaged various scenarios, including
invasion of the British colonies further north. This idea was pondered in
some American newspapers. After the South was beaten, the rumor continued to spread. There were dreams of revenge against Britain.

The participation of French Canadians in the American Civil War

Between 10,000 and 15,000 French Canadians who had emigrated to the United States in earlier decades served as soldiers in the northern armies. These soldiers were young, often from disadvantaged backgrounds. They dreamed of adventure and sought to improve their lot. Many were drawn in by the prospect of regular pay. But this was war of a new kind: It was an industrial war, a precursor to the inhumane battles of World War I. There were many desertions, especially among soldiers of French-Canadian origin. When they realized that real war was more brutal and less heroic than they had imagined, the temptation to return home was great. That said, many French Canadians took part in the great battles of the Civil War, especially the Battle of Gettysburg in July 1863. From 1861 to 1865, approximately one French Canadian soldier out of every seven perished in the war.

The possibility of an American invasion sent chills down the spines of leaders in the Province of Canada. If the Americans were ever to move into action, no army worthy of the name could stop them. The gradual withdrawal of British troops from the North American colonies in the 1850s accelerated during the Crimean War of 1855. To support the war effort, a Canadian militia was established that year. A few years later, however, volunteers were scarcer. The inhabitants of the Province of Canada felt highly vulnerable. By then, hardly anyone was calling for annexation to the United States. Many felt the colony should build a real army. This future army could ensure control of the vast prairies of western Canada. In the mid-19th century, these lands belonged to a private company and were coveted by settlers in the American West.

The Fenians attack

Fear of invasion was nurtured by real attacks that occurred in 1866, orchestrated by Irish Catholics in the United States. Grouped in semi-clandestine associations, these "Fenians" planned to attack the British colonies to the north to put pressure on England over the Irish question. A Fenian attack in southern Ontario on May 31, 1866, was easily repulsed. Though the troops assembled by these Irish revolutionaries were far from impressive, the fear of other border attacks spread like wildfire — authorities feared the worst. These fears gave ammunition to those calling for the establishment of a standing army.

The economy hits a roadblock

In the mid-1860s, military concerns were not the only ones on the minds of people in the Province of Canada. For the colony to become truly prosperous, it needed railways, along with access to a large market for its agricultural surpluses. Its prospects for attaining either of these goals were grim.

No more access to the American market

After adopting its own free-trade policy, Britain agreed to allow the Province of Canada to trade freely with the United States. In 1854, the colony signed a reciprocity treaty with its southern neighbor. In particular, the Americans obtained the right to fish in Canadian waters in return for inhabitants of the Province of Canada being able to sell their wood, wheat, coal, and fish in the United States free of customs duties.

This agreement was enormously useful to merchants in the Province of Canada and made political annexation to the United States pointless. However, in the early 1860s, the American government informed the Canadians that this ten-year treaty would not be renewed. This prospect aroused great anxiety among the merchants. The idea of uniting all the British colonies in the north with the aim of establishing a large market began to take shape in people's minds.

The British North American colonies in 1860

In 1860, Britain had the following colonies in North America:

✓ **The Province of Canada:** Formed after the Act of Union of 1840, the Province of Canada encompassed the former Upper Canada (Ontario) and Lower Canada (Quebec).

✓ **Newfoundland:** It was a while before non-Aboriginal settlers came to live on this island, long used as a fishing station. Britain granted Newfoundlanders representative institutions in 1832 and ministerial responsibility in 1855. Closely tied to the British economy, Newfoundland didn't join the Canadian Confederation until 1949.

✓ **Prince Edward Island:** This island, the former Île Saint-Jean, long inhabited by Acadians, became British after the Conquest. Large landowners divided the land among them and formed the first House of Assembly in 1773. The colony joined Confederation in 1873, with the condition that a bridge connect it to the mainland. The 12.8-kilometer (8-mile) bridge was opened — in 1997!

✓ **New Brunswick:** Formed by Loyalists who fled the American Revolution, as well as by Acadians who returned after being deported and by Irish and Scottish immigrants who arrived in the 19th century, New Brunswick became a colony in 1784 and gradually acquired representative institutions. It joined Confederation in 1867.

✓ **Nova Scotia:** Strongly British after the deportation of the Acadians, Nova Scotia was given colonial status in 1758. In 1820, Cape Breton Island, where the French had built the famous fortress of Louisbourg, was annexed to the colony, which joined Confederation in 1867.

✓ **British Columbia:** In 1843, British traders erected Fort Victoria, at the continent's western edge on the Pacific coast. In 1849, Vancouver Island became a "royal" colony, and a governor was sent there. The discovery of gold in the area was a driving force behind its development. British Columbia, formed in 1866 when Vancouver Island was united with the mainland colony, joined Confederation in 1871.

Railways

Then there were the railways, indispensable for the economic development of countries in the West at the time, especially for a territory as vast as the Province of Canada. In the mid 19th century, the colony lagged far behind, at least in comparison with the United States. Railway companies, supported by many politicians and financed mostly by municipalities and the public treasury, began building new lines. From 1850 to 1860, the network grew from 100 kilometers (62 miles) to 3,300 kilometers (2,051 miles). The aim was to unite the territory from east to west.

In 1859, the first railway bridge across the St. Lawrence opened (named the Victoria Bridge in honor of the British sovereign) — a technical feat for the time. These companies borrowed huge sums to develop railway infrastructure. The loans were usually backed by the colony's government, which itself had limited means. In the early 1860s, the railway barons turned to British banks, but the results of these overtures were disappointing. Again, the idea of uniting all the British colonies seemed to be the best solution. The new state, these businessmen hoped, would be in a strong position to back the development of railway lines stretching from the Atlantic to the Pacific.

A Solution: Confederation

Ending political instability, protecting the borders, and getting the economy moving — these were the priorities of the political elites in the Province of Canada, desperately seeking a way out of the impasse. Everything was pointing toward a union of the British colonies. But the task of devising a constitution and imagining institutions that could accommodate each colony and most parties remained.

Before that point was reached, many issues had to be debated. Was a unitary government, as in France or Britain, what was needed, or would a confederation of autonomous states, as in the United States, do the trick? In a confederation, which powers would go to the central government? Which would go to the federated states? And who would decide when there were jurisdictional conflicts?

A draft constitution

The political circumstances were favorable, and high-level conferences at Charlottetown, the capital of Prince Edward Island, and Quebec City, the *vieille capitale* of the Province of Canada, put the plan for a union of the colonies in increasingly concrete form.

The Great Coalition of 1864

On June 22, 1864, there was a dramatic turn of events in the Parliament of the Province of Canada. The Conservative leader, John A. Macdonald, newly designated as premier by the governor following a vote in the Legislative Assembly, announced that George Brown and several members of the Liberal Party had accepted positions as ministers in the government. Brown set only one condition for this grand coalition: the establishment of a federation of British colonies.

Much like the French Canadians of Quebec, Brown wanted the future province of Ontario to be able to manage its internal affairs autonomously. This support from the Ontario Liberals provided a solid base for the Macdonald government, putting an end to political instability. But this support depended on the success of the union plan.

The Charlottetown and Quebec conferences

In September 1864, the British Maritime colonies organized a conference in Charlottetown. The aim was to discuss a project for Maritime union. Initially, inviting delegates from the Province of Canada was not considered. But they showed up anyway, and they came well prepared! No resolution was adopted officially, though they agreed to get together again soon.

On October 10, 1864, a second conference opened in Quebec City. This one would be decisive. Delegates from the five British colonies gathered to discuss the future of their communities. They would later be referred to as the Fathers of Confederation. Only four of the 33 delegates were French-Canadian. Their names? George-Étienne Cartier, Hector-Louis Langevin, Jean-Charles Chapais, and Étienne-Paschal Taché. This wasn't so much a question of reaching an agreement on an equal basis between two founding peoples — one of French descent, the other of British descent — as it was of discussing the terms of an agreement among five colonies, each with a history and interests to defend. A majority of the delegates sought to preserve the autonomy of their respective colonies. After several days of debate and negotiation, the delegates agreed to 72 proposals. A draft of the future constitution of the Dominion of Canada was essentially on paper.

The key ideas in this document were as follows:

- ✔ **A monarchy:** There was no question of becoming a republic like the United States. The delegates agreed that the future colony's head of state would be the British sovereign, represented by a governor general and lieutenant governors.

- ✔ **A federal union:** The sovereignty of the future colony would be shared between a central government, later called *federal,* and local governments, later called *provincial.* The federal government would be responsible for all general matters, while the provincial governments would handle local issues. Each federated state would have an equal number of senators in the Legislative Council of the central Parliament, to be called the Senate. In the Legislative Assembly, however, the number of representatives would be in proportion to population.

- ✔ **The powers of the central government:** The central government would be responsible for the army, the post office, the mint, the coastal fisheries, the census, criminal law, marriage and divorce, transportation infrastructure between colonies, customs duties, and, especially, "all matters of a general character, not specially and exclusively reserved for the local governments and legislatures."

This last power is referred to as "residual." For example, in 1867, radio and television did not exist. In the name of this "residual" power, the federal government would later insist that telecommunications came under its jurisdiction. Quebec would challenge this idea, regarding these new sectors as being outlets for the expression of a culture.

- **The powers of the local governments:** The responsibilities of the local governments would include education, public lands, social institutions assisting the ill and the destitute, municipalities, licenses for inns, and direct taxation.

- **In case of dispute, the central government would decide:** But what would happen if the two orders of government disagreed on a power? Proposal 45 of the Quebec Conference was very clear: In case of conflicting interpretations, the laws of the central government would prevail. The specifics of this power of disavowal were gradually defined by the Privy Council, a British court that would serve as arbiter, and then by the Supreme Court of Canada, which was established in 1875 and would have full jurisdiction over constitutional issues as of 1949.

- **The powers granted to Quebec:** In the future colony, the Province of Canada would be cut into two provinces — Ontario in the west and Quebec in the east. Each entity would have its parliament and its government. In the central Parliament and the Quebec Parliament, the French language would have the same status as English. In the Legislative Assembly of the central Parliament, Quebec would have 65 representatives. This number of representatives would be guaranteed even if future censuses were unfavorable to Quebec. Its *civil laws* (those governing relationships between individuals), based on those of France, would be preserved. The continued existence of its Catholic educational system would also be guaranteed, on condition that the rights of Quebec Protestants were assured.

Women and the Civil Code of 1866

A few months before Confederation was approved by London, the Parliament of the Province of Canada adopted a civil code that would apply in the future territory of the Province of Quebec. Inspired by the Napoleonic Code and the *coutume de Paris,* this key legislation confirmed Quebec's legal specificity. Along with language and the Catholic religion, civil law formed a pillar of Quebec's distinctiveness.

The Civil Code of 1866 consolidated the powers that men held over women in the society of the time. Once married, women were viewed under the law as minors or simpletons. They could not sign contracts or initiate legal action. It was clearly stated that a woman had to submit to her husband, in exchange for which he would ensure her protection. It went without saying that she had to take her husband's name. Engaging in an occupation different from her husband's was forbidden, and opening a business without his authorization was a heresy! The few women who worked outside the home had to hand over their wages to their husbands. However, when a woman's husband died, she was responsible for his debts!

Women who wished to maintain a level of independence had to remain "old maids" *(dunmarried)* or join a religious order. Younger ones accepted positions as teachers in rural schools. These women were poorly paid and had to leave their jobs when they married.

Supporters and adversaries

Before going to London for approval, the 72 proposals from the Quebec Conference had to be debated in the legislature of each colony, on a take-it-or-leave-it basis. In the Province of Canada, the coalition government backed the plan, with only the Quebec Liberals opposed.

George-Étienne Cartier: Politician or businessman?

In Quebec, one of Confederation's most ardent supporters was George-Étienne Cartier (1814–1873). He came from a relatively well-off family in Saint-Antoine-sur-Richelieu, and he attracted attention early. As he began his career as a lawyer in Montreal, he moved in Patriote circles, signed manifestos, and composed a song, *Ô Canada, mon pays, mes amours*. In September 1837, he was among the 500 young Patriotes who founded an association called the Fils de la Liberté (Sons of Liberty). On November 23, he took part in the victory of Saint-Denis and then took refuge in the United States.

When Cartier returned from exile, he was a changed man. Not only did he back LaFontaine's reform policy, but he also became a great admirer of Britain. As an anglophile, he was proud to spell his first name *George* rather than the French *Georges*. Elected to the Assembly for the first time in April 1848 and reelected repeatedly until his death, he became LaFontaine's successor, formed an alliance with John A. Macdonald, and founded the Conservative Party. An ardent monarchist, he energetically opposed universal suffrage and often called for the vote to be restricted to property owners. In addition to being an influential politician, George-Étienne Cartier was a lawyer and a leading businessman who defended powerful interests, notably the Sulpicians of Montreal and the big railway companies. In 1853, he became the lawyer for the Grand Trunk Railway Company, which, during the 1860s, was planning to build an "intercolonial" railway, a huge project requiring plenty of capital. Worldly and comfortable in circles of wealth and power, George-Étienne Cartier was a man to be reckoned with.

On February 7, 1865, it was his turn to speak out in support of the Quebec Conference's proposals. In a speech given in French, he struck a reassuring note. French Canadians had nothing to fear. Their rights and privileges would be protected by the Quebec Parliament. Though he dreamed of creating a "new nationality," Cartier was opposed to the "unity of the races" — a utopia, he said. Confederation, with its federal principle, ensured respect for the diversity of cultures while favoring a union of strengths and talents. In reality, he argued, the people of the British colonies had only two options: "to have a confederation of British North America or to be absorbed by the American confederation."

After raising the specter of invasion by the United States, he explained that French Canadians had never wanted to live in a republic:

> We, who have had the advantage of watching republicanism at work for a period of 80 years and seeing its defects, have become convinced that purely democratic institutions cannot produce peace and prosperity.

Confederation, he insisted, would benefit the economy of the Province of Canada. By joining with the Maritime colonies, the merchants of Montreal and Toronto would have year-round access to the sea. He also enjoyed the support of the clergy and depicted his opponents as dangerous extremists.

And where were the people in all this?!

Soon after, on February 16, the Liberal leader replied. Antoine-Aimé Dorion (1818–1891) was the grandson of Pierre Bruneau, a former member of the legislature, a great admirer of Papineau, and a fervent defender of the Patriote cause. With his brother Jean-Baptiste-Éric, he founded the newspaper *L'Avenir* in 1847 and called for universal suffrage. Influenced by the 1848 Spring of Nations, calling himself "a democrat in conscience and a French Canadian in origin," Dorion believed that each nationality should look after itself, and peoples should be consulted when their destiny was at issue. Though he rejected radical action and remained a practicing Catholic, his positions were naturally linked with those of the anticlerical *rouges* who dreamed of establishing a republic. To give his movement a more moderate vision, Dorion founded the newspaper *Le Pays* in 1852. Elected to Parliament in 1854, he took part in several governments and built alliances with George Brown, to the dismay of the Catholic Church.

In his speech, given in English, Dorion didn't beat around the bush. The official reasons Cartier gave to justify the Confederation plan were hiding something else. The government was being guided not by the common good but by powerful financial interests for which Cartier was the spokesman. If the Parliament of the Province of Canada came under pressure to enter into a new confederation, he believed, this was primarily to satisfy the top executives of the Grand Trunk Railway Company, who were seeking new sources of financing. Dorion saw in this project a barely disguised legislative union, "the aim of which is to assimilate the people of Lower Canada."

On what did he base this judgment? On the major powers that the central government and the Crown would hold. Rather than being named by the provinces, the future senators in the federal Parliament would owe their appointments to the prime minister in the central government. This plan, he lamented, was not submitted to the people and reflected a hierarchical vision of society: "We find ourselves with the most conservative constitution ever to be instituted in a country ruled by a constitutional government." Though fervently opposed to the plan submitted by Cartier, Dorion wasn't closed to the idea of a confederation. He sought to form a more democratic union consisting of the former Upper Canada and Lower Canada, in which French Canadians would be in a stronger position demographically and politically.

Médéric Lanctôt: The first labor leader

While the British North America Act was being negotiated in London, opposition forces had no intention of sitting idly by. Médéric Lanctôt (1838–1877), the son of a Patriote exiled in Australia, raised to worship republicanism and freedom, a member of the Institut Canadien, and one of the people behind the newspaper *L'Union Nationale,* did a remarkable job of mobilizing the opposition in the spring of 1867.

Lanctôt viewed Canadian Confederation, a project of capitalists and bosses, as hostile to the interests of the people. He created the Grande Association pour la Protection des Ouvriers du Canada (Great Association for the Protection of the Workers of Canada) to represent workers. On March 27, 1867, nearly 5,000 people answered his call and assembled on the Champ-de-Mars in Montreal. On June 10, nearly 8,000 people demonstrated in the streets of Montreal — something unheard of! Every trade was well represented, and it all

went smoothly. People waved the green, white, and red flag of the Patriotes. Lanctôt had a base in the numerous mutual-aid societies founded by workers over the years. The experience of the mutual-aid societies inspired him to start people's bakeries, but these did not have the success he hoped for.

The Conservatives' response was merciless. Depicted by his adversaries as a "priest eater" and a "revolutionary," Lanctôt was defeated in the federal election in the fall of 1867. This political setback dealt a fatal blow to his Grande Association but did not shake his convictions. In 1872, he published a document calling for an "association of capital and labor." Rather than adopt the Marxist line of class struggle, Lanctôt favored open collaboration between bosses and workers and a better sharing of wealth. In his eyes, "it is the human conscience and the sympathetic force of charity incarnate that command us all to associate and unite!"

The British North America Act

On March 10, 1865, the Legislative Assembly voted on the government's Confederation proposal. It was backed by 91 members, with 33 voting against. Among Quebec members, the vote was closer, with 37 in favor and 24 opposed. August 15, 1866, was the final day of the last session of the last legislature of the Province of Canada. The coalition government had gotten the go-ahead. A delegation left for London to have the project approved.

A British law

In December 1866, a final conference opened in London. The negotiations were vigorous. George-Étienne Cartier and Hector-Louis Langevin tried to resist pressure from John A. Macdonald to establish a strong central government. On July 1, 1867, the British North America Act, adopted without much debate by the British Parliament, came into effect. The separation of legislative powers, set out in the key articles 91 and 92 of the new constitution, was in accordance with the proposals adopted at the Quebec Conference.

What stood for a Canadian constitution was, in fact, just an ordinary piece of legislation voted on by members of a foreign parliament. This colonial link would last until the Canadian constitution was "repatriated" in 1982 (see Chapter 20). From 1867 to 1982, all constitutional changes had to go through London. The Canada born in 1867 was a "Dominion" that could not sign international treaties or declare war — powers it would be granted in 1931. It was autonomous in internal matters, although the monarch's representative could, in theory, refuse to ratify laws adopted by Parliament.

The Canada of 1867 had four provinces: New Brunswick, Nova Scotia, Ontario, and Quebec. Six other provinces would join later: Manitoba (1870), British Columbia (1871), Prince Edward Island (1873), Saskatchewan (1905), Alberta (1905), and Newfoundland (1949). According to the 1871 census, the new Dominion had a population of 3.5 million. With 1.2 million people, Quebec was a heavyweight.

Birth of the "province" of Quebec

Quebec as we know it today was born on July 1, 1867. Despite pressure from Montreal interests, Quebec City became the capital of the new federated state. Like the central Parliament, Quebec's Parliament consisted of two chambers: the Legislative Assembly, with 65 elected members, and the Legislative Council, equivalent to the Senate, with 24 members appointed for life by the lieutenant governor. In 1968, just over a century later, the Legislative Council was abolished, and the Legislative Assembly became the "National" Assembly.

The British North America Act contained protections for the Anglo-Protestant minority, with 12 seats set aside for it in the Legislative Assembly. Education came under the Quebec government, but Protestant denominational schools were protected. If the Catholic majority ever chose to abolish them, the Protestant minority could ask the central government to intervene and restore its rights.

Part III
Survival
(1867–1939)

The 5th Wave By Rich Tennant

1867 THE CONFEDERATION OF CANADA IS COMPLETED. PRIOR TO SETTLING ON THE TERM "DOMINION" OF CANADA, A DISCUSSION ENSUES...

Let's see, "The Kingdom of Canada". Too pretentious. "The Land of Canada". Not pretentious enough. "The Very Proper Area of Canada". No. "The Vast and Chilly Domain of Canada". No. "The Highly Wooded Vastness of Her Majesty's Canada". No, no. "The Federal Kingdom of the Vast and Chilly Land of Canada". "Her Majesty's Wild Realm of Mountains and Meadows though Mostly Mountains of the Region Known as Canada". We'll never fit that on a document.

In this part . . .

Here, I reveal how French Canadians used political and economic means to survive. Forming a majority in Quebec but a minority in Canada, French Canadians mobilized against the hanging of Métis leader Louis Riel. They fought British imperialism and the 1917 conscription act. Above all, they became more aware of the economic backwardness of the French-speaking majority in Quebec and the Americanization of their economy, and they gradually began to imagine government action as a way to gain greater control of their destiny.

Like other Western peoples, Quebecers were hit hard by the Depression of the 1930s and sought various solutions to end it. In this part, I show you how.

Chapter 11

"Riel, Our Brother, Is Dead" (1867–1896)

In This Chapter

▶ Recognizing the church's dominance in education

▶ Tracing the beginnings of Quebec's pro-autonomy stance

▶ Considering French Canadians' economic inferiority

*O*n the surface, the period after the British North America Act came into effect was a very calm one. No war or revolution disturbed the tranquility of the St. Lawrence Valley! And yet, basic elements were being put in place, and a national life was taking shape.

The domination of the Quebec Conservative Party continued, but ultra-orthodox Catholics were making waves. Divided between a moderate wing and more intransigent Catholics, the Conservatives abolished the Department of Public Instruction and turned the education sector over to the church. The Liberals, meanwhile, took more conciliatory positions on religious questions. Their new leader, Honoré Mercier, championed Quebec's autonomy and defended the French-Canadian cause when the Métis leader, Louis Riel, was hanged in 1885. Two years later, Mercier came to power.

The most striking feature of this era was the economic inferiority of French Canadians. For Quebec's French-speaking majority, the Industrial Revolution meant a decline in social position. With no prospects for the future, many French Canadians emigrated to the United States and served as cheap labor in the textile mills of the American east coast. Others settled in Montreal and accepted pathetic working conditions. With a few exceptions, a small elite made up of Montrealers of British origin was in control of the real levers of economic power.

The Church Grabs Hold of Education

From 1867 until the early 1880s, the Conservatives dominated political life in Quebec, as the Liberals continued to be linked with dangerous *rouges*. But the Conservatives' star was beginning to fade. Under the influence of ultramontane bishops, some Catholics put pressure on the Conservative government to submit even further to the views of the church, especially in education.

Chauveau: Premier by default

The first premier in the modern history of Quebec was Pierre-Joseph-Olivier Chauveau (1820–1890). He had many outstanding qualities and was a highly literate man who in his youth had been a poet and written short pieces for the American French-language newspaper *Courrier des États-Unis.* Chauveau was the author of one of the first novels in French-Canadian literature: *Charles Guérin: Roman de mœurs canadiennes,* published in 1852. Running as a reformer, he won a dramatic election victory in 1844 against the veteran John Neilson in Quebec riding.

After serving as a minister in a variety of governments, Chauveau was appointed superintendent of public instruction in 1855. It was a heavy responsibility because the number of schools in Quebec increased from 1,569 to 3,826 between 1844 and 1866, and the number of students from 57,000 to 206,820. Chauveau's major concerns as superintendent were providing the students with competent teachers and persuading the school commissioners to pay them decently. The church was suspicious of him because he was a moderate conservative who wanted education to remain in lay hands. A man of his time, he also sought to develop technical education that kept up with progress.

Ottawa calling: Can you hear me now?

In early 1867, Chauveau was on tour in Europe, discussing educational matters with authorities in Ireland, France, Belgium, and Germany. There was no Internet or telephone to reach him, which was too bad, because he was being offered the position of premier of Quebec! Initially, George-Étienne Cartier and Hector-Louis Langevin, who were the real masters of the Conservative Party and preferred to work on the federal scene, had favored another candidate, Joseph-Édouard Cauchon, but for various reasons Cauchon sent shivers down the spines of the English-speaking minority. So, Chauveau was the second choice. When they finally reached him, he accepted, but on the condition that he retain his educational portfolio. Although the church wasn't favorably disposed, it was agreed that a Department of Public Instruction, headed by Chauveau, would be established.

Quebec: A branch plant of Ottawa?

The way Chauveau was chosen says a lot about how Canada functioned in its early days. In the minds of Quebec's first political leaders, the real power was in Ottawa, at the federal level. Everyone saw the Quebec government as subordinate to the federal government, and the Quebec Conservative and Liberal parties were branch plants of the federal parties.

This situation was the result of two main factors:

- **The double mandate:** From 1867 to 1874, it was possible to be a member of the federal and provincial parliaments at the same time. Nineteen of the 65 members elected to the Quebec Legislative Assembly in the fall of 1867 had this "double mandate." Most of the time, these members used their position to carry out the decisions of the central government. This conflict of loyalties soon came under criticism, not only in Quebec but in other provinces as well.

- **The Quebec government's limited room to maneuver on budgetary matters:** The most serious limitation on the powers and autonomy of the new Quebec government was its dependence on federal subsidies. Even if they had had the power to do so, provincial governments at the time would never have dared to tax the income of their citizens directly. In 1869, 60 percent of the Quebec treasury's income was made up of federal subsidies. This proportion gradually declined: In 1874, it was 50 percent, and in 1896, it was only 25 percent. There were other constraints as well: The Quebec government inherited part of the debt of the old Province of Canada, and it made massive infrastructure investments in railways and roads. It had very limited room to maneuver.

Despite his good intentions, Premier Chauveau's hands were tied, and he couldn't develop the great educational and cultural institutions he dreamed of. Instead, he was caught up in the needs of the economy. And on top of that, he always had to deal with his ultramontane wing.

The Catholic Program

The most intransigent Catholics believed that French Canadians — their politicians included — should always submit to the decisions of the church. Strict separation of church and state? A heresy! Truth shouldn't be confined to the private sphere, but disseminated everywhere. The pope was a leader, not just a spiritual guide. Meanwhile, Pope Pius IX was under threat from the Italian republicans, and he asked for support from Catholics the world over. In Quebec, ultramontanes scoured the countryside recruiting soldiers to defend the pope. Between November 1867 and September 1869, more than 500 young French-Canadian volunteers left for Italy. Their motto was *Aime ton Dieu, va ton chemin* (Love your God, go your way). When they came back, these contingents of papal regiments received a triumphal welcome.

Although not everybody shared their zeal, the ultramontanes were influential and carried considerable political weight. Supported by the pastoral letters and writings of the bishops of Montreal (Ignace Bourget) and Trois-Rivières (Louis-François Laflèche), the ultramontanes also had their newspapers and propagandists. One of them was the writer and journalist Jules-Paul Tardivel, publisher of the newspaper *La Vérité* and one of the first intellectuals to advocate the independence of Quebec. The ultramontanes were an active group that moved forward in tight formation, and they formed an essential element of the Conservative coalition.

More Catholic than the archbishop!

On April 20, 1871, these ultramontane activists published the "Catholic Program," which issued a warning to all candidates who wanted to obtain the voters' support: "It is impossible to deny that politics and religion are closely related, and that the separation of Church and State is an absurd and impious doctrine." The *programmistes,* therefore, called on voters to vote for candidates "with principles that are perfectly healthy and dependable." While acknowledging that the Conservative Party was "the only one that offers serious guarantees for religious interests," the *programmistes* believed that "this loyal support must be subordinated to the religious interests that we must never lose sight of." In other words, submit to the church or we won't vote for you!

The archbishop of Quebec was displeased by this initiative and dissociated himself from it. Neither he nor any other member of the clergy had been consulted when the program was drawn up. In the June election, just one openly *programmiste* candidate was elected. Despite this setback, the ultramontanes continued their activity behind the scenes.

The government gets out of education

Chauveau withdrew from politics for good in 1873. He was succeeded by Gédéon Ouimet, and then by Charles-Eugène Boucher de Boucherville, who was close to the ultramontanes. As soon as he came to power, de Boucherville abolished the Department of Public Instruction. In this way, the Quebec government gave up any direct power over education. From then on, the Quebec education system would be headed by a superintendent who was responsible not to the government or to Parliament but to the Council of Public Instruction.

This reform suited the purposes of the English-speaking minority, because the new council was divided into two denominational committees: a Catholic one and a Protestant one. Each committee determined the programs offered in its system. The Quebec bishops were *ex officio* (by virtue of an office) members of the Catholic committee. The government granted funds but no longer dared have a say in the general orientations of education. "Education," de Boucherville declared, "is too important a matter to be entrusted to politicians." There were only a few fruitless objections to this reform, and it wouldn't be challenged until the 1960s.

Fighting for Autonomy

However, the Liberals were not out of the picture. Denounced as "radicals" and "subversives" by their opponents, they nevertheless continued to offer voters an alternative path for governing. Noteworthy leaders soon joined their ranks, with new positions on liberalism and provincial autonomy that marked them as different from their predecessors. They also knew how to take advantage of their opponents' mistakes.

Influence peddling — and moderation

And the Conservatives made plenty of mistakes! The system of awarding government contracts at the time, it must be said, was conducive to scandal. "Patronage" was a normal and regular practice. Government contracts were obtained by supporting the party in power with a donation to its election fund. Boundaries between politics and the business world were porous. A number of ministers of the Crown sat on the boards of directors of large companies. Natural resource extraction firms most often had direct access to power. Thanks to gifts or favors provided to key ministers or sometimes even the premier himself, some companies obtained cutting rights in Quebec's forests at an absurdly low price.

"Scandal, Mr. Speaker!"

In 1873, it came out that Cartier and John A. Macdonald had promised a lucrative contract to the Montreal businessman Hugh Allan for the construction of the Canadian Pacific Railway, which had been promised to the people of British Columbia and would link east and west. In return for the federal government's generosity, Allan paid $350,000 into the Conservative Party's election fund.

The scandal was enough to bring down the federal Conservatives, who lost the 1874 election to the Liberals. A few months later, Quebec's Conservative premier, Gédéon Ouimet, was forced to resign. His government had purchased a farm at an exorbitant price (25 times its value — a good deal for a few Conservative members of the Legislative Assembly who pocketed the profits!).

Liberals in politics, good Catholics in religion

To gain the confidence of the people, the Quebec Liberals also had to reassure them and shed their antireligious image. This is what Wilfrid Laurier tried to do in a major speech in Quebec City on June 26, 1877. Laurier was a young lawyer, born in 1841, educated at McGill University, and completely at ease in both French and English. Elected as a Liberal to the Quebec Legislative Assembly in 1871 and then to the federal Parliament three years later, he was appointed to Prime Minister Alexander Mackenzie's cabinet in 1877.

A coup d'état in 1878!

Luc Letellier de Saint-Just, who had been federal minister of agriculture since 1874, was appointed lieutenant governor of Quebec in December 1876. A Liberal activist and a man who liked to wield power, he was not easily reconciled to the reticence that his office imposed on him. As soon as he took up his duties, he insisted on being consulted by the Conservative premier, de Boucherville. Formally, no law or proclamation could come into effect unless he signed it.

In March 1878, Letellier de Saint-Just sent a memorandum to the premier who, he complained, had not listened to him or consulted him on important decisions. He refused to give his assent to a railway bill. This decision touched off a political crisis without parallel in Quebec history. Premier de Boucherville promptly submitted his resignation, and the lieutenant governor called on the Liberal leader, Henri-Gustave Joly, to immediately form a new government. The Conservatives were quick to denounce this "coup d'état." In the next election, the Liberals obtained one seat fewer than the Conservatives but managed to govern for a few months. In October 1879, the Joly government fell and Letellier de Saint-Just was removed from office.

Laurier was a politician who understood perfectly the bicultural framework of the new Dominion of Canada. In his speech, Laurier started by taking account of an important fact: "We French Canadians are a conquered race. This is a sad truth to tell, but it is nevertheless the truth." The positive side of things, he said, is that this "race" had inherited British liberties that allowed it to choose the representatives who best embodied its aspirations. Of course, the priests and the church had the right to give advice on political matters, but they didn't have the right to prevent citizens from taking the side of one party or the other. According to Laurier, it was possible to be a good Catholic and believe that the progress of science and civilization was a good thing — to the extent that the rights of the church were respected, of course.

Laurier's speech came at an opportune time, because a number of bishops wanted the Quebec church to speak with a single voice. As a papal emissary saw it, doctrinal disputes had to stop and the clergy had to demonstrate "the greatest reserve" at election time. Now that the church controlled the education system, it had to leave current affairs to the politicians and keep its distance from political life.

The rise of the Liberals

In 1882, the Conservatives were tainted with another scandal. Premier Adolphe Chapleau's Quebec government sold the Montreal–Quebec City portion of the publicly owned Quebec, Montreal, Ottawa, and Occidental Railway (the QMO&O) to a group of businessmen led by one Louis-Adélard Senécal, a

Conservative bagman and confidant of the premier. This influence peddling was regarded as scandalous even by the ultramontanes, who denounced this flagrant breach of morality.

Circumstances were highly favorable for the Liberals. Popular discontent was having an effect; power was within reach. They needed only two ingredients to be able to grab the prize: a leader and an event.

Mercier: Champion of Quebec's autonomy

A lawyer and a journalist with the *Courrier de Saint-Hyacinthe,* Honoré Mercier (1840–1894) had been an opponent of Confederation in his youth. His long-standing dream was to found a national party that would unite French Canadians, whether their loyalties were Liberal or Conservative. Elected to the federal Parliament in 1872, he switched to the Quebec scene in 1879 and became leader of the Quebec Liberal Party in 1883.

A champion of provincial autonomy and more a French-Canadian nationalist than a Liberal, Mercier had flair and a commanding presence. He resisted the centralizing efforts of the federal government, because he believed that real sovereignty was located in the provinces — a point of view that was shared at the time by Ontario Premier Oliver Mowat and the British Privy Council, which was called on to settle a number of disputes between Ottawa and the provinces. In Mercier's view, the provinces had delegated powers to the federal government in 1867, not the reverse. He saw the Quebec government as an instrument for the development of a distinct people. In subsequent years, this conception of Canadian federalism would gain wide support.

The Liberals now had a solid leader who was moderate on religious questions and nationalist on political ones. An extraordinary event was all they needed to tip the balance.

50,000 people on the Champ-de-Mars

On November 22, 1885, more than 50,000 people gathered on Montreal's Champ-de-Mars. A few days earlier, Louis Riel had been hanged. French-speaking and Catholic, Riel belonged to the Métis, a people of mixed heritage descended from First Nations and French-Canadian fur traders in the west. After leading an initial insurrection in the Canadian prairies, Riel went into exile in the United States. But he came back to support his brothers in arms, who once more rebelled against the uncontrolled colonization of the west. The confrontations of 1885 were violent, and Riel was taken prisoner. During his trial, he was blamed for the murder of Thomas Scott and condemned to death. Riel's lawyers pleaded for clemency, but Prime Minister Macdonald turned a deaf ear: "He shall hang, though every dog in Québec bark in his favor."

The hanging of Riel elicited a flood of patriotic feeling among the people of Quebec. Many of the demonstrators gathered on the Champ-de-Mars even hummed a "Riel Marseillaise" that had been composed for the occasion: *Enfants de la Nouvelle-France / Douter de nous est plus permis! / Au gibet Riel se balance / Victime de nos ennemis . . .* (Children of New France / Doubting us is no longer allowed! / On the gallows Riel stands / Victim of our enemies . . .).

Wilfrid Laurier and several other French-Canadian leaders spoke to the crowd. But it was Honoré Mercier who, in simple words, expressed all the sorrow and anger of his compatriots: "Riel, our brother, is dead, a victim of his devotion to the cause of the Métis whose leader he was, a victim of fanaticism and betrayal." He issued a ringing plea for unity: "Let us unite. . . . For 20 years now I have said to my brothers, 'Sacrifice the hatreds that blind us and the divisions that kill us on the altar of the fatherland in danger.'" But, he added, this union "is not the union of one race against other races, of a religion against other religions. We don't want to rectify one crime with another crime."

A narrow, hard-won victory

Mercier's appeal was heard. He transformed the Liberal Party into the Parti National and sought to win the support of dissident Conservatives who were shocked by Macdonald's intransigence. But while many Conservatives were troubled by what had happened, very few crossed the Rubicon.

In the fall of 1886, Mercier made unity and autonomy the central themes of his election campaign. His party was elected, but with a narrow majority. He won 51 percent of the popular vote, but the Conservatives were very much alive with 49 percent. As soon as he took office, Mercier began to implement his reform program. Along with his Ontario counterpart, he organized the first interprovincial conference in October 1887. He also took action against Quebec's great scourge of the time, the emigration of its people to the United States.

Fighting for an Economic Leg to Stand On

Mercier's dream of unity and his hope that partisan disputes would fade away were also motivated by his awareness that the great tragedy that French Canadians of his time were experiencing was primarily economic. Quebec's elites saw emigration to the United States as a drain for which an effective solution had to be found at all costs.

Quebec embarks on industrialization

The drain began slowly in the mid-19th century. It happened while Quebec was going through a period of great transformation, brought on by what's called the Industrial Revolution. The Industrial Revolution began in England in the late 18th century and spread to all Western countries over the course of the 19th century. The process was the same everywhere. New inventions made it possible to produce more goods at lower cost. Subsistence agriculture was gradually abandoned and people moved from the countryside to the cities where the factories and mills sprang up. In every country, industrialization had social effects. A powerful bourgeoisie exploited the labor force, which, over time, came to band together in associations and unions to protect its interests.

Canada and Quebec, in particular, were among the last Western societies to enter the industrial era. There was a simple reason for this: Since the 17th century, the collective wealth of the society had been based on natural resources. First, there were fish and furs; then timber and, to a lesser extent, wheat. Manufactured products came from France, England, and later the United States. During the period of economic slowdown in Western countries that began in 1873, this situation could no longer be maintained. The economic survival of the Dominion of Canada was at stake.

In this context, the federal government adopted a "National Policy," consisting of very high tariffs on all foreign products to force the development of Canadian industry, along with massive investment in transportation infrastructure. It was a risky bet, but the results were not long in coming. Within a few decades, Quebec had industrialized.

Three options for farmers

Chauveau and people working in the educational sector soon began to plead for better training of farmers. In 1859, an agricultural school was established in La Pocatière east of Quebec City. Newspapers specializing in agriculture were launched as well. Farmers needed to master crop rotation techniques, become familiar with the best fertilizers available, and buy mowing and harvesting machines to improve yields from their land.

Despite these good intentions, it quickly became apparent that farm mechanization was not proceeding as fast in Quebec as in Ontario. Quebec farmers were left with three options:

- ✔ **Be a farmer in the summer and a lumberjack in the winter.** The first option, combining farming with woodcutting, was very common but not very lucrative. You could take care of the farm during the summer and be a lumberjack in the winter. Unfortunately, the lumber camps were increasingly remote, and the wages and working conditions there were often atrocious. The forestry companies held all the cards. With a government-sanctioned monopoly, they were the only employers in distant regions such as Saguenay–Lac-Saint-Jean and Lower St. Lawrence–Gaspé. Gradually, wood came to be processed where it was cut, especially in the St. Maurice Valley — into boards, and later into pulp and paper.

- ✔ **Specialize.** The second option for farmers was to find a new niche to develop. Many took this route, specializing in dairy products, livestock raising, or tobacco production. Specialized farming took root in the Eastern Townships, Bellechasse, Montmagny, and the Joliette region.

✔ **Go work in the city.** For the rest, there was a third option: to go work in the city. The industries that hired laborers — often unskilled laborers — emerged in the urban centers. Between 1881 and 1901, the rate of urbanization in Quebec grew by leaps and bounds, from 23.8 percent to 36.1 percent. The industrial sectors that were growing most quickly were textiles and especially leather. In the late 19th century, two-thirds of the shoes sold in Canada were produced in Montreal. The food-processing sector also provided numerous jobs, as did iron and steel.

Montreal: From the "Golden Square Mile" to Saint-Henri

In the late 19th century, Montreal became the economic capital of Quebec and of Canada as a whole. This was when Montreal definitively surpassed Quebec City in both population and economic stature. Montreal's population grew from 90,000 in 1861 to 268,000 in 1901, while Quebec City's grew only from 42,000 to 69,000 in the same period.

Like all large industrial cities, Montreal presented a study in contrasts. In the "Golden Square Mile" on the slopes of Mount Royal, a wealthy bourgeoisie built luxurious mansions. The workers clustered down below, close to the factories on the banks of the St. Lawrence. The slums they lived in were often unhealthy and living conditions were difficult; Montreal's infant mortality rate was among the highest in the world. In 1885, a smallpox epidemic killed 3,234 people in Montreal. The disease struck eight times as many French Canadians as other people. To combat these plagues, the Quebec government required every municipality to set up a board of health and established a provincial Hygiene Council.

The first union: The Knights of Labor

Between 1815 and 1879, there were 137 strikes in Quebec. But it wasn't until 1872 that employers were required to negotiate collective agreements. In 1885, the Quebec government developed a regulatory framework for workers. A limit was placed on the number of hours per week that women and children could work — 60 hours. For men, the limit was 72 hours. Boys under 12 years of age and girls under 14 were not allowed to work. However, the Quebec government hired only three investigators to monitor the implementation of these measures.

In the 1880s, some workers decided to band together in an organization called the Knights of Labor, which had started in the United States. The church was offended by the Knights' American origins and feared confrontation and disobedience. In 1886, Quebec's archbishops recommended that workers not join the organization. The Knights of Labor were more reformers than revolutionaries. Their efforts were directed toward obtaining healthier working conditions and wages paid on a fixed date. Between 1882 and 1887, the Knights recruited some 2,500 members.

The gap between the two worlds in Montreal was ethnic as well as social. Not all English-speaking Montrealers were rich and powerful — for example, Griffintown was a poor Irish Catholic neighborhood in southwestern Montreal. However, taken as a whole, Montreal's English-speaking minority was clearly privileged relative to the French-speaking majority. It was in charge of the major industries and controlled the financial world. The Montreal Board of Trade conducted its business in English. The layout of the city, the architecture of its large downtown buildings, and the signs on its stores all gave Montreal the look of a British city. Montreal had been majority English-speaking between 1831 and 1861, but the arrival of masses of French Canadians from the countryside changed the population balance. Still, it was not until 1882 that a majority of Montreal city councilors were French-speaking.

Taking hold of the economy, but how?

All the new possibilities that industrialization offered didn't provide a place for everyone, and large numbers of French Canadians preferred to emigrate to the United States. Even though many of them returned, emigration was seen as a hemorrhage. Between 1870 and 1900, nearly 410,000 Quebecers crossed the border. With each succeeding decade, about 10 percent of the population moved south, mostly to the textile mills of the U.S. east coast. Between 1861 and 1901, the proportion of French Canadians living outside Quebec increased from 14 percent to 45 percent. The migratory movement continued into the 1930s. A number of different solutions were envisioned to reverse the flow.

Curé Labelle's dream

The first solution put forward was the colonization of Quebec's hinterland. A colorful personality of the time made this his great project. As *curé* (pastor) of parishes near the American border for more than ten years, François-Xavier-Antoine Labelle (1833–1891) saw thousands of his compatriots leave for the United States. The image of the humble, withdrawn *curé* shut up in his rectory, accepting the fate that Providence reserved for his flock, did not apply at all to this fiery giant of a man.

Transferred to Saint-Jérôme parish in the lower Laurentians, he persuaded entrepreneurs to build a railway to the Laurentians, the *petit train du nord*. Until his death in 1891, he spared no effort in trying to attract French Canadians to the lands of the *Pays d'en haut*.

Curé Labelle's personality and the tenacity with which he pursued his work attracted attention. In 1888, Honoré Mercier appointed him deputy minister of colonization. Curé Labelle was the inspiration for some dramatic initiatives, among them the famous "hundred-acre law," which offered free land to any family with 12 children or more! However, life in the hinterland wasn't easy, and the communication infrastructure developed too slowly. There was a lot of good will, but it wasn't enough to prevent many settlers from abandoning their new lands or being unable to reconcile themselves to their life of misery.

Let us take control of industry!

Others saw the real solution as being the development of an entrepreneurial spirit. In his 1901 publication *Emparons-nous de l'industrie (Let Us Take Control of Industry)*, a French-Canadian intellectual, Errol Bouchette, asked some embarrassing questions:

> Where are the French-Canadian industrialists, shipowners, and especially engineers? Who built and profits from the railways that crisscross the country, for which we provided the money? . . . Who exploits the forests, the main source of our wealth?

Many believed along with Bouchette that the development of French-Canadian industry would be the salvation of Quebec's French-speaking majority. This aim was behind the establishment of a French-language chamber of commerce in Montreal in 1886.

Two periodicals were launched to familiarize French Canadians with the realities of modern commerce and industry: *Le moniteur du commerce* and *Le prix courant*. In addition, the Quebec government was urged to establish schools specializing in training engineers and industrialists. The government followed through, founding the École Polytechnique (1873) and the École des Hautes Études Commerciales (1907). French-speaking Quebecers were also poorly served by the English-controlled banks, so French Canadians established their own institutions, such as the Banque Nationale (1859) and the Banque Hochelaga (1874).

French Canadians' economic inferiority was the great issue of the time. Some theologians denounced the "materialism" of liberal capitalist societies and counseled French Canadians to be resigned to their fate. A more common response, however, was to try to design solutions to remedy the inequalities. But it would take decades and several political crises before that happened.

Attracting French immigrants

To counterbalance the emigration of French Canadians to the United States, the Quebec government developed its first immigration policy, essentially aimed at people from France.

One of the architects of this policy was Siméon Le Sage, who worked in Quebec's brand-new civil service from 1867 to 1888. Le Sage published a pamphlet, *The Province of Quebec and European Emigration,* of which 80,000 copies were printed. He sought to persuade French people to settle in the far-off lands of Témiscamingue, which in his view had enormous potential.

In 1882, the Quebec government appointed Hector Fabre, who was then a senator, agent general of Quebec in France. Fabre took up residence in Paris, where he also served as commissioner general of Canada. His initial mandate was to attract French immigrants and stimulate economic and cultural relations between Quebec and France. While these initiatives received the support of French intellectuals such as the historian François-Edme Rameau de Saint-Père, they did not achieve the results that were anticipated.

Chapter 12

Conscription (1897–1928)

● ●

In This Chapter
▶ Looking at Laurier, Bourassa, and British imperialism
▶ Ensuring Quebec's prosperity

● ●

During the first decades of the 20th century, Quebec expanded in size and its population doubled. Abitibi was annexed in 1898 and Ungava in 1912 — but Labrador was lost in 1927.

Between 1901 and 1931, the population of Quebec increased from 1.6 million to 2.9 million. As of about 1915, the majority of Quebecers lived in cities. Up until the 1930s, tens of thousands of Quebecers continued to try their luck in the United States, but their Liberal government was doing everything in its power to develop industries at home.

While these changes were taking place, an intense debate regarding the future of Canada was raging. These clashes mobilized Quebec elites, who were wary of Great Britain's imperial ambitions. World War I brought into sharp focus the huge gap that continued to separate the views of French Canadians from those of English Canadians on the role that Canada should play on the world stage.

Opposing Imperialism

In 1896, Liberal leader Wilfrid Laurier became prime minister of Canada. The Quebec Liberals basked in the reflected glory of this win, and came to power the following year. This was the beginning of a long Liberal reign in Quebec — one that would not end until 1936. Quebec Liberals would retain power for 39 years.

Laurier was the first French Canadian to lead the federal government. Many Quebecers felt that they had elected one of their own. His task would not be easy, because he had to deal with constituents with very different visions of the future of the Dominion.

Laurier's compromises

For many English Canadians, Canada's place was to be found as a part of the British Empire. In 1911, 834,000 Canadians, out of a total population of 7.2 million, were natives of the British Isles. Some Canadians supported the "imperialist" movement and wanted Canada to serve the grand ambitions of Britain's sprawling global empire, on which, as was often said, the sun never set. Laurier knew that his French-Canadian compatriots saw things differently, but he could not completely ignore this influential political current, which had a substantial base in Ontario and Nova Scotia.

To fight the Boers in South Africa or not?

In 1897, the English celebrated the 60th anniversary of Queen Victoria's accession to the throne with great pomp. On June 12 of that year, Laurier gave a major speech in which he asserted the loyalty of all Canadians to the British Crown. In the years that followed, Canada demonstrated this loyalty by adopting a preferential tariff for British products and by sending a contingent of 7,300 Canadian soldiers to South Africa.

In 1899, the English army went to war against the Boers, descendants of Dutch settlers in South Africa, who had founded the Transvaal Republic a few years earlier. Britain's power and prestige were at stake in a region rich in gold and other precious metals. French Canadians were against Canada's participation in this "imperialist" war. The problem was that Canada didn't yet have an independent foreign policy. The Empire's wars automatically became Canada's wars. Laurier did not challenge this understanding, but the level of Canadian participation in the Boer War to which he agreed was well below what the imperialists wanted.

The Canadian prime minister was torn between two incompatible visions — between those who supported Canadian autonomy on the one hand and the imperialists on the other. He was constantly trying to navigate these troubled waters. In 1910, Laurier announced a plan to establish a Canadian navy, which in addition to supporting the empire on occasion would primarily be responsible for protecting Canada's coasts. Once again, the plan offended the imperialists, who wanted the Canadian vessels to be incorporated into Britain's Royal Navy.

A place for French-speaking people outside Quebec?

Laurier also tried to compromise on another front: Canada's cultural and linguistic duality. In Manitoba, an officially bilingual province, a controversy raged regarding the language of instruction in public schools. Laurier reached an agreement with the premier of the province: The Catholic religion could be taught in public schools, but only after school hours; it would also be possible to teach in French, but only where the numbers of students warranted. In the neighboring provinces of Alberta and Saskatchewan, officially created in 1905, Catholics and French-speaking people were subject to the same compromise.

The "numbers" — that's what French Canadians were lacking, especially in western Canada. Clifford Sifton, the federal minister responsible for immigration policy, wanted to populate the west with Anglo-Saxon farmers. The Canada he dreamed of was Protestant and British. His efforts would be partly rewarded. Whether they were German, Austrian, or Scandinavian, most new farmers settling in the west belonged to the great Protestant religious family.

Henri Bourassa and the nationalist movement

Laurier's compromises disappointed many Quebecers who, even if they continued to vote for the Liberals, were paying closer attention to speeches from the leaders of a nationalist movement that was growing in influence.

For the independence of Canada

Up until the early 1920s, Henri Bourassa (1868–1952) was the great symbol of Quebec nationalism. He was the son of Napoléon Bourassa, a renowned artist, and the grandson of Louis-Joseph Papineau on his mother's side. Although he inherited his grandfather's panache and independent spirit, there was nothing of the revolutionary leader in Henri. A devout Catholic and an austere man who held very conservative views on social issues, he was a fierce opponent of women's right to vote and also opposed easing the rules governing divorce. For this father of eight children, the family was the foundation of the nation. In no way should it be weakened.

Feminists organize

In 1907, Marie Gérin-Lajoie (1867–1945) joined with other women to found the Fédération Nationale Saint-Jean-Baptiste (FNSJB). She had previously been active in the Montreal chapter of the National Council of Women of Canada. The FNSJB promoted the creation of women's business associations. Women made up 15.6 percent of the labor force in 1901; by 1931 this proportion had increased to 19.7 percent. Women's working conditions were so bad that in 1919 the Quebec government adopted the Women's Minimum Wage Act.

But for Marie Gérin-Lajoie, as for other early feminists, the big issue was women's right to vote. At the federal level, the right to vote was extended to women in 1917. But in Quebec, as in most Catholic societies, the church strongly opposed this measure.

Marie Gérin-Lajoie's view of womanhood was nevertheless very traditional. She believed that motherhood gave women special knowledge. They should have the right to vote primarily because they were mothers: As mothers, they understood public health issues better than men and knew better what was good for children in school. As Gérin-Lajoie explained in 1922, "It's more in the name of difference than similarity with men that women must have the electoral franchise."

Henri Bourassa was first and foremost a man of ideas, not of government. In 1910, he founded *Le Devoir,* an independent newspaper that provided him with a choice outlet for his ideas. The independence he dreamed of was not that of Quebec, but of Canada. Like his Patriote grandfather, he wanted Canada to free itself from the imperial British yoke and progress under its own steam. He also dreamed of a bi-national and bi-cultural Canada in which French Canadians would feel at home from coast to coast. At age 27, he was elected to the federal Parliament under the banner of Wilfrid Laurier's Liberal Party. When he learned that the Canadian government was participating in the Boer War, he resigned very publicly and became head of a nationalist movement.

The founding of patriotic organizations

Rising stars such as Armand Lavergne, Olivar Asselin, and Jules Fournier followed Bourassa. They founded the Ligue Nationaliste (Nationalist League) in 1902 and *Le Nationaliste,* a publication that opposed Canada's participation in imperial wars, two years later. In 1904, students at Quebec's classical colleges founded a patriotic organization called the Association catholique de la jeunesse canadienne-française (Catholic Association of French-Canadian Youth). In 1902, some people from Quebec City founded the Société du Parler Français (Society for Speaking French), which sought the promotion and protection of the French language in Canada.

"We have the right to live"

By turns an independent member of Parliament in Ottawa and of the Legislative Assembly in Quebec City, Bourassa was not the head of any party, but he was influential. Along with his struggle against British imperialism, he defended the French language — the status of which was questioned even by members of the Catholic hierarchy. Visiting Montreal in 1910 for a major international Eucharistic Congress, the head of the Catholic Church in England told his French-Canadian co-religionists that to develop, Catholics in North America must adopt English. According to him, the arrival of Irish immigrants provided ample justification for this shift.

On September 10, during a famous speech at Notre-Dame basilica in Montreal, Henri Bourassa offered a scathing reply to the English prelate: "Let us take care, yes, let us be very careful not to extinguish this intense source of light that has illuminated an entire continent for three centuries. . . . There are only a handful of us, it is true, but we count for what we are, and we have the right to live." The crowd erupted in wild applause.

But it would take more than a speech to ensure the survival of French in the other Canadian provinces. In 1912, Ontario adopted Regulation 17, which made English the only language allowed in the province's public and religious schools after grade 3. During a long court battle, Quebec mobilized fully to support the cause of French Canadians in Ontario. On January 11, 1915, Quebec Premier Lomer Gouin offered his support to those who later came to be known as Franco-Ontarians. The Quebec government also agreed to allow school boards to collect donations for the cause. In November 1916, the Privy Council in London upheld the legality of Regulation 17. Little by little, Quebecers were discovering that the rules concerning bilingualism set out in the 1867 constitution only applied to Quebec and the federal government.

The conscription crisis

These clashes about language came about at a very bad time. From 1914 to 1918, Canada was plunged into a terrible world war.

In the early 20th century, imperialism was not peculiar to Britain. Leaders in other Western countries also had a strong desire to expand their territory, corner new markets, and impose their values, language, and customs. Italians and Germans, who had completed their political unification in the 19th century, were seized with the imperialist fever, but they saw that Asia and Africa had already been divided up by other powers. This fierce competition created a lot of tension and mistrust. Germany and Austria-Hungary concocted an alliance. France tried to surround its powerful German neighbor by signing a treaty with Russia. Every country invested heavily in its military. Europe was a powder keg that exploded on June 28, 1914, following the assassination of the presumptive heir to the Austro-Hungarian throne. This was the beginning of World War I — a catastrophe for England and France, allies during the conflict that would leave eight million victims.

Canada takes action

England declared war on Germany on August 4, 1914. The Dominion of Canada and the colonies of the British Empire were automatically drawn into this war that was expected to end quickly. Robert Borden's Conservatives, in power in Ottawa since 1911, were eager to mobilize all Canada's resources to support Great Britain. By August 7, a contingent of 25,000 troops was announced. On August 22, the federal government gave itself extraordinary powers by passing the War Measures Act. Anyone who criticized the war effort or hindered its proper functioning risked censure or even imprisonment. The economy was also mobilized, and women were recruited by the armament factories.

Yes to the war effort . . .

Overall, the Quebec elite, starting with the church, supported the war effort. "Loyal subjects," wrote the archbishop of Montreal in September 1914, "recognizing it as the protector of our rights, our peace, and our freedom, we owe England our most generous support." For its part, the government of Quebec voted a sum of $1 million in 1916. The nationalists were more divided. Henri Bourassa was wary of England but did not formally oppose Canada's participation in the war. Olivar Asselin, deeply attached to the ancestral homeland, encouraged French Canadians to enlist: "Immortal France is watching us. . . . We, the French in America, we are only French because of France."

. . . but no to conscription

Even though the Canadian government formed an exclusively French-speaking infantry battalion in October 1914, Asselin's call for recruits received little response. Barely 12 percent of World War I volunteers were French Canadians. It was easy to see that they felt less affected by this war than English Canadians. Notably, nearly 40 percent of Canadian soldiers who fought in Europe were born in the British Isles. In addition, there were many available jobs in Montreal with attractive working conditions.

The war itself turned out to be far less heroic than people imagined at the outset. Following each encounter, the casualties were counted in the thousands. Soldiers endured horrific living conditions in the trenches, far from their loved ones. In October 1915, the Canadian government announced an expeditionary force of 250,000 men. As of April 1917, nearly 424,000 Canadians had volunteered — a huge contribution for a dominion of just eight million people. But for Prime Minister Borden, just back from a visit to Europe, it was not enough.

On August 29, 1917, the Canadian Parliament finally adopted the Military Service Act, which called for compulsory enlistment by all men of military age, from 20 to 35 years old, widowed or single. Borden had announced this extraordinary measure in May. In Quebec, "conscription" immediately aroused anger. On August 9, a bomb exploded at the home of the owner of the pro-conscription *Montreal Star.* Protests followed throughout Quebec, culminating on the evening of August 29. Quebec elites, themselves hostile to conscription, felt overwhelmed by the public response and feared a large-scale riot that would threaten public order.

Bourassa's arguments

With his strong distaste for disorder, Henri Bourassa launched an early appeal for calm. He feared that the riots would give ammunition to English Canada's imperialists who dreamed of muzzling the nationalists and closing down *Le Devoir.* In a series of articles published in May 1917, Bourassa explained why he opposed conscription:

- ✔ **Enough sacrifices:** Solidarity with Britain had its limits. If Canada was attacked by the Americans, would the motherland send so many men?

- ✔ **A broken promise:** The Borden government had committed itself to never enacting compulsory recruitment. It had, thus, betrayed a solemn promise, in addition to violating the most fundamental freedoms.

- ✔ **The danger of an explosion:** The opposition to conscription among French Canadians in Quebec was so strong that the government's legislation could lead to a civil war.

A "separatist" motion

These arguments failed to convince Borden who, in October 1917, formed a coalition government with Liberals who supported his agenda. Wilfrid Laurier, old and tired, led the anti-conscription wing of the divided Liberals. In the federal election held December 17, 1917, the Conservatives were soundly defeated in Quebec, getting only 4.6 percent of the vote and three seats in English-speaking constituencies. However, they won a resounding victory in the rest of Canada. Some spoke of a "race vote." In the new federal cabinet, nobody spoke for the French Canadians. The Dominion was more divided than ever.

Faced with a hostile Conservative government in Ottawa, the Liberals in power in Quebec City no longer knew how to react. In the days after the federal election, Liberal member Joseph-Napoléon Francœur rose in the Legislative Assembly and read a historic motion:

> That this House believes that the province of Quebec would be willing to accept the failure of the federative pact of 1867 if, in the other provinces, it is viewed as an obstacle to the unity, progress, and development in Canada.

Should Quebec stay in Canada or leave? For the first time since 1867, the question of Quebec independence was put on the table. A debate ensued. Premier Lomer Gouin asked the member to withdraw his motion but, along with Francœur, deplored the smear campaign orchestrated against French Canadians in the imperialist press in the lead-up to the election. "We complain of insults," he explained, "of repeated appeals to prejudice, but our fathers have always suffered these." That said, he nevertheless believed that the Canadian federation remained the "best form of government open to our country."

Riot in Quebec City: Four dead

While Quebec's elected officials reflected on the future, recruitment officers were tracking down men of fighting age. The "deserters" faced up to five years in prison. Many of them hid in the forests, with help from French-Canadian farmers who opposed the Borden government. From March 28 to April 1, 1918, riots broke out in Quebec City. Acting on the War Measures Act, the federal government suspended civil liberties. A meeting featuring the nationalist leader Armand Lavergne, banned by the authorities, turned into a confrontation. The army fired on the crowd; four men were killed, including Georges Demeule, a 15-year-old boy.

Ultimately, only 48,000 Canadian conscripts would fight in Europe. World War I ended on November 11, 1918, when the Germans finally agreed to an armistice. Canada's international status was strengthened by the conflict, but the conscription crisis left deep scars in Quebec.

The husband of a feminist stands out at the League of Nations

Following World War I, the countries that had just been at war founded the League of Nations, the forerunner of the United Nations. This international forum, it was hoped, would foster improved dialogue between countries around the world and provide greater collective security.

Raoul Dandurand (1861–1942), a lawyer, Laurier confidant, Liberal senator since 1898, and skillful diplomat, was elected president of the sixth assembly of the League of Nations in September 1925. Through his actions, Canada became a full-fledged member of this international organization.

Dandurand was the husband of Josephine Dandurand-Marchand, a writer and journalist. From 1892 to 1896, she published *Le Coin de Feu*, a magazine that promoted women's education. "The more we are educated and informed," she declared in 1901, "the more we will be good mothers." Nevertheless, she was opposed to women's suffrage.

Prosperity through Foreign Capital

Like politics, economic development was a contentious area. Ensuring Quebec's prosperity was one thing; selling its wealth to foreigners was another. And there were also social inequalities that many people could not help noticing.

Triumph of the free market

For the governing Liberals, prosperity depended on private enterprise. Only the free market could generate wealth. The government should intervene as little as possible in the economy, except to promote its smooth running through road infrastructure. In Quebec, as elsewhere in the West, this was the golden age of uncontrolled liberalism. Critics of this conception of the economy came from nationalist movements and the working class.

Prosperity above all

Starting in 1896, Canada and Quebec experienced a wave of unprecedented prosperity. Experts spoke of a second industrial revolution. The most successful sectors in Quebec were the following:

- **Hydroelectricity:** Energy continued to be the crucial element in industrial development. Instead of relying on coal like many other parts of North America, Quebec harnessed its rivers and built hydroelectric dams. Electricity production increased from 83,000 horsepower in 1900 to 2,322,000 horsepower in 1930. Unlike Ontario, which nationalized its hydroelectric companies in 1905, the Quebec government allowed large companies to control the industry. Thus, the Shawinigan Water & Power Company, Montreal Light, Heat & Power, Southern Canada Power, and several other corporations came to own exclusive rights to the waterways.

- **Pulp and paper:** This sector saw dramatic growth. Between 1900 and 1930, the value of production increased from $5 million to $130 million. This development was partly due to a ban imposed by the Quebec government in 1910 on exporting pulpwood cut on public lands. This measure required U.S. companies to process wood destined for paper production in Quebec. The St. Maurice Valley benefited greatly from the wealth generated by this sector.

- **Aluminum and mining:** By importing bauxite, Quebec became a major producer of aluminum. This sector created many jobs in the Saguenay region, particularly in Arvida, which would later be merged with Jonquière. The mining sector was also growing. Asbestos (from the town of Asbestos in the Eastern Townships) was mined by private companies, as were copper and gold (Rouyn-Noranda and Val-d'Or in the Abitibi region).

- **Manufacturing:** During the first three decades of the 20th century, food processing was the largest industry in Quebec. Beer production (Molson) and sugar refining (Redpath) created many jobs, as did the production of bread and butter. The leather industry was gradually supplanted by paper products, but the garment industry was still strong. While industrial production increased dramatically in Quebec, from a gross value of $154 million in 1900 to $1.1 billion in 1929, Quebec's proportion of industrial development in Canada as a whole nevertheless decreased slightly.

In Quebec, as elsewhere in the world, this second wave of economic and industrial development was marked by two major phenomena:

- **Wealth became concentrated in the hands of a few corporations and individuals.** The banking and financial sectors were controlled by a small and powerful elite, as were natural resources.

- **It was often foreign investment — initially British, then increasingly American — that made Quebec's economic development possible.** Quebec's Liberal premier during the 1920s, Alexandre Taschereau, saw no problem with this. In 1927, he declared, "Let capital from England and the United States come here as much as it wants and expand our industries, so that our people will have jobs. . . . I prefer importing American dollars to exporting Canadian workers."

"Masters in our own house"

Nationalists centered around Abbé Lionel Groulx (1878–1967) criticized this liberal philosophy. They lamented the weakness of the French-Canadian presence in the circles of economic power. In their eyes, the national recovery of the French-Canadian people could only be achieved through taking back control of the territory's natural resources and increasing their presence in industry. In 1922, *Action Française,* a journal dedicated to the nationalist struggle that had been founded five years earlier, published a theme issue on "our political future" that struck a chord. Abbé Groulx wrote:

> Our province's wealth is too abundant and too attractive. It is the object of tremendous greed. The problem is no longer whether these resources will be used, but whether they will be used by us and for us, or by foreigners against us. . . . The only choice remaining to us is this: either we become masters in our own house, or we resign ourselves to forever being a people of serfs.

But the solutions proposed by these nationalists were more moral than political. No question of nationalizing hydroelectric companies, for example. First and foremost, French Canadians needed to practice a "buy at home" strategy, thus encouraging French merchants. And the few French-Canadian industrialists should stop squandering their wealth and learn how to better pass it on to their descendants.

"Catholic" unions

Despite the prosperity, workers still lived in difficult conditions. The Quebec government created placement offices for the unemployed and a workers' compensation board during this period, but workers continued to organize themselves into unions to defend their interests. Between 1901 and 1931, the number of unions increased from 136 to 501. The rate of unionization of workers in Quebec kept pace with that in Ontario.

The church, initially averse to unionization, later agreed to trade unions, but only if they were "Catholic." Presenting themselves as an alternative to the Communist or workers' parties and international American unions, the Catholic unions, supervised by "chaplains," preached true collaboration between employers and workers.

In 1921, the Canadian and Catholic Confederation of Labour (CCCL) was created. In 1922, 17,600 unionized Catholic workers from 120 associations represented 25 percent of all unionized workers in Quebec. The other unionized workers continued to belong to international associations. Even though Albert Saint-Martin founded a university for laborers in Montreal in 1925, Quebec did not appear to be fertile ground for socialist ideas.

The emergence of a modern Quebec state

During the first decades of the 20th century, the Quebec state became somewhat more fully developed. Between 1900 and 1921, its workforce increased from 625 to 2,285 employees. It had much more financial autonomy than in 1867. With the main railway lines having been completed, Liberal ministers of finance brought down balanced budgets so that debt service charges were reduced. And federal subsidies accounted for only 5.8 percent of the Quebec government's revenues in 1929. Fees on lands and forests generated most of the government's revenues. Spending on roads was the biggest expenditure item. Although it had little involvement in the economy, the Quebec government was called on to address social issues.

The Public Assistance Act

Liberal capitalist societies generate their share of social inequalities. Philanthropic organizations and religious congregations were no longer sufficient to help the poor, the needy, and the destitute. Despite opposition from the church, which feared state control, the Liberal government passed the Public Assistance Act in 1921. Under this law, the cost of operating hospitals and asylums was shared equally between the Quebec government, municipalities, and the institutions involved. A new entertainment tax was introduced to finance the government's involvement.

Aurore: The child martyr

On February 12, 1920, little Aurore Gagnon, age 11, was found dead. The inquest showed that Marie-Anne Houde, the second wife of Télesphore Gagnon, the victim's father, was responsible for the tragedy. Mercilessly beaten with a log by her stepmother, repeatedly whipped with a strap, burned with a curling iron, regularly locked in the attic, the girl had suffered heavy abuse. The neighbors noticed the welts, rumors spread, but no one dared intervene directly. The trial of the accused, heavily covered by the newspapers of the time, took place from April 13 to 21, 1920. Marie-Anne Houde was sentenced to death, but her sentence was commuted to life imprisonment. The father was accused of complicity and sentenced to life imprisonment. After five years in prison, he was finally released.

The story greatly upset Quebecers. During the years that followed, they became more likely to report violence against children. The drama would be remembered through a play, first produced in 1921. Thirty years later, the film *Aurore l'enfant martyre (Aurore the Child Martyr)*, directed by Yves Bigras, opened in theaters. The public rushed to relive this sordid story. In 2005, director Luc Dionne offered another interpretation of the drama. He pointed the finger not only at the stepmother but at all the neighbors who remained indifferent to Aurore Gagnon's fate, including the parish priest who, according to him, tried to cover it up. Dionne's film brought the story to a new generation.

A liquor commission

The same year, the government established the Quebec Liquor Commission, the forerunner of today's Société des Alcools du Québec (SAQ). From the mid-19th century on, some groups had denounced the social effects of alcohol and fought for its total prohibition. Those who opposed this measure in favor of a less draconian solution feared that prohibition would give rise to an illegal trade orchestrated by unscrupulous traffickers. In creating the Liquor Commission, the government opted for a middle ground that was neither prohibitionist nor completely laissez-faire. The sale of alcohol was permitted but controlled by the government. Initially, sales were restricted to one bottle at a time! In its first year of existence, the corporation generated income of $4 million — which, oddly enough, had the effect of silencing the critics. At the time, Quebec was the only place in North America where alcohol was not completely banned.

Supporting culture

During the 1920s, the Quebec government also became involved in the field of culture, through the efforts of Athanase David, a sort of minister of culture without the title. A number of prizes were established to support the most promising students and to encourage writers. David set up schools of fine arts in Quebec City and Montreal and created the Historic Monuments Commission to ensure the survival of Quebec's architectural heritage.

Arrival of Jews and Italians

During the first decades of the 20th century, two communities — Jews and Italians — settled in Montreal in large numbers.

Jews have a historic presence in Quebec. The Hart family in Trois-Rivières had played an important role in commerce and politics. In 1871, however, records show only 74 Jews in Quebec. Thirty years later, there were more than 7,600, and in 1931 more than 60,000. Most of the newcomers were fleeing *pogroms* (organized massacres of Jews) in eastern Europe. Although many Jews demanded separate schools for their children, they were integrated into the Protestant system, which sometimes led to acrimonious debates during the 1920s. This "openness" of Protestants, however, stopped at the gates of McGill University, which restricted the admission of Jews from the late 1920s on.

The Italian community was growing during the same period. In 1931, there were nearly 25,000 in Quebec, while 30 years earlier they had numbered barely 2,800. Most came from the agricultural regions of southern Italy and were very poor. Many of these immigrants came to Quebec through the efforts of Antonio Cordasco, a recruiting agent for Canadian Pacific who promised Heaven and Earth. In 1905, Cordasco was severely criticized by a federal commission that accused him of abusing the trust of the newcomers. Businessman Charles-Honoré Catelli, along with other members of his community, founded an aid society for immigrants.

Chapter 13

The Depression (1929–1938)

· ·

In This Chapter

▶ Measuring the magnitude of the Depression and early government responses

▶ Focusing on the founding and election of the Union Nationale

· ·

*T*he 1930s were marked by the Great Depression, one of the worst economic crises of the modern era. Unemployment hit new peaks and wreaked havoc in all major Western cities. Governments had to devise new measures to help the needy through the slump and put their countries back on the road to prosperity.

Quebec was no exception to this harsh reality. Government authorities improvised solutions, but the Depression persisted throughout the 1930s. Many people wanted to get to the root of the problem, but only a few small groups considered extreme solutions. In 1936, a new party overthrew the Liberal regime. The election of the Union Nationale brought a new generation to power and raised a lot of hope.

The Effects of the Stock Market Crash

On October 24, 1929, share prices on the New York Stock Exchange collapsed. The event was less the cause than the symptom of a much deeper crisis within the economic system of the time. The crash had immediate effects on the Canadian economy, and on Quebec in particular. Politicians' reflex was to trust the market and free enterprise, and not to use government to revive the economy. But patience among the unemployed had its limits.

The defects of the liberal economy

The Roaring Twenties were followed by years of misery and distress, especially in the cities. During the 1930s, the market economy and capitalism showed their worst face. In Quebec, as elsewhere, the immediate causes of the Depression were primarily economic:

✔ **No middle class existed.** Thanks to advanced technology, new consumer products were being manufactured. But as wages stagnated, workers didn't have the means to buy them. In 1931, there were 141,000 cars on the roads of Quebec. Although they were mass produced, the average worker couldn't afford a car. The result: a crisis of overproduction.

✔ **The banking system was in chaos.** In the late 1920s, economic growth became artificial. It wasn't based on actual production and work, but on speculation in the financial world. Banks lent too easily to individuals and businesses that didn't have solid financial backing. At the slightest jolt, people and businesses were forced into bankruptcy.

✔ **The reconstruction of Europe ended.** Much of Western prosperity in the 1920s was due to the reconstruction of Europe after World War I. In 1929, the reconstruction was complete, but the European countries were heavily indebted.

When the Depression began to bite, governments didn't know how to react. They would readily agree to go into debt to construct a road or public buildings, but not to revive the economy in a time of crisis. This traditional view was challenged by an English economist, John Maynard Keynes, who developed a new concept of the welfare state. According to Keynes, in addition to better sharing the wealth between rich and poor, the government could and should stimulate growth. Inspired by this new vision of the state, U.S. President Franklin Delano Roosevelt, elected in 1932, declared a New Deal and launched an ambitious program of recovery. He hoped this would help the United States pull itself out of the Depression.

But it would take years before the effects of the New Deal were felt in Quebec. The Canadian economy was heavily dependent on the United States. Between 1929 and 1933, Canada's gross domestic product fell by 30 percent; manufacturing, by 33 percent; and exports, by 55 percent. In three years, the unemployment rate increased from 4.2 percent to 27 percent! In Quebec, the lumber and pulp and paper industries were hit hard; nearly 12,500 jobs were lost in this sector during these lean years. Many U.S. corporations closed their Canadian subsidiaries or postponed planned investments. Montreal was very hard hit. In 1934, more than 62,000 Montrealers were unemployed, representing approximately 30 percent of the workforce.

The Tin Flute

The misery of the working-class neighborhoods in Montreal was the inspiration for a then-unknown young novelist, Gabrielle Roy (1909–1983). A native of Manitoba, Roy toured Europe, settled in Montreal, and earned her living by writing articles for *Le Jour,* a liberal weekly, and *La Revue Moderne.* A series of reports on Montreal written for the *Bulletin des Agriculteurs* inspired her to write an urban novel set in the working-class neighborhood of Saint-Henri.

Published in 1945, *Bonheur d'occasion* tells the story of Florentine Lacasse and his family, very hard hit by the Great Depression of the 1930s. Unlike most major novels of the period

(Claude-Henri Grignon's *Un home et son péché,* Félix-Antoine Savard's *Menaud maître-draveur,* or Germaine Guevremont's *Le survenant,* for example), which celebrated rural life and the land, Roy's novel portrayed the city not as a place of ruin and decay but as a dynamic space where social struggles were played out.

Thanks to her — and Roger Lemelin, whose *Les Plouffe,* set among the working class of Quebec City, appeared three years later — the Quebec novel came into its own. Roy's book received huge critical and popular acclaim. In 1947, it won the Prix Femina, and came out in English translation as *The Tin Flute.*

Immediate government reactions

In Montreal and in most other cities and towns, the unemployed tried in vain to find work. The neediest lined up at the Old Brewery Mission or one of the offices of the St. Vincent de Paul Society for a bowl of soup or some firewood. Before the 1930s, such private charities had been able to meet the demand. These times of crisis, however, called for other solutions.

The failure of the Canadian New Deal

Elected in 1930, R. B. Bennett's Conservatives launched an ambitious infrastructure program and set up a federal credit agency to stimulate housing construction. To encourage foreign investment and deal with financial instability, the federal government negotiated more favorable tariffs with the United States and created the Bank of Canada in 1935.

Bennett's government went further and proposed a series of major collective insurance programs for the unemployed, the sick, and the elderly. Quebec and Ontario argued that these federal initiatives violated the 1867 constitution, under which the provinces had exclusive responsibility for social issues. The Privy Council in London agreed with them. The jurisdictional quarrel between the federal and provincial governments had only just begun! In 1937, Ottawa set up the Rowell-Sirois Commission to find a solution.

Direct relief

In Quebec, the Liberal government of Louis-Alexandre Taschereau also launched public works, but unemployment was so high that this initiative was not enough to end the crisis. A very limited number of jobs were available. Only fathers of families were eligible. As always happened, friends of the party in power were often favored. Everyone was trying to save his own skin.

But more was needed, and fast. Many families had nothing to put on the table and were barely able to heat their small apartments. A hastily designed program of "direct relief" was put together. Costs would be shared by all levels of government, but the program would be administered by municipalities, in cooperation with charitable associations.

Initially, there was no question of giving money to the unemployed. Instead, they received coupons to be used for food, firewood, and electricity. As time went on, checks were issued to the unemployed. Some municipalities required that recipients work on some public project, but most came to offer direct relief without asking anything in return.

This was a first step toward what would later be called the welfare state. But no one saw this social achievement as cause for celebration. For many fathers, receiving handouts from the government represented the ultimate humiliation.

Back to the land

Because the crisis was most prevalent in the cities, many people became convinced that the real solution was to settle the rural areas. People were starving in Montreal, so why not go live in the country! Despite his constant support for industrialization, Premier Taschereau was persuaded by the argument. "Let our unemployed workers from the cities go back to the land. Let us make colonists of them," he said in October 1931. In a letter published on July 10, 1932, the Quebec bishops saw it as "the most profound human solution."

The same year, the federal government offered a bounty of $600 to unemployed workers who decided to settle on the land. Three years later, the Quebec government instituted an ambitious program that included a series of bonuses for clearing land, building houses, and planting crops. Colonization societies got their second wind. The Lac-Saint-Jean, Abitibi, and Gaspé regions saw many "colonists" arrive with their families. During the 1930s, approximately 50,000 Quebecers participated in these colonization programs and founded nearly 150 parishes.

La Bolduc and Éva Circé-Côté: Two outstanding women

In this period of gloom, women played a key role. In town, many housewives administered the family budget, albeit with great difficulty. In addition to preparing meals and making clothing, some had no choice but to work outside the home. After all, the rent had to be paid. Although priests ranted against women who dared to "obstruct the family," many couples practiced techniques to space out pregnancies, to the extent that during the 1930s the birth rate decreased significantly.

During the Great Depression, some women distinguished themselves through song; others, through advocacy for greater social justice.

One such woman was someone who everyone familiarly called La Bolduc (1894–1941). The wife of fiddler Édouard Bolduc, born Mary-Rose-Anna Travers in Newport in the Gaspé, she was an immensely popular singer-songwriter during the 1930s. Her first album, recorded in 1929, sold more than 12,000 copies. She toured throughout Quebec, Acadia, and the United States. Singing in the informal language spoken by the people of Quebec, La Bolduc described the difficulties of the time with humor. Some of her songs gave

hope and invited people to be patient: *"Ça va venir pis ça va venir mais décourageons-nous pas / Moi j'ai toujours le cœur gai et j'continue à turlutter..."* ("The bad times will come, but they will not discourage us / I still have joy in my heart, and I continue to sing my songs..."). These well-known tunes were hummed everywhere!

Though less well known than La Bolduc and with social ideas that were shared by a small minority of educated Quebecers, Éva Circé-Côté (1871–1949) also stood out. An author and journalist, she wrote for many years under various pseudonyms — for the trade-union newspaper *Le Monde ouvrier,* she was Julien Saint-Michel. Her greatest cause was gender equality. In an article published in 1931, she deplored the fact that women who worked outside the home were often the first employees that companies would dismiss in times of crisis. The pretext? Heads of household should be favored. "In many homes," she explained, "the father squanders everything he earns, drinking most of his income, and does little more than make brief appearances at home. It is the mother and the girls who work to ensure the well-being of the little ones, pay the rent, heat, light, etc."

Whose fault is it?

Such an unprecedented crisis was fertile ground for the most subversive ideologies. Whether they attacked the bourgeoisie or the Jews, whether they were inspired by Russian Bolsheviks or Italian Fascists, revolutionaries on the left and right hoped to upend liberal democracies and establish authoritarian, even totalitarian regimes. In a number of European countries, Communist parties offered the sun and the moon. In Germany, Adolf Hitler's National Socialist Party took power in January 1933. Starting in 1936, Spain was in the grip of a terrible civil war in which the most extreme elements battled one another.

In Quebec, as elsewhere, the Great Depression led people to frustration and the depths of despair. People wanted to understand what was happening, and those who offered forceful solutions attracted the most attention. In such times of crisis and confusion, many dreamed of order and wanted to see a strong leader emerge. Liberal democracy was often blamed. Fortunately, the audience for these prophets who preached the renewal of the human race was actually quite small.

Jews and the bourgeoisie

On the fringe of Quebec's elites, there was real sympathy for the authoritarian regimes established by Mussolini in Italy, Salazar in Portugal, and soon Franco in Spain. These traditionalist regimes, close to some elements of the Catholic Church, appeared to have restored order. Nazism also had its followers, but they were rare. In 1934 an admirer of Hitler, Adrien Arcand, founded the Parti National Social Chrétien, which incorporated Nazi emblems, starting with the swastika. The enemy? Jews. "Jewry," he wrote in a pamphlet published in 1933, "because of its very essence, because of its destructive instincts, because of its age-old, ingrained corruption, because of its exclusively materialistic sense, is the greatest danger, the one, the only. . . ." His Canada-wide party, denounced by the major Quebec newspapers, had no more than 1,800 members.

Nor did the Communists gain a much larger audience in Quebec. Founded in 1921, the Communist Party of Canada followed the Russian Bolsheviks' line and promoted the dictatorship of the proletariat. However, they found it very difficult to recruit activists in Quebec. Quebec elites, with their attachment to Christianity, were repelled by the Communists' materialistic vision of social life. Inspired by the "antifascist" policy of the Comintern (an international communist organization), some English-speaking intellectuals in Montreal established the Mackenzie-Papineau Battalion and went to support the "republicans" in Spain. One of them, Dr. Norman Bethune, also became a close friend of Mao Zedong and accompanied Mao on his Long March.

Down with the electricity trust

The *trusts* (the handful of companies that controlled key sectors of the economy) were a favorite target of Quebec elites during the 1930s. The opposition to finance capitalism, to the propertied minority that was mostly English or foreign, and to Liberal politicians, some of whom (starting with Premier Taschereau) sat on boards of large companies, crystallized around these trusts.

The fiercest opposition was to the electricity trust, which many saw as controlling a natural resource that was vital for the economic future of Quebec. To reduce the pressure, the Quebec government set up a commission to study electricity, chaired by Quebec's most prominent federal Liberal MP, Ernest Lapointe, but ended up simply creating a permanent Quebec Electricity Commission in 1935.

"We will have our French State"

As the Depression continued unabated, young people developed a generational awareness. Many felt that the Depression reflected the failure of the older generation. In their eyes, the new generation would restore order and justice to a troubled world. Some dreamed of a great national recovery. A group of intellectuals founded "Jeune-Canada" in 1932 and published their articles in *L'Action Nationale*. The *Jeunesses Patriotes* (Patriotic Youth) and writers for the newspaper *La Nation* and the magazine *Vivre* openly advocated the separation of Quebec from Canada. Some of their work was xenophobic or anti-Semitic. Many of these young people dreamed of a strong leader. Such a leader would have a coherent body of thought like the historian Lionel Groulx, who gave a resounding speech on June 29, 1937, in which he declared, "Whether or not others want it, our French State, we will have."

"See, judge, act!"

Other young people became involved in a new form of Catholic social apostolate: Catholic Action. Intellectuals from this movement founded the magazine *La Relève* in March 1934. The most committed became active in Catholic Action associations founded during the 1930s — the Jeunesse Ouvrière Catholique, the Jeunesse Étudiante Catholique, or the Jeunesse Agricole Catholique — through which they developed a new concept of social commitment.

Their motto? See, judge, act! These young Catholics rejected both uncontrolled liberalism and authoritarian solutions. They believed that the crisis was, above all, moral and spiritual. However, the world could be saved if lay Christians could work with the faithful. Their ways of seeing often brought them into conflict with the hierarchy, which was eager to maintain its influence over believers and was often more fatalistic in outlook.

The Union Nationale

Faced with the Depression of the 1930s, the Liberal government was at the end of its rope. Even though it won 55.6 percent of the vote and 79 seats in the 1931 election, the Taschereau government was worn out and out of steam. In power since 1897, the Liberals controlled the major newspapers and practiced an effective system of patronage. But the domination of the Liberal Party was nearing its end.

The opposition gets organized

Criticizing the government was one thing; proposing a solid and credible alternative was another. In terms of ideas and policies, the Depression was an exuberant period. Each group had its own agenda and proposals. What remained was to bring these energies together into a broad political movement.

The Conservative Party discredited

Quebec Conservatives had never really recovered from the conscription crisis. From 1922 to 1929, they were led by Arthur Sauvé, who made no effort to distinguish his party from its federal big brother. His successor, Camillien Houde, raised some hope.

Mayor of Montreal and an effective speaker, the new Conservative leader channeled the resentment of low-wage earners. Houde came from humble origins and had been a bank clerk, representative of a biscuit company, and an insurance agent. As the populist leader of the Opposition, he had the appearance of a leader and it was thought that he could embody the anger of a scorned people. Though he was reelected repeatedly as mayor of Montreal, his star faded quickly on the Quebec scene. Defeated in the 1931 election, he resigned in September 1932.

Maurice Duplessis enters the scene

Maurice Duplessis (1890–1959) grew up in Trois-Rivières in a prominent family. His father, close to the ultramontanes, was a Conservative MP in the late 19th century and then a Superior Court judge. The young Duplessis became a lawyer and followed in his father's footsteps. After being narrowly defeated in the 1923 Quebec election, this confirmed bachelor did not give up. Deeply rooted in the region, he put his engaging personality and determination at the service of his political ambition. He was elected to the Legislature in 1927, winning a riding that had been a Liberal fiefdom for 27 years. The highly partisan Duplessis attacked the Liberals relentlessly and became one of their toughest opponents in the Legislature. In October 1933, he was elected leader of the Conservative Party. To gain power, this skilled parliamentarian had to develop a credible program for governing and rally the active forces of the opposition — not an easy task!

In search of a third way

To accomplish this difficult task, Duplessis could count on Catholic and nationalist intellectuals who developed a *Programme de Restauration Sociale* (Social Restoration Program). Brought together in the École Sociale Populaire, these intellectuals were inspired by innovations in the social doctrine of the church that had been made public in 1931. Although they were not tied to the Conservative Party, Duplessis would later use their ideas for his election platform.

Their program offered a third way. The deleterious effects of uncontrolled liberalism had been demonstrated, but the great totalitarian revolutions did not offer a humane and Christian alternative. The *Programme de Restauration Sociale* advocated increased government involvement. But instead of wholesale nationalization, its authors proposed a system that would better plan economic development by bringing together experts and representatives of major institutions in society in an economic council that would assist the government. A majority of Quebec elites of the time favored this "corporatist" solution.

A new party: The Action Libérale Nationale

This program also pleased some Liberals, and not the least prominent ones. Paul Gouin, a respected poet and the son of a former Liberal premier, openly distanced himself from the Taschereau government. In a lecture delivered before an audience of young Liberals on April 23, 1934, he argued that "we must democratize and reliberalize the Liberal Party."

Along with other dissident Liberals, Gouin founded the Action Libérale Nationale (ALN) in July 1934. The new party quickly rallied major players such as Édouard Lacroix, a businessman from the Beauce and Liberal Party fundraiser; Ernest Grégoire, the new mayor of Quebec City; and especially Philippe Hamel, a dentist and professor at Laval University. Since the 1920s, Hamel had been criticizing the electric companies' exorbitant rates and their fear campaigns against nationalization, which he favored. His well-documented arguments had a far-reaching political effect and hurt the Liberal government.

At mass meetings held across Quebec and through radio broadcasts, the ALN attacked the "old parties," slush funds, and trusts. Their program, close to the ideas of the École Sociale Populaire, was ambitious, but it was more reformist than revolutionary, and more conservative than reactionary. It called for the following:

- **Rediscovery of Quebec's agricultural vocation:** For the new party, colonization was not only a circumstantial solution to the crisis. It viewed rural life as healthier and more moral than urban life. To facilitate the return to a rural, farm-based lifestyle, it proposed establishing farm credit, electrifying rural areas, and organizing farmers into guilds.

- **Better protection for workers:** To help workers, the party proposed adoption of a labor code, disability insurance, healthier housing, and vigorous application of the Sunday Observance Act.

- **Economic nationalism:** The ALN intended to fight all trusts, starting with electricity, and did not exclude the possibility of nationalization if that was the only way to lower prices. It proposed a ban on politicians holding shares of companies receiving government contracts.

The fall of the Taschereau government

The establishment of the ALN raised a lot of hope, but its leaders feared that a divided opposition would make it impossible to oust the ruling Liberals. To avoid splitting the vote, Paul Gouin and Maurice Duplessis signed an agreement providing that, in each riding, only one opposition candidate would face the Liberal candidate. This "Gouin-Duplessis" alliance produced excellent results. In the election of November 25, 1935, the Liberals won 48 seats, only six more than the opposition. This narrow victory greatly weakened the Taschereau regime.

On May 7, 1936, Duplessis convened the Public Accounts Committee of the Legislative Assembly. The leader of the official opposition called Premier Taschereau's officials, cronies, and family members to testify. Damning revelations showed, in black and white, that patronage had reached inordinate levels and that public funds were sometimes diverted to private ends. Irénée Vautrin, the former minister of colonization, was the target of numerous attacks, as was Antoine Taschereau, accountant of the Legislative Assembly and brother of the premier.

On June 11, 1936, Premier Taschereau submitted his resignation to the lieutenant governor. Elections were triggered immediately. A triumphant Maurice Duplessis said mockingly, "With a government this dissolute, dissolution was necessary!"

A new regime is installed

For the first time since the beginning of the century, the Liberal regime was in a weakened state. As soon as Duplessis suspended the work of the Public Accounts Committee, he started in earnest to put together a formidable electoral machine. But the game was far from won. Adélard Godbout, Taschereau's successor, was a talented politician.

A party, a program, a leader!

Maurice Duplessis approached the ALN and proposed that it merge with the Conservative Party to create one big party, the Union Nationale. This proposal was rejected by Paul Gouin but supported by most members of his caucus, including Philippe Hamel. On June 20, 1936, the new party was officially launched in Sherbrooke. The election campaign that followed was an impassioned one. In late July, the Union Nationale published its *Catéchisme des électeurs* (Catechism for Voters), inspired by the short catechism that all Quebec Catholic students were required to memorize. An extremely effective propaganda document, the Union Nationale's platform was distributed to all households.

On August 17, 1936, Duplessis's party won a resounding victory. The Union Nationale captured 57.5 percent of the vote and 76 seats. This election resounded like a thunderclap in the firmament of Quebec politics. The Liberals had been in power for 39 years. Many believed that the election would finally make it possible to emerge from the Depression.

First resignations

Forming a cabinet was the first test of the new premier. Philippe Hamel, apostle of the nationalization of hydroelectric companies and scourge of the trusts, expected to receive a key position. But Duplessis offered him a position as minister without portfolio or speaker of the Assembly, shutting him out of major economic decisions.

Feeling betrayed, Hamel resigned, taking several nationalist deputies with him. This reversal did not surprise Lionel Groulx, who had always been wary of Duplessis. He wrote to one of the members who resigned, "He does not have enough personality to be of his time. . . . We must mourn the great national policy of which we had dreamed."

Civil service purges

During the three years that followed, the new government didn't propose a "great national policy." Its patronage practices were the same as those of the previous government. As soon as it came into office, staff was dismissed from the Provincial Police and the Liquor Commission. Of 6,613 appointments made between 1936 and 1939, only 120 were reappointments of staff employed under the former Liberal government. To keep or obtain a job in the public service, you had to be a Union Nationale supporter. Although Maurice Duplessis had at one time been legal counsel to Shawinigan Water & Power, the new government's links with big business were not as tight as the Liberal government's had been. A law now prohibited ministers from sitting on boards of directors.

Significant reforms

Even if it disappointed the most ardent reformers and militant nationalists, the first Union Nationale government nevertheless compiled a significant legislative record:

- ✔ **Agricultural credit:** Farmers were the Union Nationale's electoral base. One of the government's first measures addressed them directly. Thanks to the agricultural credit program established by the new regime in the fall of 1936, farmers could more easily consolidate their debts and get their children set up on adjacent land.

- ✔ **Pensions for needy mothers:** Working-class advocates had long been calling for assistance for widows and women abandoned by their husbands. Innovating in the social sphere, the new government adopted a pension program for needy mothers. To be eligible, however, a mother was required to obtain a certificate from her priest confirming her good character and irreproachable morality.

- ✔ **The National Electricity Syndicate:** Duplessis did not nationalize any of Quebec's hydroelectric companies. Like many conservatives of his time, Duplessis instinctively associated nationalization with socialism. He placed more trust in local initiatives and market forces. But he recognized that rural electrification, especially in remote areas, would require government intervention. Therefore, the new government established the National Electricity Syndicate. To better serve farmers in the Abitibi region, a small plant was built near Cadillac.

The work of Marie-Victorin

The Duplessis government replaced direct relief with public works. To obtain government assistance, the unemployed would have to work. Throughout Quebec, they contributed to major projects. They built a highway linking Chicoutimi with Tadoussac and a civic center in Trois-Rivières. In Montreal, 5,000 men were conscripted to transform Île Sainte-Hélène into a recreational park, and more than 10,000 men transformed part of Maisonneuve Park into a Botanical Garden.

This beautiful garden, comparable to large landscaped gardens in cities like London or New York, was a work conceived and coordinated by Conrad Kirouac (1885–1944), known as Brother Marie-Victorin, a member of the Christian Brothers. From a very young age, he devoted himself to the study of the flora of southern Quebec. He taught at the Collège de Longueuil and in the Faculty of Science at the University of Montreal. Cofounder in 1923 of the Association Canadienne-Française pour l'Avancement des Sciences (ACFAS; French-Canadian Association for the Advancement of Science), he published *La flore laurentienne* in 1935. This monumental work earned him international recognition and inspired a generation of scientists in Quebec. The Botanical Garden opened its doors for the first time in 1939, and it remains one of Montreal's major attractions.

Beware the Communists!

The most striking legislation adopted by the new regime targeted the Communists. The Padlock Law, passed in March 1937, gave the attorney general the power to close any facility or seize any publication promoting Communist propaganda. All but two members of the Legislative Assembly supported the new law. The law was strictly enforced and gave rise to 124 confiscation orders. Premier Duplessis sometimes used it to undermine the democratic, anti-Communist left.

The trade unions and the Civil Liberties Union, led by Professor Frank R. Scott of McGill University, tried in vain to persuade the federal government to disavow the law. In 1957, the Supreme Court declared it illegal — not because it attacked freedom of association and expression, but because it infringed on the jurisdiction of the federal government, which had sole responsibility for criminal law.

A new alliance between church and state

The Padlock Law was the occasion for a reconciliation between the Union Nationale and the Catholic Church, which had long called for such a measure. Clearly, Premier Duplessis wanted his party and his government to be associated with Catholicism. In October 1936, he installed a crucifix above the speaker's throne in the Legislative Assembly, an important decision on a symbolic level. The goal was to show that, contrary to previous Liberal governments, the new regime would comply with the principles of Christian morality.

The miracles of Brother André

Alfred Bessette (1845–1937), known as Brother André, was a member of the Congregation of Holy Cross. He was in frail health and could barely read and write. At Collège Notre-Dame in Montreal, he was the jack of all trades — he acted as porter and barber and ran errands. He also welcomed the poor and needy.

During the 1870s, many patients reported being healed by Brother André. His methods were always the same: a few drops of olive oil and a prayer to St. Joseph, declared patron saint of the Universal Church by Pope Pius IX in 1870. His reputation as a healer spread like wildfire. People came from all over to see Brother André.

To meet the demand, a chapel and a huge shrine were built on the northwest slope of Mount Royal. When he died in January 1937, more than a million people paid their respects. On October 17, 2010, 50,000 Quebecers gathered in Olympic Stadium to celebrate the canonization of Brother André by Pope Benedict XVI.

During a major Eucharistic Congress held in June 1938, Premier Duplessis offered the primate of the Canadian Church a ring and declared his "filial affection" to the Catholic religion. Cardinal Villeneuve responded with an astonishing statement: "I recognize in this ring the symbol of the union of religious authority and civil authority."

Part IV

The Quiet Reconquest (1939–1967)

In this part . . .

Progress through politics. . . . The war brought the economic stagnation of the 1930s and the emigration of French Canadians to the United States to an end once and for all. Quebec's economy recovered and became more modern and more urban than ever before. Education became compulsory, and women finally got the right to vote! Torn between their attachment to tradition and their desire to "catch up" to other Western societies, Quebecers swung back and forth between the Union Nationale and the Liberals. For the first time in their history, they began to have faith in politics. They saw that instead of dividing them, politics might be able to save them, by putting an end to their economic inferiority — and making it possible for them to become "masters in their own house."

Chapter 14

War (1939–1944)

● ●

In This Chapter

▶ Considering Canada's entry into the war and its impact on Quebec

▶ Admiring Adélard Godbout's courageous reforms

● ●

*I*n September 1939, World War II broke out. This conflict, fought on a global scale, awakened the old conscription demons in Quebec and led to a referendum. At the same time, the war effort mobilized the Quebec economy, putting an end to the terrible Depression of the 1930s.

The year 1939 was also marked by the Liberals' return to power in Quebec. Their leader, Adélard Godbout, was a reformer, open to new ideas. Quebecers have him to thank for bold reforms, greater equity between women and men, and significant changes in education. At the end of his term, however, many people accused him of having been a poor defender of Quebec's interests within Confederation.

The Shadow of Conscription

On September 1, 1939, Nazi Germany invaded Poland. For democracies in Western Europe, this was too much. Hitler had already annexed Austria and taken over Czechoslovakia. At the Munich Conference in 1938, he had sworn that he would curb his appetite for conquest. Scarred by the carnage of World War I, the French and British leaders hesitated for a long time before involving their countries in another world war. But this new affront by Hitler gave them no choice. On September 3, 1939, France and Britain declared war on Germany. Another nightmare was beginning. . . .

The election of 1939

Formally autonomous since 1931, Canada had become the sole master of its foreign policy. Its government could decide to stay out of the conflict and follow an isolationist path. That's what the United States did, but Canada's Liberal prime minister, William Lyon Mackenzie King, decided otherwise. On September 10, 1939, it was Canada's turn to officially declare war on Germany.

To participate or remain neutral?

Quebec did not give its undivided support to the federal government's decision. Liberal MP Maxime Raymond fiercely opposed the declaration of war. He said Canada should remain neutral, like Ireland or South Africa. "Why would we be fighting? Not to defend Canada's territory," he explained in the House of Commons, "It has not been attacked or threatened. . . . We have no commitments with respect to Poland." The power of Hitler and his government was the result of Western policy: "During the last 20 years, England has been the best champion of German recovery." Above all, Canada's entry into the war risked breaking up the country, as it did in 1917, as "any participation will logically lead to conscription, in the event of a long war."

Conscription — the word had been spoken! The French-Canadian lieutenant in the Mackenzie King government, Ernest Lapointe, believed that the relationship between Canada and Great Britain was too close and neutrality was impossible. But he promised that his government would not impose conscription. On behalf of his Quebec colleagues, he said, "We will never be members of a government that tries to implement conscription. . . . Is that clear enough?"

Duplessis calls an election

Well, it was not clear enough for Maurice Duplessis, the premier of Quebec, so he called a snap election on the question of conscription. In the view of the Union Nationale leader, the issues were crystal clear: A vote for the Liberals "is a vote for participation and conscription. A vote for Duplessis is a vote for autonomy and against conscription." Throughout the campaign, the premier played the nationalist card. Duplessis argued that re-electing his government, firmly committed to Quebec's autonomy, would be the best defense against conscription. This position led to the resignation of two English candidates from his own party.

The Union Nationale is defeated

Adélard Godbout, the Quebec Liberal leader, remained unruffled. In his view, Duplessis was just trying to make people forget his poor record. As for the draft, that decision rested with the federal government, not the Quebec government. As long as Liberal cabinet ministers such as Ernest Lapointe served in the federal cabinet, Quebecers had nothing to fear. Godbout went further. He promised to leave his party "and even oppose it if one French Canadian, from now until the end of hostilities in Europe, is mobilized against his will." For their part, Lapointe and the federal Liberal ministers threatened to resign if the Union Nationale was returned to power.

These arguments — some would say blackmail — bore fruit. With 54 percent of the popular vote and 70 seats, Godbout's Liberals won a dramatic victory on the evening of October 25, 1939. In the end, it's reasonable to think that the Liberal position was a fair reflection of the position of most Quebecers, who were generally in favor of participating in the war but opposed to conscription.

Prosperity returns!

The election of the Union Nationale had raised a lot of hope in 1936. In particular, people hoped that the Duplessis team would put an end to the Depression. But it was the war that would allow Quebec, and North America as a whole, to come out of the ordeal. To support Great Britain, France, and Canada in the war effort, the arms and supply industries went into high gear. In a few years, the number of Canadian soldiers increased from 9,000 to 800,000. Not only did unemployment rapidly decrease, but also with the departure of men to the front, labor was scarce. As happened during the previous war, women were called in as reinforcements. The clergy were not in favor of this development; they accused working mothers of abandoning their homes and neglecting their families.

During the war years, there were more strikes because unions had the upper hand in negotiating better working conditions, including a 45-hour work week. In 1944, the Quebec government passed the milestone Labour Relations Act, which governs the union certification process, requires employers to bargain "in good faith," and forces the parties into arbitration when negotiations stall.

General mobilization

On May 10, 1940, Hitler launched an attack on Western democracies. Within a few weeks, he invaded Holland, violated Belgium's neutrality, and won a crushing victory against France.

Shock: France has fallen

Even though the relationship between Quebec and France at the time was fairly remote (despite the links among some intellectuals and artists, or the growing number of students who spent time in Paris), France's defeat created shock waves in Quebec. This "intimate turmoil" surprised the young intellectual André Laurendeau, who believed that the attachment to the ancestral homeland only applied to a small elite. But in June 1940, he noted, the crowds in Montreal "felt the pain, disappointment, perhaps a bit of shame: the French name, with which they felt solidarity, had been shaken."

Quebecers torn between Pétain and de Gaulle

On August 1, 1940, General Charles de Gaulle, who had gone to London to continue the fight against the Nazi invaders, appealed to French Canadians: "The soul of France calls to you and seeks your help." The leader of Free France hoped Quebecers would mobilize and support the former mother country.

During World War II, two men spoke in the name of France: the old Marshal Philippe Pétain and General Charles de Gaulle. Pétain resigned himself to working with Hitler instead of fighting a merciless war. He saw France's defeat as a result of poor policy choices, the pervasiveness of the Jews, and moral laxity. Pétain suspended democratic freedoms and broke with republican ideals. For his part, de Gaulle believed the defeat of France was due solely to military failure. With British support, he tried to rally the French colonial empire to his cause.

The traditionalist elites of Quebec, long hostile to the ideals of the republic, were initially attracted by Marshal Pétain's "national revolution." Finally, someone had revived the Catholic France of Louis XIV's *Grand Siècle!* But when they saw that Petain's government was a puppet regime doing Hitler's bidding, the support of these elites declined. Although a few diehards remained loyal to the marshal, even helping some of the regime's sympathizers after the war, the majority soon saw de Gaulle as the only authentic representative of France.

A controversial federal law

Immediately after the French defeat became known, on June 18, 1940, the Mackenzie King government announced adoption of the National Resources Mobilization Act. This legislation established compulsory military service, but only for the defense of Canada; overseas service remained voluntary. Only able-bodied single men would be called. Initially, recruits underwent 30 days of training — soon increased to four months — and then returned to go about their business. After 1941, men were required to serve indefinitely.

To evade the law, many couples decided to hasten their nuptials. During the summer of 1940, the stadium in Montreal's Jarry Park was stormed by newly-weds simultaneously celebrating their eternal union.

The mayor of Montreal — in prison!

For Quebec nationalists, this federal law was a first step toward conscription. On June 19, 1940, MLA René Chaloult introduced a motion in the legislature reaffirming Quebec's opposition to conscription. Despite his solemn commitment during the 1939 election campaign, Premier Godbout voted against the motion. He declared emphatically, "If, at the moment that Canada itself is threatened, the Canadian government did not ask each of its sons to fulfill his duty and give every last drop of his blood in the defense of the country, it would be remiss."

Godbout's extreme position raised the pressure a notch. On August 2, 1940, the mayor of Montreal and independent member of the legislature for Montreal-Sainte-Marie, Camillien Houde, spoke openly against "national registration" and encouraged citizens to disobey the federal law. Despite wartime censorship by the federal authorities, two Montreal newspapers, *The Gazette* and *La Patrie,* reported the act of defiance by the former Quebec Conservative leader. On August 6, 1940, the mayor was arrested as he left City Hall and sent to Camp Petawawa in Ontario. He joined other — much less desirable — political prisoners, including Adrien Arcand, the pro-Nazi leader of the National Unity Party of Canada. Houde would not be released until August 14, 1944.

Were all Quebecers deserters?

For isolationists, most of whom were associated with the Quebec nationalist movement, fear of conscription was an effective weapon. They overlaid their memories of the previous world war onto the second one. Wary of the old British imperialism, they feared that French-Canadian soldiers would be used as cannon fodder. But the fall of France and the spectacular success Hitler achieved up to January 1943 gave ammunition to supporters of an increased contribution to the war effort. Among these was Cardinal Jean-Marie-Rodrigue Villeneuve, who in July 1941 agreed to be photographed at the wheel of a military vehicle. The primate of the Catholic Church considered Hitler the embodiment of evil and tried to convince his compatriots to take part in this great struggle for the defense of Christianity and freedom.

Over the course of World War II, 131,618 Quebecers would volunteer. Proportionately, this was fewer than in other provinces but more than in World War I. The volunteers' motivations were less patriotic than material. After the hard years of the Depression, many sought a stable income, wanted to receive a free education, and dreamed of adventure. Because of the debates about conscription, these volunteers would be forgotten or all but ignored on their return.

The 1942 vote

On December 7, 1941, the Japanese attacked U.S. bases at Pearl Harbor in Hawaii. On December 11, it was Germany's turn to declare war on the United States. Meanwhile, Hitler's troops were fighting on the Russian front, and the Nazi authorities were preparing to endorse the Final Solution, which would result in the extermination of six million Jews.

The German enemy was at Quebec's doorstep. In the spring of 1942, fisher-men in the Gaspé noticed "stovepipes" emerging from the waters of the St. Lawrence. They were not hallucinating! These were real periscopes attached to U-boats, the dangerous German submarines that were sinking ships from the merchant marine, whose mission was to resupply Great Britain. In total, 28 attacks were identified with 23 ships sunk and hundreds of people dead.

Divided Liberals

For many English Canadians, the situation was clear: The Canadian govern-ment absolutely must employ conscription; mobilizing volunteers was not enough. To defeat the Nazi enemy, Canada had to give its all. The pressure on Prime Minister Mackenzie King was very strong. The only problem: He had made a formal commitment to Quebecers never to introduce conscription. But the prime minister was a clever politician, and he decided to appeal to the people and ask the voters to release him from his commitments. On April 27, 1942, all Canadians were asked to answer the following question: "Are you in favor of releasing the Government from any obligations arising out of any past commitments restricting the methods of raising men for military service?"

The federal Liberals campaigned for a Yes vote, but those in Quebec were deeply divided. A dozen MPs and three Quebec Liberal ministers called for a No vote. Premier Godbout remained fairly quiet throughout the campaign.

The No forces

On February 11, 1942, the Ligue pour la Défense du Canada (League for the Defense of Canada) launched its manifesto. The main arguments for the No vote were as follows:

- **Defend Canada first.** The primary task of the army was not to rescue allies but to protect Canada's population and territory.

- **There are enough volunteers.** The army was finding it difficult to absorb the many volunteers who wanted to fight.

- **Human resources in Canada are limited.** Because Canada is not a very populous country, we shouldn't bleed it dry.

The League mobilized all the nationalist forces in Quebec. Its representatives spoke at numerous meetings across the province. In Quebec, the No side won 72 percent of the vote, while in the rest of Canada the Yes side garnered 80 percent. Canada emerged very divided from this vote, as it had been in 1917. Mackenzie King was well aware of this division. The Canadian military didn't resort to using conscripted troops until November 1944. All in all, 16,000 sol-diers conscripted against their will were sent to Europe. Of these, 2,500 took part in combat.

All eyes on Quebec

During World War II, British Prime Minister Winston Churchill and U.S. President Franklin Delano Roosevelt met several times to coordinate major military operations against Nazi Germany.

In August 1943 and September 1944, the meetings took place in Quebec City. At the second conference, they discussed the progress of Allied troops on the western front. Although Prime Minister Mackenzie King was the official host, he didn't take part in the discussions. Churchill believed that he alone spoke for the British Empire and its various dominions. Newsreels broadcast around the world offered beautiful images of Quebec City and gave the city international visibility.

Summit meetings were held at the Citadel, the residence of Canada's governor general, and the Château Frontenac. This luxurious hotel named in honor of a famous governor of New France, which opened on December 18, 1893, offered tourists a breathtaking view of the St. Lawrence River.

The Bloc Populaire

Proud of their success, the No activists wanted to take advantage of the fervor created by the vote. Former leaders of the Action Libérale Nationale who felt betrayed by Maurice Duplessis, along with a new nationalist guard, dreamed of a great national party that would be independent of secret campaign funds. The Bloc Populaire announced its platform in 1943. Respect for provincial jurisdiction and retrocession of Labrador to Quebec were among its more notable promises. At the time of its launch, the new party seemed to have a promising future. Early polls revealed strong support. But election results would be disappointing. The Quebec wing won only four seats in 1944, while the federal wing won two the following year.

Godbout the Reformer

While the war raged in Europe and conscription debates divided Quebec, the government of Adélard Godbout introduced many important reforms. When they were proposed, these changes generally shocked or disturbed traditionalists, who were suspicious of the state and defended the old order.

An international presence for Quebec

In April 1940, the Quebec government decided to open Quebec delegations in the major capitals of the world. If not for the war, Paris and London would've had their Quebec delegations in the 1940s.

Quebec thus renewed the international presence it had briefly had in the past. From 1882 to 1912, it was represented in Paris by an "agent general," a position held until 1910 by Senator Hector Fabre. From 1908 to 1936, Quebec had a general agency in London. Its mandate was to defend the rights of provincial legislatures before the Privy Council, which had long acted as Canada's highest court of justice.

In 1941, the Quebec government sent a sales agent to New York. This office would become Quebec's largest delegation in the United States. In 1943, an economic mission was sent to Haiti. The objective was to raise awareness of Quebec in the tourist industry, then in its infancy. It also aimed to attract economic investment.

Women get the vote!

Most Catholic societies gave women the right to vote later than Protestant countries. France first allowed it in 1944, Portugal and Italy in 1945, Belgium in 1948. In all these traditionally Catholic countries, the church was opposed to this measure. Quebec was no exception.

The new feminists

During the 1920s and 1930s, a new generation of feminists took up the fight for the right of women to vote. Idola Saint-Jean, who taught French at McGill University and published the magazine *Sphère Féminine,* founded the Alliance Canadienne pour le Vote des Femmes (Canadian Alliance for the Women's Vote) in 1927. Two years later Thérèse Casgrain, the wife of a politician and daughter of a bourgeois family, founded the Ligue des Droits de la Femme (Women's Rights League). These feminists were more focused on equal rights between men and women than their predecessors had been. Yes, most women are mothers, they said, but it's primarily as citizens that they should have the right to vote.

The activism of these movements led to significant gains. Women could now become guardians of children and keep their wages or property acquired before marriage. But voting rights had yet to be adopted. Feminists succeeded in placing a commitment to give women the vote in the Quebec Liberal Party's platform at its June 1938 convention.

The opposition goes to the barricades

In his first throne speech, Premier Godbout announced that he would introduce a bill on voting rights for women. The reactions were not long in coming. Cardinal Villeneuve believed that such legislation would "go against family unity and hierarchy," in addition to exposing "women to all the passions and all the adventures of electioneering." As he saw it, the majority of women did not claim this right. The head of the Catholic Church in Quebec was able to point to the position of the Catholic Women's League and the Cercles de Fermières, which, surprisingly, also opposed the measure. These women feared that the participation of mothers in political debates would cause discord in families. At this point, the positions of both sides were so entrenched that a Liberal member proposed holding a referendum on the issue.

"The equal of men"

The cardinal's criticism rattled the premier a bit, and he briefly considered resigning. But he pulled himself together and pressed forward. It's worth noting that most nationalists, who had once been strongly opposed to women's right to vote, rallied. On April 11, 1940, the premier delivered a passionate plea for his bill. "The conditions in which we live make women equal to men," he explained. Women now had the same duties and obligations as men, and nearly 100,000 of them worked outside the home. So, it was natural that they should contribute more concretely to political discussion, he argued. The premier believed that women, often better educated than men, would also "raise the level of our discussions." Godbout's legislation was adopted on April 25, 1940. The following year, he extended the right to vote to the municipal level and allowed women to practice law.

Compulsory education

An agronomist by training and a respected teacher at the Collège de Sainte-Anne-de-la-Pocatière, Adélard Godbout attached great importance to education. He founded the Conservatoire de Musique et d'Art Dramatique (Conservatory of Music and Drama) and the Superior Council of Technical Education and inaugurated the University of Montreal's new buildings on the north slope of Mount Royal. Since 1875, education had not really been a matter for the state. The church and school boards were in charge of programs and infrastructure.

Old resistance

Once cause was particularly close to Godbout's heart: compulsory education. The subject had long been sensitive. Honoré Mercier had believed as early as 1881 that the province should go in that direction. He saw this as the only way to "overcome parents' resistance or indifference" to school attendance. The ultramontane Catholics, fearing a takeover by atheists, were strongly opposed to compulsory education. In their view, the decision to educate children belonged to parents, not the state. Despite the risk that there would be impassioned debates on the issue, the premier decided to go ahead.

The problem of absenteeism

But before moving ahead, it was important to be informed. The data for the year 1941–1942 were very alarming. The government discovered that the rate of student absenteeism was very high: almost 10 percent of children aged 6 to 14 were not enrolled in any school. For many parents, school did not seem to be a priority. In rural areas, many farmers needed their oldest children to lend a hand on the farm and believed that what was essential was to be able to read and write.

Coercion seemed to be the only avenue to combat this mentality, making compulsory education a necessity. The need for this solution was also clear to the business world and even the church, provided that parents could continue to opt for the school of their choice for their children. And while the Union Nationale, along with some traditionalists, opposed compulsory education for children aged 6 to 14, the measure was introduced in 1943 and never challenged after that.

Economic achievements and federal incursions

Like all his predecessors, Premier Godbout had to face questions raised by Quebec nationalism, which arose in at least two ways: an economic dimension and a political dimension. Economically, many people wanted French-speaking people in Quebec to have more control over their natural resources and major industries. "We are proletarians, laborers, fodder for factories," lamented Victor Barbeau in 1936. "We are a people of small shop assistants, petty officials, small workers, small bondholders, a nation of little people." Politically, the defenders of Quebec's autonomy were adamant that the division of powers set out in the constitution of 1867 be respected. How did Adélard Godbout act with respect to these two dimensions of Quebec nationalism?

Establishment of Hydro-Quebec

Nationalization of some hydroelectric companies was in the Liberal leader's plans from 1941 on. The primary objective was to reduce electricity rates for everyone in the greater Montreal region, the economic heart of Quebec. Another objective was to enable French-Canadian engineers to develop expertise in the sector and occupy important positions within it. "We want to give our youth the opportunity to become masters in industries that will be entirely our own," Godbout said in 1941.

Creation of the Académie Canadienne-Française

In 1944, a group of writers founded the Académie Canadienne-Française. The founders included historians Lionel Groulx, Marie-Claire Daveluy, and Guy Frégault; poets Rina Lasnier and Alain Grandbois; and writers François Hertel and Ringuet. The literary community was already very dynamic. Magazines like *La Nouvelle Relève* and especially *Amérique Française* welcomed new writers working in various genres: poetry, travel memoirs, short stories, and novels. Many of these young writers made a living through soap operas broadcast by Radio-Canada and the Montreal radio station CKAC. In 1992, the Académie Canadienne-Française became the Académie des Lettres du Quebec.

Open to Quebec writers of all backgrounds, the Académie promotes French culture and the importance of literature.

The war years were a time of unprecedented growth for many Quebec publishers. From 1940 on, importing French books was no longer possible. Quebec publishers got permission from the Canadian government to reprint all the titles of the great French writers. Éditions de l'Arbre, founded in 1941 by Claude Hurtubise and Robert Charbonneau, enabled people all over the world to read French writers who had taken refuge abroad, such as Jacques Maritain, Georges Bernanos, and Antoine de Saint-Exupéry.

Three years later, he moved forward and nationalized Montreal Light, Heat & Power and its subsidiaries, to the great irritation of shareholders and Montreal's English daily newspapers. Maurice Duplessis denounced the "Bolshevik and tyrannical methods" of the Godbout government. The dams and the workforce of the former private company now came under the management of a new Crown corporation, Hydro-Quebec, which was also immediately given a mandate to accelerate rural electrification.

Federal centralization

This gesture of national affirmation was overshadowed by a series of setbacks for the Quebec government on some sensitive topics. Nationalism bent on revenge was anathema to Godbout, a sincere Canadian elected in large part thanks to the support of the federal Liberals, and he agreed to allow the federal government to encroach on jurisdictions that should have belonged exclusively to Quebec. Here are three examples:

- ✔ **Unemployment insurance (1940):** The Taschereau and Duplessis governments had never agreed to allow the federal government to take sole responsibility for an unemployment insurance program. Under the British North America Act, this was to be a provincial responsibility. In 1940, Mackenzie King raised the issue again, and finally succeeded in establishing this program after a constitutional amendment was approved by the provinces, including Quebec.

✔ **Personal income tax (1942):** The war effort made it necessary for the federal government to find new sources of revenue. The 1867 constitution provided that taxation of personal income would fall primarily under provincial jurisdiction. As a good sport, Adélard Godbout agreed to let the federal government tax individuals directly, but only for the duration of the war. As the tax collector for all Canadians, the federal government then distributed grants to the provinces. In the eyes of Opposition Leader Maurice Duplessis, this was "a real and irreparable breach in the wall of our provincial autonomy."

✔ **Family allowances (1944):** In 1944, the federal government, with the consent of the provinces including Quebec, launched a generous program of family allowances. The program created a new federal department directly involved in the social sector, which was supposed to be under provincial jurisdiction. The government check was sent directly to the mother.

All these federal actions coincided with the gradual emergence of the welfare state. In the minds of many English Canadians, Ottawa should coordinate the new government-run social programs. This view was also in line with the findings of the landmark Rowell-Sirois Report, released in 1940. The primacy of the federal government over the provinces, however, was completely antithetical to Quebecers' conception of Canadian federalism.

These concessions by Quebec, along with the federal Liberals' reversal on the issue of conscription, overshadowed the socioeconomic achievements of the Godbout government. The opposition forces had no trouble portraying Premier Godbout as Ottawa's puppet.

Chapter 15

Le Chef (1944–1959)

In This Chapter

▶ Looking at postwar prosperity and the nature of the Duplessis regime

▶ Fighting for Quebec's autonomy

▶ Considering the rise of opposition forces

The years following World War II were full of paradoxes. Like other Western societies, Quebec radically transformed during this period. A new middle class became part of the consumer society, discovered modern comfort, and absorbed new values — largely through television, which made its first appearance in Quebec homes in 1952. After the deprivation of the Depression years and the wrenching conscription controversy that followed (see Chapter 14), it was a time for renewal and optimism.

But new threats clouded this confidence in the future. Communist tyranny plunged the world into a cold war. Rapid social change led to anxiety and fear of disorder. Some people were afraid of a challenge to traditional institutions. This fear of cultural and social disturbances led a majority of Quebecers to place themselves in the hands of Maurice Duplessis and his Union Nationale, which completely dominated the postwar period.

Defending the Established Order

On May 8, 1945, World War II came to an end in Europe. The Allied armies fought fierce battles and finally reduced the barbaric Nazi regime to ashes. Japan surrendered only after two atomic bombs were dropped in August. Europe had been devastated by the repeated land battles and aerial bombardments, and reconstruction was the task at hand. Through the Marshall Plan, the United States provided generous financial support to the ravaged countries. In this way, the Americans sought to hold back the Soviet threat.

A regime in control

In the Quebec election of August 1944, the Union Nationale won a narrow victory. The electoral map, skewed toward rural areas, favored Duplessis's party, which won 11 more seats than the Liberals, even though it got fewer votes. It was just enough to gain power — which the Union Nationale maintained until June 1960. Most of the nationalists who had yielded to the temptation of the Bloc Populaire came back to the Union Nationale, and it won three more elections — in 1948, 1952, and 1956.

Jobs and babies

The conditions for Duplessis's long reign were highly favorable, in several respects:

- ✔ **Continued prosperity:** Postwar recovery benefited the Quebec economy. In 1947, the unemployment rate was 2.7 percent; ten years later, it had more than doubled, but at 6 percent was still very low by today's standards. There was strong growth in both the industrial and the service sector. Wage increases outpaced inflation, and family allowances were generous. Many middle-class families were able to buy homes, household appliances, and television sets. In 1953, 9.7 percent of Quebec households had TVs; five years later, that figure had climbed to 80 percent. In 1961, 90 percent of households had hot water, a "luxury" that only 50 percent of homes had had ten years earlier.

- ✔ **The baby boom:** In common with the whole Western world, postwar Quebec experienced a "baby boom," resulting from the combined effect of a slight increase in the birthrate and a precipitous decline in infant mortality. Widely available vaccines, better-quality water and milk, and improved medical care, especially around childbirth, all contributed to higher rates of infant survival. With these advances, life expectancy also increased, from 56 years in 1931 to 67 years in 1961 for men, and from 58 to 73 years for women.

- ✔ **An end to out-migration:** With this unprecedented prosperity, the exile of French Canadians to the United States came to an end. Furthermore, Quebec became a destination for many immigrants seeking to provide their children with a better life. These postwar immigrants came mostly from Europe. Waves of Polish, Portuguese, and Greek immigrants settled in some Montreal neighborhoods. Most often, these immigrants sought out the institutions of Montreal's English-speaking minority — which did not create social tensions at the time. Between 1946 and 1960, nearly 404,000 immigrants settled in Quebec. Quebec's population grew from 3.3 million in 1941 to 5.2 million in 1961.

A traditionalist vision

In 1936, reform movements brought the Union Nationale to power. But Maurice Duplessis had a different vision in the postwar era. It was no longer a time for criticizing capitalism or renewing democratic institutions; instead, the goal was to defend the established order and maintain stability at all costs. How was this to be done?

- ✔ **By protecting free enterprise:** Duplessis believed that in order to attract investors, the government had to intervene as little as possible, especially in the area of labor relations. The government's role was not to plan economic development or reduce inequality, but to provide basic infrastructure and ensure that order was maintained.

- ✔ **By forging alliances with traditional elites:** To maintain the social order, coercion through the law was not enough. Therefore, Duplessis relied on a close alliance with the clergy and the *notables* (local elites made up largely of doctors, lawyers, and notaries), who shared his paternalistic vision of power and had real influence on his rural electorate.

- ✔ **By defending tradition:** Duplessis believed that most of his compatriots were attached to their agricultural vocations, their churches, and their language. Defending these distinctive traits of the French-Canadian people was the motive behind his nationalism.

In Duplessis's view, criticizing the principles of his regime amounted to criticizing the province of Quebec as a whole. He was an artful politician who managed to insinuate that his detractors were peddling foreign ideas that came from Ottawa — and sometimes even from Moscow!

The cold war era

After the war, the Communist threat was a real one. The Soviet Union installed puppet regimes throughout Eastern Europe. In 1949, China fell into the Communist camp and provoked a war in Korea. Communist parties in France and Italy were gaining substantial support. The specter of nuclear confrontation became an obsession in the West, evoking fear that sometimes spilled over into paranoia.

In September 1945, Igor Gouzenko, a Soviet diplomat based in Ottawa, asked for political asylum and revealed the extent of the Russian spy network. The hunt for Communists launched by Senator Joseph McCarthy defined the early 1950s in the United States. Julius and Ethel Rosenberg, accused of having supplied the Russians with the scientific information that allowed them to build their first nuclear bomb, were executed in June 1953.

KEY DATE

Refus global

On August 9, 1948, in a small bookstore in Montreal, a group of young artists launched a manifesto entitled *Refus global (Total Rejection)*. It was written by their mentor, Paul-Émile Borduas, a teacher at the École du Meuble and an artist who was well known in avant-garde circles. Borduas was an abstract painter who drew his inspiration from the ideas of the surrealist movement, which had its origins in the 1920s. The surrealists believed in the mysteries of the unconscious and thought that the modern world had lost its way. They saw technique and cold reason as being responsible for the Great War. Most of them were rebels, and a few were revolutionaries. One, the writer Louis Aragon, became a Communist Party activist, while another, Pierre Drieu La Rochelle, became a fascist and supported collaboration with Hitler.

Borduas and his group founded a movement: the *automatistes*. Their manifesto was a merciless attack on traditional Quebec and the modern world:

> To hell with holy water and the French-Canadian tuque! . . . Enough brutal assassination of the present and future under repeated clubbings from the past. . . . Our duty is plain. We must break with the conventions of society once and for all, and reject its utilitarian spirit . . . MAKE WAY FOR MAGIC! MAKE WAY FOR OBJECTIVE MYSTERIES! MAKE WAY FOR LOVE!

The manifesto was a topic of discussion among a few intellectuals and journalists. Its ideas met with nearly unanimous disapproval. On October 21, Borduas was fired from the École du Meuble "for behavior and writings that are incompatible with the position of a teacher in an educational institution of the province of Quebec." This decision by the Duplessis government made few waves and passed almost unnoticed — as did the manifesto itself. It was only in the 1960s that Borduas would become one of the martyrs of the *grande noirceur* — the "great darkness" of the Duplessis period.

After he was fired, Borduas went into exile in Paris and New York, where he continued his work. Among his disciples, Jean-Paul Riopelle and Marcelle Ferron would be recognized as major painters.

As of 1937, Quebec had on its books the Act to Protect the Province against Communistic Propaganda, also known as the "Padlock Law." Duplessis sought to take advantage of every opportunity that arose to show that, in its own way, Quebec was contributing to the free world's struggle against Communism.

Censoring films

The premier had responsibility for the Bureau of Censorship, established in 1912. One of his notable decisions in this capacity was to ban the screening of *Our Northern Neighbour*, a wartime film made when Soviet Russia was fighting alongside the Allies against Hitler's armies. The ban was announced in August 1947. Duplessis criticized Canada's National Film Board for having made a feature film that dealt much too kindly with the Communist regime. With the cooperation of the church, a number of other films were subsequently censored because they represented a breach of moral standards or openly criticized Christian morality.

Protecting the Polish treasures

February 1948 was a time of intense activity in the struggle against Communism. On February 16, the Quebec provincial police shut down the offices of the Labor-Progressive Party, which was believed to be sympathetic to the Communist regimes. A few days later, Duplessis ordered the transfer of the Polish treasures held at the Hôtel-Dieu convent in Quebec City to the provincial museum. Among the more notable items in this collection of objects from Kraków were rare manuscripts, crown jewels, and tapestries. Representatives of the Polish government in exile had brought them to North America in 1940 to keep them safe from Nazi pillage. The treasures had been held in Ottawa for five years and then disappeared mysteriously when the Canadian government decided to recognize Communist Poland. For years, the Polish government tried to get these national treasures back, but in vain. Maurice Duplessis was on guard!

Harboring the Hungarian refugees

In October 1956, a few months after the Soviet Communist Party acknowledged Stalin's crimes, people in Budapest rebelled against Hungary's tyrannical regime. This uprising was soon suppressed by the Red Army. Nearly 200,000 Hungarians were killed and 160,000 went into exile in foreign countries.

Many immigrants arrived in Quebec during the years Duplessis was in power, but the premier refused to adopt an immigration policy with recruitment agencies in foreign countries and structures to welcome new arrivals. Such a policy could undoubtedly have made it easier for immigrants to integrate into the French-speaking majority, but in Duplessis's view these measures would've been too expensive and immigration was an exclusive responsibility of the federal government.

However, his government made one exception to this principle: helping "these unhappy victims of Bolshevism," the Hungarian refugees. In January 1957, the legislature passed a law providing for the establishment of the Provincial Relief Committee for Hungarian Refugees, along with a grant of $100,000 for the new agency.

The miners of Asbestos

It's one thing to fight Communism; it's quite another to see every worker who goes out on strike as part of the forces of subversion. The Duplessis regime frequently crossed that thin line. It rarely missed an opportunity to break a strike, even though, in the vast majority of cases, the workers simply wanted to share in the fruits of growth and democratize their workplace. Their goal was reform more than revolution. Some members of the clergy approved of their demands, and this created ripples in the church.

A dialogue of the deaf

The most dramatic and emblematic strike took place in the winter of 1949 in the small town of Asbestos in the Eastern Townships. Miners working for Canadian Johns-Manville demanded higher wages, the elimination of asbestos dust, automatic check-off of union dues (the Rand formula), and worker participation in the company's major decisions. The parties quickly dug in their heels. Company president Lewis H. Brown maintained that what the union was advocating was nothing less than "revolutionary doctrine." Maurice Duplessis accused the workers of having launched an "illegal" strike. Strikebreakers were hired, and their presence quickly provoked confrontations on the picket lines. Miners at other companies decided to walk out in solidarity. The town of Asbestos was completely paralyzed; nearly 5,000 workers were off the job. Strikers' families pleaded hunger.

A prominent supporter

On the international workers' holiday, May 1, 1949, the archbishop of Montreal, Joseph Charbonneau, called for solidarity: "Our heart is, and will remain, close to the working class." He demanded the adoption of a new labor code, more favorable to workers, and urged Catholics to support the strikers. Many churches organized special collections. Within a few days, $500,000 was collected to help families in Asbestos. Many people saw the archbishop's offensive as a challenge to the Duplessis regime. In any case, it was a first. The church and the Union Nationale, which had seemed to be in bed together, were now separated by a major disagreement. But the premier had no intention of moving an inch.

On May 5, with the archbishop's support and their compatriots' solidarity giving them strength, the strikers decided to block access to the town. The premier quickly dispatched 200 members of "his" provincial police force to Asbestos and had the Riot Act read. Duplessis felt that he was back on solid ground once Pope Pius XII himself intervened on May 7. A number of Quebec priests who were close to the corporate elite asked for his opinion, and they were not disappointed. The Sovereign Pontiff maintained that in the event of a strike or a labor conflict, the owners of companies had to "remain masters of their economic decisions."

A stinging defeat

A pastoral letter issued by the bishops in February 1950 still showed considerable openness to working-class demands. In the letter, the church denounced "the abuses of capitalism" and "economic liberalism," a system that did not always respect "the dignity of the person." However, the reform current within the church was muted and Duplessis won a total victory.

The church recalled Joseph Charbonneau under mysterious circumstances and replaced him with Paul-Émile Léger. The new archbishop was close to Pius XII and had ultramontane leanings. For him, a new evangelization of the masses was more important than workers' struggles, and he believed that the Catholic Church would be saved by families praying the rosary and an unceasing war on the degradation of urban life.

In Asbestos, the union members went back to work without having won their demands. Additional strikes at Louiseville (1952) and Murdochville (1957) were repressed by the Duplessis regime. But it was the Asbestos strike that would be imprinted in people's memories, and it was there that a number of young trade union leaders, intellectuals, and politicians waged their first battle.

Striving for Autonomy and Development

In a changing world, Maurice Duplessis stood as a guarantee of all that was solid and familiar. True to himself, he continued to defend the autonomy of Quebec fiercely. In his own way, he also encouraged Quebec's development. On these two fronts, he did not disappoint his supporters and his traditional electorate.

Income tax

It seems like a dry subject, but it's a crucial issue: Who has the power to tax personal income directly? From a strictly legal point of view, the 1867 constitution stipulates that this power belongs to the provinces, but the federal government is not excluded from it. During the war, in light of the enormous expenditures that the war effort involved, the federal government asked the provinces to renounce their power, promising to give it back as soon as the war was over. Premier Godbout agreed to this request in 1942. However, after the war, Ottawa invoked the needs of reconstruction as a reason for not giving up this important lever. Its game plan was to continue taxing citizens directly and then redistribute the money the provinces needed in the form of subsidies, pro rata according to their population.

Quebec adopts a flag

On January 21, 1948, at about three o'clock in the afternoon, a new flag flew over Quebec's parliament buildings. The decision had been made by Maurice Duplessis and was a surprise to everyone. "It is ordered," said the ministerial decree, "that the flag generally known under the name of the Fleurdelisé, that is the flag with a white cross on a blue field, and with fleur-de-lys, be adopted as the official flag of Quebec and flown on the central tower of the Parliament Building."

Many years of contention preceded this decision. The Canadiens first adopted a flag at the time of the 1837–1838 rebellions. This flag consisted of three horizontal bands (green for Ireland, white for France, and red for England), and it became a rallying point for the Patriotes who dreamed of founding a new republic. Some pro-independence activists still use this flag today in their patriotic demonstrations.

In the late 19th century, French-Canadian nationalist groups proposed a new flag, inspired by the one that Montcalm's troops carried during their brilliant victory at the battle of Carillon on July 8, 1758. This initial Fleurdelisé attained a degree of popularity, but some people objected to it. The church felt that the figure of the Sacred Heart should be added in the middle of the flag, while Duplessis would have preferred a touch of red to recognize the English presence. However, everyone accepted the solution that was finally agreed upon. As the premier explained, in contrast to the initial Fleurdelisé, the four fleurs-de-lys on the new flag would "in future stand up straight, pointing toward the sky, as a good indication of the value of our traditions and the force of our convictions."

No to "centralization"!

The federal position was formulated during two federal-provincial conferences held in August 1945 and May 1946. In a richly detailed presentation to the conference, the Quebec government explained its outright rejection of Ottawa's proposal. Quebec wanted to cooperate in the reconstruction of Canada, but without abdicating the powers provided for in the 1867 constitution. It argued in its presentation that "the sovereignty and autonomy of the provinces are the exact opposite of federal trusteeship." The federal representatives responded that what was involved was the "national" unity of Canada. Unimpressed by this rhetoric, Duplessis explained that "the federal proposals can only lead us inevitably to centralization." He was not the only provincial premier to argue along these lines. Ontario Premier George Drew was on the same wavelength.

Federal financing of universities? No way!

In 1951, the report of the Royal Commission on National Development in the Arts, Letters, and Sciences, appointed by the federal government, recommended increased federal financing of cultural institutions to counter the growing influence of American culture. Among these institutions, two were problematic: the Canadian Broadcasting Corporation, which launched its television service in 1952, and the universities. The commission argued that the universities were not under exclusive provincial jurisdiction because their goals included the "general" education of all Canadian citizens. Canada, the commission explained, is a "national entity" with its own "spiritual legacy": "It is the intangibles which give a nation not only its essential character but its vitality as well."

The report — one of whose authors was Father Georges-Henri Lévesque, dean of the faculty of social sciences at Laval University and a well-known Liberal sympathizer — got a very poor reception in Quebec. The problem wasn't just that it recommended infringing on a jurisdiction that belonged to Quebec. The whole vision of the report was one that saw Canada as a unitary country, with a single culture, and not as a pact between different nations. Hence, in 1953, the Duplessis government told the universities that they would not be allowed to receive even one cent from Ottawa. It was a matter of principle, the government said. And yet, the universities had pressing needs, as did the school boards and hospitals.

Quebec: A province like the others?

To generate new revenues and allow the Quebec government to breathe, Duplessis imposed a personal income tax in March 1954. As if it were trying to provoke a confrontation with Ottawa, his government included in its legislation the statement that "the Canadian constitution concedes to the provinces priority in the field of direct taxation." This statement was a red flag for the federal Liberals, then in power in Ottawa. Prime Minister Louis Saint-Laurent, who represented a Quebec constituency, saw it as a threat to Canadian unity. Quebec, he insisted, was "a province like the others." Saint-Laurent added, "As long as I'm here, the federal government will not recognize the provinces as more important than the country as a whole." Duplessis's reply was not long in coming: "The province of Quebec demands the recognition of its rights, pure and simple. . . . Our position is simple: cooperation always, cooperation between equals. . . . Abdication of our fundamental rights: NEVER."

After these spirited exchanges, a rapprochement occurred, and a compromise was reached in February 1955. Quebec's new legislation no longer alluded to provincial priority in the direct taxation field, and the federal government agreed to lower its personal income tax by 10 percent. For the first time in their history, Quebecers were taxed directly by their "provincial" government. The idea of having to fill out two tax returns did not seem to put Quebecers in a bad mood. With its new tax, their government could make its own choices on the basis of its own needs and values. For supporters of Quebec autonomy, this was a concrete achievement.

Developing Quebec

Maurice Duplessis also had a number of other tangible achievements to his credit. Although he was a social traditionalist and an economic liberal, he was a strong believer in technical progress and tried, in his own way, to bring its benefits to his compatriots.

Light comes to the countryside

For many farmers in the 1950s, Duplessis's reign was anything but a "great darkness." In fact, thanks to the Rural Electrification Agency, established in 1945, most of them finally saw the light! In 1960, 98 percent of farms had electricity, compared with only 20 percent in 1945.

The way the agency operated is a good illustration of the philosophy of the regime. Duplessis preferred the local initiative of electricity cooperatives to technocratic state control. To get their activities off the ground and build their initial lines, the cooperatives received technical assistance and government loans at a very low interest rate. Thus, while the Union Nationale was in power, rural electrification was accomplished through the coordinated activity of 167 cooperatives.

Hydro-Quebec

Although Duplessis relied on electricity cooperatives, he did not question the existence of Hydro-Quebec, established by his Liberal predecessor. Nor did he reopen the decision to nationalize Montreal Light, Heat & Power, even though he had fought against nationalization while he was opposition leader.

Furthermore, Duplessis depended on Hydro-Quebec to build new dams in remote regions that he wanted to open to development. The hydroelectric project on the Bersimis River was launched in this spirit in 1952, as was the dam on the Manicouagan in 1959. Aiming to conquer the land, the Union Nationale government pursued the ambitious program of colonizing the territory initially launched during the 1930s. Above all, the government wanted to train French-Canadian engineers and develop technical expertise in Quebec.

Progress in education

In 1946, the legislature passed the Union Nationale's Act to Insure the Progress of Education. The legislation provided for the creation of a special fund dedicated to education. At the beginning, nearly 50 percent of the fund's financing came from the profits of Hydro-Quebec. This money was used to help school boards, which had to build hundreds of schools across Quebec to serve the children of the baby boom. School attendance had been compulsory since 1943 — another measure Duplessis did not challenge once in power even though he had opposed it when it was adopted by his predecessor. Between

1946 and 1956, Quebec's education budget increased by a factor of six. The Duplessis government encouraged the establishment of technical schools and supported the founding of a new university in Sherbrooke, which welcomed its first students in 1955.

Seeing Impatience Grow

In June 1956, the Union Nationale won its fourth consecutive election victory. This victory left a bitter taste in the mouths of the regime's opponents, who had the sense that Quebec was stagnating, not getting anywhere. The criticism came mostly from younger generations, from impatient people on the rise who wanted to move Quebec in a new direction. The opposition to the Duplessis regime was not just partisan — it was moral, national, and intellectual.

Exasperated moralists

With its close ties to the church and its hierarchy, the Union Nationale had always presented itself as the best defender of good practices and morality in politics. A few audacious priests didn't see things that way, however, and they weren't shy about publicly condemning the regime's corruption.

A scathing pamphlet

A few weeks after the June 1956 election, Father Gérard Dion and Father Louis O'Neill published an article entitled "L'immoralité politique dans la province de Québec" ("Political Immorality in the Province of Quebec") in a small in-house journal — later reprinted as a pamphlet under the title "Le chrétien et les élections."

The two priests denounced the methods the Union Nationale used to get reelected. "The outbreak of stupidity and immorality to which Quebec has just been witness cannot leave any clear-eyed Catholic indifferent," they wrote. As they saw it, anti-Communism and defense of provincial autonomy were myths that the regime resorted to in order to fool the population.

This "moral" denunciation struck a powerful chord and cast the Duplessis government in a very bad light. The priests' denunciations echoed the complaints of many young Catholic Action activists, who were no more impressed than Dion and O'Neill with the Union Nationale's slogans and its hostility to the welfare state. These reform-minded Catholics also criticized the church from within. They wanted a more substantial role for the laity and religious practice that would be more authentic and less conformist and hypocritical.

Montreal: An open city?

As the 1950s began, Montreal suffered from a bad reputation, with magazines characterizing it as "Sin City." Illegal gambling and prostitution, controlled by organized crime, were everywhere in the downtown core. Starting in November 1949, Pax Plante, who had been fired as a police officer, published a scathing series of articles on police corruption in *Le Devoir*. Some Montreal citizens established the Comité de Moralité Publique (Public Morality Committee) and demanded an inquiry that would cast light on the alleged transgressions. Judge François Caron submitted his report in 1954, a few months before a municipal election. A finger was clearly pointed at the Montreal police force, but the city government, dominated by the colorful Camillien Houde, wasn't formally accused of anything.

The lawyer for the Comité de Moralité Publique, Jean Drapeau (1916–1999), became the leading public face of a new Montreal political movement and a candidate for mayor. He was a disciple of the historian Lionel Groulx and had been a spokesperson for the anti-conscription Ligue pour la Défense du Canada and the Bloc Populaire. Drapeau loved power — and hated sharing it! — but he was a person of integrity. He was inclined to think big, and he dreamed of turning Montreal into a major international metropolis. But in his brief first term, he ran into Premier Duplessis's authoritarianism.

Duplessis imposed the Dozois Plan, a downtown housing development that thwarted an ambitious scheme to redevelop the central city. After his 1957 defeat, Drapeau was elected mayor again in 1960 and would remain in the mayor's seat for 26 years. Among his notable achievements were the metro (subway), Expo 67, and the 1976 Olympic Games.

The Civic Action League

In 1957, Duplessis's candidate, Sarto Fournier, was elected mayor of Montreal. Fournier defeated Jean Drapeau, leader of the Civic Action League, who had been elected in 1954 in the wake of the Caron inquiry (see the nearby sidebar, "Montreal: An open city?"). This victory was costly for the Union Nationale. It alienated a new generation of middle-class Montrealers, most of whom were nationalists and deeply attached to the principles of morality and integrity. The 1957 Montreal election was marked by demagoguery and stained by numerous irregularities. Drapeau, the defeated candidate, was seen as a victim of the Duplessis regime. While the opposition Liberals were in search of a leader, Drapeau undertook an extensive tour of Quebec and was highly critical of the Union Nationale's methods.

Divided nationalists

Jean Drapeau's speeches also struck a deeper chord. In the late 1950s, many nationalists had become irritated with Duplessis's party, seeing his nationalism as too symbolic and defensive.

Harsh words for the "Negro king"

A current that soon became known as "neonationalism" developed among younger intellectuals. Neonationalists wanted the Quebec government to play a larger role in the economy and accused Duplessis of being the *roi nègre* ("Negro king") for large American companies who were exploiting the iron ore resources of the North Shore. In the political realm, they attacked Duplessis's patronage practices, the rural bias of his idea of the French-Canadian nation, and his use of the Catholic religion for electoral purposes.

The Montreal daily *Le Devoir* — where Gérard Filion had been publisher since 1947 and editorial writer André Laurendeau and journalist Jean-Marc Léger were the intellectual driving forces — was a major outlet for neonationalists. Laurendeau and Léger also wrote for the journal *L'Action Nationale*. Other neonationalists, such as Maurice Séguin, Michel Brunet, and Guy Frégault, taught in the history department at the University of Montreal. They had studied under Lionel Groulx, who founded the Institut d'Histoire de l'Amérique Française in 1946. But they gradually moved away from Groulx's conception of the past, which they saw as sentimental and religious.

Traditionalists make their presence felt

Other intellectuals, however, continued to defend the Union Nationale's traditional vision. The best known of these was the prolific historian Robert Rumilly, who in December 1956 self-published his book *L'infiltration gauchiste au Canada français (Leftist Infiltration in French Canada)*. The same year, Rumilly founded the Centre d'Information Nationale, designed as a rallying point for traditionalists who were still faithful to the Duplessis regime, even if they didn't hold back from sometimes criticizing the government. Léopold Richer and Roger Duhamel, both noted for their writing style, upheld traditionalist ideas in the newspapers *Montréal-Matin* — a popular tabloid financed by the Union Nationale — and *Notre Temps*. The same current of thought was also expressed in *Les Cahiers de Nouvelle-France, Tradition et Progrès,* and other small journals edited by younger intellectuals.

The Liberals

The opposition Liberals, led by Georges-Émile Lapalme, were unrelenting in their criticism of the Union Nationale's policies, but they couldn't shake their image as a party subordinated to their federal big brother. And, indeed, in Quebec in the 1950s, the two main outlets for Liberal thinking were drawn to Ottawa more than to Quebec City.

Cité Libre

The journal *Cité Libre,* which began publication in 1950, was a forum for debate and discussion of Quebec issues. It nurtured a number of intellectuals for whom the Asbestos strike had been a defining event, including Pierre Elliott Trudeau (1919–2000). Trudeau was the son of a French-Canadian father and a mother of Scottish origin, so his heritage encompassed Canada's two founding cultures. His family's wealth allowed him to study law at the University of Montreal and then political science at major universities in Paris, London, and Boston. He saw Quebec's problem as consisting not only of its *chef* or even its regime, but also of excessive attachment to tradition and the past. French Canadians' poor political practices and their troubled relationship with democracy and individual freedoms could be explained by their nationalism. In 1956, Trudeau edited a landmark collection of essays on the Asbestos strike.

Other important contributors to *Cité Libre* included the journalist Gérard Pelletier, who hosted the Radio-Canada radio program *Le choc des idées,* and the man of action and trade union leader Jean Marchand.

Father Georges-Henri Lévesque

Georges-Henri Lévesque was a Dominican priest and founder and then dean of the faculty of social sciences at Laval University. Close to the federal Liberals, hc was a determined opponent of Maurice Duplessis's regime and the Catholic hierarchy that supported it. On May 5, 1952, he delivered a speech at Quebec City's Palais Montcalm that attracted considerable attention:

> Because of our overly exclusive, and sometimes even idolatrous, traditional worship of authority, we are in the process of losing our sense of freedom. Authority comes from God, we are often reminded. Indeed, and we are the first to be convinced of that, but freedom also comes from God!

Throughout the Duplessis years, he trained graduates who dreamed of offering their services to a renewed, dynamic government that would plan Quebec's social and economic development.

These young graduates could barely contain their impatience — but their turn would come!

Chapter 16

The "Quiet Revolution" (1959–1962)

In This Chapter

▶ Looking at the election of the Liberals under Jean Lesage

▶ Heralding the triumph of the welfare state

▶ Recapturing the economy for French speakers

*I*n 1960, Quebec had a population of more than five million. According to the 1961 census, 44 percent of Quebecers were under the age of 19. Baby boomers took up plenty of space! The middle class continued to enjoy the fruits of postwar growth, and it wanted the same prosperity for its children. In 1960, Quebec's economy slowed slightly, and the unemployment rate reached 9.2 percent. Growth resumed in 1962, and with it the optimism that had prevailed earlier.

Quebec at this time was part of Western society and had both feet in the modern world. Infant mortality continued to decline, and life expectancy rose. The population was now more than 80 percent urban, and many Quebecers worked in the service sector, which experienced unprecedented growth starting in the 1950s. Workers were unionized in the same proportion as in Ontario. Most households had cars and started taking family vacations, often in the United States.

This more modern Quebec was reflected in its values. Gone were the fatalism and resignation inspired by old religious doctrines preaching renunciation and sacrifice. Paradise was to be sought here and now! Aspiration to happiness and personal fulfillment raised expectations of what government could provide.

But these aspirations were also collective. The aim was to put an end to French Canadians' economic and social backwardness. Again, the lever chosen to achieve this ambitious goal was government, which would intervene in the economy and, where necessary, resort to nationalization.

In 1960, Quebecers did more than elect a new party: They turned their backs on the old way of viewing politics. As always, they did so calmly and in accordance with the law. This truly was a revolution, but it was quiet, like Quebecers themselves.

Regime Change

On Labor Day, September 7, 1959, Premier Maurice Duplessis died at a hunting lodge in Schefferville in northern Quebec, following several strokes. The premier had gone to the North Shore to visit iron mines operated by foreign companies. Contrary to the stories told by his enemies, the man who had led Quebec for 18 years did not die rich. He even left a debt of $40,000, covered by Union Nationale treasurer Gérald Martineau.

Mourning and succession

Duplessis's death left a great void and forced the Union Nationale to reexamine its way of governing Quebec. How could it remain loyal to the party's founder while responding to the new aspirations of Quebecers?

Even Duplessis's adversaries were deeply touched by his death. Editorial writer André Laurendeau summed it up this way: "We loved him, hated him, judged and discussed him, but his hold over us for the last quarter-century, even if it was passionately resisted, was indisputable." Longtime opposition leader Georges-Émile Lapalme believed that Duplessis had the stature of a Roosevelt or a Churchill.

The Union Nationale founder lay in state at the Legislative Assembly, and his remains were then brought to Trois-Rivières, where a grandiose funeral was held on September 10. On that day, the curtain fell on the old Quebec.

Maurice Duplessis's successor was Paul Sauvé, whose father had been Quebec Conservative Party leader in the 1920s. A World War II veteran and longtime minister of youth, Sauvé was the heir apparent. The 21st premier of Quebec was aware that many young people were champing at the bit and that the regime he was part of was being criticized from every corner. Though he assured supporters that he would remain loyal to the heritage of the old leader, he also made sure to send a signal of renewal. From now on, things would no longer be as they had been before. As soon as he took office, he raised civil service salaries, enhanced workers' rights, and backed the holding of a world's fair in Montreal. Sadly for him and his supporters, Paul Sauvé's time was short: On January 2, 1960, he was felled by a heart attack.

Labour Minister Antonio Barrette was hastily installed to replace Sauvé as premier. Despite his good will, he had a weaker grip on his party than his predecessor. His political priorities were university financing and hospital insurance, essentially "social" issues that would lie at the heart of the greater reforms of the Quiet Revolution. The new premier also sought to open a

Quebec delegation in Paris and to reopen the one in London. To bring about these changes and obtain a mandate of his own, Barrette called an election for June 22, 1960.

A Liberal victory

The Liberals, in opposition since 1944, attempted to gather together all the forces opposed to the Union Nationale regime. Despite the Union Nationale's setbacks, they took nothing for granted.

Jean Lesage: Ready for power

In 1960, the Liberal Party was headed by Jean Lesage. Born in 1912, Lesage grew up in Quebec City and graduated in law from Laval University. He entered politics under the Liberal Party banner like one of his uncles, a Liberal senator, and was elected to the federal Parliament in 1945. On May 31, 1958, at a leadership convention, Lesage was elected to succeed Georges-Émile Lapalme as Quebec Liberal Party leader.

"Not another guy from Ottawa!" party organizer Jean-Marie Nadeau was reported to have lamented. Nadeau feared ridicule from the Union Nationale, which made provincial autonomy one of its main battle cries. But Lesage had leadership skills, along with flair and great eloquence. He was also a tireless worker. Polls in the summer of 1959 still showed Duplessis ahead. In his own riding of Quebec West, the Liberal leader was six points behind. The deaths of Duplessis and Sauvé changed things, but nothing was decided.

A bold program

While on the opposition benches, the Liberals had had plenty of time to think about their platform. Georges-Émile Lapalme, known for his lively writing style and appetite for reform, was entrusted with writing the program, which was made public on May 6, 1960.

Nowhere was there any mention of leading a "revolution," but if you read between the lines, you could see that the changes being proposed were substantial ones. The program opened with a chapter devoted to "national life." It stated:

> In the Quebec context, the most widespread element consists of the French fact, which we must develop in greater depth. It is through our culture rather than our numbers that we will make ourselves felt.

The Salvas Commission's revelations

A few months after being voted into office, the Liberal government gave Superior Court justice Élie Salvas a mandate to inquire into the Union Nationale regime's actions between 1955 and 1960. The aim was to cast light on the natural gas scandal, which had involved Union Nationale ministers in insider dealings on the eve of the 1956 election, and to delve into the former government's purchasing policies. The Duplessis regime was widely suspected of engaging in patronage. The Union Nationale leadership immediately criticized the commission. The commissioners were suspected of being close to the Liberal Party.

The investigation ran longer than expected. Hundreds of witnesses were heard during the 72 sessions held over the course of a year. The first volume of the report was submitted in August 1962. Judge Salvas confirmed insider dealings, but no charges were laid. The patronage practices of the former government were brought to light. It was shown that the government overpaid for the products and services provided. Businesses charged extra amounts to the government that were then channeled to the Union Nationale election fund as kickbacks. Alfred Hardy, the purchasing manager during the 1950s, was fined, and Gérald Martineau, the Union Nationale treasurer, was sentenced to three months in prison.

The entire program ran along similar lines. Government was mentioned on every page: If the Liberals were elected, it would play a far more central role in Quebec's social and economic life. The platform also expressed the hope of greater democratic transparency. In *Pour une politique,* a policy outline written in the summer of 1959 setting out the program, Lapalme said this about political morality:

> At present, legality is mere appearance and hypocrisy. Disdain for the law has itself become the law. Money speaks louder than voters. . . . Quebec politics has always been a politics of administration accompanied by patriotic chants.

In Lapalme's eyes, the time had come to offer Quebecers a genuine "politics" — wide-ranging, coherent, and ambitious.

The "équipe du tonnerre"

To get this program going, Lesage assembled what was called an *équipe du tonnerre* ("team of thunder" or "hell of a team"), blending experience and youth. Veterans such as Bona Arsenault, Lionel Bertrand, Émilien Lafrance, and Georges-Émile Lapalme served alongside new faces such as constitutional lawyer Paul Gérin-Lajoie and journalist Pierre Laporte (elected in 1961). *Le Devoir*'s longtime legislative reporter in Quebec City, Laporte had just brought out *The True Face of Duplessis,* a book presenting an unyielding portrait of the late premier. In 1963, Eric Kierans, a former president of the Montreal Stock Exchange, joined the team.

But in light of subsequent developments, the most important recruit was René Lévesque (1922–1987). This short, disheveled man grew up in New Carlisle, a town in the Gaspé peninsula with a sizable English-speaking minority. He began studies in law but then chose journalism. Perfectly bilingual, Lévesque was hired in December 1943 by the U.S. government's Office of War Information and covered U.S. military operations in Europe. He experienced Luftwaffe bombing in London and discovered Nazi horrors at the Dachau concentration camp. On his return, Lévesque became a reporter with Radio-Canada and covered the Korean War. A few years later, he became host of the television show *Point de Mire,* devoted to international issues. In 1959, he supported the Radio-Canada producers' strike, in the course of which he gave speeches and became a political figure. With some hesitation, he agreed to run under the Liberal banner in 1960.

A "change of life!"

With their dynamic leader, bold program, and energetic team, the Liberals hoped to persuade voters to go with something new. Their slogan? *"C'est l'temps que ça change!"* ("It's time for a change!") The election of June 22, 1960, aroused unusual interest: More than 81 percent of eligible voters turned out at the polls that day. The Liberals won 51 seats and obtained 51.3 percent of the popular vote. This was a great victory but far from the landslide they had hoped for. With 43 seats, the Union Nationale was still very much alive, especially in rural areas. Races were tight in many ridings: 34 candidates were elected by margins of less than 5 percent.

Although he was one of his party's stars, René Lévesque came very close to being defeated. Despite the narrow margin by which his party won, Jean Lesage's victory speech was emphatic: "We want to give the province of Quebec a new way of thinking. What has just happened is more than a change of government: It is a change of life."

Equal Opportunity

Since the Great Depression, and especially since the end of World War II, most Western countries had moved toward what was called the "welfare state." This was the consensus model among intellectual and political elites. The advent of the welfare state marked the second phase in the modernization of Western societies. The first phase, starting in the 19th century, sought to guarantee the most basic rights for everyone (universal suffrage, freedom of speech and association, and so on), while the second phase emphasized equal opportunity for all citizens, regardless of social origins. How could this be achieved? By offering everyone basic services in vital areas such as education and healthcare.

Emphasizing the state over the church

Maurice Duplessis resisted the welfare-state model, considering it too costly and fearing that real power would slip away from elected officials. Jean Lesage and his team were enthusiastic supporters, as was the Quebec public at large in the 1960s. After being behind, it was time to catch up — and, according to the constant refrain of the new team in power, to do it quickly. Quebec had to follow in the footsteps of other Western societies, which meant adopting a welfare state to provide social services to the populace.

The era of the technocrats

Before 1960, Quebec had adopted a number of social policies, notably the Social Assistance Act (1921) and allowances for needy mothers (1937). There were also measures from Ottawa — old-age pensions, unemployment insurance, and family allowances. Prior to the election of June 22, 1960, social concerns were viewed as the responsibility of the church or charitable associations, with government as a last resort. This outlook changed completely when the Lesage Liberals came to power. Government took charge of social solidarity.

To build this "modern" state and develop rational policies, the government hired an army of young minds trained in social sciences. These brilliant recruits included Arthur Tremblay, Claude Morin, and Jacques Parizeau. Many of them had studied abroad or worked in the federal civil service. These technocrats soon acquired substantial power. The Liberals sought to build a competent civil service that would be independent of political power, and it grew at an unprecedented pace. From 1962 to 1966, the number of civil servants rose each year by 53 percent and public spending by 21 percent.

Redefining the role of the church

A few years earlier, the church would have denounced this growth in government. But things were changing, both in Quebec and within the church itself.

Creation of the Mouvement Laïque de Langue Française

On April 8, 1961, more than 800 people joined to form an association that called for the church and religious issues to be relegated to the private sphere. This French-language secular movement said the state should ensure the neutrality of major public institutions, both to facilitate the integration of newcomers who did not share the Catholic faith and to respect the freedom of conscience of all Quebec citizens.

Vatican II

The most dramatic change was occurring within the church itself. Since the 1930s, a reform current had criticized the authoritarian philosophy that dominated the church and Catholics' conformist religious practices. These reformers, many of them laypeople active in Catholic youth movements, also denounced clerical ascendancy in the church and the disproportionate attention the church paid to temporal institutions. Instead of managing structures, the church should offer a new pastoral approach (with Mass in vernacular languages rather than in Latin, for example). With the arrival of Pope John XXIII in 1958, this point of view prevailed. The Second Vatican Council (1962–1965) marked a stunning victory for the reformers.

Although resistance did not vanish, the context was ripe for overhauling the church's role in Quebec society.

Educating the masses

The welfare state's first priority was an assault on education. If there was one area where it was necessary to catch up to other parts of the Western world, education was it. The efforts of previous governments and the church, though commendable, had proven inadequate. In 1960, only 29 percent of Quebecers from ages 25 to 34 had high school or college diplomas, and only 5 percent had university degrees, far lower than in Ontario.

For the quiet revolutionaries, education was a way of meeting the needs of the market. But first and foremost, it was a form of social policy, for in their minds promoting education meant favoring equality of opportunity and allowing less-favored classes to climb the social ladder. This mindset led to the Liberal slogan *"Qui s'instruit s'enrichit!"* ("Those who learn get rich!"), aimed at convincing the public of the vital need to invest in education.

"A word is worth a trout!": The impertinences of Brother Anonymous

The need to reform education also arose from concern over the French spoken in Quebec. In a series of letters published in late 1959, Marist Brother Jean-Paul Desbiens, known as Frère Untel (Brother Anonymous) denounced the quality of language in Quebec. These letters were collected in a hard-hitting book called *Les insolences du frère Untel (The Impertinences of Brother Anonymous),* which became a huge bestseller.

He and others characterized Quebec's spoken language as *joual,* a deformation of the word *cheval,* or horse. It was a poor language, sloppy and full of Anglicisms. Brother Desbiens's targets were the education system — public high school courses, in particular — and society as a whole for not attaching enough value to the quality of language. He clamored for increased government action: "The government protects national parks and does it well: they are common property. LANGUAGE IS ALSO COMMON PROPERTY, and the government should protect it just as rigorously. An expression is worth a moose, and a word is worth a trout!"

The Great Charter of Education

As the overseer of the great education reforms of the Quiet Revolution, Paul Gérin-Lajoie presented a "Great Charter of Education" in 1961, calling for overhauls at every level. These included

- ✓ **School attendance up to age 15:** This was one year more than Adélard Godbout's government had mandated in 1943.

- ✓ **School boards obliged to provide high school education, grades 8 to 11:** This was a new and very heavy responsibility for school boards, which previously had to assume only elementary school education, up to grade 7.

- ✓ **Free education for students ages 6 to 16, including tuition and books:** The principle of access to education meant that the costs of the education system at the primary and secondary levels would be shared by all taxpayers.

- ✓ **Creation of a system of loans and grants for college and university students:** Financial support for students in higher education would be based on their needs, not on their parents' political contacts.

- ✓ **Higher statutory subsidies to school boards and independent educational institutions:** The era of "discretionary" subsidies was over. More rational planning of education spending was the goal.

A department of education

From the moment it came to power, the new government centralized everything involving education into a single department, the Department of Youth, for the first time since 1875! This proposal fulfilled the main recommendation of the Royal Commission of Inquiry on Education (called the Parent Commission after its chair), which was appointed in 1961 and submitted the first volume of its report in 1963.

The Parent Commission and the minister, Gérin-Lajoie, felt that it had become essential to create a department of education. The minister said,

> In Quebec, spending on education devours one quarter of the government's budget. . . . It is crucial that the person holding authority over so vital a sector of society sit in cabinet and in the Legislative Assembly to defend the measures being advocated.

When it was officially established in 1964, the education department accounted for 28 percent of the Quebec budget and had 4,000 civil servants. The Superior Council of Education was created that same year to guide its major policies. Specialists in teaching methods and representatives from the new department and the clergy, as well as from various levels of education, sat on the council.

The first woman elected to the legislature

In a by-election on December 14, 1961, Marie-Claire Kirkland-Casgrain was elected as a member of the Legislative Assembly. This was a first! After studying at Villa Maria convent, she obtained a law degree from McGill University in 1952. She also completed studies in international law in Switzerland, and on her return became active in the Liberal Party. After being elected, she was appointed a minister without portfolio.

This was a major breakthrough because, even though women had voting rights, political involvement by women was looked down on in the years after World War II. Housewives were the favored model, even in a new publication such as the French edition of *Châtelaine,* which first appeared in October 1960. "Fine arts and politics," the inaugural editorial stated, "as well as education, science, and social problems are no longer the preserve of the stronger sex; it is also good for 'the honest woman' to have 'a broad overview' since her fate and that of her children are linked to the world's destiny."

Before engaging in politics, a woman had to be a competent and loving mother and a spouse attentive to her husband's needs. That, at least, is how things were seen in that era, when one of the most popular American television series was *Father Knows Best* (broadcast in French starting in 1960).

Crucifixes there to stay

To promote more rational management of the education system, the government forced the amalgamation of school boards (the aim was to reduce their number from 1,500 to 55). The Mouvement Laïque de Langue Française, meanwhile, called for the establishment of language-based, rather than religious-based, school boards. The government moved cautiously, preserving the denominational school board structure and maintaining the Catholic and Protestant committees that approved religious programming in schools. There was no question, for the moment, of removing crucifixes from schools!

For the more ardent reformers, this agreement between the government and the church was a disappointment and a missed opportunity to bring Quebec into a new era, while traditionalists who defined French Canadians first and foremost by their adherence to the Catholic religion heaved a sigh of relief.

Comprehensive high schools

Although the Lesage government guaranteed free education up to age 16, it also allowed parents to register their children at private institutions. This ensured the continuation of prestigious institutions such as Collège Brébeuf in Montreal and the Séminaire de Québec.

In most cases, however, students were sent to comprehensive high schools. This new type of educational institution typified the excesses of the Quiet Revolution. To comply with the modern ideas of the time, enormous impersonal bunkers were built, each serving up to 4,000 students. These comprehensive schools aimed to reflect a new and more egalitarian society. They welcomed boys and girls alike, in a general stream for students headed to university and a vocational stream. Teachers — who, like civil servants, obtained the right to strike in 1965 — now emphasized their pedagogical skills more than the "vocation" or "knowledge" that had once defined the teaching profession. Nurtured by the era's prevailing trends in child psychology, they advocated more "open" and less authoritarian methods.

Healthcare for all

In 1960, healthcare was a matter of concern for many Quebec households. In the view of the new government, promoting equal opportunity meant providing basic care for all, regardless of income.

Prior to 1960, the Quebec government provided assistance to asylums and subsidized what were called "health units," intended to educate the public in hygiene, prevent the spread of contagious disease, and administer vaccines to newborn infants. In 1966, they employed about 1,000 people, mostly nurses. These health units, spread across Quebec, kept growing in number, rising from 30 in 1936 to 64 in 1950 and 77 in 1968. Four years earlier, the Lesage government decided to organize them so that each unit served a population basin of 100,000. But the results of this initiative were far from conclusive. Starting in 1970, "popular clinics" provided additional support. Two years later came the advent of Centres Locaux de Services Communautaires (Local Community Service Centers), or CLSCs.

Prevention was vital, but people still sometimes had to go to the doctor or be taken to the hospital when they got sick. In 1960, 57 percent of Quebecers had no private insurance covering the costs of hospitalization. The very poor received charitable assistance, but middle-class Quebecers were left to their own devices. If they fell ill, it was at their own expense. A hospital stay was expensive and often put people deeply into debt. In 1947, the Saskatchewan government introduced hospital insurance for all citizens. Ten years later, the federal government offered the provinces co-financing of a similar program across Canada. In keeping with its notions of provincial autonomy, the Duplessis government refused to take part in the program. Jean Lesage was more open.

In 1961, his government's hospital insurance bill was passed by the legislature. Its impact on Quebec's finances was quickly felt. In the first year it was in effect, new patients flooded in — 150,000 rather than the forecast number of 90,000. The hospital insurance budget grew from $140 million in 1961 to

$343 million five years later. And that was just the start! In 1970, in cooperation with the federal government, Quebec launched an even more ambitious free universal health insurance program.

Masters in Our Own House

The government now provided all Quebecers with basic healthcare and made education accessible to the vast majority. The quiet revolutionaries were betting that everyone, regardless of social origin, could more easily choose their destiny and gain personal fulfillment. But they weren't going to stop there! They were ready to tackle another, and perhaps even bigger, problem: the economic backwardness of the French-speaking majority.

Breaking through the glass ceiling

Up until the 1960s, Quebec elites took the view that government and economy did not mix. Liberals and traditionalists swore by market forces. Some of them were quick to associate government intervention with atheistic socialism. However, despite the handful of economic institutions created by the French-Canadian bourgeoisie (the Chamber of Commerce, the Desjardins Group, the École des Hautes Études Commerciales), the French-speaking majority did not make its presence felt in the business world. Big business, controlled by foreign or English-Canadian interests, had little room for French Canadians. Even if they spoke English and were well educated, French speakers often had the impression that they had hit the ceiling. Once in power, the Lesage team attacked this problem.

And with reason! In hindsight, the signs of this economic backwardness were obvious. In 1961, the outlook of French Canadians in the 25-to-29 age bracket was gloomier than that of American blacks of the same age. On average, French Canadians had completed ten years of schooling, one year less than American blacks. Their income was also lower, equal to 52 percent of the average income of the English-speaking minority. This gap was two points wider than that separating American blacks from the dominant social group in the United States. Added evidence came from comparisons of average income by ethnic origin in Canada: In 1961, the average income of Canadians of French descent was $3,185, far below the $4,940 average among Canadians of British or Scandinavian descent. Excluding First Nations, only Canadians of Italian descent had a lower average income.

For the French-speaking majority, this situation gave the education slogan "Those who learn get rich" a very particular meaning. Even a reformed education system better suited to the modern economy could not, on its own, reverse their structural inferiority. Something more was needed. The government would have to intervene to encourage innovative ideas and support the most promising entrepreneurs.

In June 1962, the Liberal government set up the Société Générale de Financement (SGF). A $20-million fund was established by the government, the Desjardins Group, and private partners. It had a dual mission: to provide venture capital to projects that would have an impact on the structure of Quebec's economy, and to encourage Quebec control of some large companies, especially in the natural resources sector. It took some time for the SGF to find its true niche and for its chief executive, Gérard Filion, to grasp the institution's economic and nationalist mission.

One thing was sure: This new type of government intervention in developing the economy was part of a broader movement of economic reconquest, echoing the nationalistic program of the 1920s.

Completing the nationalization of hydroelectricity

It was generally agreed that this economic reconquest involved greater government control of natural resources. In the mining sector, for example, it was felt that the time had come for a radical revision of the pact between the government and the private sector. Until then, the government awarded exploitation rights to private companies, often on an exclusive basis, in return for financing infrastructure in the region concerned, hiring Quebec technicians, and paying a small sum in royalties to the public treasury. But most of the profits remained in company coffers, often heading to parent companies in the United States or elsewhere.

Starting in the 1960s, there was a call for the government to intervene more actively in both exploring and exploiting ore bodies. With this in mind, the SGF established Sidérurgie Québec (Sidbec) in 1964, and the government authorized creation of the Société Québécoise d'Exploration Minière (SOQUEM) in 1965.

Natural resources rather than "old codgers"

This interventionist philosophy suited René Lévesque perfectly. Soon after the election, Jean Lesage wanted to name him minister of social welfare. But Lévesque turned this down: He had no desire to be the "minister of old codgers"! The premier then offered him responsibility for hydraulic resources, where he could show his full potential. In line with an election promise, the Lesage government created the Department of Natural Resources.

Hydro-Quebec already existed. This government-owned enterprise, founded in 1944 by the Godbout government following the nationalization of hydro-electric companies in the Montreal area, provided a good return to the Quebec treasury. People began to think about nationalizing electricity cooperatives in other regions along with all hydroelectric companies. Though the Liberal program of 1960 stated that "exploitation of these resources must occur in such a way as to benefit the people of the province first," it stopped short of advocating nationalization.

Natural Resources Minister Lévesque surrounded himself with a team of brilliant young advisers. One of them was Michel Bélanger. With a background in economics, this former federal civil servant was given a mandate to produce a study on this issue. His "blue paper," written in the summer of 1961, argued strongly for bringing the hydroelectric companies under government ownership. The numbers spoke for themselves. Private companies' profits were leaving Quebec, Bélanger lamented in his report. Furthermore, the position of French-speaking engineers in these companies often left much to be desired. As for electricity rates, they varied far too much from one region to another. Completing the nationalization of all the hydroelectric companies would help remedy these problems. But hadn't Ontario not done the same thing . . . back in 1906?

The Lac à l'Épaule meeting

Lévesque was committed to the idea, but he had to persuade his cabinet colleagues. Some of them saw nationalization as synonymous with socialism. On September 5, 1962, during an important meeting at Lac à l'Épaule near Quebec City, the natural resources minister set out his main arguments. Getting Lesage to allow him to defend his project was already quite a feat! A few months earlier, the premier had been very reticent. He felt things were moving too quickly. He feared the reaction in English-speaking business circles, and he wanted to give Quebecers more time to digest the various reforms initiated since the 1960 election. But Lévesque gradually won over the premier and most of his colleagues to his cause.

Down with "economic colonialism"

Lévesque may well have won his gamble, but Lesage still wanted to win a mandate from the people before nationalizing 11 private companies. A snap election was called for November 14, 1962. The decision came as a surprise, because the Liberals could have kept governing for another two years. But Lesage decided to go for broke. The 1962 Liberal program stated:

> The era of economic colonialism is over in Quebec. Unification of the electricity networks — a key to the industrialization of all Quebec regions — is needed as a primary condition of our economic liberation.

Colonialism, liberation — the Liberals were clearly making this a nationalist issue. The Liberal slogan *Maîtres chez nous* (Masters in Our Own House) hammered home the same message.

No more "drawers of water"

The Liberal leader caught the opposition completely off guard. The divisions created by the Union Nationale's 1961 leadership convention had still not healed. The party's new leader, Daniel Johnson, wanted the election theme to be the Liberal record, which he saw as very costly, but this went nowhere. René Lévesque, the former television host, created a sensation during the election campaign.

He traveled across Quebec, a cigarette dangling from his mouth and a piece of chalk in his hand. Standing in front of a blackboard, he would give lessons on government ownership of hydroelectricity. His charisma was crowd-pleasing and his way of presenting things was highly persuasive.

"There has to be a way of not only being onlookers, drawers of water, and hewers of wood!" Lévesque repeated in his campaign speeches. "We arrived here something like 300 years ago. There should be a way of making us feel more at home here." This was a politician who didn't talk like a bureaucrat or a college professor! Lesage's team won a smashing victory, taking 56.5 percent of the popular vote and 63 seats.

New York, New York!

Despite the election result, there was resistance from the English-speaking financial cartel in Montreal. There was no way they would finance this "socialist" project. In the face of this defiance, the government turned to a Wall Street firm to find the $600 million needed for the operation. "In 25 minutes, the matter was concluded," recalled Jacques Parizeau, then a young economic adviser. "That type of experience leaves a lifelong impression!"

On February 22, 1963, Hydro-Quebec made an official bid to acquire the hydroelectric companies that then shared the Quebec market. In the course of 1963, the number of employees at the government-owned company increased from 8,665 to 15,500, and its subscriber base jumped from 589,291 to 1,363,390. Hydro-Quebec would become a breeding ground for executives and engineers, and its expertise would be solicited around the world.

Chapter 17

The Reforms Continue (1963–1967)

In This Chapter

▶ Continuing the Quiet Revolution

▶ Seeking "special status" for Quebec

▶ Watching the surprising return of the Union Nationale

*I*n Quebec, as elsewhere in the world, people's increased expectations of the welfare state and collective desire to be on their own helped make the 1960s a time of turmoil.

Even the Americans, normally so strongly attached to individual freedoms and the market economy, elected a president in 1964 who believed strongly in a role for government in ending social inequality. The "Great Society" promised by Lyndon B. Johnson, who assumed the presidency when John F. Kennedy was assassinated on November 22, 1963, aimed for greater fairness and solidarity, paying more attention to citizens who were left behind. This political approach appealed to the Southern black pastor Martin Luther King, Jr., a stirring orator and heroic advocate of civil rights.

This yearning for emancipation and freedom spread around the world. The decade of the 1960s was the peak time of decolonization. Everywhere, people were struggling for independence and breaking away from colonial powers. After India and Pakistan (1947) came Morocco and Tunisia (1956), Togo and Ghana (1957), and then Madagascar, Côte d'Ivoire, and both Congos (1960). Algeria gained its independence in 1962 after a long war led by the National Liberation Front against French troops. All these national liberation struggles influenced and inspired a significant fringe among Quebec youth.

The Liberals under Jean Lesage, re-elected on November 14, 1962, with a broad majority, had a free hand to continue and consolidate the major reforms of the Quiet Revolution. The means and the ends remained the same, with reliance on government to combat social exclusion and put an end to the economic backwardness of French Canadians. The winds of change sweeping Quebec seemed irresistible. Even the conservative Union Nationale, which regained power in 1966, couldn't stand in the way.

Fighting Social Exclusion

Government social and economic intervention would now extend beyond the education, health, and natural resource sectors. The goal was not only to ensure equality of opportunity but also to fight social exclusion by bringing old laws up to date and developing programs tailored to current needs. In the economic field, the government decided to nationalize a portion of Quebecers' retirement savings.

Women's rights

Though women could now vote, run for election, and be active in politics, the struggle for equality was far from over.

Granting equal rights to married women

Until Bill 16 became law in 1964, women who married lost most of their rights. A married woman could practice a trade or be a guardian only with her husband's explicit consent. This amounted to married women having the same status as minors or the feeble minded. Despite some adjustments to the Civil Code in 1866, this legal inferiority of women had been maintained. The Liberals' reform ended this situation. Married women now had equality with their husbands and full legal capacity, and they could leave their husbands if they felt threatened. In many respects, these changes to the Civil Code merely reflected changed male-female relations, characterized by greater equality of the sexes.

Becoming more educated and self-reliant

Although society still generally believed that women's work was in the home, a growing number of married women were working outside the home. In 1951, only 17 percent of women in the labor market were married. Twenty years later, married women accounted for 48 percent of the female workforce. Parents — and mothers, in particular — increasingly encouraged their daughters to study and choose an occupation, even in sectors that were not traditionally friendly to women. The Parent Commission stated that "preparing young girls for life must not be limited to domestic training. . . . On the other hand, all young girls should be interested . . . in the role of housekeeper." But it also argued that "every young girl should receive some practical training so that she can earn a livelihood before or during her married life." This line of thinking represented a "quiet evolution" in attitudes. The role of women in the home was still favored, but women didn't have to feel imprisoned there.

Getting organized

The year after Bill 16 became law, a coalition of women's associations announced the establishment of the Fédération des Femmes du Québec (FFQ), open to Quebec women of all ethnic origins and religions. This new group sought to defend women's interests in every sphere of society, from the working world to conjugal relations. In particular, its members demanded equal wages with men and the establishment of government-run child-care centers. At its initial convention in 1966, divorce and abortion were sensitive issues that stirred lively debate among the activists, who did not all share the same values.

The FFQ largely represented women in urban areas. To give a stronger voice to women in outlying regions, members of the Union Catholique des Femmes Rurales (Catholic Union of Rural Women) and the leaders of the Cercles d'Économie Domestique (Domestic Economy Circles) founded the Association Féminine pour l'Éducation et l'Action Sociale (Women's Association for Education and Social Action) in 1966. Their main demand was greater recognition for women's work in the home and in family businesses.

The very poor

Prior to the welfare state, the very poor were looked after by the family, the church, or charitable organizations. Except in times of major crisis or high unemployment, a government-guaranteed minimum income was unthinkable.

Inspired by major social reforms elsewhere in the West, a review committee on public assistance, chaired by Judge Émile Boucher, issued a major report in 1963. Government, the committee argued, should play a far more active role in the area of assistance, should no longer defer to any private organization, and should develop broad and coherent policies. The Quebec government should uphold the principle that any individual in need is entitled to government assistance; in the committee's view, this assistance should be assumed by government services.

Although there was a consensus on the social role of government, another question arose: Which government would have this responsibility? In 1966, the federal government adopted the Canada Assistance Plan. Four years later, Ottawa moved forward on a new unemployment insurance program benefiting nearly all wage and salary earners. The Boucher committee suggested that the Quebec government should control assistance programs and "opt out" of federal programs, with financial or tax compensation.

A confrontation was taking shape. Which of the two governments would shape and manage these social policies? The issue wasn't just administrative. Two competing governments had the same goals — both claimed to speak on behalf of a people or nation, and each defended its own view of Canadian federalism.

The Caisse de Dépôt et Placement

It was in this context that a showdown between the federal and Quebec governments was looming over the establishment of a retirement plan for all citizens. This confrontation involved the creation of an economic institution that would play a fundamental role in Quebec.

A proposal worthy of "national socialism"?

Since the early 1960s, the federal government had been considering creation of a Canada Pension Plan, a retirement plan for all Canadians. The Lesage government approved the principle but wanted Quebec to create its own plan. The quiet revolutionaries sought to have retirement savings in Quebec managed by and for Quebecers. At its 1962 convention, the Confederation of National Trade Unions envisaged the possibility of creating a fund (a *caisse*) that would manage the sums set aside for a new retirement plan. The union delegates saw this sort of institution as "the finest economic planning instrument that a society could dream of," something that would hasten "the economic liberation of Quebec."

In April 1963, Premier Lesage took up the idea and announced the creation of a "general retirement fund." A few months later, the premier stated that "our economic liberation cannot truly be achieved if the people of Quebec remain uninvolved in the choices guiding the use of their savings." This Quebec project outraged Judy LaMarsh, the minister of national health and welfare in Ottawa. LaMarsh said:

> The power of a government with so much money would be frightening. By controlling investment capital, it would be in a position to dominate business. We would then risk ending up with a sort of national socialism, as it was practiced in Nazi Germany.

A powerful lever

Not until 1965 did things move forward. That year, the government established the Régie des Rentes du Québec to run a universal and compulsory retirement plan. Each worker had to contribute to the plan on the basis of a percentage of income set by the Régie. As of 1966, more than two million workers were contributing. The accumulated funds went straight into the Caisse de Dépôt et Placement, also founded in 1965. This new institution stood as a symbol of the spirit of economic reconquest by the French-speaking majority.

The Caisse had a dual mission: to make Quebecers' savings grow and to support Quebec's economic and social development. How? By buying a portion of the bonds issued by the Quebec government, thereby helping to finance social programs and basic infrastructure. The Caisse's capital would make Quebec more autonomous financially and less dependent on foreign banks. The Caisse could also become a shareholder in ventures, often ones with their head offices in Quebec, that would have an impact on the structure of Quebec's economy. It would also back the most dynamic Quebec entrepreneurs who sought to export their products or know-how.

The legislation governing the Caisse de Dépôt et Placement required the institution to be independent of government. Its management team would report to a board of directors. The Caisse opened its doors in January 1966. When he took up his new position, Claude Prieur, the Caisse's first president, had only a pen — which was borrowed! On December 31, 2011, the Caisse had assets of $159 billion.

Fighting for the Independence of Quebec

Through these government reforms, the quiet revolutionaries created a new state of mind. Unlike their Union Nationale predecessors, they were not content simply to oppose federal initiatives and say no. They suggested alternatives and asserted themselves. This was not just a matter of controlling financial levers but of being on one's own — in Canada and in the world. And for some people, though not yet for many, this meant making Quebec a truly independent country.

Special status

The confrontation over the Régie des Rentes clearly illustrated the new contentious issues pitting the Quebec government against Ottawa. Far from being just administrative matters, these issues involved politics and identity.

From French Canadians to Québécois

In the 1950s, many people were becoming alarmed over the high assimilation rate of French Canadians outside Quebec. The Canadian census of 1951 was studied very thoroughly by Jesuit priest Richard Arès. His conclusions, published in *Relations* magazine, convinced a new generation of nationalists that the Quebec government was probably best positioned to defend and promote French culture in North America. After agreeing to have stamps and currency printed in English and French, the Canadian government announced in 1962 that all federal checks would be bilingual. Too little, too late, some people said. French was absent from most Canadian institutions, and French Canadians who broke into the federal civil service were the exception rather than the rule.

The decline of French explained in part the emergence of a new Québécois identity. Until the 1960s, French-speaking Quebecers referred to themselves as French Canadians. Gradually, they began calling themselves Québécois. Their homeland was Quebec, and they intended to have this new identity recognized in the Canadian constitution, whose 100th anniversary was set to be celebrated in 1967.

Reviewing the constitution

In 1961, the Lesage government created the Department of Federal-Provincial Relations and began holding annual meetings with its counterparts in other provinces. The Lesage team showed up with a new concept of the role to be played by the Quebec government. Discussions focused on the establishment of new social programs and the repatriation of the constitution. Many people wanted Britain to give up its power to amend the Canadian constitution, so that Canadians would be the sole masters of their basic law. As a former federal minister, Jean Lesage agreed with the idea of repatriation. But the talks soon stumbled on issues that were delicate for Quebec:

- **The amending formula:** Once the constitution was repatriated, how much weight would Quebec have when the time came to bring in new changes? Could it block any constitutional change affecting its powers in education and culture, for example? In other words, would it have "veto power"? Talks would often run into snags over this issue.

- **Distribution of powers:** Though Lesage shared the federal government's eagerness to repatriate the constitution, some members of his government believed a thorough examination of the distribution of powers set out in the 1867 constitution was needed. Such an examination would help delineate the powers of the federal and Quebec governments more clearly in many areas (international relations, higher education, telecommunications, and so on).

It was amid these discussions that the idea of "special status" for Quebec emerged. Many people hoped a new Canadian constitution would explicitly recognize specific powers for Quebec. As the political expression of French Canada, the Quebec government spoke both on behalf of its own inhabitants and on behalf of one of Canada's founding nations.

Playing in the big leagues

Quebecers wanted not only to be recognized by Canada but also to speak in their own name on the world stage. In 1961, Quebec's trade office in New York was given the status of General Delegation. On October 5 of that year, the Quebec Delegation in Paris was inaugurated with great pomp and was virtually accorded the status and privileges of an embassy. The following year, Quebec reopened a London office that had been closed since 1935.

"What does Quebec want?"

This new demand left many English Canadians feeling puzzled. One question kept coming up: What does Quebec want? Would Quebecers be satisfied with the special powers that the rest of Canada was prepared to grant them? Would a subsequent government ask for more?

In 1963, with this in mind, the federal government under Prime Minister Lester B. Pearson established the Royal Commission on Bilingualism and Biculturalism, often referred to as the Laurendeau-Dunton Commission after the names of its co-chairs. Its mandate was not only to inquire into Canada's bilingual and bicultural character but also "to recommend what steps should be taken to develop the Canadian

Confederation on the basis of an equal partnership between the two founding races."

In a preliminary report, issued in 1965, André Laurendeau and Davidson Dunton concluded that Canada "is going through the most critical period of its history since Confederation." Despite several years of consultation, with hundreds of briefs received and analyzed and vast expertise solicited, no consensus could be achieved. Should bilingualism be implemented from coast to coast or should Quebec be guaranteed special powers to help protect the French language? The commission didn't come down on one side or the other.

In 1965, two key events took place:

- ✔ **First agreement with a foreign government:** On February 27, the Quebec and French ministers of education signed an agreement calling for closer cooperation in that field. This was the first time the Quebec government signed an agreement with a sovereign state.

- ✔ **The "Gérin-Lajoie doctrine":** On April 12, Education Minister Paul Gérin-Lajoie gave a major speech to the consular corps in Montreal. Backed by André Patry, a multilingual jurist and influential senior official, Gérin-Lajoie explained that Quebec was a federated state and, hence, sovereign in its areas of jurisdiction. It was this status that allowed it to sign an agreement on education and participate in international forums on education and culture.

Accepting or rejecting the Fulton-Favreau formula

This self-affirmation by Quebec made constitutional discussions more delicate. In 1966, under public pressure, the Lesage government ended up rejecting the so-called Fulton-Favreau amending formula, which it had approved two years earlier. The formula devised by federal justice ministers Davie Fulton and Guy Favreau would require the unanimity of all governments for any future constitutional changes affecting the distribution of powers, areas of provincial jurisdiction, or the use of the French and English languages.

However, any reforms of the monarchy, the Senate, or the Supreme Court would require only the agreement of seven provinces representing at least 50 percent of the population.

The nationalist opposition attacked this amending formula and the entire repatriation process. The Union Nationale denounced this "straitjacket" that "would virtually shut the door to any future extension of Quebec's powers." Several Liberal ministers — especially René Lévesque — were swayed by opposition arguments. Lévesque halfheartedly defended the agreement in March 1965 before students at the University of Montreal. On the eve of an election, Jean Lesage backtracked. This was the first in a long series of constitutional failures.

Birth of the independence movement

As the quiet revolutionaries moved into action, some young people dreamed of revolution and independence. In October 1963, a group of intellectuals founded *Parti Pris* magazine, which called openly for revolution and urged a secular, socialist, and pro-independence Quebec. A program of this kind appealed to many educated young baby boomers, who compared the Quebec cause to that of oppressed peoples struggling for national liberation.

The first FLQ bombs

Inspired directly by the ideology and revolutionary practices of Algeria's National Liberation Front, several young Quebecers founded the Front de Libération du Québec (FLQ) in 1963. They saw Quebec as a colonized nation. The economic and social backwardness of French Canadians resulted from the political domination instituted after the Conquest of 1760. Political and religious elites had become corrupted by the conquerors, and the people had developed a loser's mentality. To break this yoke, there was only one solution: revolution.

The FLQ militants, initially few in number, split off into cells, hoping that others would join the resistance. "Students, workers, peasants," declared their initial communiqué, "form your clandestine groups against Anglo-American colonialism. Independence or death!" Death was something these apprentice terrorists were prepared for, even though, in their early years, they didn't carry out any kidnappings or political assassinations. They chose instead to raise mass awareness of their cause by planting bombs in places that symbolized "colonial" power. On April 21, 1963, one of these bombs killed a night watchman at the Canadian Army Recruiting Station in Montreal. On January 30, 1964, some FLQers stole military equipment and founded the Armée Révolutionnaire du Québec.

The "three wise men" head to Ottawa

In September 1965, three influential Quebecers announced that they would run for Parliament under the banner of the Liberal Party of Canada. The two best-known members of the trio at the time were Jean Marchand and Gérard Pelletier, renowned earlier for their opposition to the Duplessis regime.

However, it was the least known of the three, Pierre Elliott Trudeau (1919–2000), who soon became the most famous. The product of a prosperous, bicultural family (Scottish and French-Canadian), he completed studies in law and political science at top-flight institutions in Paris, London, and Boston. After founding the *Cité Libre* journal, fighting the Duplessis regime,

and being active in the socialist movement, he made the leap into active politics and cast his lot with the federal Liberals, who elected him their leader in 1968.

The aim of the "three wise men" was to ensure a strong French-Canadian presence in Ottawa. All three disapproved of the nationalistic turn that the Quiet Revolution had taken. From 1962 on, Trudeau would later explain in his *Memoirs,* instead of greater openness to universal values, we heard only about being masters in our own house: "Were we to leave the abusive tutelage of our Holy Mother Church . . . only to throw ourselves now under the shadow of our Holy Mother Nation?"

The RIN

While revolutionary and anticolonial rhetoric held a fascination for some, most of the early independentists rejected terrorist violence. The Rassemblement pour l'Indépendance Nationale (RIN; Rally for National Independence) was founded in 1960 and was turned into a real political party three years later.

One of RIN's founders, Marcel Chaput, soon became known to the general public. This federal civil servant, who held a doctorate in biochemistry from McGill University, was fired in 1961 for his pro-independence stance. The same year, he published *Pourquoi je suis séparatiste (Why I Am a Separatist).* For the first time, Chaput grounded the idea of independence in a modern set of arguments, and his book became a huge bestseller. "That is the glory of the French-Canadian people — to have survived in the adverse conditions it experienced," he wrote in his conclusion. "But survival is not an end in itself. It has meaning only inasmuch as it leads to life."

Nightstick Saturday

Between 1960 and 1964, independentists built a dynamic organization. They founded the newspaper *L'Indépendance,* recruited devoted activists in every region of Quebec, and found effective speakers.

One of these speakers was Pierre Bourgault. He rose through the ranks of the movement and became RIN leader in 1964. Born in 1934, this unemployed actor became a convert to the idea of independence in his mid-20s. His impassioned, insurrectionary speeches drew crowds. His party held large numbers of meetings and noisy demonstrations, some of which turned violent. Nothing strange there: Its emblem was a ram!

A visit by Queen Elizabeth II to Quebec City on October 10, 1964, was preceded by a long RIN campaign. Bourgault suggested several times that things could turn nasty for the queen and that she should stay home. On the day of the visit, very few people showed up. Along the route of the procession, all the queen could see were soldiers and police officers, ready to put down the pro-independence demonstrations. That day became known as *samedi de la matraque* (nightstick Saturday).

Dissidence: Ralliement National

With some reluctance, Pierre Bourgault condemned the actions of the FLQ. In some of his writings, he took up the idea of revolution, even though the party program was social democratic. This left-wing version of independence irritated some activists, who were annoyed at seeing Quebec compared to third-world countries. In the Cold War context, they rejected having the cause of independence associated in any way with a Marxist outlook.

Based mostly in the Quebec City area, these independentists slammed the door on the RIN in August 1964, founding a party that soon took the name Ralliement National. In their manifesto, they condemned "any form of violence," promised a "democratic state," denounced "totalitarianism in all its forms," and committed themselves to respecting the historic rights of the English-speaking minority. Their approach was resolutely democratic and reformist.

One person who was pleased with this approach was René Lévesque, who on December 9, 1964, made a statement that did not go unnoticed: "I am not a separatist, but I could become one." But the means used would have to be "peaceful."

Seeing the Union Nationale Back in Power

After six years of reforms, some of which disrupted daily life (especially school reform, which was under mounting attack), Premier Lesage sought a new mandate. The Liberal campaign focused on the leader's record and personality, while top figures in the Union Nationale nicknamed the premier "Ti-Jean la taxe" (Johnny the Taxer). The Liberals' reforms were costly for Quebecers and raised the public debt. The Union Nationale promised, if elected, to control spending and defend national interests more effectively. Its slogan was "Québec d'abord" (Quebec First).

The 1966 campaign was marked by the presence of two pro-independence parties, poor in resources but rich in the enthusiasm of their young activists. Pierre Bourgault's hard-hitting speeches and the RIN slogan *"On est capable"* ("Yes, we can") grabbed attention and raised hopes among many young people, who could now vote starting at age 18.

The results on June 5, 1966, caught everyone off-guard. The Liberals got the most votes (47.2 percent) but won only 50 seats. The Union Nationale, with 56 of its candidates elected, would form the new government, even though the party, headed by Daniel Johnson, won only 40.9 percent of the votes. This surprising result was due to a distorted electoral map, which gave disproportionate weight to rural ridings. The two pro-independence parties together got 8.8 percent of the popular vote, a noteworthy breakthrough.

Choosing continuity

Some people were worried by the Union Nationale's return to power. They feared that the welfare state would be called into question, the new educational system would be dismantled, and the old, more defensive nationalism would be brought back. But none of this happened.

The technocrats stay put

As a party of local *notables* and small-town lawyers, the Union Nationale was scorned in intellectual and university circles. The party did not have a team of top people with social-science backgrounds who could take over from the technocrats appointed by the Liberals. Lacking these people, the new government had to hang onto the young public officials who had devised and implemented the various Quiet Revolution reforms.

That said, after the new premier was sworn in, he sent them a clear message: "Theories are all very well. But I want ministers who can remind the technocrats, from time to time, that these theories do not always meet the people's desires."

Education: "Plus ça change . . . !"

This warning would have no effect on education, which continued to be animated by the same spirit of innovation, expansion, and occasional excess.

✔ **The creation of Cegeps:** In 1967, the Johnson government created the *collèges d'enseignement général et professionnel* (general and vocational training colleges, or Cegeps). These institutions provided two-year general programs leading to university, as well as three-year vocational or technical programs preparing students for the labor market. All students had to take the same compulsory courses. Like the comprehensive high schools, the Cegeps brought young people with varied social and vocational profiles into the same institutions. At the start of the 1968–1969 school year, 30 Cegeps had opened their doors. In many cases, the buildings they occupied were those of former church-run classical colleges nationalized by the government.

✔ **The founding of the Université du Québec:** A year later, the same government founded the Université du Québec, a public institution consisting of research centers, colleges, and regional universities. This network's largest campus was the Université du Québec à Montréal (UQAM). Montreal finally had a second French-language university.

✔ **"Framework programs" in French:** Under the Union Nationale, the sky was the limit when it came to theoretical experiments in pedagogy! New "framework programs" at the high school level favored "open" methods focused on oral communication and learning by sound. Systematic teaching of grammar through dictations and the more traditional methods of conveying knowledge were discredited — it was too "retro," according to the experts at the time. The Superior Council of Education encouraged this type of approach.

An interventionist government

The Union Nationale ended up relying heavily on the state — sometimes for better and sometimes for worse! In the economic sphere, it continued the previous government's moves toward greater state control of natural resources. While complaining that Hydro-Québec did not consult his government enough, Premier Johnson backed its development choices. The Société Québécoise d'Initiatives Pétrolières (SOQUIP) in the oil exploration sector and the Société de Récupération et d'Exploitation Forestière du Québec (REXFOR) in the forestry sector were founded in 1969, again with the aim of enhancing control over natural resource development.

Government was also called on to revive declining regions, especially the Lower St. Lawrence and Gaspé peninsula, which had falling populations and rising unemployment. Starting in 1963, the government made this a pilot region, creating the Bureau d'Aménagement de l'Est du Québec (Eastern Quebec Development Bureau), which submitted an extensive report in 1966 suggesting a series of solutions to revive the area. An ambitious development plan, backed by the federal government, was launched in 1968, but it led to an outcry in several small communities that the plan, in true technocratic fashion, was slated for elimination.

Equality or independence

The Union Nationale really only stood out from the Liberals on what was known as the "national question." A year before becoming premier, Daniel Johnson issued a book with the provocative title *Égalité ou indépendance (Equality or Independence)*. His argument was simple but very bold: Either Canada should amend its constitution radically or Quebec should become independent. The constitutional reform advocated by Johnson, and by many Quebec nationalists in the mid-1960s, called for "associated states." A reconstituted Canada would be a pact between two equal nations, each with real powers and neither one subservient to the other. If English Canada rejected this reform, Johnson argued, there remained the option of separation. "Confederation is not an end in itself," he wrote. But this option was a last resort for him, a final fallback position.

"Quebec needs you"

Johnson showed his true colors as soon as he was elected. He demanded and obtained increased taxing powers that helped finance the development of the Quebec government apparatus. But to obtain the fundamental constitutional changes he sought, he would have to strike boldly. In May 1967, Johnson was received in Paris by French President Charles de Gaulle. The official aim of the meeting was to invite the president to visit the Montreal world's fair, the major highlight of the summer of 1967. The Quebec premier was also hoping for the great man's backing in his constitutional battle. "General, Quebec needs you," he said. "It's now or never." The former leader of the French resistance in World War II would not allow this great rendezvous with history to pass him by!

Expo 67

Montreal was the host in the summer of 1967 of a Universal Exposition, or World's Fair. The most recent ones had been held in Brussels (1958) and New York (1964), and the next ones would occur in Osaka (1970), Seville (1992), Hanover (2000), and Shanghai (2010). These large fairs date back to the mid-19th century and celebrate progress, civilization, and peace among the nations. Faithful to this tradition, the theme of Expo 67 was *Terre des homes* (Man and His World), inspired by the title of a novel by Antoine de Saint-Exupéry.

Quebecers had the impression that summer that their largest city lay at the center of the world. More than 50 million visitors from Quebec and elsewhere came to admire the pavilions of the various countries represented, each of which showed off its finest dishes and its greatest technical achievements. With its futuristic pavilion, Quebec projected a very modern image. The youth pavilion, with shows every evening, became a gathering place for baby boomers on the threshold of adulthood.

"Making up for France's cowardice"

Charles de Gaulle rejoiced in Quebec's moves toward self-affirmation. He hesitated briefly before deciding to visit Expo 67: He didn't want to take part in celebrating the centennial of Canadian Confederation, which, in his eyes, put French Canadians at a disadvantage and was a reminder of a French defeat. To comply with protocol, the French president would've had to begin his journey in Ottawa, the Canadian capital, but this was out of the question. To get around this obstacle, it was decided that the general would travel by ship, aboard the *Colbert,* a French cruiser. He set off on July 15 from Brest in Brittany. "I intend to hit hard," he told a member of his inner circle. "Sparks will fly. But it's necessary. This is the last opportunity to make up for France's cowardice." On July 23, 1967, 208 years after the defeat on the Plains of Abraham, the *Colbert* arrived in Quebec City.

On the "Chemin du roy"

On the morning of July 24, the French president, accompanied by Premier Johnson, headed to Montreal along the *Chemin du roy* (King's Highway), an old road inaugurated in 1737 along the north shore of the St. Lawrence. Along the way, Quebecers marked the general's passage by adorning their houses with Quebec fleurs-de-lys and French tricolor flags. Even the asphalt was painted in fleurs-de-lys over a 200-kilometer (124-mile) stretch! The procession stopped in Donnacona, Sainte-Anne-de-la-Pérade, Trois-Rivières, Louiseville, Berthier, and Repentigny, towns and villages founded in the era of New France.

In each of his speeches, the French president saluted the vigor of Quebec's self-affirmation: "The French-Canadian people, the Canadian-French people, must depend only on itself. . . . And this is what is happening. . . . I see it. I feel it." The role of France, he repeated, is "to assist French Canada in its development." Johnson appreciated the general's support but feared the excessive enthusiasm. "If it continues like this," he was overheard to say at lunch, "in Montreal we will have separated."

"Vive le Québec libre!"

The speeches were carried live on the radio, and interest in this unusual visit grew by the hour. Between Repentigny and Montreal, more than half a million people saluted the presidential procession, which, with difficulty, worked its way to Montreal City Hall at about 7:30 p.m.

After being greeted by Mayor Jean Drapeau, de Gaulle stepped forward to address the enthusiastic crowds, in which nationalist militants and RIN members joined with the merely curious. "This evening here, and all along my route, I found myself in the same kind of atmosphere as at the Liberation," he said. President de Gaulle then praised the "immense effort at progress, development, and, accordingly, emancipation" in Quebec, made up of "elites, factories, businesses, and laboratories that will be a revelation for everyone and that, one day, I am quite sure, will enable you to assist France." And he concluded, "All of France knows, sees, and understands what is happening here. And I can tell you that she is the better for it. *"Vive Montréal! Vive le Québec! Vive le Québec libre! Vive le Canada français et vive la France!"* ("Long live Montreal! Long live Quebec! Long live free Quebec! Long live French Canada and long live France!")

Fear and trembling

General de Gaulle's speech created a shockwave that was felt around the world, forcing even the Chinese to create a new *ideogram* (symbol) representing Quebec! On July 28, 1967, François Aquin, Liberal member of the legislature for Dorion riding, left his party and became Quebec's first elected official to declare himself openly in favor of independence. Daniel Johnson and René Lévesque exulted in the new life that the speech breathed into the Quebec nationalist movement but were less approving of the general's somewhat intemperate manner, with his use of a partisan pro-independence slogan.

The English-Canadian and foreign press condemned what they saw as an intrusion in a Canadian internal debate. Many people in France, including some Gaullist supporters, did not understand their president's speech. They wondered if the 77-year-old general still had his wits about him. Needless to say, Canada's federal government strongly condemned General de Gaulle's speech, saying in an official news release:

> The people of Canada are free. Every province of Canada is free. Canadians do not need to be liberated. Indeed, many thousands of Canadians gave their lives in two world wars in the Liberation of France and other European countries. Canada will remain united and will reject any effort to destroy her unity.

A poll released two weeks later found that 58.7 percent of Quebecers did not consider the general's act as an intrusion in an internal affair. Some 48.9 percent approved of "Vive le Québec libre," 31.7 percent condemned it, and 16.9 percent said they had no opinion.

The French president had expressed his point of view on the Quebec question. It was now up to the people of Quebec to decide.

Part V
Province or Country? (1967 to Today)

The 5th Wave   By Rich Tennant

"In or out—make up your mind."

In this part . . .

An existential choice, and a deeply emotional one: Did Quebecers want to remain in a reformed Canada or found a new country? Both options had their political parties, their charismatic leaders, and their radical activists. Twice — in 1980 and again in 1995 — referendums focused all of Quebecers' political energy and attracted the attention of the world.

Other issues were also extensively discussed: the role of the trade-union movement and the welfare state, the decline of social solidarity, and the rise of individualism. In competing manifestos, *Lucides* and *Solidaires* laid out their plans for the future. Quebecers were looking for new political options. Was this the end of a cycle?

Chapter 18

Revolt (1967–1972)

● ●

In This Chapter

▶ Seeing how the Parti Québécois was founded

▶ Considering the growing violence and social radicalization

● ●

*I*n the late 1960s, a fever struck the youth of the West. They didn't want to be bound by the chains of tradition any longer. Reform wasn't enough. They had to do something spectacular! Elections? Only fools would fall into that trap! Raise awareness among the masses to develop revolutionary consciousness? That takes too long! They felt the need to act immediately — the better to fight against imperialism, racism, local leaders, employers, the military, the consumer society, and on and on. This sense of agitation took hold of French youth in May 1968. It was also evident among American youth opposed to the Vietnam War and among African Americans who embraced the revolutionary theories of Malcom X in the wake of the 1968 assassination of Martin Luther King, Jr., a leading advocate of nonviolence.

Youth challenged their parents' values, as well as their political choices. Life had to be transformed in all its aspects. This meant putting an end to patriarchy, radically rethinking the family, and reexamining what schools are for. This was the time of the sexual revolution, of communes and drugs, of hippies and flower power — and the time when John Lennon and Yoko Ono, during their "bed-in" in Montreal in 1969, composed their famous song "Give Peace a Chance."

The fever struck Quebec youth as well, and it showed in both their political views and their value systems. They rejected the church their parents attended. Rosary, family prayer, pilgrimages, devotional images, fasting? They were over all that. With his statements against allowing priests to marry and the birth control pill, the new pope, Paul VI, only drove them further away. There were more empty seats at Sunday Mass, and seminaries were emptier still. Priests, brothers, and nuns left their orders to get married — and to work in the department of education! Instead of Catholic Action associations, politicized young people opted for the student movement or revolutionary groups.

The Founding of the Parti Québécois

René Lévesque was aware of the impatience of many Quebec youth. Like many reformers of his generation, he was entranced by youth mobilization. But he feared that it might go too far, that it might spill over into violence. He focused above all on channeling all that energy into a great political cause.

Sovereignty-association

In the summer of 1967, Lévesque, the former Liberal cabinet minister, put down some ideas on paper and developed a new concept that would be a defining issue in the coming years: sovereignty-association. Lévesque presented this document to activists in his constituency on September 18, and the solution he proposed lay at the intersection of two great movements of the time: "freedom of peoples and voluntary economic and political associations."

Because "we are Quebecers" and Quebec is a nation, Lévesque explained, it was essential for Quebec to affirm its "sovereignty" as soon as possible. After Quebec became a sovereign state, it could more easily negotiate, on equal terms, an economic association with the rest of Canada. The new partnership outlined by Lévesque would resemble the association among the countries of Europe: "Such an association seems perfectly tailored to allow us, without the hindrance of old constitutional structures, to pool . . . that which would best serve our economic interests: a customs union, common tariffs, debt management." Thus, a sovereign Quebec could keep the Canadian dollar.

The founding of the MSA

Supported by Liberal activists in his constituency and the more nationalist wing of his party, Lévesque brought his proposal to the Liberal convention that opened in Quebec City on October 13, 1967. The next day, he explained his position at length to the delegates. But most of them were not interested. In their eyes, the former minister was embracing "separatism." After four hours of discussion, Lévesque decided to withdraw his proposal and resign from the Liberal Party.

A month later in Montreal, he and his followers founded the Movement Souveraineté-Association (MSA; Sovereignty-Association Movement). He explained:

> The reasons that direct us toward this constitutional future are reasons of survival. For serious dangers currently threaten our ethnic group. Demographically, the reality is disturbing. Our birth rate, once the highest in Canada, is now the lowest, and it is declining constantly.

Furthermore, immigration works against us. Historically, we have been overwhelmed by a wave of nonfrancophone immigration that, for one reason or another, we have failed to integrate.

Sovereignty-association, he added, would also put an end "to waste and duplication of energy."

A break with the Franco-Ontarians

From November 23 to 26, 1967, the Estates General of French Canada met in Montreal. This was a gathering of old-school nationalists connected to the Saint-Jean-Baptiste societies, and for them it was time to take stock. To ensure the development of French Canada, was it better to seek a thorough transformation of Canada or gain sovereignty for Quebec?

Very soon, a split emerged between activists from Quebec and those from other provinces. The Quebecers presented a motion stating the following:

1. French Canadians constitute a nation.

2. Quebec constitutes the national territory and the principal political center of this nation.

3. The French-Canadian nation has the right to determine its own purposes and to choose freely the political regime under which it intends to live.

After bitter, heart-rending discussions, the motion was finally adopted. Franco-Ontarians felt abandoned and betrayed, and from that point on regarded Quebecers as estranged brothers. These "Estates General" ended with the breakup of traditional French Canada and conversion of the more conservative Quebec nationalists to the idea of sovereignty.

The Trudeau-Johnson confrontation

Although the idea of sovereignty made its way into people's thinking, the Union Nationale government continued to advocate a major reform of the Canadian constitution. On February 5, 1968, Premier Johnson laid out his perspective before his colleagues from other provinces and federal government representatives.

The federal minister of justice, Pierre Elliott Trudeau, squarely rejected Johnson's arguments:

Requesting special powers is an affront to French Canadians. What they want is linguistic equality. Once this is done, they will not need special powers. A "dual Canada" will lead necessarily to special status, then to associated states, and finally to separation.

Johnson responded immediately:

> We delude ourselves if we imagine that Quebec will be satisfied simply because we can speak French in the other provinces! The problem is deeper than that and cannot be cured with aspirin. The two languages will be on an equal footing when the two nations are. It is the entire federal system that must be renegotiated.

Daniel Johnson was not intimidated, but it was Trudeau's vision that made an impression.

A new party

Positions on the future of Quebec were becoming increasingly clear. With Trudeau as prime minister of Canada, Quebec reformers of federalism had to grin and bear it. Quebec would not become an "associated state" tomorrow! In such a context, sovereignty-association as proposed by René Lévesque became an attractive alternative for many Quebec voters. But a real political party had yet to be created.

Negotiations were undertaken between the MSA and the Ralliement National, and the two movements quickly came to an agreement. Talks with the leaders of the Rassemblement pour l'Indépendance Nationale proved much more difficult. Lévesque was "allergic" to the RIN's violent protests and Pierre Bourgault's inflammatory speeches. The two movements also had diametrically opposed views on the language issue. The RIN supported French as the only language and refused to recognize any rights for the English-speaking minority. For Lévesque, this position was unacceptable, and he broke off negotiations altogether.

The founding convention of the Parti Québécois (PQ) was held in Montreal from October 11 to 14, 1968. A few days later, the RIN activists scuttled their party and decided to join the PQ as individuals. Until his retirement from politics, these more radical activists would continue to be the bane of René Lévesque's existence.

The Saint-Léonard crisis

During the months following the creation of the PQ, the language question dominated the political scene. Quebecers gradually became aware that most newcomers enrolled their children in English schools. So, the question arose: Is choosing one's children's language of education a right? The governing Union Nationale and opposition Liberals said yes; the Parti Québécois and the nationalist movement said no.

Trudeaumania!

Pierre Elliott Trudeau viewed Canada as a society of individuals, not as a pact between two nations. The primary role of the federal government was to protect the individual rights of all citizens, whatever their ethnic or cultural origins. To recognize special rights for French Canadians, in his view, was tantamount to believing that they were individually too weak to develop and assert themselves — which was an insult. As long as they could live in their language anywhere in Canada, French Canadians, as people, had absolutely no need for special status.

A few days after his confrontation with Johnson, Trudeau announced his candidacy for the leadership of the Liberal Party of Canada. Even though he didn't have deep roots in the party, the Liberal delegates elected him on April 6, 1968. Being a bachelor and a bit of a dandy enhanced his appeal to women. Trudeau's charisma and clear ideas also attracted many Canadians. Fluently bilingual, he appeared to many to epitomize a modern Canada, open to the world, capable of transcending the two founding cultures.

Immediately after being sworn in as prime minister, he called a general election. Canadians were fascinated and bewitched by the personality of the young Liberal leader. Many went so far as to speak of "Trudeaumania"! On the evening of June 24, the Liberal leader was in the grandstand on Sherbrooke Street in Montreal to watch the traditional Saint-Jean-Baptiste Day parade. Pierre Bourgault and the independentists considered this an affront. Some protesters chanted *"Trudeau au poteau!"* ("String him up!") and threw projectiles at the dignitaries.

Unlike the other notables, Trudeau did not flinch; instead, he challenged the troublemakers. In English Canada's eyes, he had stood up to the separatists. The next day, his party was returned to power with a comfortable majority. Trudeau received a message from Johnson: "I offer you the collaboration of the government of Quebec to ensure the prosperity of our country and the development of the two nations that constitute it."

Welcoming immigrants

This emotional debate took place at a time when Quebec was receiving many immigrants and experiencing a decline in its birth rate. The fertility rate of Quebec couples (the number of children per woman of childbearing age) decreased from 3.77 in 1961 to 1.62 in 1981. Meanwhile, more immigrants were entering Quebec. Between 1946 and 1982, Quebec welcomed 965,075 immigrants. Some of these "new Quebecers" (Poles, Portuguese, and Hungarians) were fleeing dictatorships; others wanted a better future for their children. Until the early 1970s, the vast majority were European and Christian. Between 1961 and 1971, Quebec's Jewish population grew from 74,677 to 115,990, and its Greek population from 19,390 to 42,870. To facilitate the reception and integration of these newcomers, in 1968 the Quebec government created a Department of Immigration and Orientation and training centers for immigrants (*centres d'orientation et de formation des immigrants,* or COFIs).

The death of Daniel Johnson

Premier Daniel Johnson was a sick man. Since 1964, his doctors had suggested that he leave politics and seriously address his heart problem, but he decided to ignore that advice. On the morning of July 3, 1968, his heart stopped, and he was on the brink of death. He was rushed to the hospital and then flown to Bermuda. On his return in September, he began to reflect on the Saint-Léonard crisis and considered adopting legislation that would give primacy to French in Quebec.

Time was against him, however. His doctors found that he had not really recovered. After receiving their verdict, he told a friend: "I'm going to die standing up, this week." On the morning of Thursday, September 26, 1968, Premier Johnson was found dead in his bed. The race for the Union Nationale leadership turned into an acrimonious confrontation between two ministers: Jean-Guy Cardinal and Jean-Jacques Bertrand. The winner was Bertrand, who was formally elected head of his party on June 21, 1969.

The powder keg

Between 1961 and 1971, the Italian community grew dramatically (from 108,552 to 169,655). A significant number of Italians lived in Saint-Léonard, a small suburban municipality on Montreal Island. In 1963, to accommodate the Italians' demand for better education in English for their children starting in primary school, the Saint-Léonard school board set up bilingual classes. Eighty-five percent of Italian-speaking parents enrolled their children in English high schools. Inside and outside the classroom, their children studied in English, socialized in English, lived in English. It quickly became clear that these newcomers would join the ranks of the English-speaking minority.

To reverse this trend toward Anglicization, some Saint-Léonard parents created the Mouvement pour l'Intégration Scolaire (School Integration Movement). On June 27, 1968, the elected members of the Saint-Léonard school board decreed that French would be the only language taught in primary schools. This decision lit a fuse and provoked sharp clashes. Parents of Italian origin felt that they had been toyed with. In their minds, Canada was a bilingual country and English offered a better chance of upward mobility. Why deny them that opportunity? However, in the climate of national affirmation, the French school trustees opposed having a minority Anglicize itself at the expense of the majority. The two positions were irreconcilable: It would be up to the government to decide.

The Official Languages Act

While this debate raged on, the federal government of Pierre Trudeau adopted the Official Languages Act in 1969. English and French, according to section 2, have equal "status . . . rights, and privileges as to their use in all federal institutions, in particular with respect to their use in parliamentary proceedings."

The Trudeau government opted for pan-Canadian institutional bilingualism. Gone were the notions of "English" Canada and "French" Quebec; they were replaced by a single bilingual Canada from coast to coast. Receiving services from the federal government in French and English across Canada became an individual right guaranteed by the state. And respect for this right would now be closely monitored by a commissioner of official languages, who would report regularly on the progress of bilingualism. This legislation, which gave no special responsibility to the Quebec government, got a very cool reception from many of Quebec's elites, but French-speaking people in other provinces saw it as a great victory.

Bill 63: The Act to Promote the French Language in Quebec

The new federal law reassured Saint-Léonard parents who wanted their children to have unlimited access to English schools. However, since education was still within Quebec's jurisdiction, it was up to the Union Nationale government to decide. The dilemma was not easy to resolve: How to choose between the individual rights of a minority and the collective rights of the majority?

To gain clarity, in December 1968, the government set up the Commission of Inquiry on the Position of the French Language and on Language Rights in Quebec, chaired by Jean-Denis Gendron. But it would take time for the Gendron Commission to suggest anything concrete.

On October 23, 1969, to prevent the conflict in Saint-Léonard from escalating further, the Bertrand government introduced a bill, the Act to Promote the French Language in Quebec. It was a strange kind of "promotion." In effect, this legislation guaranteed all parents the freedom to choose their children's language of instruction. Section 2 stated that classes "shall be given in the English language to any child for whom his parents or the persons acting in their stead so request at his enrollment."

The Italian community of Saint-Léonard rejoiced. First, the federal government was on their side, and now the Quebec government! Opponents wrote letters of protest. Because it would facilitate the Anglicization of newcomers, they referred to the legislation by its English name, "Bill 63." On October 31, 1969, a massive demonstration was held in front of the parliament building in Quebec City. But this mobilization failed to bend the Union Nationale government and the Liberal opposition. Bill 63 was passed on November 20, 1969. In the short term, this put an end to the Saint-Léonard crisis. But opponents of the law had not said their last word.

Defeat of the Union Nationale

The language crisis and the founding of the Parti Québécois were major blows to the Union Nationale, and the results of the Quebec election of April 29, 1970, showed the impact of these developments. The ruling party won 17 seats but got fewer votes than the PQ (19.6 percent versus 23.1 percent). René Lévesque's party nevertheless elected only seven members. Lévesque himself was defeated in his constituency. But for a party that had been founded less than two years earlier, it was a major breakthrough.

The big winner of the election was the Liberal Party, which collected 45.4 percent of the vote and won 72 seats. Liberal leader Robert Bourassa, at 36, became the youngest premier in Quebec history. A lawyer and economist, he promised to create 100,000 jobs if his party was elected. Bourassa was a prudent politician, a clever strategist, and a skillful tactician. Constitutional questions and issues of national identity were of little interest to him; his passion was the economic development of Quebec. As he explained in *Bourassa Québec! Nous gouvernerons ensemble une société prospère (Together We Will Govern a Prosperous Society),* a short book that he launched on the campaign trail, it was through becoming richer that Quebecers would become truly free and independent.

Violence and Radicalization

Unfortunately for the young leader, Robert Bourassa, Quebec nationalism quickly caught up with him. Quebec, and indeed the West in general, was like a pot that was heating up and could explode at any time. Many Quebec youth questioned everything: Quebec's political status, the exploitation of workers, the domination of women by men. To rapidly transform society, some were open to the use of violence.

The October Crisis

It was in this context that members of the Front de Libération du Québec (FLQ) took action. Disappointed with the April 1970 election results, these young pro-independence activists were convinced that "bourgeois" democracy would never allow their ideal to triumph. They also believed in the need for direct and dramatic action. By making an impression and striking a blow, they wanted to administer a kind of shock to the general population. At the time, the Tupamaros of Uruguay were regularly making headlines. In July, these revolutionaries kidnapped several well-known figures, and the population followed the latest developments with bated breath.

On Monday morning, October 5, 1970, the Libération cell of the FLQ struck, kidnapping British trade attaché James Richard Cross. Made up of a dozen militants, the cell immediately made its demands known: money and the release of "political prisoners," FLQ members who had been imprisoned following criminal acts. Authorities took things seriously but showed no signs of panic. Premier Bourassa refused to cancel a visit to New York scheduled for October 7. Hoping for early negotiations with the FLQ, the federal government agreed to have the FLQ manifesto read on Radio-Canada on the evening of October 8.

The caustic manifesto held people's attention when it was read on the air:

> The people in the Front de Liberation du Québec are neither Messiahs nor modern-day Robin Hoods. They are a group of Quebec workers who have decided to do everything they can to assure that the people of Quebec take their destiny into their own hands, once and for all.

The FLQ demanded

> total independence for Quebecers; it wants to see them united in a free society, a society purged for good of its gang of rapacious sharks, the big bosses who dish out patronage and their henchmen, who have turned Quebec into a private preserve of cheap labor and unscrupulous exploitation.

There was no longer any question of having confidence in democracy and in "the electoral crumbs that the Anglo-Saxon capitalists toss into the Quebec barnyard every four years." In their view, Quebec was a "society of terrorized slaves, terrorized by the big bosses," by "the Roman capitalist Church," and by "those exclusive clubs of science and culture, the universities." The manifesto ended with a call to rise up:

> There are more and more of us who know and suffer under this terrorist society, and the day is coming when all the Westmounts of Quebec will disappear from the map. . . . We are Quebec workers and we are prepared to go all the way.

On the evening of October 10, Quebec Justice Minister Jérôme Choquette announced on television that no "political prisoner" would be released. However, he promised safe conduct to Cuba for Cross's kidnappers. At approximately 6:20 p.m., the Chénier cell kidnapped Pierre Laporte, deputy premier of Quebec.

Escalation...

For the FLQ, Laporte was a very big catch. This second kidnapping created the impression that the FLQ was well organized and ready to go all out to overthrow the regime. A letter from Laporte published on October 12 reinforced this perception. The number-two person in the government suggested that Quebec was "in the presence of a well-organized escalation that will end only with the release of 'political prisoners.'" On a more personal note,

Laporte pleaded with his boss to exercise caution: "I am the sole head of a large family. . . . My departure would bring about irreparable sorrow. . . . This no longer concerns me alone but a dozen people, all women and young children."

On October 14, union representatives, the publisher of *Le Devoir,* and the leader of the Parti Québécois called on the government to talk with the kidnappers to prevent the execution of hostages. This appeal for caution was very poorly received by the main players, who believed that this initiative amounted to the beginning of the formation of a parallel government.

The next day at the Paul Sauvé Arena in east-end Montreal, a meeting of the Front d'Action Politique (FRAP), a left-wing municipal political party, turned into a pro-FLQ demonstration. The revolutionary Pierre Vallières, author of *Nègres blancs d'Amérique,* a searing account of the Quebec condition published in 1968 (later translated as *White Niggers of America*), rallied the 3,000 activists gathered: "You are the FLQ, you and all grassroots groups who fight for the liberation of Quebec." Robert Lemieux, the FLQ's legal negotiator, shouted his famous *"Nous vaincrons!"* ("We shall overcome!"), which was replayed over and over by the television channels covering the event. These images, which suggested that public opinion was increasingly favorable to the FLQ's demands, led authorities to fear the worst.

For security reasons, the premier and all cabinet members were cloistered in a large hotel downtown. Overwhelmed by these extraordinary events, the police demanded special powers. They were also assembling lists of all activists who, directly or indirectly, might support the FLQ agenda.

Without a warrant, however, it was impossible to raid the activists or stop the presumed sympathizers. Since 1917, the federal government had had access to special legislation under which the authorities could suspend all rights and freedoms if they believed they were facing an "apprehended insurrection." However, not knowing what the real strength of the FLQ was, the Trudeau government hesitated to use this legislation. Although the FLQ was closely monitored by the Royal Canadian Mounted Police, the government did not know how many members it had. The prime minister, who was known as a great defender of individual rights, shied away from taking sole responsibility for this draconian measure. He would not go forward unless the mayor of Montreal and the premier of Quebec made a formal request.

Trudeau received a letter from the premier of Quebec on the evening of October 15:

> We are facing a concerted effort to intimidate and overthrow the government and democratic institutions . . . ; it is clear that the individuals engaged in this effort totally reject the principle of freedom within the rule of law.

At 1 a.m. on October 16, 1970, the federal government invoked the War Measures Act. The Canadian military was deployed in the greater Montreal area to ensure the safety of public places. Without warrants, at night, the police entered hundreds of homes in search of people on their lists. More than 500 people were arrested and imprisoned without seeing a lawyer or knowing the charges against them. Among them were trade unionists, activists, politically engaged poets — and federal Secretary of State Gérard Pelletier, who was confused for an activist of the same name! Many mistakes were made in the largely improvised police operation. Most of the suspects were quickly released.

On October 17, the body of Pierre Laporte was found in a car trunk on Montreal's South Shore. According to the coroner's inquest, the deputy premier had been strangled by his kidnappers a few hours earlier. Members of the Chénier cell would later clearly claim responsibility for the assassination. Laporte's death acted as a cold shower on the movement, and as a call to order. The revolution could cause loss of human life; violence and terrorism could lead to broken families. "Québec libre" perhaps — but not in blood.

The assassination of Pierre Laporte was denounced by all. In Premier Bourassa's eyes, the perpetrators of the crime were "forever unworthy of being Quebecers, unworthy of being French Canadians." Shaken, René Lévesque denounced the "cold fanaticism" of the FLQ: "If they really thought they had a cause, they killed it along with Pierre Laporte, and in dishonoring it thus, we were all more or less tainted."

After an extensive search, the authorities finally found the Libération cell's hideout. On December 3, the kidnappers of James Richard Cross — who was released after 59 days — were exiled to Cuba. Three weeks later, Pierre Laporte's killers were found and arrested; several were eventually convicted of kidnapping and murder. The October Crisis was over.

Social radicalization

The death of Pierre Laporte may have caused people to take another look at their thinking, but it did not discourage the most militant activists for social change. For many, it was the governments, which had refused to negotiate and had invoked the War Measures Act, that were really responsible for Laporte's death. Some even believed that his death served as a pretext to discredit the left and the independence movement. Thus, there was no question of giving up. The struggle against the bourgeois state, big money, and male power had to continue.

Quebec women rise!

Around 1970, a significant fringe of the feminist movement became more radicalized and gave a wider meaning to the fight for women's rights. In addition to demanding equal pay for equal work — an important demand of the Common Front in 1972 — many argued for greater control over their bodies. Amendments to Canada's Criminal Code in 1969 removed the ban on advertising and selling contraceptives and legalized abortion for therapeutic purposes.

That same year, the founders of the Front de Libération des Femmes (Women's Liberation Front) — which became the Centre des Femmes (Women's Center) in 1971 — challenged a Montreal bylaw that outlawed demonstrations. "We wanted to demystify the symbol of the passive and gentle woman who submitted to all decisions," they later wrote.

Approximately 165 were arrested and detained. These women believed that national emancipation and empowerment of women went hand in hand. "No women's liberation without liberation of Quebec. No liberation of Quebec without women's liberation" appeared on the cover of *Québécoises deboutte,* the newspaper they launched in November 1972. The women defined themselves as "slaves of slaves." They were dominated within a society that was also dominated. Their demands included free access to abortion at no charge and a complete redefinition of the "family unit, the traditional base of our society, where the woman becomes the servant of her husband and children."

Union militancy

The fight for social justice took many forms in the early 1970s. Many activists were involved in community groups dedicated to specific causes: "social" housing, public health, abortion, child protection, and so on. Others saw the trade-union movement as the main agent of social change. For these more committed activists, unions should go beyond improving the working conditions of their members. They had no use for this "petty-bourgeois" reformism, and their preferred option was a radical transformation of society. Strikes enabled workers to make gains but also raised awareness of social injustices among the masses. This perspective was widespread within the Confederation of National Trade Unions (CNTU) and the Centrale des Enseignants du Québec (CEQ; Quebec Teachers' Corporation), which, unlike the Quebec Federation of Labour (QFL), represented mainly employees in the public and state-controlled sectors, less vulnerable to fluctuations in the market economy.

From 1968 on, Marcel Pepin, president of the CNTU, spoke of the need to open a "second front." He argued that the mission of the trade union was not only to negotiate better agreements, but also to support political parties and grassroots groups fighting against social inequality. In 1971, the CNTU and the QFL published *Ne comptons que sur nos propres moyens (Rely Only* on *Our Own Resources)* and *L'État, rouage de notre exploitation (The State, Instrument of Our Exploitation),* two anti-capitalist manifestos that advocated radical economic and social reforms. The following year, the CEQ published *L'École au service de la classe dominante (Schools in the Service of the Ruling Class),* which adopted the same anti-capitalist rhetoric. Instead of promoting equal opportunities and conditions, it said, schools in the capitalist system ensured the domination of the strong over the weak. The new mission of the teachers was to put an end to this bourgeois ideology.

Three union leaders imprisoned

This ideological background is important for understanding the fierce struggle that pitted the Bourassa government against the trade-union Common Front in 1972. To increase their strength relative to the government, the CNTU, QFL, and CEQ decided to unite their 200,000 members working in the public and parapublic sectors.

Among the demands put on the table by the Common Front was minimum pay of $100 a week, regardless of the job involved. The government said this would be too expensive. As negotiations stalled, a general strike was launched on April 11. Quebec was completely paralyzed. On April 21, the government passed special legislation suspending the right to strike. Anyone who defied the law would be subject to stiff penalties.

Although the CNTU was divided, its president, Marcel Pepin called on his members to disobey the law, as did Yvon Charbonneau of the CEQ and Louis Laberge of the QFL. This act of defiance earned the three union leaders sentences of one year in prison. Their noncompliance with the law led to a split in the labor movement and the creation of the Confédération des Syndicats Démocratiques (Confederation of Democratic Trade Unions).

This strategy of common fronts would come back to haunt governments and Quebecers in general, who were taken hostage by these labor disputes. But it would benefit public-sector employees in the 1970s, who would get their $100 a week and working conditions that were often better than those in the private sector. To mitigate the effects of these strikes, the government passed legislation in December 1972 that identified Hydro-Quebec as an "essential service." Three years later, social services and health services would also be required to provide the public with basic services.

A red Quebec

The ultra-radical left was split into two wings. Members of one wing were involved in the labor movement and supported the Parti Québécois. They were willing to make common cause with more conservative nationalists and focus on the issue of Quebec sovereignty. The other wing created a myriad of small groups on the extreme left. Mao's China inspired them more than the

Soviet Union; they saw the Chinese leader's Cultural Revolution as evidence that he remained faithful to the true principles of Marxism-Leninism. The Quebec Maoists thought along sectarian lines and infiltrated community groups, local unions, and a number of university departments. They were fierce opponents of the PQ, which in their eyes was a bourgeois party in the pay of American imperialism. But the people they hoped to inspire refused to follow them. In 1976, the workers brought a sovereignist party to power, a first in the history of Quebec.

Chapter 19

The Opening of James Bay and the Election of the Parti Québécois (1973–1979)

. . . .

In This Chapter

▶ Getting hydroelectric development in the north

▶ Declaring French the official language

▶ Seeing what a sovereignist government looks like

. . . .

*O*n October 29, 1973, Robert Bourassa's government was reelected with an overwhelming majority. Of the 108 members in the new National Assembly, 102 were Liberals. With the Union Nationale virtually wiped off the map, the Parti Québécois (PQ) won 30.2 percent of the vote and became the official opposition with six seats. The economy remained the Liberals' chief talking point. "An economically weak people can always have a past, but it can never have a future," the young premier declared.

The Liberals portrayed the PQ's sovereignty-association proposal as a risky plan, an expensive and dangerous adventure. During the 1973 campaign, they printed mock banknotes with René Lévesque's image on them. To reassure the population, the PQ presented a "budget for year 1" as a way of showing that a sovereign Quebec would be economically viable. Few were convinced by the exercise. The war of numbers did not play out to the sovereignists' advantage.

However, the PQ's platform still embodied renewal and fed the dreams of young Quebecers. The Liberals were well aware of this, and they had no intention of abandoning the entire nationalist field to the PQ. In 1971, Premier Bourassa had refused to sign the Victoria Charter, a constitutional agreement proposed by Pierre Elliott Trudeau's federal government. Although it settled nothing, this gesture reassured nationalists. After his reelection, Bourassa intended to introduce bold measures to protect the French language. However, his efforts were not enough to stop the irresistible rise of the PQ, which would adopt a number of major reforms after it gained power in 1976.

From Robert Bourassa to René Lévesque

The year 1973 was dominated by the energy crisis. The price of oil exploded, and its rise had an immediate effect on inflation. Energy became a major factor in development. Some leading figures in the PQ believed that Quebec needed to turn to nuclear power, just as France had. Although he approved the construction of an initial nuclear plant at Bécancour, Premier Bourassa was resistant to nuclear power. First, he was concerned about safety — nuclear power is risky, and no one knew what to do with radioactive waste. Plus, Quebec's expertise was primarily in the hydroelectric field. Instead of dotting the landscape with nuclear plants, the government proposed to harness untamed rivers and build large dams. Because hydroelectricity is both renewable and the cleanest form of energy, it was a very wise choice.

The James Bay development

Once the government had settled on the hydroelectric option, the next question was where development would take place. After assessing a variety of factors, Hydro-Quebec made its choice: the La Grande River, an immense natural basin in the heart of the James Bay region.

Marching to the promised land

With great pomp, the Bourassa government announced in April 1971, exactly a year after it was first elected, that it would undertake a massive hydroelectric project. The project would involve a $6-billion investment and the creation of 125,000 jobs. The area it would affect was huge: 350,000 square kilometers (135,136 square miles), or two-thirds the area of France. The James Bay Development Corporation would supervise every stage of the project. A 725-kilometer (451-mile) road between Matagami and Fort George would be built to facilitate access to this remote region. Construction began soon afterward.

Thousands of workers spent time at the construction sites, far from their families. The work took a long time because of the size of the project. The LG-2 dam was opened in 1979, and was in full operation by 1982. Two years later, the LG-3 and LG-4 dams began producing electricity. Huge hydro towers had to be built to support the transmission lines that linked the dams to southern Quebec and the United States, to which Quebec began to export some of this green energy. Sections of forests were cut down, lands were expropriated, and some landscapes were stripped bare, but it was a technical achievement.

Reaching agreement with Aboriginal nations

In November 1973, a Quebec Superior Court judge upheld the claims of the Aboriginal peoples who had lived on the lands surrounding the La Grande River forever. The Cree and Inuit maintained that they had ancestral rights to these lands, which had been annexed to Quebec in 1898 and 1912. A long series of negotiations began between representatives of the Aboriginal nations and the Quebec government.

The James Bay And Northern Quebec Agreement was signed on November 11, 1975. It provided for the following:

- ✔ Cession of territorial rights by the two Aboriginal peoples involved

- ✔ Compensation of $225 million paid to the Cree and Inuit by the Quebec government in exchange for ceding their rights

- ✔ Preservation of traditional Aboriginal hunting and fishing activities

- ✔ Right of compensation on future Quebec government development projects in the region, especially in regard to their environmental impact

This agreement was unprecedented in Quebec. Since 1867, and especially since Canada's Indian Act was passed in 1876, the federal government had been directly responsible for Aboriginal people. Parked in reserves on the basis of strictly ethnic criteria, Aboriginal people living in Quebec had never maintained relations with the Quebec government.

In 1978, another agreement along the same lines was signed with the Naskapi of northeastern Quebec. As a result, the construction of dams could continue.

Surveying a scene of destruction

The James Bay construction sites had plenty of well-paid jobs. For the Confederation of National Trade Unions (CNTU) and the Quebec Federation of Labour (QFL), James Bay was a prime area for recruiting new members. Both union federations tried to gain dominance, and the struggle between them was fierce, with the force of argument often giving way to intimidation by strongmen working for the union locals.

In the competition to get workers to sign up, nothing seemed to be out of bounds. On March 21, 1974, a QFL business agent working for André (Dédé)

Desjardins — later known for his links to organized crime — crashed his bull-dozer into the three generators that provided electricity to the camp where the LG-2 workers were housed. By the time he was finished, he had also ruptured two storage tanks holding 135,000 liters (35,663 gallons) of gasoline and diesel fuel. The result: a fire, an emergency evacuation by chartered planes, enormous material damages amounting to $31 million, and a two-month delay in construction.

The perpetrator, Yvon Duhamel, explained his action in trade-union terms: Working conditions at the construction sites were unacceptable. But the Bourassa government sensed that something else was going on, and it established the Cliche Commission to investigate the exercise of trade-union freedom in the construction industry. Judge Robert Cliche, known for his left-wing sympathies, was joined on the commission by trade-union representative Guy Chevrette and management representative Brian Mulroney. A parade of union activists and construction-site bosses passed before the commissioners. With the help of wiretap evidence, allowed at the time, the commission uncovered infiltration by organized crime and troubling links between some shady characters and Premier Bourassa's entourage. The Cliche Commission's extensive report was released on May 2, 1975. A number of union locals were placed in trusteeship.

French: Quebec's official language

While Quebec developed its economy, new immigrants continued to send their children to the schools of the English minority. Figures published by demographer Louis Duchesne in November 1973 spoke for themselves. In the year 1972–1973 alone, 86.3 percent of the 60,800 "allophone" students (students of neither French nor English origin) went to English schools. These statistics accentuated the French-speaking majority's sense of cultural insecurity and confirmed the most alarmist hypotheses put forward by nationalists. The PQ missed no opportunity to go after the Bourassa government on this sensitive issue.

The Gendron Commission's conclusions

The Gendron Commission, established by Premier Jean-Jacques Bertrand in the middle of the Saint-Léonard crisis, finally submitted its report on December 31, 1972. The report, based on technical expertise and 155 briefs submitted at public hearings, was very thorough. The commissioners put their cards on the table in their first recommendation:

> We recommend that the Quebec government adopt as a general objective the establishment of French as the common language of Quebecers, that is, a language that everybody knows and that can therefore serve as an instrument of communication in situations of contact between francophone [French-speaking] and nonfrancophone Quebecers.

In their view, for French to become the normal and usual language of all inhabitants of Quebec, the government needed to regulate workplaces and commercial signs. However, there was no recommendation on the most delicate subject, the language of education. The analytical framework outlined in the report would be the inspiration for the major language legislation to come.

Bill 22: The language bill

After being reelected in 1973, the Liberals decided to introduce a language bill that would be bolder than the previous Union Nationale government's legislation. "In Quebec, we can live in French without destroying the country," Premier Bourassa said repeatedly. It was both a conviction and a gamble.

Bill 22, which received royal assent on July 31, 1974, contained the following provisions:

- ✔ **French was proclaimed "the official language of the province of Québec."** This was a first in the history of Quebec, and a powerful symbol! Supporters of Canadian bilingualism were unhappy with this formulation; they saw it as contrary to the spirit of the federal Official Languages Act.

- ✔ **French would be the official language of public administration.** All official texts and documents of the government and public administration had to be drawn up in French. If there was an English version, only the French version had legal force.

- ✔ **French must also be the language of work.** Companies wanting to obtain Quebec government assistance or benefits had to get a "certificate of francization." Among the requirements for such a certificate were knowledge of French by the company's management and capacity of its personnel to communicate in French with one another and with management.

- ✔ **Access to English schools would be restricted.** Language of education would no longer be a matter of free choice. The schools of the English minority would be available only to children who already had "a sufficient knowledge" of English. Students' level of knowledge would be evaluated through language tests.

Unfortunately for the Bourassa government, everyone was unhappy with the legislation. Nationalists felt that its provisions regarding the language of work lacked teeth and that those regarding the language of education could well turn out to be ineffective. For English-speaking Quebecers, the law was an outrage, even a scandal. Some accused the Liberals of trampling on the rights of new immigrants, while others deplored the lack of respect shown to English.

The saga of the 1976 Olympic Games

Hosting the Olympic Games was an ambition that Montreal had held for many years. Mayor Camillien Houde had led a bid for the 1932 Olympics, and again for the 1956 games. Each time, another city had come out ahead. In the mid-1960s, the idea was revived. A year before Montreal's 1967 World's Fair, Mayor Jean Drapeau launched a bid for the 1972 games, which were eventually awarded to Munich. Drapeau — a visionary according to some people, a megalomaniac according to others — would not take no for an answer. On May 12, 1970, Montrealers heard the good news: The Games of the XXI Olympiad of the modern era would be held in Montreal in 1976. The mayor had won!

The next task was to build the huge athletic complex where the 6,084 athletes from 92 countries would compete. The application Mayor Drapeau submitted to the International Olympic Committee included a total budget of $120 million for the games. But this budget was soon deemed unrealistic, especially in light of the mayor's grandiose architectural ambitions. Entranced by the Parc des Princes soccer stadium in Paris, Drapeau had his heart set on getting the French architect Roger

Taillibert — whom some people called "the Michelangelo of concrete" — to design the Olympic stadium.

Early on, the governments of Quebec and Canada had to contribute to the financing of the games. An Olympic lottery was launched in 1973. However, poor management and several work stoppages led to a delay in construction, to the point that the Bourassa government established the Olympic Installations Board in November 1975 and took control of the construction site. The 70,000-seat stadium was completed on time, but without its inclined tower, which was finished later.

From a budgetary standpoint, many people consider the Olympics a fiasco. All in all, the Olympic adventure burned through a cool $2 billion. From an athletic standpoint, however, the games were a huge success for Montreal and Quebec. More than 3.2 million spectators attended the 198 competitions in the 21 Olympic sports. These events were shown on television around the world. After the games ended, the Olympic Stadium was home to a number of professional sports teams, including the city's National League baseball team, the Montreal Expos.

The Election of the Parti Québécois

The organizational shambles of the Olympic Games, the allegations of collusion between organized crime and some leading figures in the Liberal Party, and the criticism of Bill 22 weakened Robert Bourassa's government. At the same time, more conservative voters were hesitant about switching to the Parti Québécois and sought reassurance.

A new step-by-step strategy

In the 1970 and 1973 elections, a vote for the Parti Québécois was clearly a vote in favor of sovereignty-association. A PQ government, having won a majority of the seats in the National Assembly, would begin the process leading to secession — even if the sovereignists had won fewer than 50 percent of the votes cast. In the 1973 election, the most the PQ leadership promised was that, after negotiations with the rest of Canada had been completed, the new constitution of a sovereign Quebec would be submitted for ratification by the people in a referendum. But this promise was not clearly put forward.

A sharp turn

At its November 1974 convention, the PQ decided to change the process for acceding to sovereignty-association. Officially, the reason for the change was to make the process more democratic; unofficially, tactical and electoral considerations played a significant role. The PQ now promised that if it formed a government it would proceed by *étapes* (steps): first the election of a good government; then a referendum on giving the government a mandate to negotiate sovereignty-association; finally, if Quebecers voted Yes, the beginning of negotiations with Canada.

This *"étapiste"* strategy did not meet with universal acclaim. It was denounced both by federalists and by hardline independentists, with both camps accusing the PQ leadership of opportunism or of trying to hide its option. Some referred to the strategy sarcastically as *"étapette,"* a play on a derogatory French term for a homosexual.

Thus, when the Bourassa government called an election in the fall of 1976, the PQ ran on a platform that emphasized "good government." The Lévesque team harshly criticized the Liberal government's record and promised to govern more transparently and competently. As in 1970 and 1973, the Liberals raised the specter of a brutal, painful separation from Canada if the PQ was elected. Meanwhile, the Union Nationale had a new leader, Rodrigue Biron, and a platform that included a promise to restore parents' free choice of the language of their children's education if it was elected. This promise by the party that Maurice Duplessis had founded was very attractive to the English-speaking and *allophone* (those whose native language was neither English nor French) minorities, who were distressed by Bill 22.

"Something like a great people"

On the morning of November 15, 1976, it was impossible to know who would win that day's election — the most recent polls were sending mixed signals. What was clear was that there was a lot of interest in this election — more than 85 percent of the electorate voted that day. The PQ's victory took shape early in the evening; in the end, it took 41 percent of the vote and 71 seats. Premier Bourassa was defeated in his own riding by a 36-year-old poet, Gérald Godin. The Liberals won only 26 seats and just 34 percent of the popular vote. With 11 seats and 19 percent of the vote, the Union Nationale appeared to have risen from the ashes, but its new flame would be short-lived.

Robert Bourassa quickly conceded victory to the PQ and suggested to investors that they proceed cautiously. Meanwhile, the new premier of Quebec, René Lévesque, made a triumphal entrance into Paul Sauvé Arena, where more than 10,000 celebrating supporters were waiting for him. The PQ leader was stirred by his victory, but not necessarily in a mood to party. Eyewitnesses are unanimous in reporting that the victory came as a surprise to him. Suddenly he felt the weight of the political and historical responsibility that had been placed on his shoulders. After being painfully hoisted up onto the platform, carried by the crowd but closely followed by a horde of photographers and reporters from around the world, Lévesque began his victory speech. He said he was proud of being a Québécois and then cried out in his characteristic hoarse voice, "We are not a small people. Perhaps we are something like a great people!" The celebrations continued through the night. But no matter how excited the winners were or how stunned the losers were, it all happened in an orderly fashion.

A victory for the "separatists" — and for the "petty bourgeoisie"!

Less than ten years after General de Gaulle's *"Vive le Québec libre!"* (see Chapter 17), Quebec was once again a front-page story around the world. "Separatists win in Quebec," read the headline in the *New York Post* the day after the PQ victory, and it was echoed in a number of other daily newspapers in world capitals. *The New York Times, The Washington Post, Le Monde,* and *Le Figaro* devoted editorials to the event, most of them hostile to the new government's constitutional option. Even *Pravda,* the official organ of the Communist Party of the Soviet Union, contributed its analysis — Quebecers, it explained, had chosen a "petty bourgeois" party!

In the days following the election of the PQ, there was some volatility in the markets, and the share prices of some Quebec companies fell. On the whole, however, people agreed to give the new government a chance. Lévesque reiterated that he would undertake negotiations with the federal government only after having received a clear mandate from the people in a referendum. Despite his reassuring words, the English-speaking population of Quebec would shrink by 95,000 between 1976 and 1980.

In a televised address on November 24, Canadian Prime Minister Pierre Trudeau also struck a reassuring note: "Quebecers have chosen a new government; not a new country. Mr. Lévesque has no mandate to bring in separation." Trudeau committed himself to demonstrating that "it is possible to be, at the same time, a good Canadian and a good Quebecer." Supporters and opponents of sovereignty-association would confront each other on the battleground of democracy. Their weapons in the war that had just begun would be words, arguments, and speeches.

The first sovereignist government

Immediately after being sworn in on November 25, 1976, René Lévesque announced to Quebec's senior civil servants that there would be no purge. But he was counting on their loyalty and respect for democracy. In a solemn ceremony that same day, he presented his cabinet, one of the most highly educated in Quebec history. It was a politically diverse group: Some tended to be pro-union, while others were more conservative; some were in a hurry to implement sovereignty, while others were more open to a thorough reform of federalism.

In the middle of all these currents, René Lévesque would act as referee — and orchestra conductor. After introducing all his ministers, Lévesque set a very high standard:

> Never in living memory have a group of men and women carried so many hopes at the same time. . . . If we have to disappoint Quebecers, it will be a blow to our confidence in ourselves as a people. We simply don't have the right to miss our chance.

Lévesque and Jefferson: Fighting the same fight?

Outside Canada, there was considerable interest in the November 15 election. Invitations poured in. The first major prestigious international platform offered to the new premier was the Economic Club of New York, where magnates of finance and business and influential politicians would be in the audience. Lévesque's speech to that audience on January 25, 1977, was much anticipated — but it fell completely flat. Lévesque compared Quebec to the British colonies before the 1776 revolution. For many in the audience, the comparison was not just lame but offensive. The financiers were more likely to relate the Quebec sovereignists' campaign to the position of the Southern states that provoked the Civil War in the mid-19th century.

In the end, however, Wall Street's concerns were not so much political as economic: Would Quebec become the Cuba of the north? Was the new government planning to carry out a wave of nationalizations? Lévesque did not answer these questions clearly. His inept speech was no help to the people who were trying to sell Quebec bonds to the Wall Street financiers or borrow money from large American banks.

Parizeau: Money Talks!

Lévesque and his colleagues sought to diversify the Quebec government's sources of financing and income, so that they could bypass the large English-Canadian and American financial syndicates. The person called in to accomplish this was the new minister of finance, Jacques Parizeau.

From an upper-class family — and proud of it! — Parizeau was born in 1930. He received his secondary education in a French *lycée* in Montreal's wealthy enclave of Outremont before being admitted to the École des Hautes Études Commerciales. His teachers soon decided to send this brilliant student to the best schools in Europe.

At the London School of Economics, Parizeau obtained his doctorate under the guidance of a future Nobel laureate. He came back from London with a British accent and three-piece suits. His erudition and his forceful personality made a strong impression. During the Quiet Revolution, he was drafted to provide technical advice on the nationalization of hydroelectricity and conceptualize the rough outlines of the Caisse de Dépôt et Placement. In the new sovereignist government, he held the purse strings.

His first concern was to show the world that Quebec securities were sound and investing in Quebec was still good business. Accompanied by a small team, he toured the planet's financial centers, from Frankfurt through Zürich and London to Tokyo. His arguments were convincing and his charm had its effect. The Quebec government would not have any trouble finding financing.

The Parti Québécois: "A crime against the history of mankind"

While Jacques Parizeau was rounding up millions in the world's major financial capitals (see the nearby sidebar), Pierre Elliott Trudeau was trying to demonstrate that if the PQ was successful, it would be not only harmful to Canada but a tragedy for humanity. Trudeau was invited to address a joint session of the U.S. Congress on February 22, 1977 — the first such invitation issued to a Canadian prime minister.

"The only hope for humanity," he explained, "is the willingness of peoples of differing complexions and cultures and beliefs to live peaceably together." Canada, Trudeau maintained, seeks this peaceful coexistence by providing French Canadians with language rights that allow them to develop and choose their own destiny:

> I am confident that we in Canada are well along in the course of devising a society as free of prejudice and fear, as full of understanding and generosity, as respectful of individuality and beauty, as receptive to change and innovation, as exists anywhere.

Consequently, the failure of Canada would be a "crime against the history of mankind." In a grave tone, Trudeau said that a victory for the sovereignists "would create shock waves of disbelief among those all over the world who are committed to the proposition that among man's noblest endeavors are those communities in which persons of diverse origins live, love, work, and find mutual benefit." In Trudeau's view, Canadian federalists were promoting the cause of all humanity. Their struggle was not just a political one but a moral one as well.

A Gaullist love-in

The PQ victory received a cool reception in the United States, but this was not the case in France, which from November 2 to 4, 1977, welcomed René Lévesque as if he were already a head of state. Wrapped up in European issues, some French politicians perceived the Quebec sovereignists as courageous resisters of American hegemony. "We will not allow France to become the Quebec of Europe!" declared a former prime minister under General de Gaulle a few weeks after the PQ victory.

Lévesque also benefited from a division among the heirs of Gaullism. After serving as prime minister under President Valéry Giscard d'Estaing for two years, Jacques Chirac had resigned dramatically and founded a new party hostile to Giscard. Having meanwhile become mayor of Paris, he gave Lévesque a splashy welcome at city hall in an effort to appropriate one of the general's legacies. President Giscard d'Estaing also wanted to associate himself with the PQ victory, which many French people saw as confirming General de Gaulle's prophecy.

Red carpets were rolled out, the Quebec flag flew over the National Assembly, and the Quebec premier was invested as a "grand officer of the Legion of Honor." Did this mean that France openly supported Quebec sovereignty? Not quite. The diplomatic formula that was adopted would remain in place for many years: "noninterference" but "nonindifference"! France wouldn't tell Quebecers how to vote, but it would follow their discussions closely and support their decision, whatever it was.

The charter of the French language

While the PQ's plans were being explained in New York, Washington, and Paris, in Quebec the media spotlight was on the new government's initial reforms.

Dr. Laurin: The "father of Bill 101"

Among the heavyweights of the Lévesque cabinet was Camille Laurin (1922–1999), or Dr. Laurin as he was generally known. The son of a small shopkeeper in Charlemagne northeast of Montreal, he pursued higher education in Boston and Paris. His ambition was to follow in the footsteps of Sigmund Freud and become a famous psychiatrist. On his return, he became director of the Institut Albert-Prévost, a Montreal institution for people with mental illnesses, and a professor in the faculty of medicine at the University of Montreal.

"Je me souviens" — but what exactly do I remember?

In 1978, the Lévesque government decided to place the motto *"Je me souviens"* ("I remember") on Quebec license plates. It replaced *"La Belle Province,"* more of a tourist slogan, which the French still use to describe the territory of their Quebec "cousins."

"Je me souviens" has been Quebec's official motto since the adoption of the Quebec coat of arms on December 9, 1939. The motto refers neither to values (as does France's motto of *"Liberté, égalité, fraternité"*) nor to territorial limits (as does the Canadian motto of *"A mari usque ad mare"*). Instead, it's an enigmatic formula whose significance is still under discussion. Tourists and new immigrants often find it intriguing.

Some people see *"Je me souviens"* as stoking the fires of resentment against the English, assuming that it means "I remember the defeat on the Plains of Abraham and will avenge it." Others believe that the motto, formulated in the late 19th century by Eugène-Étienne Taché, architect of the Quebec parliament building, is actually unifying and liberal. Until recently, the phrase "I remember that, born under the lily, I grow under the rose" was attributed to Taché. The architect, who had *"Je me souviens"* engraved in stone over the main door of the parliament building, believed that Quebec was born of France, owed its freedoms to British institutions, and belonged to Canada.

Whatever its exact significance, the motto shows that the past is at the heart of the Quebec identity. Since the early 1960s, whenever a new history curriculum has been proposed by the department of education, it has been examined in great detail and vigorously debated.

In the course of his practice, he observed that French Canadians were most often hesitant, indecisive, torn. Their personal identity and personality lacked dynamism. Laurin attributed these deficiencies to centuries of colonial domination. "I concluded that collective psychotherapy was needed," he wrote in 1972, two years after being elected as a PQ member of the National Assembly. In his view, only political independence would make it possible for Quebecers to regain their self-confidence.

He was defeated in the 1973 election, but regained his seat in 1976 and was named minister of state for cultural development. The thorny language issue came under his portfolio.

A Quebec as French as Ontario is English

On April 1, 1977, Laurin released a white paper explaining the major principles that would guide the government on the language issue. The white paper was written by prominent sociologists Guy Rocher and Fernand Dumont, and represented their thinking.

A basic premise was that language is not just a simple instrument of communication. Instead, as Laurin explained in a speech in the National Assembly on July 19, 1977, it is "the very foundation of a people, the basis of its self-recognition and recognition by others, which takes root in its being and allows it to express its identity." The language question is primarily a collective issue. If individuals are bilingual or speak several languages, so much the better, but if a people is to develop in a coherent manner, an official language is needed, common to all.

Quebec needed to become as French as Ontario is English, Laurin insisted. And all this could be done without trampling on the rights of the English-speaking minority, which would retain its institutions. To get there, Laurin believed that French needed to become "the normal and habitual language of work at all levels of business, among managers and professionals, in terminology and advertising, in internal and external communication." For language was also a social issue in Quebec. Even though French was the language of the majority, in many cases it was a barrier to career advancement or was looked down on by executives of large corporations.

Controversial provisions

The PQ's language bill, commonly called "Bill 101" and passed on August 26, 1977, was truly a "charter of the French language." These were some of its boldest — and most widely criticized — provisions:

- ✔ **French became the only language of legislation and justice.** Not only did trials have to be held in French, but judgments had to be rendered in French as well. This provision contravened Section 133 of the British North America Act, which provided for justice in both languages in Quebec.

- ✔ **Commercial and public signs had to be in French only.** English signs were banned. All businesses had to post their signs in French only, or else they would be fined. Corporate names also had to be francized.

- ✔ **Access to English schools was limited to children of the English-speaking minority.** No more language tests! English schools would be accessible only to children whose parents had themselves attended English schools in Quebec. This provision would even apply to an English Canadian from another province — unless that province maintained a publicly funded French school system. Its greatest impact was on immigrants who arrived after Bill 101 was passed, who would now be required to enroll their children in the French system through the end of high school.

Two agencies were established to implement the provisions of Bill 101: the Office Québécois de la Langue Française and the Conseil Supérieur de la Langue Française. All businesses with at least 50 employees were required to obtain a certificate of francization as soon as possible.

A merciless attack!

Bill 101 was discussed extensively in cabinet before being presented publicly. Some ministers feared that businesses would close. René Lévesque himself thought that the bill went too far. He wasn't happy with the provisions regarding commercial signs. But he came around to supporting the bill, as did the entire cabinet.

When it was released, the bill caused a stir among Quebecers. A number of immigrant associations denounced the bill as unjust. Claude Ryan, the publisher of *Le Devoir* and future leader of the Quebec Liberal Party, called the signage provisions "contrary to the most elementary principles of freedom of expression." Pierre Elliott Trudeau criticized it as "ethnic" legislation, which, he said, sought to create a "monolithic society."

But while the critics were merciless, the government held firm. Nationalists were ecstatic. "We have just lived through . . . the greatest moment in our history since, it might be said, the founding of Quebec in 1608," wrote François-Albert Angers in the journal *L'Action Nationale*. In the decades that followed, Bill 101 was amended several times and went through some reversals, but its spirit was maintained and there was a broad consensus in its favor. The language of education provisions weren't challenged by successive governments.

A blizzard of reforms

The first PQ government was impressive in its reforming zeal, introducing one piece of major legislation after another in rapid succession.

No more secret election funds

Ever since he had first entered politics, René Lévesque had dreamed of cleaning up Quebec's political practices. He was disgusted by the shadowy influence of some big bosses and the existence of secret election funds. On August 26, 1977, the Act to Govern the Financing of Political Parties, brought before the National Assembly by the minister of state for parliamentary reform, Robert Burns, was finally passed. The following were some of its notable provisions:

- ✔ **Only citizens registered on voters' lists could make contributions to political parties.** No contributions could be made by companies, unions, associations, or clubs of any kind.

- ✔ **Contributions to political parties would be limited to a maximum of $3,000.** It would no longer be possible to "buy" a party or a candidate. The reform aimed to have political parties financed by the people. Contributions would be partially tax deductible.

> ✔ **Contributions would be transparent.** The director general of elections would make public all contributions of $100 or more.

> ✔ **Public financing would be increased.** The government would assume a larger share of election expenses.

Many people believe that subsequent events have made a mockery of the spirit of this legislation. Nevertheless, it remains a point of reference in Quebec, in Canada, and elsewhere in the world.

Protection for agricultural lands

Like all Western societies, Quebec in the 1970s was overwhelmingly urban. In 1981, its agricultural workforce represented only 2.6 percent of its total workforce. But while there may be fewer farmers than there used to be, their farms are larger and their approach to agriculture is more industrial. The proportion of Quebec's vast territory consisting of good arable land is only 2 percent. Jean Garon, the new minister of agriculture, persuaded his colleagues to adopt measures to protect these lands from uncontrolled suburban development. In late 1978, a series of decrees was issued for this purpose. The Commission de Protection du Territoire Agricole (Agricultural Land Protection Commission) was established to ensure respect for the new zoning regulations.

Boat people "sponsored" by Quebecers

In the late 1970s, many Vietnamese fled the Communist government that took over their country after the Americans left in 1975. They were called "boat people" because they traveled onboard makeshift boats where people were crushed under a mass of bodies and the hygiene conditions were barely imaginable. Images of their tragic odyssey were transmitted to the four corners of the world.

Many Quebecers wanted to provide relief for these unfortunate people. To organize this outpouring of humanitarian feeling, Immigration Minister Jacques Couture established a sponsorship program in July 1979. Quebecers who participated in the program made a commitment to support the integration of these refugees and subsidize their needs for at least a year. Almost 8,000 Vietnamese, spread among 215 Quebec municipalities, benefited from this program up to March 1981. Quebec writer Kim Thúy, very grateful for having been welcomed so warmly when she was a little girl, told her story in *Ru* (published in French by Libre Expression in 2009 and in English translation by Random House Canada in 2012). The book was a runaway bestseller in Quebec and elsewhere.

A few years earlier, Quebecers had welcomed other refugees fleeing authoritarian regimes, especially Jean-Claude Duvalier's Haiti and Augusto Pinochet's Chile. These women and men established roots in Quebec. Many have distinguished themselves in politics, sports, and the arts, and have brought luster to Quebec. One such person is the acclaimed writer Dany Laferrière, who has been recognized with several awards. In 2009, his novel *L'énigme du retour* (later translated as *The Return*) won the prestigious Prix Médicis.

An agreement on immigration

As a society's birth rate declines, its interest in immigration tends to increase. Its concerns are economic — it wants to bring in a skilled, dynamic workforce. In the case of Quebec, however, cultural concerns predominate. The hope is that new immigrants will integrate into the French-speaking majority. In 1978, Quebec Immigration Minister Jacques Couture and his federal counterpart signed a major administrative agreement that increased Quebec's autonomy. The agreement did not deal with "political refugees" or family reunification. Instead, it concerned "independent immigrants" — those who freely chose to leave their countries of origin. Quebec could now determine the number of immigrants it would receive each year. It could also develop its own selection grid for new immigrants and, hence, encourage the immigration of French-speaking people.

Chapter 20

Federalism: A Risk Worth Taking (1980–1987)

....

In This Chapter

▶ Facing a referendum on sovereignty-association

▶ Questioning the welfare state

....

*I*n the 1980s, Quebec, like the rest of the Western world, felt the impact of a major economic recession. To combat inflation, which had been rampant since 1973, central banks raised interest rates dramatically, causing many bankruptcies and a general economic slowdown. The increasingly indebted welfare state was in no position to act effectively to curb this new crisis. British Prime Minister Margaret Thatcher, who came to office in 1979, and U.S. President Ronald Reagan, elected in 1980, even believed that, economically speaking, government was more part of the problem than the solution. In their view, to allow free enterprise to create new wealth, government should deregulate the economy and privatize some public enterprises — in short, remove obstacles to the free market. Many Canadian and Quebec politicians embraced this "neoliberal" philosophy.

In Quebec, however, people were preoccupied more with political than with economic issues. In Quebec, the constitutional question dominated the news of the 1980s. The major concern of the political class was to settle, once and for all, the question of Quebec, either through sovereignty-association or through reform of the Canadian constitution. Whether they worked on the federal or the Quebec scene, whether they were Liberal or PQ, Quebec politicians were keenly aware of this sensitive issue hanging over their heads.

The Parti Québecois's Ordeal

The 1980s were akin to a severe hangover for the Parti Québécois. The PQ government was reelected with a large majority on April 13, 1981. However, after the euphoria of the 1976 victory and the adoption of major reforms, it suffered a series of bitter setbacks on the constitutional front — at the same time that it was grappling with the economic recession.

The defeat of the "yes" side

René Lévesque had made a formal commitment to his party activists to hold a referendum during his first term in office. Although polls indicated that sovereignty-association would not receive the support of a majority of Quebecers, the PQ leader would not renege on this commitment.

The controversial question of the question

It went without saying that Quebecers would be consulted, but what specific question would they be asked? The idea of having them approve a declaration of independence or the constitution of a sovereign Quebec was quickly rejected. The 1976 platform had imagined a referendum to seek a mandate to enter into negotiations that might lead to sovereignty-association. This is also what was announced in *Québec-Canada: A New Deal,* a document presenting the main arguments in favor of the PQ project that the government published in 1979. Lévesque's ambition was to establish a partnership of equals with Canada. In his eyes, the hyphen between *sovereignty* and *association* was inescapable, even essential. In no way, however, did he want to rush Quebecers. He was well aware that his government's draft constitution raised concerns.

On December 19, 1979, the PQ cabinet members worked hard to find a question that would be both clear and relevant. Every word was weighed. They finally came up with the following:

> The Government of Quebec has made public its proposal to negotiate a new agreement with the rest of Canada, based on the equality of nations; this agreement would enable Quebec to acquire the exclusive power to make its laws, levy its taxes, and establish relations abroad — in other words, sovereignty — and at the same time to maintain with Canada an economic association including a common currency; any change in political status resulting from these negotiations will only be implemented with popular approval through another referendum; on these terms, do you give the Government of Quebec the mandate to negotiate the proposed agreement between Quebec and Canada?

The Yvette gaffe

The tide began to turn against the Yes camp on March 9, 1980. In a speech to PQ supporters, Lise Payette, a former TV star who had become minister of state for the status of women, humiliated the wife of Claude Ryan, leader of the Quebec Liberal Party and head of the No camp, by comparing her to "Yvette." Yvette was the name of a docile girl in a sexist school textbook from which Payette read an excerpt during a speech at a PQ meeting. The character embodied the stereotype of the submissive woman who took care of the housework and whose greatest pleasure was pleasing her man. Somewhat carried away, she ended up attacking Claude Ryan as a retrograde fear monger who wanted to keep women in a state of subjugation. Nothing surprising, she added, because "he's married to an Yvette."

This statement caused a scandal, in part because the charge was unfair and hurtful. Politicized, engaged Madeleine Ryan didn't have to take any lessons from Lise Payette. In addition, this attempt to link No supporters to submissive wives deeply insulted many housewives. Despite the PQ minister's efforts to apologize, the damage had been done. On April 7, a huge gathering of "Yvettes" was held in Montreal. The No side now had the wind in its sails.

Rightly or wrongly, this huge gathering of "Yvettes" was often later presented as a backlash against the feminist movement. Lise Payette's controversial statements provided an opportunity for more conservative women, tied to traditional family values, to express their beliefs loudly and clearly.

The wording was severely criticized. Federalists found it twisted while some sovereignists found it confusing. But despite the critics, it would be put before the people of Quebec on May 20, 1980.

As soon as the question was announced, the referendum debate became all-consuming. The Referendum Act, adopted by the PQ government in 1978, provided that the referendum would entail the creation of two opposing camps: the Yes and No sides. Both sides were subject to spending controls, but the Yes camp accused the No side of taking advantage of federal money to better their odds. The sovereignists sought to strike a reassuring note, promising that a Yes vote would not bring any major changes. Their spokespeople stressed the need to resolve the constitutional impasse. The federalists, in turn, highlighted the economic risks of "separation": A Yes vote, they repeatedly insisted, would undoubtedly cause upheavals with unpredictable consequences.

In early March 1980, the National Assembly debates were broadcast live on television. The PQ Assembly members were better prepared than their Liberal opponents. This was reflected in some polls, which gave a slight edge to the Yes camp.

"We're putting our seats on the line"

On February 18, 1980, Pierre Elliott Trudeau's federal Liberals were returned to power. In Quebec they won a clear victory, with 68 percent of the vote and 74 of the 75 seats. Once again prime minister of Canada, Trudeau saw the referendum campaign as the fight of his life. On May 14, he addressed his supporters, already pumped by recent polls that indicated a victory for the No camp. There were banners that read *"Mon non est québécois"* ("My No is Québécois"), an effective slogan that sent a clear message to the undecided: It was possible to be deeply attached to Quebec while still wanting to remain Canadian.

Trudeau's speech was a compendium of his most fundamental convictions:

- **Canada also belonged to French Canadians.** With patriotic zeal, the prime minister said that Canada was partly founded by French-Canadian ancestors. By separating themselves from Canada, Quebecers would turn their backs on the heroic history of the great explorers and confine themselves to a much smaller territory.

- **The PQ project would be based strictly on "ethnicity."** From the beginning, Trudeau suspected the PQ of distinguishing "true" from "false" Quebecers. He accused René Lévesque of having attributed his rejection of sovereignty-association to his Scottish roots, inherited from his mother — an Elliott who was born in Quebec.

- **There would be no association if the Yes camp won.** The Lévesque government's project was based on a partnership with the rest of Canada. But Trudeau announced that regardless of the outcome, his government had no intention of negotiating.

- **A No vote would also allow for changes.** That said, the prime minister made a solemn commitment to begin a process of constitutional renewal if Quebecers voted No. He and the Quebec MPs promised to resign if this renewal did not take place:

  > We put our necks on the line, we, members from Quebec, because we say to you, the other provinces, that we will not agree to have a No vote interpreted by you as an indication that all is well and that everything can remain as it was before. We want change; we are putting our seats on the line to have change.

  What changes exactly did he have in mind? It is difficult to know for certain. Many people interpreted his "we" associating himself with Quebec as a reference to Quebec's historical demands.

A 60 percent vote for the No side

On May 20, 1980, 85.6 percent of registered voters exercised their right to vote. The campaign had been long and arduous. It had polarized Quebecers like never before. Many did not hesitate to show their colors, proudly wearing badges or waving banners from their balconies. As soon as the first preliminary results were announced, the No took the lead, and it soon proved insurmountable. French-speaking voters were divided, with half of them opting for a No vote.

At 9:30 p.m., René Lévesque conceded defeat. His face was sad, but his speech was sober and his voice hopeful: "I remain convinced that we have a rendezvous with history, a date that Quebec will keep, and we will be there together, you and I on that day." He then asked his followers to sing the poet Gilles Vigneault's song "Gens du pays," and he concluded with a modest *"À la prochaine"* ("Until next time").

Claude Ryan's speech was more triumphalist, less in tune with the atmosphere of bitterness and gloom that pervaded people's spirits that night. Ryan called for elections as soon as possible.

Speaking briefly to reporters late in the evening, Pierre Elliott Trudeau was more magnanimous:

> I cannot stop thinking about all those supporters of the Yes camp who fought with such conviction and must tonight put their dream away and abide by the verdict of the majority. And this thought takes away any desire for a loud celebration of the victory. To my fellow Quebecers wounded by defeat I just want to say that we all come away from the referendum having lost something. If we count the broken friendships, strained romances, wounded pride, there is no one among us who does not have some bruising of the soul to heal in the days and weeks to come.

Repatriation of the Canadian constitution

With the referendum over, the time for such moods had passed; it was now time for action. The Canadian government began working to repatriate the constitution, once and for all. What passed at the time for a Canadian constitution was just a series of British laws (see Chapter 10). The only way to make any change or amendment was to go to London and persuade the British MPs. This is what the Trudeau government, in a hurry to get this issue out of the way, set out to do. Meanwhile, in London and in the provinces, questions were raised about the repatriation process. Could the federal government act "unilaterally"? Or did it have to obtain agreement from the provinces?

The Trudeau plan condemned by the court

On August 20, 1980, the premiers met in Winnipeg to discuss the constitution. That same morning, a leaked secret federal government memo informed them that Ottawa intended to act unilaterally if no agreement was reached with the provinces. On October 2, in a televised speech, Pierre Elliott Trudeau confirmed that his government would go ahead without the provinces. Two weeks later, seven of the provinces, including Quebec, condemned the process.

On December 7, 14,000 Quebecers gathered in Montreal to denounce the federal plan. The Manitoba, Newfoundland, and Quebec courts of appeal were asked to rule on the legality of unilateral repatriation. The Newfoundland court was unequivocal: The Trudeau government's action was unconstitutional, illegal. Since Canada was a federation, its sovereignty was shared between two levels of government. The constitution could not be repatriated without consulting the provinces.

On September 28, 1981, the Supreme Court of Canada also rendered a judgment. The federal project might be "legal," explained the judges of the highest court in Canada, but it was "illegitimate" in the context of a federation. A few days later, on October 2, the Quebec National Assembly passed a nonpartisan resolution condemning the unilateral approach of the Trudeau government by a large majority.

Quebec isolated

The Supreme Court judgment, along with pressure from the British government, forced Trudeau to organize a last-ditch federal-provincial conference. The conference opened on November 2, 1981. The first rounds did not bode well. Most of the provinces formed a bloc against the Trudeau plan. But on the morning of November 5, against all odds, it emerged that an agreement had been reached, signed by all — except Quebec. What happened? There were two versions.

- ✔ **The federal version:** During the conference, Trudeau put forward the idea of holding a referendum on the draft constitution. René Lévesque seemed to be in favor because he was convinced that a majority of Quebecers would reject the federal government's proposal. Lévesque's position irritated several of his allies in the other provinces. Fiercely opposed to holding such a referendum, they detached themselves from the Quebec government and began negotiations with Ottawa. According to this version, it was Lévesque who had dropped his allies, not the reverse.

- ✔ **The Quebec version:** The Quebec delegation's view was diametrically opposed. René Lévesque argued that the agreement was negotiated in secret during the night, while the Quebec representatives were sleeping peacefully in their hotel. According to this version, English Canada dropped Quebec that night.

As many Quebecers conceive it, the night during which this isolation of Quebec occurred was the "night of the long knives." It's a very strong expression, but it has continued to be commonly used. Originally, it referred to Hitler's decision during the night of June 29–30, 1934, to assassinate many of his opponents and critics.

The Constitution Act of 1982

On April 17, 1982, Prime Minister Trudeau and Queen Elizabeth II affixed their signatures on the Constitution Act of 1982. With the adoption of this act, Canada became a completely independent country. But historic as this moment may have been, not everyone wanted to take part in the celebrations. The ceremony took place without the presence of any officials from Quebec. Not even Claude Ryan, a hard-core federalist, was in attendance. On November 18, the National Assembly had passed a motion condemning the proposed repatriation of the constitution because, among other things, it did not recognize Quebec as a "distinct society through language, culture, institutions." Federal Liberal MPs and ministers from Quebec didn't pay too much attention to the absence of the Quebec officials. After all, hadn't Quebecers overwhelmingly rejected the PQ's option in the 1980 referendum? Had they not also voted overwhelmingly for the federal Liberals in the February 1980 election?

So, what was this new constitution all about anyway?

- ✔ **No veto power for Quebec:** There would be three ways to amend the constitution: provincial unanimity on some very important issues; the consent of seven provinces making up at least 50 percent of the population on other important issues; one province in agreement with the federal government on very specific subjects. One thing was clear: No formal veto was recognized for Quebec on any constitutional changes to come. The Supreme Court of Canada would even render a decision according to which Quebec did not have and never had a veto on constitutional changes.

- ✔ **A Charter of Rights and Freedoms, which greatly increased the power of judges:** In addition to recognizing the basic rights of every citizen, the Charter gave both French speakers and English speakers the right to education in their own language (Section 23). This provided a strong legal basis for minority French speakers in other provinces who wanted to be educated in their own language, but it also invalidated the portion of Bill 101 prohibiting access to English schools in Quebec for English-speaking citizens from other provinces.

- ✔ **Multiculturalism, an official doctrine of the Canadian state:** In addition to confirming the language rights of speakers of both languages, the Charter provided that "any interpretation of this Charter shall be consistent with the objective of promoting the preservation and enhancement of the multicultural heritage of Canadians" (Section 27). This was an important victory for some ethnic and religious minorities, which would later require "reasonable accommodation" (see Chapter 22).

The 1982 constitutional repatriation was a crushing defeat for René Lévesque and his government. After losing his referendum, the PQ leader watched helplessly as Canada adopted a constitution that did not recognize any special status for Québec. Pierre Elliott Trudeau kept his promise. He certainly renewed the Canadian constitution — but he did it without taking into consideration the most fundamental grievances of Quebec governments since the beginning of the Quiet Revolution. That's why, to this day, no Quebec government — federalist or sovereignist — has signed the Constitution Act of 1982.

This double failure demoralized many Quebec artists and intellectuals who had been heavily involved in the sovereignist cause. The disappointment that marked this period became known as "post-referendum syndrome."

Recovery from Recession and Political Impasse

As this constitutional saga unfolded, harsh clashes pitted the PQ government against the trade unions. It happened because Quebec was hit by a severe economic recession that greatly affected youth and led to profound questioning of the role of government.

Confrontation and cooperation

René Lévesque had often cited his "favorable bias" toward workers, and some of his accomplishments illustrate this bias. In 1977, his government banned the hiring of strikebreakers (scabs) and required employers to collect union dues at source. But for activists on the far left of the union movement, these advances were not enough. Negotiations with public-sector employees that took place in 1979 were sometimes strained. "If it is not Yes, it will be No" could be seen on some placards. Either the Lévesque government would offer union members what they wanted, or they would vote No in the referendum.

Issuing a series of decrees

The recession that hit Quebec starting in 1981 left the government no choice but to review the generous collective agreements that had been negotiated in previous years. In 1982, mortgage interest rates were above 20 percent and the unemployment rate was around 13 percent. With negotiations dragging on, the government determined the wages and working conditions of 320,000 public-sector and parapublic-sector employees by decree. Worse, it cut their wages by 21 percent during the first three months of 1983. These extreme austerity measures brought $700 million to the government coffers but alienated many voters who would never forgive this move. Unions once again formed a common front and triggered a series of illegal strikes. But the government was convinced that public-sector wages were still higher than those in the private sector, and it did not flinch.

To get out of the recession, the PQ government chose to rely more on the private sector than on the state. After having nationalized the asbestos industry — a mistake, according to experts — the government opted to encourage small investors to support the Quebec economy through their savings. In early 1980, Finance Minister Parizeau launched the Quebec Stock Savings Plan (QSSP), providing a tax deduction for money invested in shares of Quebec companies. The QSSP not only brought Quebecers into the stock market but also increased the availability of venture capital.

Reforming capitalism from within

The other exit route from the recession involved cooperation with leading socioeconomic partners. Through orientation conferences, consensus would be reached, and direction would be provided for the future. The 1982 decrees made this avenue difficult to put into practice, but another kind of dialogue began to take shape. At the Quebec Federation of Labour (QFL), the severe recession of 1981 brought a new awareness among some union leaders. Members of this large federation, which represented mostly private-sector workers, were hit hard by layoffs and plant closures.

A lost generation?

The recession had a severe impact on many young people born in the early 1960s, who were just entering the labor market. Stable, permanent jobs, and especially jobs in the public and parapublic sectors, were becoming increasingly rare. They had been convinced (as had been their parents) that their education would open up many opportunities for them, but these young men and women hit a wall. The phenomenon was so widespread that a youth summit was held in 1983.

Two years later, scholars addressed the problem at a conference. Sociologist Fernand Dumont compared the young people of the mid-1980s to a "new kind of proletariat" that would camp "outside the city." Others spoke of a "lost generation" or "Generation X." In time, some of these young people come to accuse their "baby boomer" elders of being inconsistent: Supporters of the state, the baby boomers talked about solidarity, but when it came time to negotiate their collective agreements, they looked out only for the interests of their own generation.

Generation X would also be the first to experience the effects of the revolution against tradition, the first to experience the effects of divorce, free love, and stepfamilies. Because of these economic and cultural upheavals, this generation was often slow in developing social and political commitments.

The boy from Baie-Comeau

Born in Baie-Comeau on March 20, 1939, Mulroney was the son of a humble electrician who worked for a paper mill on the North Shore that Maurice Duplessis had opened in 1937. His parents were Catholic and of Irish descent. As a child, he spoke English at home but French in the streets. Very early on, he acted as a bridge between the two major linguistic communities.

After completing his undergraduate education in Nova Scotia, Mulroney studied law at Laval University in the early 1960s, when Quebec's Quiet Revolution was in full swing. He moved to Montreal and quickly became a recognized specialist in labor relations, hired by employers. Everyone recognized his negotiating skills and

appreciated his warm and inclusive personality. Judge Robert Cliche called on him to be a member of the commission of inquiry on the exercise of trade-union freedom in the construction industry (see Chapter 19).

In 1977, he was appointed president of the Iron Ore Company of Canada, a subsidiary of an American multinational corporation that extracted iron ore on the North Shore. Early on, Brian Mulroney joined the Progressive Conservative Party of Canada and established an impressive network of relationships. After an unsuccessful initial attempt in 1976, he was elected party leader in 1983.

In response, QFL President Louis Laberge launched a completely new idea: a "Solidarity Fund" financed by contributions from workers whose primary purpose would be to support struggling companies. The government viewed the initiative favorably and immediately announced tax breaks for those who contributed to the fund, regardless of whether they were members of the QFL.

Laberge's idea was a milestone in the history of trade unionism in Quebec. Gone was the goal of destroying capitalism or working toward the disappearance of the "bourgeois state" that had characterized the QFL during the 1970s. Instead, the QFL now proposed to reform the economic system from within by supporting private initiatives or developing partnerships with promising companies.

The QFL Solidarity Fund became a key player in the economic development of Québec; in 2011, its assets totaled $8.2 billion. The Confederation of National Trade Unions (CNTU), representing mainly public-sector workers, severely criticized this pragmatic approach. The QFL was accused of turning away from its trade-union mission or playing the game of big capital. In 1996, however, the CNTU imitated its main rival by setting up an organization called Fondaction, with essentially the same mission as the QFL's Solidarity Fund.

A changing of the guard in Ottawa and Quebec

Societies don't stay mired in political gloom for long. Democracy always offers an outlet for those who hope for renewal. In the mid-1980s, Quebecers turned to new teams, new faces, which they believed would help them revive the economy and get out of some of the dead ends in which they found themselves trapped.

In February 1984, Pierre Elliott Trudeau announced his retirement from politics. Even though his influence would at times continue to be felt, it was time to turn a page — the Liberal leader had dominated Canadian politics since 1968. Canadians were ready to try another team and new proposals for the future. In 1984, it was Brian Mulroney who embodied this change.

"With honor and enthusiasm"

Since the 1960s, Brian Mulroney had urged his party to invest more effort in Quebec. Apart from John Diefenbaker's ephemeral success in 1958, Canadian Conservatives had never managed to break into Fortress Quebec, which almost always went to the Liberals. The new leader hoped to change this situation.

Immediately after winning the leadership, he brought together an impressive team of Quebecers, many of whom were nationalists, including some who had voted Yes in 1980. One of these was his friend Lucien Bouchard, a Chicoutimi lawyer, whom he had met at the Laval law school. Bouchard was assigned the task of preparing an important speech, which Mulroney delivered in Sept-Îles on August 6, 1984, in the middle of a federal election campaign. The Conservative leader condemned the Liberal constitutional mess: "There are in Quebec — it is blindingly obvious — wounds to heal, concerns to dispel, enthusiasms to revive, and trust to restore." Pierre Elliott Trudeau, he lamented, had taken advantage of the referendum turmoil to hit Quebec with "constitutional ostracism." If his party were elected, he promised, the goal he would pursue would be to "convince the National Assembly of Quebec to give its assent to the new Canadian constitution with honor and enthusiasm."

On September 4, 1984, the Progressive Conservatives won 211 seats, a stunning victory. In Quebec, Brian Mulroney's party harvested 50.2 percent of the vote and 58 seats.

Pope John Paul II's visit: A great success!

From September 9 to 11, 1984, Pope John Paul II made a very important visit to Quebec. On arrival in Quebec City, he said,

> Greetings to you, Quebec, the first church in North America, the first witness of faith, you who planted the cross at the intersection of your highways and spread the gospel in this blessed land! Greetings to you, the people of Quebec, whose traditions, language, and culture give your society such a special place within North America.

This was the first time that a pope had come to meet Catholics in Canada. For three days, Quebecers followed the pontiff's movements and listened to his speeches, which were broadcast on television.

The success of this visit, which culminated in a huge rally at Olympic Stadium in Montreal, surprised some. Fewer Quebecers attended Sunday Mass; recruiting priests was difficult; and the church's positions against the pill, abortion, gay marriage, and married priests irritated them. Nevertheless, they continued, until the turn of the millennium, to identify as Catholics and remained attached to the most basic rituals of their church (baptisms, weddings, funerals, and so on). Quebecers who welcomed the Pope in 1984 no longer practiced their religion as they had in the 1950s, but they still adhered to Catholic culture. For the vast majority of them, this legacy continued to have meaning.

The implosion of the Parti Québécois

René Lévesque welcomed the election results and announced that his government would once again participate in federal-provincial conferences, which it had boycotted since 1981. This position surprised many people, because at its most recent convention Lévesque's party had taken a hard line on the sovereignty issue, putting the *étapiste* strategy and the "good government" program back on the shelf. The PQ leader, however, ignored this.

Worse, he was ready to challenge the most fundamental plank in his party's platform. On September 22, 1984, Lévesque explained the prospects that, in his view, had emerged for Quebec since the federal election:

> If the Conservative government's collaboration should improve, would that not risk stifling our fundamental option and shelving sovereignty indefinitely? Clearly, there is an element of risk. But it's a *beau risque* [a risk worth taking].

A few weeks later, the premier drove the point home in a position paper entitled *Pour que la discussion prenne fin (Bringing the Discussion to a Close)*. In the next Quebec election, he said, "sovereignty is not to be an issue: neither in whole nor in more or less disguised parts." With the stroke of a pen, he had invalidated the convention's decision and wiped out the most important item on the PQ agenda. "This nation-state that we have believed was so close and so totally indispensable" must disappear from the radar screen, according to him.

For Jacques Parizeau, Camille Laurin, and some other ministers, members of the National Assembly, and activists, this shift was absolutely unacceptable. On November 22, 1984, they quit en masse. René Lévesque's *"beau risque"* sapped the motivation of the most determined activists and led to internal wars. Plagued by illness and fatigue, the PQ founder resigned on June 20, 1985.

The Meech Lake Accord

While the PQ was imploding and choosing Pierre Marc Johnson to succeed René Lévesque, the Quebec Liberal Party was gaining strength and adopting a new platform.

The return of Robert Bourassa

In October 1983, Robert Bourassa was once again elected leader of the Quebec Liberal Party. In the aftermath of the 1976 defeat, he had spent time in Brussels studying European integration. He also lectured and conducted seminars at several European and American universities. Claude Ryan's election defeat in 1981 reopened the doors of power for him. The inauguration of the LG-2 dam at James Bay in 1979 reminded many people of his astute economic choices.

Recognition of Aboriginal nations and the death of René Lévesque

Just before leaving the political scene, René Lévesque had the National Assembly pass a motion recognizing the existence of the ten Aboriginal nations living in Quebec. The event took place on March 20, 1985. The motion clearly recognized that these nations had the right to "autonomy within Quebec"; the right "to their culture, their language, their traditions"; the right "to own and control their land"; the right "to hunt, fish, trap, gather, and participate in wildlife management"; and "the right to participate in the economic development of Quebec and benefit from it." This motion is one of the many legacies of René Lévesque, who made his mark on Quebec as had few politicians before him.

After leaving politics, the founder of the Parti Québécois wrote *Attendez que je me rappelle . . .* (published in English under the title *Memoirs*), a book of memories that enjoyed tremendous success. Lévesque also went back to his work as a journalist, his first passion. This return to normal life was brutally interrupted. On November 1, 1987, he collapsed in his living room, felled by a heart attack. The news took everyone by surprise — he was only 65 years old. For several days, Quebec mourned the death of its former premier. The epitaph on his tombstone was written by the poet Félix Leclerc: "The first page of the true beautiful history of Quebec just ended. Henceforth, he will be part of the short list of liberators of peoples."

A summit of the Francophonie in Quebec City

In the early 1980s, the idea of holding a regular summit of French-speaking countries was gaining ground. The writer Léopold Sedar Senghor, president of Senegal from 1960 to 1980, had been an early advocate of such meetings. French President François Mitterrand, elected in 1981, wanted to organize a first Francophone Summit before the end of his seven-year term. However, the idea was delayed by the Quebec question. Would Quebec speak in its own name or would it be represented by Canada? Pierre Elliott Trudeau and René Lévesque had diametrically opposed views on this issue.

The logjam was broken, however, when the Mulroney Conservatives and the Bourassa Liberals came to power. An agreement was sealed on November 7, 1985. Quebec would participate in the Canadian delegation, but it would speak in its own name on most issues.

The first Summit of the Francophonie was held in Versailles in February 1986. Quebec City hosted the second summit from September 2 to 4, 1987. Ten years later, the member countries developed the Organisation Internationale de la Francophonie (OIF). In 2012, 56 states and governments were members of the OIF.

The mandate of the Francophonie's institutions is not always clear. Is their goal to promote French language and culture or to reaffirm universal values of sharing and openness? Quebec continues to contribute to the discussions as a federated state.

On the constitutional front, the Liberals believed that they were in a better position than the PQ to respond to the outstretched hand of Brian Mulroney's new team. Robert Bourassa felt he had shown that he knew how to defend Quebec's interests in constitutional matters. Because the Liberals sincerely believed in the virtues of Canadian federalism, he felt confident that no one could accuse them of bad faith. On December 2, 1985, with 99 seats and 55 percent of the vote, the Liberals came to power.

From welfare state to business state

During the 1985 election campaign, Robert Bourassa returned to one of his favorite themes: the economy. He promised a second phase of the James Bay development and rationalization of government spending. The tone of the Liberal agenda, influenced by the neoliberal philosophy that was in vogue at the time, was strongly anti-bureaucratic.

Bourassa also recruited some familiar faces from the business community who intended to apply private-sector methods to the public sector. One of these was Paul Gobeil, a former senior manager with the Provigo grocery chain, who was appointed president of the treasury board. Gobeil filed a highly controversial report calling for a complete overhaul of the management of large public networks. He advocated making government employees more accountable and introducing the principle of competition between services offered by the public sector and ones that could be offered by the private sector. His report also criticized the proliferation of public agencies — there were 200 agencies in 1984 compared with 47 in 1964. To generate savings and improve the performance of the public system, Gobeil proposed a drastic remedy: the elimination of 79 agencies.

Two other similar reports would be made public. One suggested significant deregulation, while the other recommended privatization of some public corporations. Without going as far as the reports suggested, the Bourassa government followed some of these recommendations. Several provincial corporations — SGF, SOQUEM, SIDBEC, and REXFOR — were divested of assets that the government judged the private sector better able to develop.

Quebec's minimum conditions

The return of the Liberals to power made it easier to launch a new round of constitutional discussions. On April 30, 1987, the federal government and the ten provinces agreed on the wording of an agreement which, once approved by the provincial legislatures, would allow Quebec to ratify the Constitution Act of 1982. The agreement was signed at the prime minister's retreat on the shores of Meech Lake, just outside Ottawa.

Quebec's five minimum conditions for returning to the constitutional fold were:

- ✓ **Status of "distinct society":** In the amended constitution, Quebec would be clearly recognized as a "distinct society." When judges had to rule on a case concerning Quebec, they would have an obligation to interpret the constitution in light of this provision.

- ✓ **Recognized immigration powers:** The administrative agreements previously reached with the federal government in the area of immigration would be "constitutionalized." The federal government would, therefore, not be able to retract the arrangements.

- ✓ **Limiting the federal spending power:** In areas of exclusive provincial jurisdiction, the federal government would have to limit its spending or consult with the government of Quebec.

- ✓ **Changing the amending formula:** With respect to future constitutional amendments, Quebec would have veto power.

- ✓ **A new process for appointing judges to the Supreme Court of Canada:** Because Quebec is the only province that uses the Civil Code from the French tradition, its government would be consulted on appointments to the highest court.

The Meech Lake Accord was generally well received in Quebec. Many people saw it as an opportunity to finally bring the thorny constitutional issue to a close. The signatories, however, would have three years to ratify the agreement — an eternity in politics!

Chapter 21

Almost a Country (1987–1995)

In This Chapter

▶ Focusing on the failure of the Meech Lake Accord

▶ Looking at Quebec's second sovereignty referendum

*I*n the weeks after the Meech Lake Accord was reached, it received strong support from Quebecers. Polls conducted in June 1987 showed that more than 60 percent of them favored the agreement between the provinces and the federal government. But clouds soon appeared in these blue skies. Opposition came both from sovereignists and from federalists.

The failure of the Meech Lake Accord plunged Canada into an unprecedented political crisis. Quebec Liberals seemed perplexed. Some considered secession, while others insisted that Quebec should stay in Canada at whatever cost. Unfortunately for Quebec federalists, the Charlottetown Accord, a desperate attempt to get out of this constitutional impasse, was rejected in a referendum by Quebecers and English Canadians alike. Some Quebecers felt humiliated by these rebuffs. However, a majority still hesitated to embrace sovereignty, although the creation of a broad sovereignist coalition sent shivers down federalist spines.

Canada in Crisis

A country's constitution usually embodies its most fundamental values. It's intended to bring citizens together. By repatriating the constitution without the Quebec government's consent, English Canada had given sovereignists extra ammunition. Instead of uniting Canadians, the Constitution Act of 1982 sowed seeds of division. It was precisely to remedy this situation that the Mulroney Conservatives devised the Meech Lake Accord, which encompassed Quebec's five minimum conditions for signing the Constitution Act (see Chapter 20).

A looming failure

Voices were soon raised in opposition to the Meech Lake Accord, both in Quebec and in English Canada. This opposition soon plunged Canada into turmoil. Instead of bringing Quebec and the rest of Canada closer together, the Meech Lake Accord left Quebec more isolated than ever.

The "Meech Lake monster"

The first people to oppose the constitutional agreement were sovereignists. Pierre Marc Johnson, René Lévesque's successor as leader of the Parti Québécois, denounced the "Meech Lake monster." He said that instead of a "distinct society" clause, subject to interpretation by federally appointed judges, what Quebec needed to defend its language, culture, and institutions was real powers. This view was shared by Jacques-Yvan Morin, a renowned constitutional lawyer and a former minister under René Lévesque. By signing this agreement, Morin believed, Premier Bourassa was giving up on a new sharing of powers between the federal government and Quebec, a basic demand since the 1960s. After the Meech Lake Accord was signed, "Quebec will find itself hemmed in and locked into its areas of jurisdiction," he lamented.

The PQ took the position that the *"beau risque"* phase of federalism initiated by René Lévesque was very clearly over. It would use any argument to fight the Meech Lake deal. The hasty departure of Pierre Marc Johnson, whose new "national affirmation" approach was seen as excessively vague by the more staunchly pro-independence wing of his party, and the choice of Jacques Parizeau as PQ leader on March 19, 1988, confirmed this back-to-basics turn. "The primary role of the Parti Québécois is to achieve the sovereignty of Quebec," Parizeau stated the evening he was voted in as leader. "It must clearly put forward its sovereignist position, before, during, and after elections." His party would no longer consider discussing the terms of any kind of renewed federalism.

A "total mess"

The reaction from the sovereignists was expected. But the position of former Prime Minister Pierre Elliott Trudeau took everyone by surprise. On May 27, 1987, the Montreal newspaper *La Presse* published a harsh assault by Trudeau on the Meech Lake Accord, which he called "a total mess." In Trudeau's view, the "distinct society" clause was an insult to the French Canadians of Quebec. He said it suggested an inferiority complex among nationalists, whom he labeled a "bunch of crybabies [and] spoiled adolescents." Trudeau continued: "The rising generation of businessmen, scientists, writers, filmmakers, and artists of every kind has nothing in common with the siege mentality in which the elites of past eras huddled." To confront the great modern-day challenges, Quebecers "have absolutely no need for crutches in order to walk."

No free trade with the United States without Quebec

During the recession of the 1980s, many American politicians felt protectionist measures were needed. More than 300 bills introduced in the U.S. Congress clearly aimed to restrict imports of foreign merchandise. To counter this trend toward protectionism, the Canadian government sought to persuade Americans to reach a free trade agreement. Ideological convergence between ruling Conservatives in Ottawa and Republicans in Washington, both proponents of deregulation and free markets, facilitated the discussions.

When agreement in principle was reached, Prime Minister Mulroney called a general election on this issue, which left English Canadians deeply divided. Many business people favored free trade, but unions, fearing lower wages and poorer working conditions, opposed it. People on the left also feared that the Canadian government might weaken social programs to compete with the U.S. tax system. At another level, having more to do with identity and symbols, many intellectuals believed the agreement was a long-term threat to Canadian sovereignty. They saw greater economic integration as a step toward Canada's absorption into the American empire.

A significant majority of Quebecers did not see things in this light. Union and business circles in Quebec denounced or supported free trade for essentially the same reasons as in English Canada. What set Quebec apart was the support for free trade from sovereignist forces, which believed that free trade provided a new argument for their cause. Their adversaries had always asserted that the Quebec market was too small to support a modern economy. But now, like small countries in the European Community, Quebec would be able to rely on a vast pool of consumers. A free trade agreement would make the Quebec economy less dependent on the Canadian market.

On November 21, 1988, Mulroney's Conservatives were reelected. In Quebec, they won 60 of the 75 seats and got 52.7 percent of the popular vote, an even stronger showing than in 1984. In the rest of Canada, however, Conservative support fell compared to the previous election. Without this massive support from Quebecers, the Canada-U.S. Free Trade Agreement, which took effect officially on January 1, 1989, might not have been adopted, because the Liberals under John Turner and the New Democrats under Ed Broadbent campaigned strongly against free trade. Some English Canadians accused Quebecers of selling out Canadian sovereignty, which did little to encourage adoption of the Meech Lake Accord.

All signs indicate that the opening of the U.S. border to trade has benefited the Quebec economy. In 1994, when the Canadian dollar was at its lowest, 81.73 percent of Quebec's exports went to the United States. In 2008, this proportion was 72.1 percent. In 1994, Mexico was brought into the North American free trade zone.

He also criticized what he saw as the agreement's "balkanization" of Canada. He felt the powers yielded to Quebec would weaken the central government. By acting in this way, Prime Minister Brian Mulroney was attacking the great dream of a "single Canada, bilingual and multicultural," united by a charter of rights. Trudeau blamed Quebec's isolation following the 1982 repatriation on "inward-looking politicians" from Quebec who had been blocking all attempts at constitutional reform since the 1960s.

French on the outside, bilingual on the inside

On December 15, 1988, the Supreme Court of Canada issued a controversial ruling on Quebec's language law. The judges of Canada's highest court invalidated provisions requiring commercial signage to be in French only (Section 58). These provisions were a serious attack on individual freedoms "in a free and democratic society," they wrote in their ruling:

> Language is so intimately related to the form and content of expression that there cannot be true freedom of expression by means of language if one is prohibited from using the language of one's choice.

Reactions to this ruling were not long in coming. The Mouvement Québec Français, a grouping of a number of nationalist associations, came out against the "bilingualization" of Quebec spelled out in this ruling and asked the government to maintain Section 58.

Caught between a rock and a hard place, Premier Robert Bourassa reacted quickly. On the one hand, the English-speaking community supported his party but wanted full compliance with the ruling. On the other hand, the French-speaking nationalist wing of his party hoped the premier would make use of the "notwithstanding" clause in the Constitution Act, a provision allowing exemptions from Supreme Court rulings in areas involving some sections of the Charter of Rights. In a speech after the ruling was announced, the premier admitted that it was difficult "to conciliate protection of French culture, which obviously is an absolutely essential and vital goal for Quebec and for Canada, with, at the same time, respect for individual rights." True to himself, Bourassa went halfway and suggested a compromise (Bill 178). While outdoor commercial signage would remain French only, signage inside businesses could be in both languages.

This compromise led several members of the National Assembly from English-speaking ridings to leave the Liberal Party and form the Equality Party. In the general election held on September 25, 1989, in which the Liberals were easily reelected, the new party won four seats.

The tide turns in English Canada

Robert Bourassa's compromise on the language of signs gave ammunition to opponents of the Meech Lake Accord outside Quebec. English Canadians who felt attached to the Charter of Rights and Freedoms bequeathed by Trudeau accused the Quebec government of sacrificing the rights of the English-speaking minority and violating a basic individual freedom. Influenced by the former prime minister's attack on the Meech Lake Accord, some of them came to believe that the "distinct society" clause would allow for the suppression of minority rights protected by the Charter.

The Polytechnique massacre

On December 6, 1989, 14 female students at the École Polytechnique de Montréal were brutally murdered by 25-year-old Marc Lépine. Since around 4 p.m. that day, Lépine had been wandering around the institution, the engineering school affiliated with the University of Montreal. At about 5:10 p.m., he entered a classroom carrying a semi-automatic weapon, fired at the ceiling, and ordered the male students to leave. He approached ten women cowering at the back of the room and coldly fired an initial round of bullets. He hit nine people, six of whom died on the spot. Lépine then left the room and fired randomly at the women he came across. After stabbing some of them, he took his own life.

In a letter he wrote before the massacre, Lépine gave a political meaning to his act. "Being rather backward-looking (except for science) by nature," he wrote in his clumsy way, "feminists have always had something to enrage me. They want to hold onto the advantages of women ... while grabbing those of men." The letter contained the names of a number of prominent women whom he also intended to kill. The actions of this delusional anti-feminist were the subject of highly emotional discussions in Quebec.

Polls clearly indicated that a majority of English Canadians opposed this clause, and opposition gradually began to grow among politicians as well. Three new premiers — Frank McKenna of New Brunswick, Gary Filmon of Manitoba, and later Clyde Wells of Newfoundland — rescinded their predecessors' signatures and demanded substantial changes to the Meech Lake deal, which, it was argued, contained nothing for French-speakers outside Quebec or for Aboriginal people.

The Charest Report

The clock was ticking, and the Meech Lake Accord was still not approved. The opposing provinces held back on ratifying the deal, putting greater pressure on the federal government. Three months before the deadline of June 23, 1990, Brian Mulroney gave a young cabinet minister, Jean Charest, the job of touring the provinces and seeking a new consensus. This initiative was not well received in Quebec, because of fears that the agreement might be watered down. These fears appeared to be well founded.

Charest's report, submitted on May 17, 1990, suggested holding a new first ministers' conference and adopting a set of accompanying resolutions that were supposed to help clarify certain issues. For example, one of the resolutions would state that the distinct society clause "in no way impairs the effectiveness of the Charter of Rights" and "does not compromise the rights and freedoms it guarantees." Supporters of the Meech Lake Accord were taken aback by this wording, which they saw as an attempt to restrict the scope of one of the agreement's most important clauses.

Indian summer

On July 11, 1990, the Sûreté du Québec, the provincial police force, launched an assault against a barricade set up at Oka by members of the Mohawk nation, leading to violent confrontations. Police Corporal Marcel Lemay was mortally wounded by a bullet. For months, the Mohawks of Oka had challenged a decision by the municipality to develop a golf course and allow the building of condominiums on land they said belonged to them. In protest, the Mohawks had erected a barricade and decided to disregard two court injunctions ordering them to abandon this pressure tactic.

The Sûreté du Québec had intervened on July 11 to enforce these court orders. The police operation not only ended in failure but also produced strong reactions from other Mohawks living on the South Shore of Montreal. A barricade was set up in Châteauguay, blocking access to the Mercier Bridge linking the South Shore with Montreal Island. This pressure tactic caused great inconvenience to many residents of the area who went to work in Montreal each morning.

The Oka crisis made headlines throughout the summer of 1990, drawing substantial media attention in Quebec and around the world. A crisis unit was established, and the federal government, with jurisdiction in First Nations matters, was called in as reinforcement. Despite the appointment of a mediator, Judge Alan B. Gold, irate citizens formed groups, adding to the enormous tension. The government authorities even felt the need to bring in the Canadian Army. The Mohawk Warrior Society, armed to the teeth and linked to organized crime, stood its ground and demanded numerous concessions from the authorities.

The barricades were lifted after 78 days of intense negotiations. The Bourassa government was obsessed with avoiding further deaths. Some people accused it of negotiating with smugglers and weakening government authority.

The Alma telegram

A few days after the Charest Report was submitted, the PQ held a Quebec-wide council meeting in Alma. The federal MP for that region was Lucien Bouchard, minister of the environment in the Mulroney government and a strong supporter of the Meech Lake Accord. While on a trip to Europe, he sent a telegram of welcome to PQ leader Jacques Parizeau that had an explosive impact. Its content was so fraught with consequences for Bouchard that Parizeau feared it might be a hoax! Bouchard wrote to the PQ delegates:

> Your meeting, will mark the tenth anniversary of an important time for Quebec [the referendum of May 20, 1980]. Commemorating it is an opportunity to provide a reminder, loud and clear, of the openness, pride, and generosity of the Yes side, which we supported under the leadership of René Lévesque and his team. The memory of René Lévesque will unite us all this weekend, for he enabled Quebecers to discover the inalienable right to decide on their own destiny.

This last sentence was greeted with thunderous applause. Lucien Bouchard had just changed sides.

Lucien Bouchard, a lawyer born in 1938 at Saint-Cœur-de-Marie in the Lac-Saint-Jean region, regarded the Charest Report as the straw that broke the camel's back. A supporter of the Yes side in 1980, Bouchard, like René Lévesque, had bet on the *"beau risque"* of Canadian federalism. He had no reason to doubt the good faith of Brian Mulroney, an old friend he had met during their student days at the Laval law faculty in the early 1960s. Once he became prime minister, Mulroney named Bouchard Canadian ambassador to Paris. After coordinating the 1987 Summit of the Francophonie, Bouchard was appointed to the federal cabinet and became the prime minister's Quebec lieutenant. In May 1990, this old friendship came to an end. On May 21, Bouchard sent his letter of resignation, explaining the meaning of his Alma telegram. He said the process of adopting the Meech Lake Accord showed that English Canada understood nothing about Quebec's just grievances:

> What was supposed to be a demonstration of generosity and respect for Quebec has, on the contrary, emphasized the divisions in this country and given free rein to a resurgence of prejudice and emotion that are not a credit to anybody.

Repairing the damage

With Lucien Bouchard's resignation, the constitutional crisis took an extraordinary turn. In the end, Elijah Harper, a First Nations member of the Manitoba legislature, denied the unanimous consent the legislature needed to hold a vote, and Newfoundland Premier Clyde Wells, going back on a solemn commitment, refused to let his House of Assembly vote on the agreement. On June 22, 1990, supporters of the Meech Lake Accord had to face the facts. This attempt to end Quebec's isolation proved to be an abject failure. The time had come to repair the damage — and, for federalists, to play for time to prevent things from getting worse.

A "free society"

Up until the last minute, Premier Robert Bourassa believed there would be a final push toward approval of the deal. He was convinced that even if some English Canadians had reservations, English Canada would accept the accord if only to put an end to a constitutional saga that was paralyzing the country. But he underestimated the strength of the opposition.

On June 22, 1990, he finally faced the facts. That evening, he had to make a statement in the National Assembly. Surveys told him that Quebecers were deeply shocked by the failure of the Meech Lake Accord. During the weeks and months that followed, support for sovereignty reached an unprecedented 60 percent in the polls. What could he say? He would have to convey something of the disappointment and anger felt by Quebecers, but without going too far. Ill at ease with political emotion, he had to find just the right tone. Members in the chamber keenly awaited his speech. After briefly reviewing the events leading to the agreement's failure, he concluded with these words: "Whatever may be said or done, Quebec is a distinct society, today and always, free and capable of assuming its destiny and its development." Was Bourassa about to switch to the sovereignist side? Some people thought so, and others hoped so — including Jacques Parizeau, who extended a hand to the premier. In reality, Bourassa remained resolutely hostile to the sovereignist option. But on that day he held back from saying so.

During the days that followed, Quebecers took to the streets and celebrated Saint-Jean-Baptiste Day with unusual fervor. These were days of high emotion. At a time when former Soviet republics were proclaiming their independence, many Quebecers were convinced they were on the verge of having their own country.

One reaction: The Bélanger-Campeau Report

In more concrete terms, Premier Bourassa made two announcements:

- ✔ An end to constitutional talks involving players other than Quebec and the federal government

- ✔ Establishment of a major commission mandated to make recommendations on Quebec's constitutional future

This commission was intended to be nonpartisan, with one co-chair, Michel Bélanger, chosen by the Liberal Party and the other, Jean Campeau, chosen by the PQ. The Bélanger-Campeau Commission's members included the leaders of both parties, as well as Lucien Bouchard and various "civil society" representatives drawn from business and union circles in particular. The commission traveled to every region of Quebec to hear presentations from numerous associations and individuals interested in Quebec's political future. Following a period of very intense negotiations, the commission released its report in March 1991. Its recommendations were the following:

- ✔ **Holding of a referendum on Quebec sovereignty no later than October 26, 1992:** With English Canada having rejected Quebec's minimum demands, Quebecers should express their views on sovereignty as soon as possible.

- ✔ **Creation of two special parliamentary committees on Quebec's political and constitutional future:** The first committee would have a mandate "to examine matters relating to the accession of Quebec to sovereignty." The second committee would have a mandate to "assess all offers for a new constitutional partnership made by the Government of Canada." While the first committee laid the groundwork for sovereignty, the second would address new proposals from English Canada.

Another reaction: The Allaire Report

While the Bélanger-Campeau Commission took the pulse of the populace, the Liberal Party consulted its members and outlined a new constitutional position. Jean Allaire, who chaired his party's constitutional committee, released his report on January 29, 1991. It proposed major changes. Never had a Liberal Party report gone this far.

The report favored a complete overhaul of the Canadian political framework, enabling Quebec to benefit "from exclusive and total jurisdiction in most areas of activity." This would put an end to areas of overlap and to the federal spending power. The only powers maintained by the central government would be defense, territorial security, customs, and foreign policy. Canada as viewed by the Allaire Report was merely a large free trade area. At any time, Quebec could withdraw from it without difficulty.

Unless such changes were made, the Allaire Report suggested holding a referendum on Quebec sovereignty no later than the fall of 1992. Although the report got a very cool reception from the party's moderate federalist wing, it became the official position of the Quebec Liberal Party.

Rejection of the Charlottetown agreement

The conclusions of the Bélanger-Campeau and Allaire reports pushed the federal government to launch a new round of constitutional talks in the fall of 1991. A joint Senate–House of Commons committee heard briefs from Canadian associations and individuals in a round of public hearings. In March 1992, the committee laid out its proposals.

What was involved was no longer just satisfying Quebec's demands but also reforming the entire Canadian constitution to incorporate proposals regarding First Nations, the Senate, and various other issues. Despite the commitment he made after the failure of the Meech Lake Accord, Robert Bourassa agreed to take part again in constitutional discussions with the federal government and the other provinces.

The deal reached in Charlottetown on August 28, 1992, was immediately denounced in Quebec, even by prominent Liberal Party members. Jean Allaire and the youth wing, headed by Mario Dumont, rebuffed their party and founded the "Liberal Network for the No Side." On October 26 the same year, the agreement was submitted to a cross-Canada referendum. More than 56 percent of Quebecers voted against it. It was back to square one.

The Second Quebec Sovereignty Referendum

This new failure was the death knell for constitutional negotiations and marked an end to the political careers of Brian Mulroney, who stepped aside on February 25, 1993, and Robert Bourassa, who resigned on September 14, 1993, after undergoing numerous treatments for skin cancer. This new failure also made sovereignists more comfortable in their convictions. The only option that remained open to Quebec, they believed, was sovereignty. But first Quebecers would have to be convinced.

Creation of the camp for change

To convince Quebecers of the need for sovereignty, sovereignists would have to show that their cause belonged not just to one party and not to a single leader or person. It would have to be open to people of varied political views and sensitive to the fears and apprehensions of newly minted sovereignists.

The Bloc Québécois

In the days and weeks following Lucien Bouchard's resignation, he came under pressure to found a new party. The failure of the Meech Lake Accord had led to other resignations among Conservatives and federal Liberals alike.

On July 25, 1990, Bouchard and the other MPs who had left their parties laid the foundations for the Bloc Québécois, a sovereignist party that would operate on the federal scene. Section 2 of the protocol adopted that day stated, "Our national allegiance is to Quebec. Our home territory is Quebec, the motherland of a people of French culture and language whose sovereignty we intended to promote."

Although it was a federal party, the Bloc Québécois would present candidates only in Quebec ridings. In the founders' view, the Quebec National Assembly was "the supreme democratic institution of the Quebec people." When sovereignty was won, the party would be dissolved.

In a by-election on August 13, 1990, Bloc Québécois candidate Gilles Duceppe easily won the east-central Montreal seat of Laurier–Sainte-Marie. A former communist activist who later became a militant trade unionist, the first Bloc MP was known above all as the son of the great actor Jean Duceppe. His election gave real legitimacy to the party Lucien Bouchard had founded. Polls soon showed great enthusiasm among Quebecers for the Bloc Québécois and its leader's personality.

Her Majesty's official opposition

The federal general election of October 25, 1993, was a historic one. The Bloc Québécois, which won 54 of Quebec's 75 seats and 49.3 percent of the popular vote, made a stunning entry into the Canadian Parliament. In the House of Commons, there was now a party devoted solely to the interests of Quebecers. Even more incredibly, the Bloc formed Her Majesty's official opposition!

Bouchard's party benefited from the collapse of the Progressive Conservative Party, whose historical foundations had been undermined by the repeated constitutional failures. The collapse took place not only in Quebec but also in western Canada, which had given birth to the Reform Party, a new right-wing group that won 52 seats. This collapse was especially beneficial to the Liberals under Jean Chrétien, who were swept into office with promises to focus on the economy.

One of the new prime minister's firmest commitments was not to talk about the constitution anymore. Chrétien had been a cabinet minister under Trudeau, and in his mind the matter had been settled in 1982. Reality would soon catch up with him, however.

Dissident Quebec Liberals form a new party

Jean Allaire and the Liberal youth wing grouped around Mario Dumont left their party for good after it supported the Charlottetown agreement. They first created a think tank, the Groupe Réflexion Québec, which brought together people from various nationalist tendencies but was fairly conservative in its political views. These were people who no longer saw themselves reflected in the Liberal Party, which they felt was willing to accept just about any federal offer, but could not make the leap to the PQ under Jacques Parizeau, which they viewed as too radical or too close to the trade unions.

In the early 1990s, some of them sought to create a third way, oriented more toward autonomy than independence but resolutely nationalist. On January 18, 1994, Jean Allaire and Mario Dumont founded the Action Démocratique du Québec (ADQ). The ADQ's program contained the main features of the Allaire Report but also backed positions close to the neoliberal thinking that was in vogue during the 1980s. In May 1994, at age 24, Mario Dumont became the party leader.

The PQ back in power

In 1994, sovereignists had the wind in their sails. In Quebec City, they were champing at the bit, biding their time on the opposition benches. To call a new referendum on Quebec independence, the PQ first had to win power and sit at the controls. This was accomplished on September 12, 1994, when the PQ won 77 seats, enough to form the next government.

But this victory was not the triumph they were hoping for. The PQ won 44.7 percent of the popular vote, compared to 44.3 percent for the Liberals. It was some distance from the result obtained by the Bloc in 1993, and even further from the 50 percent plus 1 they would need to win the next referendum. Meanwhile, ADQ leader Mario Dumont was elected in his riding, and his party won 6.5 percent of the vote. This was a political force the new premier would have to reckon with if he wanted to win the next referendum.

Forward march!

After being elected, Jacques Parizeau was driven by a sense of urgency, and he wasted no time as he began his mandate. There were marked differences between his approach, endorsed by his party's members, and that of René Lévesque. Parizeau's outlook was as follows:

- ✔ **The initial goal was not to provide good government for a province but to prepare for the advent of a country.** In 1976, Lévesque wanted to reassure the populace by showing that sovereignists were capable of governing. In Parizeau's view, Quebecers no longer doubted the PQ's ability to govern. In his early weeks in power, he put the Quebec government to work to advance the referendum agenda.

- ✔ **The next referendum would be "executive," not "consultative."** In 1980, the sovereignist forces were asking the people for permission to engage in talks with the rest of Canada, with a second referendum to ratify the conclusions of the negotiations. Jacques Parizeau believed that Quebecers had gone far enough in exploring the avenues of renewed federalism. A Yes in the next referendum would enable the government to set the secession process in motion.

- ✔ **Association with the rest of Canada was no longer essential.** In a context of free trade with the United States, Parizeau felt that economic association with the rest of Canada, though desirable, was no longer a prerequisite to achieving sovereignty.

Jacques Parizeau was clear in his ideas. To bring Quebecers together, he would have to cast a wider net and team up with more moderate nationalists who still dreamed of a renewed federalism. On November 5, 1994, the new premier asked party activists to turn their backs on "radicalism," "parochialism," and "partisanship."

Broad consultation

Pressed by reporters, Parizeau refused to set a date for the next referendum, but he assured them it would take place very soon. As the PQ saw it, before the referendum date was announced, a large-scale popular consultation needed to be carried out. On December 6, 1994, the premier submitted a draft bill on Quebec sovereignty. Through a series of commissions, Quebecers would have an opportunity to speak out on the approach suggested by the Parizeau government. They would also be asked to ponder the preamble of a future Quebec constitution, intended to reflect their most basic convictions and values. The consultation would lead to improvements in the bill, and only after it was completed would the people be called on to endorse or reject the bill in a referendum. In short, there would be a transparent process and a simple question.

But things did not work out exactly the way Parizeau had expected.

1995, when everything seemed possible

The public consultations failed to arouse the enthusiasm that was hoped for. The Liberals denounced the whole exercise and refused to take part in it. Though it was supposed to be about sovereignty and the draft bill, various lobby groups took advantage of this forum to present lists of demands.

Tensions regarding the date

Early in 1995, a spring referendum was still a possibility. The premier wanted to keep his troops at the ready. But Parizeau's firm resolve had some people worried. On February 19, Lucien Bouchard stated on television, "I cannot consider a hypothesis under which we would deliberately agree to expose Quebec to a No vote on sovereignty, knowing what would follow."

The Bloc leader and several top ministers in the Quebec government tried to persuade Parizeau to postpone the referendum. Launching a campaign when they were so low in the polls seemed suicidal. "I do not wish," said Deputy Premier Bernard Landry, "to be the second in command of the light brigade, which was exterminated in 20 minutes in Crimea because of its leaders' irresponsibility." It was a pointed analogy.

Though he did not much appreciate the deputy premier's touch of humor, Parizeau nevertheless agreed to postpone the referendum until the fall.

A "shift" is imposed

But the referendum date was not the only issue causing a problem. Lucien Bouchard called Parizeau's entire approach into question. In late March 1995, only 41 percent of voters surveyed would have answered Yes to a clear question on Quebec independence. The Bloc leader felt that the premier's resolutely pro-independence approach did not square with the wishes of most Quebecers, who wanted to maintain ties with the rest of Canada. On April 7, at the opening of his party's convention, Bouchard suggested bringing the idea of economic association back into the independence project.

"The sovereignist project must shift quickly … to open the way to a credible future for new relations between Quebec and Canada," he said. What should be offered to Quebecers in the coming referendum, Bouchard added, was not simply independence but a sovereignty-partnership plan close to what René Lévesque had previously suggested.

What the Bloc leader was seeking to impose on the sovereignist movement was very clearly a "shift." In the days following his speech, Bouchard threatened not to take part in the coming referendum campaign if his ideas were not taken into account. The sovereignist camp was facing a split.

The June 12 agreement: A "major coup"

After a few difficult weeks, representatives of the Parti Québécois, the Bloc Québécois, and the Action Démocratique du Québec negotiated a new plan to be submitted to the people. This task was not easy. Jacques Parizeau's first choice was independence, while Mario Dumont preferred a highly decentralized Canadian confederation. But each party was open to compromise, and so an agreement was reached.

The "camp for change" presented its outline at an official ceremony that attracted wide attention. The so-called June 12 agreement included the following:

- ✔ **A new approach:** A Yes vote in the next referendum would mean two things:
  - The National Assembly could proclaim Quebec's sovereignty.
  - Quebec would be required to propose a treaty to English Canada covering "a new economic and political partnership."
- ✔ **A clear timeline:** English Canada would have one year to respond and negotiate Quebec's proposal. After that time, either of two scenarios could arise:
  - If the negotiations failed, the National Assembly would proclaim sovereignty.
  - If the negotiations succeeded, the National Assembly would proclaim sovereignty and ratify the partnership treaty reached between the new sovereign state and the rest of Canada.

Things had changed very suddenly. The U.S. consult in Quebec City wrote to his superiors:

> For months, analysts in Ottawa have been ridiculing the Parti Québécois's independence project. Everything here indicates, on the contrary, that they have been seriously misled. . . . The tripartite agreement that has just been signed between Parizeau, Bouchard, and Dumont, resulting from a diligent courtship, is a major coup for the independence movement.

Meanwhile, in Paris and Washington . . .

While these negotiations were going on, the Parizeau government rolled out a diplomatic "great game" and prepared for the days following a Yes vote. To exercise sovereignty, a country must be recognized by other nations. For obvious reasons, involving General de Gaulle's heritage and the role France still sought to play in the world, sovereignists were counting heavily on immediate recognition from the former mother country. During an official visit to the French capital in January 1995, the Quebec premier obtained this assurance from both Édouard Balladur and Jacques Chirac, the two leading candidates in the presidential campaign then underway. He also received a very warm welcome from National Assembly President Philippe Séguin, who was put in charge of the Quebec issue in the new French government after Chirac was elected in May. This ardent Gaullist prepared a positive French response to a Yes vote.

In Washington, things were more complicated. The complications began with James Blanchard, then the U.S. ambassador to Canada, who was strongly opposed to Quebec independence. In addition, sovereignists had little success in penetrating the inner circle of U.S. decision makers. On a visit to Ottawa early in February 1995, U.S. President Bill Clinton met Lucien Bouchard, but nothing came of the discussions.

However, despite repeated pressure from the Canadian government, the United States refused to condemn the independence proposal. "Now the Canadian people, the people of Quebec, will have to cast their votes as their lights guide them," was as far as Clinton would venture at a news conference on October 25, 1995. "But Canada has been a great model for the rest of the world and has been a great partner for the United States, and I hope that can continue."

The question

On September 7, the Quebec government unveiled the question to be decided in the October 30 referendum:

> Do you agree that Quebec should become sovereign after having made a formal offer to Canada for a new economic and political partnership within the scope of the bill respecting the future of Quebec and of the agreement signed on June 12, 1995? Yes or no?

The federalist side immediately denounced this question, which lacked words such as *separation* or *independence*. The question was a trap, they kept repeating. It was a trick.

These harsh criticisms seemed to strike a chord, with initial polling not at all favorable to the Yes side. Supporters of Canada also emphasized economic arguments, as they had done in 1980. A Yes vote, they said repeatedly, would lead to serious instability and would cause heavy job losses. Owners and executives of large companies called for a No vote and urged their employees to follow suit. Other corporate leaders with more nationalist leanings tried to calm things down. "It is not the role of the heads of companies to send letters to their employees and try to influence how they vote," said Pierre Péladeau, the chief executive officer of Quebecor Inc.

The Bouchard effect

To breathe new life into their campaign, sovereignists announced that, if the Yes side won, Lucien Bouchard would lead the negotiations for a partnership treaty with the rest of Canada. This announcement, made on October 7, galvanized the troops.

The Bloc Québécois leader was enormously popular at the time. A year earlier, this father of two young children had come close to death. Flesh-eating bacteria had forced doctors to amputate one of Bouchard's legs. This human drama kept Quebecers in suspense for many days. His quick recovery and his determination to return to work impressed many people. In October 1995, some felt he had been saved by a miracle and regarded him as an icon. His cane and his slow step reminded everyone of his personal ordeal. His passionate speeches attracted growing crowds. Everywhere he went, he stirred genuine enthusiasm. By October 20, the Bouchard effect had taken hold, the tide had turned, and the Yes side pulled ahead in the polls.

In the No camp, panic reigned. On October 24, Prime Minister Jean Chrétien gave a major speech at the Verdun Auditorium. There was no need to vote Yes to get real change, he promised. This was too little, too late, the sovereignist leaders replied. The Yes side's lead shook up many English Canadians. Some phoned individual Quebecers directly to try to persuade them to vote No. Others boarded buses, trains, and even airplanes to take part in an impressive demonstration on Friday, October 27, in downtown Montreal. This great "love-in," as it was called, flouted Quebec laws on referendum campaign financing and irritated many Quebecers who felt the decision belonged to them.

A tie game

On the morning of October 30, 1995, nobody knew if the Yes or the No side would win. The latest polls showed the two sides neck and neck. On that day, 93.5 percent of registered voters exercised their voting rights, a historic high for Quebec (and for Canada). In the evening, excitement filled the air. The early results gave the Yes side a comfortable lead. But as the evening wore on, the gap narrowed. At 9:36 p.m., it was a tie. And then the No side took a slight lead and held onto it. In the end, the No side won by a margin of 54,288 votes (No: 50.58 percent; Yes: 49.42 percent).

More than 60 percent of French-speaking Quebecers had voted for the Yes side, while non-francophones (English-speakers and immigrants combined) massively rejected the independence proposal. This split angered Premier Parizeau who, in his concession speech, stated, "It is true we were beaten, yes, but by what? By money and the ethnic vote, essentially." These words shocked many people, sovereignists and federalists alike. Accusations of intolerance and xenophobia poured in from everywhere. Despite the tension, no incidents were reported during the night following the announcement of the results.

On the next day, Jacques Parizeau resigned. Lucien Bouchard was named leader of the Parti Québécois and became premier of Quebec.

Chapter 22

Balanced Budget and Reasonable Accommodation (1996–2012)

. . . .

In This Chapter

▶ Striving for budgetary rigor under Bouchard

▶ Looking at Quebec's quest to find itself

. . . .

*T*he years following the 1995 referendum were marked by heated discussions on the size of government, the constitutional impasse, and national identity. For both the Parti Québécois, which held power until 2003, and the Liberals who came after it, putting Quebecers through a new referendum campaign or seeking to renegotiate Canadian federalism was out of the question. Instead, it was a time for cleaning up public finances and focusing on economic development. The "reasonable accommodation" crisis that arose in the middle of the new century's first decade put the issue of national identity back on the front burner, however. Though Quebecers seemed in no hurry to be consulted on their political future, they insisted on respect for their cultural heritage and their Western values.

The Bouchard Years

For Quebecers who were hoping to put an end to the existential debate on Quebec's future, the years following the 1995 referendum (see Chapter 21) were like a dose of strong medicine. Political ferment gave way to budgetary rigor. Instead of sensitive discussions on Quebec's place in Canada, there were austerity programs. And English Canadians, shocked by how close the 1995 referendum had been, were in an uncertain mood: sometimes open and sometimes firm, going back and forth between reconciliation and indifference.

The return of "good government"

Lucien Bouchard, who was sworn in as premier on January 29, 1996, was convinced that public finances had to be put in order before a new offensive on the sovereignty front could be considered. Like his predecessor, René Lévesque, Bouchard believed that winning public confidence first required boosting the economy, running the government more efficiently, making the right choices, and providing "good government."

"Yes to language, yes to identity, yes to sovereignty, but also yes to jobs," he told party activists in November 1996. "Because the sovereignty fight will also be won on the jobs front."

The goal: A balanced budget

The Bouchard government felt that consulting employers and unions before launching its austerity drive would be prudent. This consultation took the form of two major socioeconomic summits held in the spring and fall of 1996. The premier, a skilled negotiator, managed to get a consensus in favor of achieving a balanced budget. The government had run a deficit in every fiscal year since the 1960s. When it came to power in 1994, the PQ inherited a deficit of $5.8 billion for the current fiscal year. The cumulative effect of these annual deficits meant that servicing the debt was cutting more deeply into the Quebec government's annual budget — 13 percent of spending for 1994–1995. To end this debt spiral, the unions agreed that taxing the rich was not enough. Government administration and collective agreements had to be reviewed. The target was set for 2000. The government and its partners gave themselves just over four years to meet this ambitious goal.

Retirements and "orphan clauses"

Implementation of this zero-deficit policy had visible effects. Soon after it was announced, the Bouchard government closed a number of Quebec delegations abroad. Municipalities had to contribute more toward financing improvements to road infrastructure that needed to be modernized. The Quebec government sent a $375-million bill to cities and towns, which easily reached agreement with their unions. They did this by concentrating the cuts on the youngest workers — most commonly on the backs of employees who had not yet been hired. In 1998, the Human Rights Commission denounced these "orphan clauses," which created two categories of employees.

The government's cuts were also felt in the Quebec public service. In just a few months, nearly 30,000 public and parapublic employees agreed to the terms of an early retirement plan, taking experience and know-how with them. The consequences of their departure soon became clear, especially in the healthcare sector. Overworked nurses launched a campaign of pressure tactics, which included defying an order from the Essential Services Council imposing work schedules in May 1999. Despite public sympathy, the nurses backed down and agreed to the government proposals.

Battlefield medicine

The Bouchard government's nemesis would be the healthcare system. Health Minister Jean Rochon, a former senior official of the World Health Organization, led a major overhaul upon taking office in 1994. He proposed a shift to ambulatory care, seeking to move some patients out of hospitals and develop home care — but not without stirring up a major controversy. In the name of local care, the government closed a number of small hospitals (seven in the Montreal area alone). In addition to creating enormous confusion, this reform occurred as the government was trying desperately to balance the budget.

The government was accused of lacking compassion for sick people stuck waiting for hours in overcrowded emergency rooms. When a neglected patient was found dead on her stretcher in a drab waiting room at Maisonneuve-Rosemont Hospital in Montreal on February 3, 1998, it was headline news. Emergency room physicians denounced the "battlefield medicine" practiced at major Montreal hospitals and demanded immediate adjustments. In the context of an aging population, the poor organization of the system was a source of great anxiety. From 1998 on, healthcare would be the central issue in every election campaign.

A spectacular ice storm

On the night of January 4–5, 1998, an ice storm hit the Montreal area. Although the icy coating from layers of freezing rain provided a splendid sight, the city's hydroelectric infrastructure crumpled under the weight of the ice. Pylons in the Montérégie region east of Montreal gave way, one after another, and after a few days 1.4 million Hydro-Quebec customers were in the dark. On Friday, January 9, only one high-tension line linked Montreal to the electricity network. Water filtration plants had stopped working, and people feared that drinking water would run out. Even firefighters were asked to conserve water.

The crisis caused by the ice storm led to some wonderful demonstrations of solidarity. Many Quebecers, driven from their homes by cold and darkness, found refuge with family members for days on end. Others slept in improvised shelters set up in schools and community centers. Firewood was sent to the 89 Montérégie municipalities affected by the crisis. Premier Bouchard managed the crisis well, providing a televised update each evening. As Quebecers stuck together, Hydro-Quebec was busy repairing the pylons. Backed by 800 reinforcements from electric utilities in the United States, courageous linemen gradually restored electricity to the directly affected areas.

The ice storm showed just how much Quebecers were dependent on hydroelectric power. In addition to building a new high-tension line between Des Cantons and Hertel, top Hydro-Quebec officials, with an eye on diversifying the energy supply, suggested opening a gas-fired thermal plant (the Suroît plant). However, the project was attacked by environmental groups and never went ahead. The new power plant, it was claimed, went against the Kyoto Protocol, which many countries, including Canada, had signed in 1997, agreeing to reduce greenhouse gas emissions to fight global warming.

Five-dollar-a-day daycare

While seeking to balance the budget, Lucien Bouchard continued to pursue the major social goals of the welfare state. In addition to building a new central library in Montreal to house the Bibliothèque et Archives Nationales du Québec, his government established a universal childcare system in 1997. The new public daycare centers, the Centres de la Petite Enfance (CPEs), served children from early infancy to age 5 for the modest sum of $5 a day (raised to $7 a day in 2003). This program, long demanded by the feminist movement, was popular from the start. Although new spaces were added over the years, waiting lists grew longer, leading to bitterness among many parents. Home-based daycare and subsidized commercial daycare centers rounded out the system.

The constitution: A lull followed by an impasse

In the wake of the 1995 referendum, most English Canadians were still having trouble understanding what had led 60 percent of French-speaking Quebecers to vote for sovereignty. After all, weren't Prime Minister Jean Chrétien and several of his key ministers Quebecers, and wasn't Canada an officially bilingual country? And given that repatriation of the constitution and introduction of the Charter of Rights seemed to be among Quebec's major grievances, how could Quebecers be opposed to the most basic individual rights?

Even as English Canada struggled with these questions, a number of federal politicians and other Canadians sought a political response to the close referendum results. But there were differences of opinion as to what that response should be.

Plan A: Opening and rapprochement

In the final days of the referendum campaign in October 1995, Jean Chrétien promised constitutional changes favorable to Quebec. During the months following the referendum, the federal government followed up on this commitment. Plan A relied on openness and rapprochement. The aim was to show that the message from Quebec voters had been heard, as shown by the following moves:

  ✔ **Distinct society motion:** On December 11, 1995, the Chrétien government introduced a motion in the House of Commons recognizing that "Quebec is a distinct society within Canada." This motion was symbolic, however, and had no constitutional bearing.

> ✔ **Workforce agreement:** On the basis of its responsibility for unemploy-
> ment insurance, the federal government had set up an employment
> integration system. The Quebec government saw this as encroaching
> on its jurisdiction. In the fall of 1997, an agreement put Quebec in sole
> charge of workforce matters. More than 1,000 federal civil servants were
> transferred, and Ottawa turned $2.4 billion over to the Quebec treasury
> to handle this responsibility.

> ✔ **Language-based school boards:** The British North America Act of 1867
> gave Quebec Catholics and Protestants the right to denominational
> school boards. But with the new realities of immigration and a more
> secular society, these structures had become less relevant. In the fall of
> 1997, the Quebec and Canadian governments reached an agreement to
> move forward with a constitutional amendment so that school boards in
> Quebec would henceforth be language based.

Provincial governments also showed openness toward Quebec. In September
1997, representatives of the nine English Canadian provinces and the two
northern territories unanimously adopted the "Calgary declaration," recognizing that the "unique character of Quebec society" was "fundamental to the
well-being of Canada." This statement, which all observers at the time saw as
far more cautious than the Meech Lake Accord, did not call for a new round
of constitutional negotiations.

Plan B: Making sovereignty illegal

Along with Plan A, there was a far less generous Plan B. Many people saw the
post-referendum period as a time not for an outstretched hand but for greater
firmness. Quebecers had to understand that secession was an illegal act and
that there was no constitutional provision for a province to leave Canada. This
was the view of Stéphane Dion, a political science professor at the University of
Montreal who was appointed minister of Canadian intergovernmental affairs in
January 1996.

In August 1996, the Supreme Court of Canada agreed to hear a motion from
lawyer Guy Bertrand, who sought to show that a unilateral declaration of
independence would be illegal. A few weeks later, on September 26, the federal government followed up with a series of questions to the judges on the
legality of Quebec secession.

On August 20, 1998, the Supreme Court finally issued a ruling: "A clear majority
vote in Quebec on a clear question in favor of secession would confer democratic legitimacy on the secession initiative which all of the other participants
in Confederation would have to recognize." This key part of the ruling was
interpreted in two ways:

✔ Sovereignists argued that, in addition to recognizing the democratic legitimacy of their project, the ruling would require English Canada to negotiate in the event of a future secession.

✔ Federalists, on the other hand, emphasized the notions of "clear majority" and "clear question." They had long accused sovereignists of posing sneaky questions and hiding their project's true nature.

The Clarity Act: Tightening the screw

Because the judges specified that it would be "for the political actors to determine what constitutes 'a clear majority on a clear question,'" the federal government introduced the Clarity Act, passed by Parliament on June 29, 2000. This controversial legislation stated that the federal government could negotiate secession only if the House of Commons had approved the wording of the question. In the future, a Yes vote would have to indicate clearly "whether the province should cease to be part of Canada and become an independent state." By this criterion, both referendum questions, in 1980 and 1995, would have been invalid.

Quebec quickly attacked the Clarity Act and reaffirmed the right of Quebecers to choose their destiny freely. On February 28, 2001, the National Assembly passed a law to this effect, with Section 1 reading as follows:

> The right of the Québec people to self-determination is founded in fact and in law. The Québec people are the holder of rights that are universally recognized under the principle of equal rights and self-determination of peoples.

The ephemeral "social union" of the provinces

At the same time that it was pursuing legal means to invalidate Quebec's secession from the rest of Canada, the federal government launched the Canadian Foundation for Innovation, the Millennium Scholarship program, and later the ambitious Canada Research Chair program. All these initiatives involved the education sector, supposedly an area of provincial responsibility.

The provinces signed a "social union" agreement, supported by Quebec, reaffirming provincial jurisdiction in education and urging the federal government to consult them before launching new social programs. On February 4, 1999, Quebec withdrew from this common front after the English Canadian provinces agreed to a broader federal role in the social sector.

A surprise resignation and the "Michaud affair"

On January 11, 2001, Lucien Bouchard announced he was leaving politics. In his resignation speech, he said that he had been unable to mobilize Quebecers around the sovereignist cause. "My efforts to rekindle quickly the debate on the national question have been in vain," he stated. "Therefore, it was not possible to relaunch a referendum within the short time frame we anticipated." With some chagrin, he noted that "Quebecers have remained astonishingly unmoved by the federal offensives."

This resignation came after the National Assembly passed a motion on December 14, 2000, denouncing "the unacceptable remarks toward ethnic communities and, in particular, toward the Jewish community, made by Yves Michaud." Michaud, an ardent defender of the French language, had lamented the monolithic vote of some ethnic communities in the 1995 referendum and suggested in a radio interview that some Jewish spokespersons occasionally minimized the pain of other peoples who had suffered genocides. Some PQ members of the assembly, still troubled by Jacques Parizeau's "ethnic vote" speech, immediately denounced Michaud's remarks. Other sovereignists, who viewed Michaud as an irreproachable activist despite these remarks, considered the December 14 motion an act of censorship.

This greatly irritated Bouchard, who, in his resignation speech, said:

> This, unquestionably, is a core issue. First, I declare that Quebecers, without distinction, may exercise their right to vote as they see fit, without being accused of intolerance. Second, I declare that the Holocaust is the supreme crime, a systematic attempt to eliminate a people, a negation of human conscience and dignity. Jews cannot be blamed for being traumatized by it. This unspeakable tragedy suffers no comparison.

The whole episode showed that the wounds from the 1995 referendum had still not fully healed.

Quebec in Search of Itself

The year 2000 marked the 40th anniversary of the election of the Liberals under Jean Lesage and the start of the Quiet Revolution. The builders of modern Quebec took the opportunity to look back over their achievements and marvel at how far they had come. In economic terms, French-speaking Quebecers no longer lagged behind, in part as a result of institutions such as the Caisse de Dépôt et Placement. In social terms, Quebec offered free education through the pre-university level and $5-a-day childcare. This was something to be proud of. Plus, Quebec continued to create numerous "new economy" jobs and reached a "peace of the Braves" with the Cree in 2002, allowing for exploitation of the hydroelectric potential of Quebec's far north.

And yet, self-satisfied as Quebec was, it couldn't fully put to rest dissonant voices that were increasingly critical of the "Quebec model." The difficulties young couples faced in finding family doctors, unacceptable high school dropout rates, underfinancing of universities, the public debt, high taxes, union corporatism, lack of job security — all these issues led to substantial questioning of the heritage of the Quiet Revolution. On top of these problems, there was the "fiscal imbalance." The federal government taxed citizens almost as much as the provinces did and racked up budget surpluses, but the Quebec government had to manage the costliest services. Many people felt a new approach was required, but there was no consensus on solutions.

Quebec was also searching for itself in terms of identity. The "reasonable accommodation" crisis that sprang up mid-decade led Quebec's French-speaking majority to reflect on its deepest values.

Which way for the Quebec model?

At the turn of the millennium, the Quebec model began to come under heavy criticism. The unions and the Parti Québécois were bastions of the model's supporters. In their eyes, the Quebec model favored cooperation over confrontation and state intervention over market forces. As an instrument of social solidarity and an engine of economic development, government lay at the heart of the model. Challenging its goals, its scope, or its operation meant attacking one of the most important legacies of the Quiet Revolution.

The rise of the Action Démocratique du Québec

Bernard Landry took over from Lucien Bouchard as leader of the Parti Québécois and premier of Quebec. A former minister who had held the economic and finance portfolios, Landry was an ardent promoter of the Quebec model. For him, nothing in the model needed to be changed. This view was disputed by the Action Démocratique du Québec (ADQ), which to almost everyone's surprise won four by-elections in the spring of 2002.

Party leader Mario Dumont was one of the harshest critics of the Quebec model. He denounced union inflexibility, bureaucratic complacence in government, and the waste of public funds. Two of the reforms he suggested were especially noteworthy:

- ✔ **The ADQ wanted to give parents school vouchers to create healthy competition in education.** The more a school appealed to parents, the more they would be willing to contribute to its financing.

- ✔ **The ADQ wanted a flat tax to simplify tax regulations.** All taxpayers, regardless of income levels, would pay the same percentage of their income in taxes.

Defenders of the Quebec model immediately denounced these proposals, accusing Dumont of pandering to particular constituencies and setting the rich against the poor.

"We are ready": The Liberals come to power

After leading in the polls during the summer of 2002, the ADQ began to lose ground. In a speech in Toronto in September 2002, Dumont announced that "the constitutional issue is no longer on the ADQ's radar screen." This former defender of the Allaire Report said he had moved on to other things, a statement that alienated some nationalists. And his neoliberal proposals scared away more conservative voters.

These strategic missteps played into the hands of the Quebec Liberal Party, led since 1998 by Jean Charest. While endorsing some of the ADQ's criticisms of the Quebec model, the Liberal leader put forward a more moderate program and a more experienced team. He, too, pledged to cut taxes and reduce the size of government. Above all, he promised to do away with long delays in emergency rooms and waiting lists for seeing specialists — all without turning to the private sector.

Unlike the ADQ, the Liberals promised to reestablish dialogue with English Canada, while adopting a new strategy. With confrontations between Quebec and Ottawa having become sterile, Charest's party preferred to rely on enhanced cooperation among provinces. The Liberal slogan in the 2003 election was "We are ready," a clever way of suggesting that the ADQ, which had slipped up a few times during the campaign, may not be mature enough to govern. On April 14, 2003, the Liberals won 76 seats and 45.9 percent of the popular vote, and were set to form the next government.

Massive demonstration against the war in Iraq

Like everyone else in the Western world, Quebecers were deeply shocked by the terrorist attacks on September 11, 2001. This solidarity with the United States had its limits, however. On February 15, 2003, in the bitter cold, about 150,000 Quebecers marched through the streets of downtown Montreal to protest against the war in Iraq that the United States, under President George W. Bush, was preparing to launch. Nowhere else in Canada did this cause mobilize as many people. On the same day, about 30,000 Canadians marched in Toronto, 20,000 in Vancouver, and 2,000 in Ottawa. Three days before the U.S. invasion of Iraq began on March 20, the Canadian government announced that it would refuse to support the military operation. Polls at the time showed that only 33 percent of Quebecers wanted Canada to send troops, compared to 60 percent of Albertans.

This hostility to the war in Iraq led to interesting debates on Quebecers' relationship with the United States. Although Quebecers had been highly favorable to free trade and increasingly asserted their status as a North American society, were they becoming anti-American? Or was this hostility to the war just a sign of their congenital pacifism? In hindsight, we can see that the major irritant was Bush's foreign policy. It was not the United States or war as such that Quebecers were rejecting as much as a warmongering and protectionist president — who, on top of all that, opposed the Kyoto Protocol. The election of Barack Obama in 2008 restored friendlier feelings.

"We are concerned": The "Lucide" manifesto

Critics of the Quebec model who were hoping for major reforms following the election of Jean Charest's team were soon disappointed. A number of government initiatives (for example, labor-code reform to favor outsourcing in the public sector, partial privatization of the Mont Orford park, and cuts to student loans and grants) were abandoned following great uproars. These mobilizations took Charest by surprise.

On October 19, 2005, former premier Lucien Bouchard and 11 other figures from political, intellectual, and business circles issued a manifesto, *Pour un Québec lucide (For a Clear-eyed Vision of Quebec).* The manifesto created a shockwave. "We are worried," they wrote. "Concerned for the Quebec we love. Concerned for our people, who have weathered many storms but seem oblivious to the dangers that today threaten its future."

The pitfalls that concerned them were demographic decline leading to much higher healthcare costs, fierce competition from Asia in the manufacturing sector, trade-union inflexibility that blocked innovation, and income-tax rates that deterred initiative. To meet the great challenges of the 21st century, the "Lucides" suggested reducing the public debt, investing heavily in education (including ending existing tuition freezes), raising electricity rates, and taxing consumption rather than work.

Reaction from the left

The reaction from the political left and from supporters of the Quebec model was not long in coming. Barely two weeks after the "Lucides" published their manifesto, the "Solidaires" issued a response:

> We, too, are concerned about our children's future. Above all, we do not want to leave them a battered planet, forests that have been destroyed, greater social and economic inequalities, or wars for control of what water is left. We want to pass on to them something more than the idea that we have no choice but to give in to whatever the market dictates.

Though Quebec faces problems, the signatories stated, this is because its leaders have succumbed too readily to the lure of neoliberalism. In the view of the "Solidaires," wealth exists but is poorly distributed. Instead of reducing public services, tax evasion should be cut down and taxes on the rich should be raised. As a proportion of gross domestic product, healthcare costs are lower in Quebec than in the United States, and the public debt is under control. When it comes to competing with China, a race to the bottom must be avoided. Instead of accepting lower wages and poorer working conditions, Quebec workers would do better to help Chinese workers raise their standard of living.

The Liberal Party of Canada tainted by the sponsorship scandal

In the view of many English Canadians, so many French-speaking Quebecers voted for independence because they were misled by separatist propaganda. In July 1996, the federal government established an Information Bureau to increase the visibility of Canada's presence in Quebec and to run a sponsorship program. This meant that the federal government would support sports and cultural events across Quebec. In return for the funds they received, organizations had to fly the maple-leaf flag as a way of showing Ottawa's generosity and Quebec's place in Canada. But the program was put together in a great hurry, and the management of public funds soon led to questions.

Following a number of revelations in the Toronto *Globe and Mail,* along with embarrassing questions from the Bloc Québécois in the House of Commons and a devastating report from the auditor general of Canada, Chrétien's successor, Paul Martin, mandated Judge John Gomery to shed light on the program's operation. Throughout 2005, Quebecers followed the Gomery Commission's hearings attentively. Month after month, the commission's lawyers grilled politicians, political advisors, civil servants, heads of advertising firms, and Liberal Party of Canada officials, all connected to the program in one way or another. Gomery's aim was to find out whether the $332 million sunk into the sponsorship of special events had actually served the purposes set by the government.

Judge Gomery's report was consistent with the revelations at the hearings. It showed that advertising firms often overbilled or submitted false invoices, and that hypothetical and apparently nonexistent studies sometimes cost taxpayers millions of dollars. These anomalies resulted from political interference and fraudulent actions by some civil servants, the judge said. The hearings showed, above all, that some of the funds that went into the sponsorship program had helped finance the Liberal campaigns in the 1997 and 2000 federal elections. A number of criminal charges were laid following the commission's revelations.

The sponsorship scandal greatly tarnished the federal Liberals' image in Quebec. In the federal election of June 28, 2004, the Bloc Québécois won 54 seats, its best showing since 1993. Throughout the campaign, Gilles Duceppe, the Bloc leader since 1997, took full advantage of Quebecers' anger. Years later, the party once led by Pierre Elliott Trudeau still had not recovered from this scandal in Quebec.

The birth of Québec Solidaire

For a long time, people on the political left had been active mostly in the Parti Québécois. But the Bouchard government's austerity policy and the deferral of the next sovereignty referendum moved some "progressives" away from the party René Lévesque had founded.

In June 2002, several tiny, far-left groups, including the Communist Party of Quebec, established the Union des Forces Progressistes. This new party won only 1 percent of the vote in the 2003 election, but in some urban ridings its candidates did significantly better. Others later joined this left-wing party, including a number of activists with the Fédération des Femmes du Québec, a feminist organization that initiated the 2000 World March of Women. In 2004, Françoise David, the group's spokesperson, founded Option Citoyenne, which emphasized feminism and ecology.

In February 2006, the Union des Forces Progressistes and Option Citoyenne merged to form Québec Solidaire. Primarily left leaning but also sovereignist, the new party stood out with its dual leadership. Amir Khadir and Françoise David were designated the party's "co-spokespersons." In their view, the Quebec social model should not only be protected but also be developed and extended.

The crisis of reasonable accommodation

Since 2001, the growth of Quebec's population had depended more on immigration than on natural growth. This was a new phenomenon with significant consequences, and it meant Quebec had to adapt. Although most newcomers were recruited by a Quebec government department, they were immigrating to Canada, a country that has made multiculturalism an official doctrine. In Canada, it was the host society that had to accommodate newcomers, not the other way around. But how far could this accommodation go? Very far, in some cases.

In December 2001, the Montreal civic administration named the traditional Christmas tree put up each year in front of City Hall a "tree of life." Montreal was a city with many cultures and religions, so its elected officials were reluctant to display a Christian and Western symbol. This decision was immediately denounced. In December 2004, a report commissioned by the Ontario government argued that religious arbitration should be allowed when requested by Muslim families. This opening to "Islamic courts" greatly shocked Quebecers, who saw it as a potential attack on women's rights.

On May 26, 2005, the National Assembly unanimously passed a motion introduced by Fatima Houda-Pepin, a member of Moroccan descent, rejecting religious courts, whether in Quebec or elsewhere in Canada.

A controversial ruling on kirpans

This unanimity was shattered, however, when the Supreme Court of Canada issued a ruling on March 2, 2006, allowing young Gurbaj Singh Multani to wear a *kirpan* (a traditional dagger of the Sikh religion) at his Montreal school. The school board and the Quebec Court of Appeal had found this accommodation excessive and unreasonable, even in a free and democratic society. But Canada's highest court, in the name of religious freedom and multiculturalism, agreed to permit the young Sikh to attend school armed with a kirpan. Many Quebec intellectuals, journalists, and analysts felt that the Supreme Court ruling should be respected in the name of accepting others, but polls showed that a large majority of people were opposed.

Tension rises

As debate over kirpans raged in the media, other similar cases cropped up in the news, and "reasonable accommodation" became a hot topic. Here are a few examples:

- ✔ **Frosted windows at the YMCA:** In a Montreal neighborhood inhabited by many members of an Orthodox Jewish community, a YMCA branch agreed to install four frosted windows to avoid distracting males in this religious group who could see women in training outfits. Shocked by this decision, YMCA members circulated a petition to have these windows removed. After the controversy made headlines in the newspapers, YMCA management backtracked and reinstalled regular windows, with curtains.

- ✔ **Separate bathing:** In May and December 2006, two instances of separate bathing were reported in the newspapers. When taking swimming tests in public pools, some Muslim parents and women insisted that all men leave. The school and YMCA in question complied with the wishes of these Muslim women, who did not want men to see them in bathing suits.

- ✔ *Halal* **(sanctioned by Islamic law) menu at a childcare center:** At a government-financed facility, a Muslim man demanded that his children not consume any non-halal meat. A ruling from the Quebec human and youth rights commission, issued on March 20, 2007, backed the father and ordered the center to pay him $4,000 in "moral damages for violating his rights."

These examples of reasonable accommodation all nurtured a debate that was becoming increasingly sensitive and emotional. With the authorities not quite sure how to react to these initiatives, Hérouxville, a small municipality in the St. Maurice Valley, adopted its own "code of conduct." As a place that welcomes newcomers, the document says, "it is not up to us to give up our values. We are tolerant and willing to facilitate the integration of immigrants, but not at any price." This document made headlines. Four years later, André Drouin, the municipal council member who developed this "code of conduct," acknowledged that his main goal had been to provoke a thorough debate on the issue.

Dumont catches the rebound

The chattering classes were embarrassed by this debate and feared a rise of xenophobia. Only ADQ leader Mario Dumont came out clearly against accommodations, which he called "unreasonable." In November 2006, he said:

We are pleased that people are coming to be with us, but let them do so in keeping with who we are. And in my view, these are principles that we cannot defend halfheartedly while down on our knees. . . . Here in Quebec we are a majority that has no need to live in fear of being called intolerant.

Meanwhile, Parti Québécois leader André Boisclair believed that the court decisions should be respected. He even asserted that the crucifix should be removed from the Blue Room of the National Assembly, a suggestion that stirred up a lively reaction.

The Bouchard-Taylor Commission

To cool tempers, on February 8, 2007, Premier Jean Charest announced the establishment of the Consultation Commission on Accommodation Practices Related to Cultural Differences. Philosopher Charles Taylor and sociologist Gérard Bouchard, two renowned intellectuals, chaired the commission, which received more than 900 briefs and held 22 citizens' forums all across Quebec. Broadcast live on television, these gatherings stirred considerable interest. Everyone seemed to have an opinion on the issue. The two co-chairs also consulted experts and commissioned studies. The Bouchard-Taylor Report, released a year later, blamed the media, criticized the uneasy attitude of the French-speaking majority, and urged the government to reflect deeply on secularism. But it was not acted on.

Political effects of the crisis

The reasonable accommodation crisis was a major backdrop to the March 2007 election campaign. For only the second time in Quebec history, voters brought a minority government to power. With 48 seats and 33 percent of the popular vote, the Liberals finished first — but just barely. The ADQ made the biggest breakthrough in its history. With 41 members elected and backing from 1.2 million voters, Mario Dumont's party outpolled the Parti Québécois under André Boisclair and became the official opposition. All signs indicated that the ADQ's positions on reasonable accommodation had paid off in electoral terms. A large part of the French-speaking nationalist electorate had shifted from the PQ to the ADQ.

This crushing PQ defeat led to the leader's resignation and his replacement by Pauline Marois, an experienced politician who had served as a minister in the Lévesque, Parizeau, and Bouchard governments. From the moment she took up her position as leader, Marois shifted the party's focus to identity issues, presenting a private member's bill that called for the institution of Quebec citizenship, which would include requiring knowledge of French to vote in elections. Nationalists gradually returned to the fold, and the PQ once again formed the official opposition after the 2008 election, which resulted in a Liberal majority government.

Many people, both on the right and on the left, felt that the PQ's sovereignist position no longer had the same relevance as before. This did nothing to shake the beliefs of leading Parti Québécois members. Even though they remained unclear about the date of the next referendum, they promised to be faithful to "Quebec values" — left-wing values, in their view — and to govern as sovereignists.

Right, left, right, left . . .

Quebec's search for itself has continued and intensified since 2008. The traditional polarization between sovereignists and federalists was wearing thin. Young people, intellectuals, and artists were no longer as concerned about the decline of French in Montreal and the political status of Quebec within Canada. In their eyes, what appeared to set Quebec apart now was less a history, a language, and a culture than social policies and environmental concerns. Meanwhile, others with little interest in the national question or identity issues saw Quebec as a stagnant society, paralyzed by debt and corporatism and threatened by demographic and economic decline.

The "Plan Nord" and "real business"

Two options were open to those who believed Quebec had to change the way its government operated, revive its economy, and deal with the major challenges of the future.

The first option was promoted by Jean Charest's Liberal government, with its heavy boosterism for "Plan Nord," an ambitious natural resource development program in northern Quebec above the 49th parallel The exploitation of this natural wealth would require substantial public and private infrastructure investment. But allegations of collusion between the Liberal Party and the construction industry led to opposition criticism and public mistrust — and to a commission of inquiry, headed by Judge France Charbonneau. Many people also feared that the royalties the companies exploiting this wealth would pay were not high enough.

The second option for those concerned above all with Quebec's economic future was that of the Coalition Avenir Québec (CAQ). Founded in 2011 by François Legault, a former PQ minister, the CAQ called for more stringent management in the public sector and a fight against corruption. Following Mario Dumont's resignation in 2008, ADQ members of the National Assembly agreed to scuttle their former party and join the new group. Liberals and CAQ members agreed on the need to keep the national question off the political agenda. Neither suggested new powers for Quebec or a reform of federalism. Constitutional matters were associated with old clashes that divided Quebecers. In the view of the Liberals and the CAQ, sound management and a more prosperous economy were the only "real business" of any consequence.

The left and the "maple spring"

Facing two such "neoliberal" parties, the left mobilized and showed its teeth. In 2008, an initial Québec Solidaire member, Amir Khadir, was elected to the National Assembly in Mercier riding, in the heart of Montreal's Plateau-Mont-Royal district. Khadir's speeches, whether on losses incurred by the Caisse de Dépôt or the building of a publicly financed arena in Quebec City, were often hard hitting.

While taking on the Quebec Liberals and the CAQ, the left also fought against the federal Conservatives under Stephen Harper, prime minister since January 2006. The Harper government's pro-American and pro-Israeli positions, as well as its opposition to the Kyoto Protocol and its law-and-order policies, appalled the Quebec left. Although much of the political left remained sovereignist, in the federal election of May 2, 2011, a large proportion preferred the New Democratic Party (NDP) — whose leader, Jack Layton, had only a few months to live — to Gilles Duceppe's Bloc Québécois. The scope of this "orange wave" (so called after the NDP's color) took most observers by surprise.

The same was true of the "maple spring" (following soon after the "Arab Spring"), which mobilized a significant portion of Quebec youth in the spring of 2012. Night after night, countless thousands of students and other citizens wearing the movement's trademark red square, with backing from the Parti Québécois and much of the union movement, took to the streets to denounce the higher tuition fees decreed by the Charest government.

A woman premier

In the Quebec election of September 4, 2012, the Parti Québécois under Pauline Marois finished first but formed a minority government, winning 54 seats with just under 32 percent of the popular vote. Despite sky-high dissatisfaction rates shown in poll after poll, the Liberals managed to win 50 seats with 31 percent of the vote, coming in ahead of the CAQ, which saw 19 candidates elected and received 27 percent of the vote.

Beaten in his own riding, Jean Charest announced the next day that he was leaving politics. This was a historic election: For the first time, a woman would hold the position of premier. But with this political configuration, it was hard to say how the PQ program, which pledged to "achieve Quebec sovereignty following public consultation through a referendum held at a time it judges appropriate," would fare.

Part VI
The Part of Tens

The 5th Wave   By Rich Tennant

QUEBEC CITADEL

"I'm from maintenance—where do you want the welcome signs?"

In this part . . .

This wouldn't be a *For Dummies* book without a Part of Tens. In this part, I offer up ten personalities, ten symbols, and ten landmarks — all of which have put their stamps on Quebec.

Why were Quebecers so drawn to personalities such as Louis Cyr, Maurice Richard, and Gratien Gélinas? Where does the arrow sash come from? How do Quebecers swear? Who wrote *L'homme rapaillé?* Is Mount Royal a volcano? Are the Plains of Abraham just a Canadian national park? And is Wendake no different from other First Nations reserves? I answer these and other questions in this part.

Chapter 23

Ten Mythical Personalities

In This Chapter

▶ Considering people who have made their mark on Quebec

▶ Finding inspiration among famous Quebecers

*P*ortraits of important political figures appear throughout this book. But other personalities have also left their mark on Quebec, especially those who have excelled in the arts and in sports. Young people have often viewed them as role models or idols. They're all legends — or in the process of becoming ones. In this chapter, I introduce ten famous Quebecers who made their mark on the world.

Maurice Richard and the Riot of 1955

Maurice Richard (1921–2000), the legendary hockey player nicknamed "the Rocket," began his professional career in October 1942 and retired in September 1960. He played 1,111 regular-season and playoff games for the Montreal Canadiens and scored 626 goals. A mighty scorer full of raw energy, he was an inspiration to all his teammates. Intense and combative, he accumulated 1,473 minutes in penalties! One of his feats was to score five goals on December 28, 1944, after having moved a family member that same day. He was also the first player in National Hockey League (NHL) history to score 50 goals in 50 games.

In March 1955, NHL president Clarence Campbell deprived French Canadians of their idol. The Rocket was suspended for hitting a Boston Bruins player with his stick. On March 17, Campbell made the mistake of attending a game at the Montreal Forum between the Canadiens and the Detroit Red Wings. The extremely hostile crowd threw all kinds of projectiles at him. After a tear gas bomb exploded, the police evacuated the Forum. Outside, a riot broke out, resulting in $100,000 worth of damage and dozens of arrests. Richard went on the radio to appeal for calm.

If Maurice Richard became a personality of mythic proportions, it's because the Quebec people as a whole recognized itself in him. "French-Canadian nationalism seems to have taken refuge in hockey," wrote André Laurendeau in *Le Devoir* on March 21, 1955, a few days after the riot. "The crowd that manifested its anger last Thursday night was not motivated only by the love of sport or a sense that its idol had suffered an injustice. It was a people who are frustrated, who were protesting against the conditions in which they find themselves." Some believed that this riot was one of the seeds of the Quiet Revolution.

Louis Cyr: Strong Man

As longtime farmers and loggers, French Canadians greatly admire strong men. Cyprien Noé Cyr (1863–1912), also known as Louis Cyr, was an athlete renowned in his time for his Herculean strength. He grew up in a typical 19th-century agricultural setting and left school at the age of 12 to work in lumber camps, where everyone was impressed by his physical strength. When he was 14, he moved 15 bushels of grain, weighing about 408 kilograms (900 pounds), a distance of 4.5 meters (15 feet). At the age of 18, when he and his family were living in Lowell, Massachusetts, Cyr participated in his first test of strength. As the crowd held its breath, he managed to lift a horse! The following year, he lifted a huge stone weighing 234 kilograms (517 pounds) up to his shoulders. More than 4,000 people witnessed this feat.

During the years that followed, Cyr's reputation as a strong man continued to grow, in both Quebec and the eastern United States. He started performing in shows in 1883. Thousands of people came to see him on his initial tour. He lifted heavy weights with the middle finger of his right hand, pulled carts containing up to 15 people, and in one motion with one arm lifted barrels of flour, often weighing more than 90 kilograms (200 pounds), from the ground. His tours made headlines, and he quickly became a star. Recruited by traveling shows, he performed in Canada and the United States.

In 1886, in Quebec City, Cyr won the title of strongest man in Canada. His fame soon transcended national boundaries. He traveled to Europe and faced European champions. Louis Cyr never lost a competition. By the end of his career, Cyr had held 2,500 performances. He was the pride of French Canadians, who saw in him an illustration of their own potential. Stories of his exploits were perennial favorites in the homes of old, traditional Quebec.

Albani: The Great Singer

During the same period as Cyr's (see the preceding section), but in a completely different setting, a singer from Quebec enjoyed immense success. Emma Lajeunesse was born in Chambly in 1847. Her father, a music teacher, recognized her raw talent and taught her everything he knew. She was soon known as a child prodigy. Not that her success came without effort: She practiced piano and voice six hours a day. She made her first stage appearances at the age of eight. In 1862, her father organized a benefit concert to raise funds to allow the young artist to pursue her studies. Six years later, Lajeunesse crossed the Atlantic and settled in Paris, where she studied under the great masters. She then studied with Francesco Lamperti in Milan. It was in Italy that she adopted the stage name under which she would become famous: Albani. In 1871, she became the singer in residence in London's Covent Garden. Her international career had been launched.

Albani performed on the great stages of the world. She had a captivating talent and a fascinating personality. Her collection of jewelry and dresses was the envy of women everywhere. In 1873, in St. Petersburg, she received congratulations from Tsar Alexander II in person. The following year, she performed for Queen Victoria in a private concert at Windsor Castle. She rubbed shoulders with the great personalities of her time and was the stuff of headlines. On August 6, 1878, she married Ernest Gye, the son of Covent Garden's manager, with whom she later had a son.

In 1883, at the end of a North American tour, she finally returned to Montreal. More than 10,000 people came to see her. The mayor himself welcomed her at City Hall and presented her with an ode written by the poet Louis Fréchette: "Overseas they gave you fame and fortune; now your home country, so proud of you, has come in turn to offer you its most fervent tribute and most tender love." In 1896, she performed at Covent Garden for the last time. Ten years later, on a farewell tour, Emma Lajeunesse returned to her country. She died on April 3, 1930, after experiencing financial difficulties.

Céline Dion: International Star

Another diva would distinguish herself a century later. Born in 1968 in the small town of Charlemagne near Montreal, Céline Dion learned to sing with her older brothers and sisters. She never lacked musicians to accompany her. In the Dion household music was sacrosanct, and everyone played an instrument. Her mother wrote the piece for which she first became known, "Ce n'était qu'un rêve" ("It Was But a Dream"). In 1981, Dion released her first album and achieved immediate commercial success. The best songwriters in Québec, including Luc Plamondon, wrote brilliant lyrics for her.

Despite her youth and sensitivity, her voice and style made her a commanding presence. Her biggest fan was René Angélil, her impresario who later became her husband. Of Lebanese origin, the former member of the group Les Baronets knew how to market his artists. From the beginning he was convinced that Céline Dion was a singer of international caliber. Acting on this intuition, he entered her in major international competitions, and she handily won contests in Japan and Europe during the 1980s.

In the 1990s she tried to break simultaneously into the French and American markets. In France, she teamed up with singer-songwriter Jean-Jacques Goldman. Her album *Deux* was a huge success. In 1996 and 1997, she became a bona-fide star with her albums *Falling Into You* and *Let's Talk About Love,* each of which sold more than 30 million copies. In 1998, her song "My Heart Will Go On," from the soundtrack of the American film *Titanic,* became one of the top-selling songs in music history, with sales exceeding 15 million copies.

To date, Dion has won five Grammys, three Victoires de la Musique awards, 39 Félix awards, 21 Junos, and 12 World Music Awards. Sales of her albums have surpassed 200 million copies. Although she lives in Las Vegas and performs internationally, she returns regularly to Quebec. She and her husband are also major philanthropists, as the directors of Sainte-Justine Hospital in Montreal can attest.

Leonard Cohen: The Soothing Voice

Coming from a completely different environment than Céline Dion, with a different artistic style and songs in a very different register, Leonard Cohen is also a major international star. Born in 1934 in the very posh English enclave of Westmount on Montreal Island, Cohen grew up in a Jewish family of Polish origin. As a youth, he devoured books, read Sartre and Camus, and enrolled at McGill University to study history. His deepest desire was to become a poet. In 1956, while still a young student, he published his first book of poems, *Let Us Compare Mythologies.* Over the next decade, he pursued his writing career, producing four more books of poetry and two novels.

In 1968, the poet transformed himself into a musician and launched his debut album, *Songs of Leonard Cohen*, in the United States. "Suzanne," one of his greatest hits, was on that album. "Hallelujah," undoubtedly his greatest success, was on *Various Positions,* which came out in 1984. Four years later, he launched *I'm Your Man.* Even as a singer, Cohen is first and foremost a poet. Each one of his compositions creates an exquisite ambience, a cocoon-like atmosphere. He gives the impression of coming to us from another world. There is a very special quality to the sound, melodies, and lyrics. His songs have also been covered by numerous artists.

As with many artists of his generation, Cohen's life and work have all the trappings of a spiritual and mystical quest. A follower of Zen Buddhism, he has spent long sojourns meditating in the California desert.

In May 2012, he received the Glenn Gould Prize in Toronto. The citation noted his "outstanding contribution to music and communicating music through the use of communications technologies." Instead of pocketing the $50,000 award, he chose to turn it over to the Canada Council for the Arts.

Émile Nelligan: The Accursed Poet

Another poet who had a great impact on Quebec was Émile Nelligan. The son of Patrick Nelligan, a postal worker of Irish origin, and Émilie Hudon, a French Canadian from Rimouski, Nelligan was born in Montreal in 1879. As a student, Nelligan was undisciplined, shy, and lacked motivation; he also attended several educational institutions. He discovered poetry at an early age and wanted to devote himself entirely to it, as had his favorite French poet, Paul Verlaine. His father was not at all supportive of Émile's passion for poetry, but this didn't bother the young Nelligan, who published his first poems under the pseudonym of Émile Kovar in September 1896.

His talent was quickly noticed. Robertine Barry (also known as Françoise), a respected literary columnist, took him under her wing and introduced him to Montreal's cultural milieu. He forged a friendship with Louis Dantin, Quebec's outstanding literary critic at the turn of the 20th century. Nelligan was also part of a group of young artists that on November 7, 1895, created the École Littéraire de Montréal. This group held regular public meetings at the Château Ramezay, where notable personalities came to hear their latest compositions. This was how Nelligan introduced some of his poems to the public.

Between 1896 and 1899, Nelligan's most productive period, he composed nearly 170 poems. They were romantic and melancholy. Here is one stanza from "Vaisseau d'or" ("Ship of Gold"), his most famous poem: "It was a great ship carved from solid gold / Its masts touched the skies over uncharted seas / Venus, goddess of love, her hair streaming, her flesh bare / Flaunted herself on the prow beneath a blazing sun."

On April 9, 1899, Émile Nelligan was taken to the Saint-Benoît-Joseph-Labre asylum, where he was treated for what was deemed "mental degeneration." He was held there until his death in 1941. Seemingly the victim of a literary curse, Nelligan became a kind of myth. His friend Louis Dantin later compiled his major poems, and his works were reprinted in many editions. A musical play was written to pay tribute to his work, with the lyrics composed by none other than the playwright Michel Tremblay.

Michel Tremblay: Putting "Joual" on Stage

Born in Montreal in 1942, Michel Tremblay came to public attention in 1968 with the opening of his play *Les belles-sœurs,* directed by André Brassard. The play had been rejected in a competition in 1966, but the Théâtre du Rideau Vert finally agreed to produce it. The script caused a scandal. It wasn't an avant-garde play intended to revolutionize established theatrical formats. On the contrary, the play was easy to follow and the staging was very realistic. It was simply a group of women discussing the ups and downs of their daily lives.

So, what caused the uproar? The language. The dialogue was written in *joual,* the vernacular language popular among the Quebec working class. Many theatergoers were shocked. It was unclear whether Tremblay was mocking this segment of his society or whether he wanted to promote the language, which some considered vulgar. This use of slang offended many people's very conception of "culture." Instead of reflecting the least educated, shouldn't culture serve to elevate people? The play sparked a major controversy about the language spoken in Quebec. Condemning Parisian linguistic colonialism, Tremblay's supporters believed that joual was the true language of Quebecers. One of these was Léandre Bergeron who, in 1980, published his *Dictionnaire de la langue québécoise (Dictionary of the Quebec Language).* The opponents of joual argued that use of this slang has only isolated Quebecers.

Michel Tremblay did not stop with one play. *Les belles-sœurs* was followed by many other plays that became widely known: *À toi pour toujours, ta Marie-Lou* (1970), *Sainte Carmen de la Main* (1976), *Albertine en cinq temps* (1984), and *Le vrai monde?* (1987). A number of these were translated and performed throughout the world. Tremblay's works include stories and novels as well. His best-known series of novels, the *Chroniques du Plateau-Mont-Royal —* which included *La grosse femme d'à côté est enceinte* (1978) and *Des nouvelles d'Édouard* (1984) — achieved great popular success.

Gratien Gélinas

Whether rich or poor, French-speaking Quebecers who sometimes went to the theater during the 1940s and 1950s have a vivid memory of the actor Gratien Gélinas. Born in Saint-Tite in the St. Maurice Valley in 1909, he first became known as a radio performer. His character Fridolin was a naïve young French Canadian who offered a satirical look at Quebec society between the two world wars. Although he spared the church and the clergy, Fridolin did not shy away from ridiculing politicians' corruption and arrogance, the stupidity of the police, or the shenanigans of some businessmen. He put the spotlight on the deficiencies of the public education system and the anti-intellectualism of the elites. As a nationalist, he made fun of the fatalism of his compatriots, who were sometimes more interested in sports and trivialities than in the political future of French Canada.

This somewhat ingenuous child attracted a large public following. Dressed in a Montreal Canadiens sweater, the character Gélinas created soon made the transition to the stage. Gélinas's theatrical career took another big step forward in 1948 with the runaway success of his play *Tit-Coq.* Acclaimed by French-speaking audiences, the play was translated into English and had a run of more than 600 performances in all. His second play, *Bousille et les justes* (1958), was also very successful in Quebec and abroad. Without endorsing joual, Gélinas used a colorful vocabulary — expressions and phrases understood by all French-speaking Quebecers.

Supported by the government of Maurice Duplessis, Gratien Gélinas established the Théâtre de la Comédie Canadienne in 1957. At a time when most theatrical presentations were of French or American origin, Gélinas sought to stimulate the creation of Quebec works. Many playwrights — including the renowned Marcel Dubé, then at the height of his popularity — took advantage of this initiative. A highly talented standup comedian, Gelinas influenced a number of the great comedians of the 1960s, such as Yvon Deschamps and Marc Favreau. With his *Fridolinades,* he showed that it was possible to be funny and sensitive at the same time, and that humor could also have political significance. Regarded as one of the fathers of Quebec theater, Gélinas died in 1999.

Olivier Guimond: A True Comedian

Considered the greatest comic of his time, Olivier Guimond (1914–1971) was deeply loved by the Quebec public. His father, known by his stage name "Ti-Zoune," was also a popular comic. The younger Guimond's stage career began at the age of 18, and in 1934 he was recruited by the theatrical troupes of Arthur Petrie and Jean Grimaldi. Guimond's world was burlesque. He performed in variety shows that included dance numbers, songs, magic tricks, and comedy skits. These skits, which were especially popular with burlesque audiences, were often very brief. People laughed not so much at scripted exchanges as at the actors' antics and their improvised repartee. Some of the skits that contributed to his fame involved Guimond portraying an intoxicated man trying to hide his drunken state from his wife.

Actors trained in the major theater schools often snubbed the burlesque comedians. This condescension never bothered Guimond, who hosted his first broadcast on Radio-Canada in 1955. He also played roles in popular soap operas, including *Le survenant.* But it was with Télé-Métropole, a new private television channel launched in 1961, that he reached the height of his popularity. He played the role of Basile Lebrun in the highly successful sitcom *Cré Basile,* which ran on Télé-Métropole from 1965 to 1970. In *Bye Bye 1970,* Radio-Canada's year-end news magazine, he performed in an unforgettable skit about the October Crisis.

Like all burlesque comedians, Guimond had "straight men" who set up his lines. Among them were Paul Desmarteaux and especially Denis Drouin. He was also very close to Gilles Latulippe, the founder of the Théâtre des Varieties in Montreal, which kept the burlesque tradition alive. Olivier Guimond, a kind of Québécois Charlie Chaplin, died in 1971.

Guy Laliberté: A Clown in Space

Born in Saint-Bruno, on the South Shore opposite Montreal, Guy Laliberté became a stilt walker, an accordionist, and a public entertainer. In 1984, during the celebrations of the 450th anniversary of Jacques Cartier's first voyage, he founded Cirque du Soleil along with Daniel Gauthier. The company was quickly recognized for its completely new approach to the circus. No more elephants and tigers — now it was all about acrobatic performances and elaborate sets!

The Cirque mounted its first show the year it was founded. Presented in 11 cities and towns throughout Quebec, it was a great success. The following year, Guy Laliberté's team embarked on an extensive tour of Canada. In 1987, Cirque du Soleil created *Le cirque reinventé (We Reinvent the Circus),* its first big show, acclaimed in the United States, England, and France. The company's reputation has continued to grow and it has gone on more and more tours ever since.

In 1993, Cirque du Soleil presented its first show in Las Vegas. Five more were to follow in that city, which became the company's launching pad and its main venue. In 1994, the show *Alegría* was a smash hit. Far from slowing down, Guy Laliberté's cast has strengthened its position in the entertainment world with shows like *Zumanity* (2003), *KÀ* (2004), *LOVE* (2006), and *Zaia* (2008).

Today, Cirque du Soleil employs 5,000 people, including 1,300 artists. There are 2,000 employees in its Montreal headquarters alone. Its shows are presented in major cities around the world, including Las Vegas, New York, Dubai, Tokyo, and Macau. The company estimates that in 2012 alone, approximately 15 million people attended its shows.

Laliberté is also socially engaged. In 2007, he established the One Drop Foundation, whose mandate is to promote access to safe drinking water in poor countries. Two years later, the Cirque du Soleil founder took a ride aboard the Russian *Soyuz* spacecraft and flew into space. In addition to drawing attention to his foundation, he fulfilled a long-standing dream that cost him $35 million!

Chapter 24

Ten Quebec Symbols

In This Chapter

▶ Seeking out symbols of Quebec culture

▶ Finding community in the symbols of Quebec

A ll cultures have their symbols. These symbols are derived from history and from a people's mindset, as well as from artists and creators of varied schools and genres. They bring members of a community together. Some are serious and solemn, while others cause people to laugh or swell up with pride. In this chapter, I introduce you to ten symbols of Quebec.

Saint-Jean-Baptiste Day: French Canadian or Québécois Celebration?

In the era of New France, Saint-Jean-Baptiste Day was a pagan festival celebrating the summer solstice, the longest day of the year. Great bonfires were a prelude to long bouts of drinking that lasted well into the night. The Catholic Church moved quickly to take control of this sometimes debauched celebration and to give it a religious meaning, channeling the day's festive spirit toward nobler aspirations! During the 18th century, the festival gradually lost its meaning and disappeared almost entirely.

The idea spread quickly among the people, with bonfires blazing again in towns and in the countryside. Religious authorities got on the bandwagon and made John the Baptist the patron saint of French Canadians. It wasn't until 1925, however, that the Quebec government officially recognized June 24 as a Quebec-wide public holiday.

Ludger Duvernay, editor of the newspaper *La Minerve* and an ardent supporter of the Parti Canadien led by Louis-Joseph Papineau, gave it a new and far more political, patriotic significance. On June 24, 1834, he invited the political elite to a large banquet. This was his way of celebrating the Lower Canada Assembly's adoption of the 92 resolutions, the Parti Canadien's ambitious reform program. That gathering persuaded him that Saint-Jean-Baptiste Day would become the official holiday of the colony's inhabitants, fighting to defend their rights.

In addition to bonfires, typical festivities included a big parade, religious ceremonies, and patriotic speeches. At the end of the parade, the crowd always greeted a child with curly blond hair seated next to a lamb. In the 1970s, the religious content was removed from the celebrations, and the lamb, which many saw as symbolizing the submission and alienation of older French Canadians, was eliminated. Preference went instead to big variety shows, like the one held in 1975 on Mount Royal.

The meaning of Saint-Jean-Baptiste Day remains a subject of debate. French-speaking people in the other Canadian provinces, as well as the federal government, see it primarily as a French-Canadian celebration — a holiday observed by a specific ethnic community. But most people in Quebec see it as a "national" celebration open to everyone living there. Each year, the Mouvement National des Québécois is asked by the government to organize a major celebration. Every June 24, more than 20,000 volunteers help put together neighborhood festivities, fireworks, and parades. In addition, enormous shows draw thousands of people to Maisonneuve Park in Montreal and the Plains of Abraham in Quebec City.

"Gens du pays": The Unofficial Anthem

Composed in just two days by poet Gilles Vigneault, the song "Gens du pays" was first performed in 1975 at a Saint-Jean-Baptiste Day celebration before a crowd of hundreds of thousands of people on Mount Royal. That evening, Vigneault, Louise Forestier, and Yvon Deschamps, in chorus, sang the famous refrain *"Gens du pays, c'est votre tour de vous laisser parler d'amour"* ("People of our land, it's your turn to let yourselves speak of love"). Already, this brand-new Quebec hymn to friendship and fellowship was stirring hearts and minds.

Lasting two minutes, "Gens du pays" is certainly one of the best-known songs in Quebec, hummed by people of all generations. At birthday celebrations, its famous refrain has gradually replaced "Happy Birthday." This is exactly what Gilles Vigneault was hoping for. The songwriter from Natashquan, a small village on the Lower North Shore, sought to offer Quebecers an alternative to an insipid translation of "Happy Birthday." He had long dreamed of an original and truly Québécois song to mark happy occasions.

The song's success was instantaneous. Not only did Quebecers use it at family celebrations, but it also became a kind of national anthem, sung at major rallies. In addition to being a vital part of Saint-Jean-Baptiste Day celebrations, the song has been heard at key moments in Quebec history — the night of the 1980 referendum, for example — and at the funerals of major figures.

L'homme rapaillé: "I Have Never Traveled Anywhere but to You, My Country"

L'homme rapaillé is the most widely read and most admired Quebec poetry collection, both in Quebec and worldwide. It has been studied by researchers and was reissued in many editions. The first edition of this collection appeared in 1970. Gaston Miron (1928–1996) saw it as the work of a lifetime. Every line was the object of careful meditation, reflection, and reworking. The early poems in the collection appeared at scattered intervals during the 1950s and 1960s in various newspapers and magazines, which venerated him as a "national poet." Before him, this title had been bestowed only on the 19th-century poets Octave Crémazie and Louis Fréchette.

This coveted title is fully deserved. Gaston Miron was an ardent defender of the French language and a keen activist for Quebec independence. He disdained *joual,* the informal, patois-like dialect that some advocates of a distinct Quebec identity fervently defended in the 1970s. Miron nevertheless gave his poetry a wholly unique Quebec flavor, in part by using certain common words in Quebecers' colloquial language. One such word is *rapaillé;* an *homme rapaillé* is someone who regains control, puts his house in order, and focuses on what is essential. Poems such as "For My Repatriation" ("one day I'll have said *yes* to my birth"), "Companion of the Americas" ("Quebec, my bitter land my almond land"), and "October" ("we will make you, land of Quebec") inspired many pro-independence activists. Miron was also a great love poet, as can be seen in such poems as "I Write to You" and "The March to Love."

Gaston Miron founded Les Éditions de l'Hexagone, a publishing house whose authors included Quebec's most talented literary figures. He also vigorously promoted Quebec's cultural life and charmed his contemporaries with his engaging personality. *L'homme rapaillé* made him famous. The book and his overall contribution to the world of letters earned him several awards: Ludger-Duvernay (1978), Guillaume-Apollinaire (1981), and Athanase-David (1983).

The Plouffe Family: A True Québécois Saga

The story of the Plouffe family, told initially in a novel by Roger Lemelin (published in 1948), and then for years on the Radio-Canada radio and television networks, had a deep influence on Quebecers in the postwar years. The television series, broadcast in a time slot just before the weekly wrestling matches, achieved top ratings at a time when television was just coming into people's homes.

The story focused on a working-class family in Quebec City. The father, Théophile, was a typographer and a fervent nationalist. The mother, a house-wife, reigned over her home and took advice from her priest. Cécile, an older unmarried daughter, was seeing a married man. Three sons made sure that things were never dull in the Plouffe home. Napoléon, the eldest, loved sports and photography. He acted as trainer to his younger brother Guillaume, who excelled in baseball, the American game that a growing number of French Canadians were playing. Ovide, a music lover, Francophile, and self-taught scholar, dreamed of becoming a Dominican priest but was held back by his hidden longing for Rita Toulouse!

Many people in Quebec recognized themselves in this modest but optimistic family with a rebellious streak. The Quebec of the Plouffes did not disavow its connection to America, its French roots, or its Catholic heritage. This was a Quebec anchored in tradition but open to modernity. The characters were endearing, and the actors playing them were memorable. This story became a classic of sorts. It was also the subject of a 1981 feature film by Gilles Carle, one of the great Quebec directors of his generation. The film was an immediate box-office success.

Swearing in Quebec: A Throwback to an Earlier Era?

Distinctive expressions and a particular accent are not the only elements that give a language its flavor, liveliness, and originality. There are also its swear words! Swearing says something about a culture's taboos. In Quebec, the religious connotation of the most resonant swear words says plenty about Quebecers' relationship with the Catholic Church.

In the era of New France, the swear words that have been identified were nearly all imported from Old France. People swore by God or his body — the most common swear words were *sacredieu* (holy God), *mort Dieu* (by the death of God), *ventre Dieu* (by the belly of God), *nom de Dieu* (in God's name), and *tort Dieu* (by God's error). At the time, blasphemy was a criminal offense, and uttering these words in public was risky. The religious authori-ties frequently denounced the use of these words. But fear did not put an end to swearing, which was common, and not only among *habitants* and manual workers. In the mid-19th century, the courts gradually stopped bringing blas-phemy cases to trial.

This was when swear words began to change. Since the old ones no longer seemed to carry the same weight as before, a whole new set of swear words developed. God gave way to Christ and to liturgical objects: *câlisse* (chalice), *ciboire* (ciborium), *hostie* (host), *tabernacle,* and so on. The words were different, but the same taboos were being transgressed. People swore to defy what the church held as sacred.

Religious taboos fell with the advent of the Quiet Revolution, but the swear words lingered, forming part of Quebec speech. Some artists, politicians, and social activists began using these words to show a connection to the common people. Many people considered this practice demagogic and increasingly pointless.

The Arrow Sash: Patriote Symbol

The arrow sash, a symbol from the Quebec folk tradition, is one of the items of clothing that is most representative of the 19th-century *habitant.* Its exact origin remains a mystery. Was this cloth band around the waist introduced by Acadians, Scots, or Native people? Or was it a "purely" Quebec item? It's hard to say.

The first mention of the arrow sash is found in a document dating back to 1798. Produced in some places near Montreal, notably in L'Assomption, the arrow sash was initially intended for the voyageurs of the North West Company and the Hudson's Bay Company. They offered these belts as gifts to Native people or traded them for furs. The *habitants* also wore them in the winter. They helped keep people warm by closing the front of the *capot,* a popular style of coat at the time. The width of the sash also provided lumbar support, which could relieve backaches and hernias.

The arrow sash gradually became a symbol of North American French-speaking people. In 1837, Parti Patriote members wore it proudly — it showed they sided with the Canadien cause. In a famous image devised by Henri Julien in the late 19th century and taken up by the militants of the Front de Libération du Québec, a Patriote wearing an arrow sash brandishes a rifle.

Production of arrow sashes peaked between 1830 and 1880. Their use gradually disappeared in the early 20th century, and they receded to the status of handicrafts. Some saw the arrow sash as symbolizing rootedness and respect for tradition, while others saw it as outdated attachment to the past.

Square Dancing: "And Swing Your Partner!"

When dancing is mentioned in the early documents on New France's beginnings, it's usually in the context of Aboriginal rituals. The first bishop of New France did not have a favorable view of dancing or celebrations. For that matter, did the early settlers really have the time and energy to get together and dance?

It was only gradually, starting in the second half of the 18th century, that "traditional" dances came to be held in the villages. The contribution of the Scots and Irish appears to have been significant. These dances required little training or special talent. People danced in groups, paying careful attention to instructions from a caller. With a touch of humor, the caller would indicate which way to go: "Women in the middle, men around them — and swing your company!" These dances were places where you might meet someone, with delightful results: People could go alone and dance with several partners in succession.

The *set carré,* or square dance, was the most common form of traditional dance. It usually involved four couples who passed from one partner to another after executing several steps ordered by the caller.

The Sugar Shack: An Indigenous Heritage

The French discovered maple sap early on, thanks to the Aboriginal people who used it to cook their game. The sweet taste of the sap immediately pleased the Europeans, who lost no time in tapping the maple trees of the St. Lawrence Valley. Techniques were rudimentary. Sugar shacks did not yet exist, and facilities were makeshift. Even so, production was substantial. In the early 18th century, it is said, up to 13,000 kilograms (30,000 pounds) of syrup could be produced each year in the Montreal area alone.

It was not until the early 19th century that the first true sugar shacks made their appearance here and there. The traditional shack was made of wood. Its gabled roof provided openings to let the vapor from the boilers escape. Ideally, it was located in the middle of the maple bush. The work was hard and kept the sugar maker very busy from mid-March to mid-April. To harvest the maple sap, they had to go from tree to tree on snowshoes or walk on melting snow in the spring. The precious sap was then brought to the boiler.

For many farmers, maple sugar provided substantial supplementary income, augmenting what they could earn from the summer harvests.

The sugar shack was also a meeting place, where the entire community could socialize. The sugar period coincided with spring, a time of renewal and re-acquaintance. The weeks following Lent — when people give up things they love — were especially well suited to celebrating. And a person could enjoy culinary pleasures and indulge his sweet tooth without feeling too guilty!

Nowadays, a few old traditional shacks still exist. But most syrup producers use industrial processes. Quebec accounts for 90 percent of Canada's maple syrup production and 75 percent of world output. Among the largest foreign consumers are the Japanese.

The Bombardier Ski-Doo

The history of snowmobiles in Quebec begins with Joseph-Armand Bombardier (1907–1964) and the company — now a multinational — that bears his name today. Starting in the 1920s, this inventor worked to develop a more effective means of getting around during Quebec's snowy winters. A personal tragedy drove home the importance of making available a device of this kind. In the winter of 1934, a violent storm struck Valcourt, his home town in the Eastern Townships. The weather was so bad that Bombardier was not able to bring his sick son to the hospital, nor could the doctor make it to Bombardier's house without risking his own life. Lacking an adequate means of transportation, Bombardier saw his son die in front of him.

Between 1922 and 1934, he produced several snowmobile prototypes. It was not the snowmobile as such that he invented but a totally new track system that enhanced the ability to move across snowy surfaces. In 1934, Bombardier launched his first snowbus, the B7, which could carry up to seven people. It achieved immediate success. Customers ranged from ordinary individuals to public services transporting schoolchildren or the ill.

In 1949, the Quebec government instituted a policy of clearing snow from the main roads, making Bombardier's snowbus less essential. It was during this period that the snowbus, a utility vehicle, became the snowmobile, a recreational vehicle. Once again, Bombardier anticipated the market and became one of the world's three major snowmobile makers with his famous Ski-Doo. Postwar prosperity enabled many people to buy these vehicles.

Today Bombardier is one of the world's largest aircraft makers, with its head office in Montreal. A separate division produces rail passenger equipment. The company, with 70,000 employees, reported revenues of $18.3 billion in 2011.

The Montreal Canadiens: A Hockey Dynasty

The first ice hockey game was played in Montreal on March 3, 1875. Two teams from McGill University, with nine players each, fought over a piece of wood using sticks that resembled upside-down canes. Two years later, rubber pucks were introduced, and only seven players from each team were on the ice at the same time. Games were divided into two 45-minute periods. Paddle sticks appeared in the late 1880s.

Teams were established in a number of large Canadian cities. The teams that founded the Amateur Hockey Association of Canada on December 8, 1886, dreamed of holding large cross-Canada tournaments. The Montreal teams had a long head start, but the Ontario teams decided to create their own association. To bring the teams together and make hockey a great Canadian sport, the governor general, Lord Stanley, commissioned a prestigious silver trophy. Starting in 1893, hockey teams fought for the Stanley Cup, a symbol of success and excellence.

In the late 19th century, Montreal had several English-speaking teams, including the Victorias, the Crystals, and the Shamrocks. Meanwhile, French-speaking Montrealers began to show interest in the sport and even to play it. "There has never been a French-Canadian hockey club that can brilliantly uphold our name," lamented Jos Marier in *La Patrie* on February 3, 1900. To remedy this situation, the Montreal Canadiens hockey club was founded on December 9, 1909. Talented Quebec players soon stood out.

In North America and worldwide, the Montreal Canadiens are one of the oldest and most prestigious professional sports organizations. The team has had its ups and downs but holds the National Hockey League record for the greatest number of Stanley Cup championships, at 24. In the course of the 20th century, the likes of Maurice Richard, Jean Béliveau, and Guy Lafleur have thrilled Montreal Canadiens fans.

Chapter 25

Ten Quebec Landmarks

In This Chapter

▶ Identifying notable places in Quebec history

▶ Finding inspiration in Quebec's past

▶ ▶ ▶ ▶ ▶

*T*he collective consciousness of all societies is marked by unusual or historic places that enchant tourists, recall memories, and inspire poets and politicians. Quebec is no exception. In this chapter, I fill you in on ten Quebec landmarks that are sure to inspire.

The Plains of Abraham and the Battle of Memory

At the time of the French regime, these plains were located outside Quebec and were used as pastureland for livestock. They were named in honor of Abraham Martin *dit l'Écossais* ("called the Scot"), who arrived in New France in 1619. He was one of the first settlers in the colony and the first *pilote du roi* (royal pilot) to navigate the St. Lawrence. It was on the heights of the Plains of Abraham that the French and British armies squared off against each other for possession of Quebec on September 13, 1759. In order to get there, General James Wolfe's troops had to climb an imposing rocky cape. It was partly because of that exploit that this victory so impressed the English.

In 1908, for the 300th anniversary of the founding of Quebec City, the Canadian government gave the Plains of Abraham back to the people by buying the land and existing buildings and landscaping a large public park. Under federal jurisdiction through the National Battlefields Commission, the Plains of Abraham are part of the beautiful Battlefields Park, in the heart of Quebec City on Cap Diamant along the St. Lawrence River. Over time, this park has become a central focus of collective memory both for French-speaking Quebecers, who continue to commemorate a defeat, and for English Canadians, who celebrate the birth of British Canada.

But the Plains of Abraham isn't only a place to think about the past. It's the gathering space where people who live in Quebec City converge to celebrate Saint Jean-Baptiste Day every June 24 or to attend top-quality performances at festivals or celebrations. It's also a beautiful green space in the heart of an active, dynamic city. There, in both summer and winter, Quebec City residents practice their favorite sports.

Mount Royal: An Extinct Volcano?

Located in the heart of Montreal Island, Mount Royal is a small hill with three peaks. Contrary to what many believed, Mount Royal was never an active volcano, despite the presence of magma there. It was named after Francis I, king of France at the time of Jacques Cartier's second voyage to North America. Guided by Iroquois from the village of Hochelaga, Cartier climbed Mount Royal in 1535. Once on the heights, he looked out for a river route that could lead him toward the west, where he hoped to find China.

Not until Montreal was industrialized did Mount Royal become a site of urban development. The city's rapid growth encouraged municipal authorities to protect Mount Royal, coveted by the wealthy bourgeoisie, as a green space. The city bought some of the land and hired Frederick Law Olmsted (1822–1903) to design a park. Olmsted was a leading landscape architect, having designed Central Park in New York City. On May 24, 1876, Mount Royal Park was opened to the general public. From 1885 to 1918, people could go to the top by cable car. In 1938, a large artificial pond called Beaver Lake was completed.

Thanks to its green spaces and hiking trails, Mount Royal Park became a peaceful haven for Montrealers from all parts of the city. When you're there, it's hard to believe that you're in the heart of central Montreal. A lookout also offers a stunning view of the city. In winter, many people go cross-country skiing or tobogganing down the hills.

The Saguenay Fjord and Its "Incredible Depth"

"Saguenay" was the name the Aboriginal people first encountered by Cartier had given to a fabulous kingdom, where diamonds, gold, and precious stones could be found. But even though he explored the mouth of the Saguenay River, Cartier did not succeed in finding the treasure that would have made him rich and famous! It wasn't until the summer of 1603 that Samuel de Champlain methodically explored the fjord and Saguenay River, which empties into the St. Lawrence at Tadoussac. Champlain cast a sounding line on the waters of the fjord and was amazed by its "incredible depth." He noted that "mountains and rocky headlands" covered the shores of the Saguenay River, which were poorly equipped to receive settlers.

The Saguenay fjord is the result of a very rare geological formation dating from the ice age. The mountains and cliffs offer spectacular scenery. The Saguenay extends over 100 kilometers (62 miles) between Tadoussac and Lac Saint-Jean. The site contains an unusual marine ecosystem where freshwater and saltwater species live together. It's also an ideal place to closely observe several species of whales, including the blue whale and the humpback. For a long time, the beautiful beluga could be seen there, but those white whales, long the target of hunters, have all but disappeared.

Sainte-Anne-de-Beaupré: Sanctuary for the Faithful

Sainte-Anne-de-Beaupré is the oldest pilgrimage site in Quebec, and one of the most popular. Each year, more than 250,000 Catholics converge on its impressive basilica. Filmmaker Bernard Émond used it as the starting point for his critically acclaimed 2005 film *La neuvaine (The Novena)*. Through the internal drama of a woman, the film explored the link between contemporary Quebecers and their Catholic roots.

Veneration for St. Anne, mother of Mary and grandmother of Jesus, dates back to the time of New France. Very early on, the settlers believed that she was responsible for miraculous healings, including the healing of a worker during the building of the first chapel in 1658. Many adventurers, sailors, and soldiers also attributed their good fortune to her. Very quickly, St. Anne became one of the most popular saints in New France. The first bishop of Quebec, François de Laval, encouraged devotion to her.

Over the centuries, places of worship at the site have taken a variety of shapes. After the two initial chapels (1658–1661), a first church was built in 1676; it was replaced by a true basilica two centuries later. The current basilica was built between 1923 and 1926 after a fire destroyed the previous one. Several jewels of Quebec's religious heritage are located there, including an important collection of thanksgiving plaques (letters of thanks for wishes granted), which date back to the time of New France. This is where the Redemptorists, guardians of the sanctuary since 1878, welcomed Pope John Paul II on September 10, 1984.

Île d'Orléans: Birthplace of French America

Île d'Orléans is located on the St. Lawrence River, just east of Quebec City and Lévis, where the river's two banks come closest to each other. This island, with an area 34 kilometers (21 miles) long and 8 kilometers (5 miles) wide, has six municipalities. It's one of the oldest areas of settlement in Quebec. More than 300 of Quebec's old families have ancestors native to Île d'Orléans. The first land was granted in 1636, and five parishes were established between 1669 and 1679. Its economy grew thanks to the prosperity of its agriculture. For a long time, Île d'Orléans was considered the breadbasket of Quebec City and its region.

Île d'Orléans is the largest historic district in Quebec, with at least 600 historic buildings. These include many stone houses dating back to the French regime and some of the oldest Quebec churches. The charms of Île d'Orléans and fears that destruction of its heritage might be imminent were immortalized by the poet Félix Leclerc, who lived there from 1970 until his death in 1988, in his song "Le tour de l'île." Espace Félix Leclerc, located in Saint-Pierre-de-l'Île-d Orléans, traces the life and work of the popular singer-songwriter. In addition to its heritage, the island is known for its bucolic landscapes, the astuteness of its people, and its beautiful inns.

The Magdalen Islands: Acadian Refuge after the Deportation

Briefly explored by Jacques Cartier and mapped by Samuel de Champlain, this archipelago is situated in the heart of the Gulf of St. Lawrence, between Prince Edward Island and Newfoundland, 215 kilometers (134 miles) from the Gaspé coast. François Doublet, who was granted the islands in the middle of the 17th century, named the archipelago in honor of his wife Madeleine. The people of the Mi'kmaq nation, in their quest for fish and seals, were the first to reach the archipelago. Basque fishermen also resided there on occasion.

The real settlement of the Magdalen Islands began only after the deportation of the Acadians in 1755. A small number managed to escape and find refuge in the islands. A few years later, other Acadians from the French islands of Saint-Pierre and Miquelon rejected the ideals of the French Revolution and moved to the archipelago.

Long isolated from the rest of the continent, the islanders have developed their own unique lifestyle. The lobster fishery and tourism are the islands' main economic activities. In the summer, the islands' population triples with the arrival of tourists in search of green spaces and wide horizons, not to mention the 300 kilometers (186 miles) of beachfront! The seven inhabited islands of the archipelago have a population of approximately 13,000.

The Quebec Citadel: Remains of a Fortified City

The Quebec Citadel was part of the fortifications of the Quebec capital. The fortifications are still in plain sight, reminding people of the old military vocation of the city and offering one of the last North American examples of what a fortified site, ready to defend itself, would've looked like. Perched on Quebec City's heights, long nicknamed the "Gibraltar of America," the Citadel ensured control of navigation on the St. Lawrence and defense of the colony against invaders. Some of its buildings date back to New France, but it was under British rule that it was fully completed in the early 1830s. The work of Lieutenant Colonel Elias Walker Durnford, the Citadel was inspired by the plans of the French engineer Sébastien Vauban.

Quebec has not been attacked since the winter of 1775–1776, so the Citadel was primarily used to garrison British troops stationed in Quebec. It was later home to the Royal Regiment of Canadian Artillery and, since 1920, to the only French-speaking regiment in the Canadian Forces, the 22nd Regiment, founded at the beginning of World War I.

During World War II, the Citadel hosted the deliberations of the two Quebec conferences that brought together British Prime Minister Winston Churchill and U.S. President Franklin Delano Roosevelt. The Citadel has also been the summer residence of the governor general of Canada since the 19th century.

Percé Rock: Gateway to the St. Lawrence

Percé Rock is one of Quebec's best-known natural monuments. The imposing rock formation is 475 meters (519 yards) long and up to 88 meters (96 yards) high. It creates a kind of natural gateway in front of the village of Percé that you cross in the Gulf of St. Lawrence before entering the river leading to Quebec City, Trois-Rivières, and Montreal. At low tide, you can get there on foot — but don't think of climbing it! The authorities are committed to preserving the integrity of the rock monument and protecting the birds that have settled there.

Erosion by the waters of the Atlantic Ocean has pierced the rock, creating a large arch. From the beginning of settlement, people found the rock fascinating. Jacques Cartier, the first Basque fishermen, and sailors have all noted its existence. Samuel de Champlain already called it by its name.

The face of the rock has changed over time. Observers described it as having two or even three arches. It has been in its current shape since 1845, when one of the two arches collapsed, leaving a large rock column alongside. Every year, Île-Bonaventure-et-du-Rocher-Percé National Park, created in 1985, attracts thousands of tourists who, in addition to contemplating the amazing rock, take the opportunity to travel around neighboring Bonaventure Island, recognized as one of the largest gannet sanctuaries in the world. The uninhabited island and its unique fauna inspired the writer Anne Hébert, whose work *In the Shadow of the Wind,* published in 1982, won the Prix Fémina.

Wendake: Last "Reserve" of the Hurons

The Jesuits first had the idea of creating "reductions" for Aboriginal people. The first of these reserves was founded in 1637 in Sillery, near Quebec City. These somewhat artificial small villages aimed at converting Aboriginal people to Christianity and gradually assimilating them into the European way of life. The Jesuits' efforts quickly yielded results. In 1638, 38 Natives were baptized. Eight years later, Sillery had converted 167 people. Later, the idea of Native "reserves" became widespread, and the Indian Act, passed in 1876, institutionalized this kind of closed community.

The village of Wendake, located in a suburb of Quebec City, is an ideal place to discover the tormented history of the First Nations of Quebec and the Huron-Wendat nation in particular. The Hurons, traditional allies of the French at the time of colonization, settled in the region of Quebec around 1653, after losing the war against the Iroquois who sought to wipe them off the map. Desperate and starving, some 300 Huron survivors sought the support of the French and were initially settled on Île d'Orleans and then in Sillery before being moved to the current village site in 1693.

About 1,300 Hurons currently live in Wendake. The reserve is one of the most urbanized in Quebec and enjoys considerable economic vitality. Artisans continue to manufacture traditional snowshoes. Tourism also plays an important role in the economic development of the Huron nation. Museums, interpretation centers, and events such as the great pow-wow offer many reasons to visit Wendake.

Manic-5: The Pride of a Conquering People

Inaugurated on the eve of Premier Daniel Johnson's death on September 26, 1968, Manic-5 is a hydroelectric dam located in the North Shore region, nearly 483 kilometers (300 miles) from the town of Baie-Comeau. At a length of 1,300 meters (1,421 yards) and a height of 214 meters (234 yards), the equivalent of a 50-story skyscraper, it is the centerpiece of an extensive hydroelectric network that continues to ensure Quebec's energy independence. The impressive structure is the largest multiple-arch buttress dam in the world. When it opened, the central dam broke records for daily production of electricity.

Built by Hydro-Québec, Manic-5 is often considered one of the greatest technical feats of Quebec engineering. For many Quebecers, the huge project represented the conquest of nature and passage to technical modernity — tangible proof that Quebec had emerged from its long preoccupation with survival. Accustomed to being subjected to the economic development projects and grand investment schemes of American capital, Quebecers could at last be proud of their own great economic achievement that would allow them to exploit a majestic natural resource. It was a great symbol of the Quiet Revolution, because Manic-5's generating station would serve the entire population.

Located in the Manicouagan-Uapishka World Biosphere Reserve, the dam created a huge reservoir covering 2,100 square kilometers (811 square miles). The Manicouagan reservoir lies in one of the largest and oldest meteorite craters known in the world.

Index

• A •

Abenaki, 56, 62
Abercromby, James, 77
Aboriginals. *See* First Nations
absenteeism, student, 200
Académie Canadienne-Française, 201
Académie des Lettres du Quebec, 201
Acadia (Acadians), 22, 58, 59, 68, 74, 75, 77, 84, 348
Act of Union of 1840, 123–124, 126, 138
Act to Govern the Financing of Political Parties, 276
Action Démocratique du Québec (ADQ), 305, 308, 318–319, 324, 325
Action Française (journal), 172
Action Libérale Nationale (ALN), 183, 184
agriculture and farmers
   Action Libérale Nationale, 183
   credit program, 185
   crisis of 1815, 109
   18th century, 64
   options for farmers, 159–160
   protection for agricultural lands, 277
   17th century, 29
   subsistence, 64, 109, 159
Albani (Emma Lajeunesse), 330–331
Algonquians, 13, 21, 23, 28, 36, 39
Allaire, Jean, 303, 305
Allaire Report, 303, 305, 319
Allan, Hugh, 155
Alma telegram (1990), 300–301
ALN (Action Libérale Nationale), 183, 184
aluminum, 171
American Revolution, 85, 91–96
Amherst, Jeffery, 82, 83
Ancien Régime, 60–67
André, Brother, 187
Angers, François-Albert, 276
Anglo-Americans, 74–75, 77
annexation to the United States, 134–135, 138
Anse au Foulon, 80
Aquin, François, 245
Arcand, Adrien, 180
Arès, Richard, 235
Armée Révolutionnaire du Québec, 238
Arnold, Benedict, 94
arrow sash, 341

Asbestos (town), 208–209
Asselin, Olivar, 167, 168
Assembly. *See* Legislative Assembly
assimilation of Canadiens, 87, 89, 111, 124, 235
austerity policy, 312, 321
autonomy, 155, 157, 158, 164, 209. *See also* independence, of Quebec
Aylmer, Baron, 115
Aymar de Chaste, 20, 21

• B •

baby boom, 204
Bagg, Stanley, 115
Bagot, Charles, 128
Baie-Saint-Paul, 79
Baillairgé, François, 99
Baldwin, Robert, 127–130, 138
Balladur, Édouard, 309
Barbeau, Victor, 200
Barrette, Antonio, 218
Basques, 19, 22, 23
beau risque, 290, 291, 296, 301
Beauport, 33, 54, 78, 80
Beaver Club, 88
Bédard, Pierre, 104–108, 111
Bégon, Michel, 64
Bélanger, Michel, 229, 302
Bélanger-Campeau Commission, 302, 303
Belvèze, Paul-Henry de, 136
Bennett, R. B., 177
Bertrand, Guy, 315
Bertrand, Jean-Jacques, 254, 255, 266
Bessette, Alfred (Brother André), 187
Bigot, François, 77, 82, 83
bilingualism, 167, 235, 237, 255, 267
Bill 16, 232, 233
Bill 22, 267, 269
Bill 63, 255
Bill 101, 275, 276, 285
Biron, Rodrigue, 269
Blackburn, Hugh, 88
Blanchard, James, 309
Blanchet, François, 106, 107
Blanc-Sablon, 16
Bloc Populaire, 197, 204, 214
Bloc Québécois, 304, 305, 308, 310, 321, 326

Boer War, 164, 166
Boisclair, André, 324
Bolduc, Édouard, 179
Bombardier, Joseph-Armand, 343
Bonne, Pierre-Amable de, 99–100
Borden, Robert, 167–169
Borduas, Paul-Émile, 206
Bouchard, Gérard, 324
Bouchard, Lucien, 289, 300–302, 304, 305, 307–314, 316–318, 320, 321, 324
Bouchard-Taylor Report (2008), 324
Boucher, Émile, 233
Boucher, Pierre, 38, 43, 44
Boucherville, Charles-Eugène Boucher de, 154, 156
Bouchette, Errol, 162
Bougainville, Louis-Antoine de, 76, 79, 80
Boullé, Hélène, 26
Bourassa, Henri, 165–168
Bourassa, Robert, 257, 259, 261, 263, 264, 266–270, 291–293, 296, 298, 300–304
Bourgault, Pierre, 240, 241, 252, 253
bourgeoisie, 109, 159, 180, 270
Bourgeoys, Marguerite, 38
Bourget, Ignace, 125, 133–136, 138, 154
Brébeuf, Jean de, 34, 37
Briand, Jean-Olivier, 88, 94
Brisay, Jacques-René de (Marquis de Denonville), 48, 51, 52
British North America Act (1867), 147–148
"British Party," 89
British Rifle Corps, 118
Broadbent, Ed, 297
Brother Anonymous (Frère Untel), 223
Brown, George, 138–139, 142, 146
Brûlé, Étienne, 28
budgets, 101, 114, 116, 119, 124, 153, 173, 312
Burke, Edmund, 91, 98
Burns, Robert, 276
Byng, John, 76

• C •

Caisse de Dépôt et Placement, 234–235
Caldwell, John, 114
Calgary declaration (1997), 315
Callière, Louis-Hector de, 54
Calvet, Pierre du, 95
campaign financing, 276–277
Campbell, Clarence, 329
Campeau, Jean, 302
Canada, origin of the word, 17

Canadiens. *See also* French Canadians; New France; settlers
  American Revolution, 93–94
  assimilation of, 87, 89, 111, 124, 235
  departure of Canadiens (1759–1760), 83
  language used in the Assembly, 100
  petition of 1773, 90
  Quebec Act (1774), 90–91
Cape Breton (Ile Royale), 74, 78, 84
CAQ (Coalition Avenir Québec), 325, 326
Carignan-Salières Regiment, 45, 65
Carleton, Guy, 89–91, 95
Cartier, George-Étienne, 143, 145–147, 152, 155
Cartier, Jacques, 14–18, 48, 346, 348, 350
Catéchisme des électeurs, 184
Catholic Action, 181, 213
Catholics. *See also* Roman Catholic Church
  Conservative Party, 151
  Laurier, 155–156
  Test Oath, 87, 90
  ultramontanes, 135, 153–154
  young people, 181
Cegeps, 242
censorship of films, 206–207
Centrale des Enseignants du Québec (CEQ), 260, 261
centralization, 201–202, 210
Centre des Femmes, 260
Centre d'Information Nationale, 215
Centres de la Petite Enfance (CPEs), 314
Chaloult, René, 194
Champlain, Samuel de, 19–33
Chapais, Jean-Charles, 143
Chapleau, Adolphe, 156
Chaput, Marcel, 239
Charbonneau, France, 325
Charbonneau, Joseph, 208, 209
Charbonneau, Yvon, 261
Charest, Jean, 299, 319, 320, 324–326
Charest Report, 299, 301
Charles I, King of England, 32
Charlottetown Accord (1992), 303
Charlottetown conference (1864), 143
Charter of Rights and Freedoms, 285, 298, 299
Chauveau, Pierre-Joseph-Olivier, 152–154, 159
Chemin du roy, 64, 244
Chénier, Jean-Olivier, 122
childcare, 314, 317, 323
Chiniquy, Charles, 132
Chirac, Jacques, 273, 309
Choiseul, Duc de, 83–85
cholera epidemic (1832), 116
Chrétien, Jean, 305, 310, 314

Churchill, Winston, 197
Circé-Côté, Éva, 179
Cirque du Soleil, 336
Citadel, Quebec, 349
Cité Libre (journal), 215–216
Civic Action League, 214
Civil Code of 1866, 144, 232
civil law, French, 88–90, 93, 98, 144
civil service, 185, 218, 222
Civil War, United States, 139–140
Clarity Act (2000), 316
Cliche, Robert, 266
Cliche Commission, 266
Clinton, Bill, 309
Closse, Lambert, 37
Coalition Avenir Québec (CAQ), 325, 326
Cohen, Leonard, 332
Colbert, Jean-Baptiste, 41, 43, 46, 48, 49, 62, 65
Colborne, Sir John, 122
Cold War era, 205–206
colonization, 9, 161, 178, 183. *See also* New
    France; settlers
Common Front, 260, 261
Communists, 180, 186, 205–206
Compagnie de la Nouvelle-France, 31–33, 37, 44
Confederation, 142, 143, 145–147
Confederation of National Trade Unions (CNTU),
    234, 260, 261, 265, 288
conscription, 167–169, 191–197, 202
Conservatives (Conservative Party), 135, 138,
    145, 152, 154, 155, 182, 184, 218, 288, 305.
    See also elections; *specific leaders*
    and issues
  1882 scandal, 156–157
  1860s–1870s, 151, 152, 154, 155
  1920s–1930s, 182
Constitution Act of 1982, 285–286, 295
constitution of 1867, 143, 146–148, 167, 177, 200,
    202, 210, 211, 236
Constitutional Act (1791), 98, 99, 106
constitutional issues, 243, 270, 283–286, 289,
    292, 293, 295, 296, 298, 301–305, 307, 315,
    319, 325. *See also specific issues*
conversion of Aboriginals to Christianity,
    35, 36
Couture, Jacques, 278
Craig, James, 106, 107
Cree, 13, 265, 317
Crémazie, Octave, 136, 339
crisis of 1810, 105–107
Cross, James Richard, 256, 259
culture, 174, 211, 235. *See also* language
currency, 29, 63, 235, 280
Cyr, Cyprien Noé (Louis Cyr), 330

Dalhousie, Earl of (George Ramsay), 114
Dandurand, Raoul, 170
Dandurand-Marchand, Josephine, 170
d'Avaugour, Baron Pierre Du Bois, 41, 43
de Gaulle, Charles, 194, 243–245, 273, 309
de la Dauversière, Jérôme Le Royer, 35
Déat, Antoine, 69
Declaration of the Rights of Man and of the
    Citizen, 102
Deerfield, Massachusetts, 56, 65
Denonville, Marquis de, 48, 51, 52
department of education, 224
Department of Federal-Provincial Relations, 236
Department of Natural Resources, 228–229
Department of Public Instruction, 152, 154
Department of Youth, 224
des Groseilliers, Médard Chouart, 49, 50
Desbiens, Jean-Paul, 223
Deschambault, 79
Desjardins Group, 228
Deux-Montagnes region, 122
Dion, Céline, 331–332
Dion, Father Gérard, 213
Dion, Stéphane, 315
Dionne, Luc, 173
direct relief, 178
"distinct society" status, 293, 314–315
Dollard des Ormeaux, Adam, 38, 39
Donnacona, 16, 17
Doric Club, 118, 122
Dorion, Antoine-Aimé, 146, 245
double mandate, 153
Dozois Plan, 214
Drapeau, Jean, 214, 268
Drouin, André, 323
Duceppe, Gilles, 304, 321, 326
Dugua de Mons, Pierre, 21–22, 24
Duhamel, Yvon, 266
Dumont, Fernand, 274, 287
Dumont, Mario, 303, 305–306, 308, 318, 319,
    323–325
Duplessis, Maurice, 182–187, 192, 193, 197,
    201–216, 218–220, 222, 226, 239, 269, 288, 335
Durham, Lord, 124
Duval, Jean, 23
Duvernay, Ludger, 337

earthquake of 1663, 39
Eastern Quebec Development Bureau, 242

Eastern Townships, 104, 113, 116, 131, 160
École Polytechnique de Montréal, 299
Economic Club of New York, 271
economic colonialism, 229–230
economic nationalism, 183
economy
 Bourassa, 292–293
 down-turn of the 1830s, 116
 eighteenth-century, 63–66
 glass ceiling, 227–228
 government finances (1830s), 115
 Great Depression, 175–177, 179–181, 193
 industrialization, 158–159
 inferiority of French Canadians, 151
 Johnson government, 242
 late 19th century, 161–162
 mid-1860s, 140–142
 nationalists, 172
 postwar, 204
 prosperity, 170–171, 193, 204
 recession of 1981, 286–287
 under Talon, 47
 after World War I, 170–172, 176
education and schools, 101, 162, 174, 212, 213,
  225, 316, 317
 Action Démocratique du Québec (ADQ)
  policy, 318
 Bill 101, 275
 British North America Act (1867), 148
 Chauveau government, 152, 153
 comprehensive high schools, 225–226
 compulsory, 199–200
 constitution of 1867, 144
 Department of Public Instruction, 152, 154
 1840s, 128
 federal financing of universities, 210–211
 first half of the 19th century, 101
 government role, 154
 language in, 164, 166, 252, 254–255, 267, 275,
  285, 315
 1940s-1950s, 212
 reforms of the Quiet Revolution, 223–226
 Saint-Léonard, 254–255
 school boards, 225, 315
 student absenteeism, 200
 Union Nationale (Johnson government),
  241–242
education department, 224
elections
 1792, 99
 1832, 114
 1834, 117
 1841, 127
 1886, 158

1917, 169
1935, 183
1936, 184
1939, 192–193
1944, 197, 204
1956, 213
1960, 219, 221
1966, 241
1970, 255–256, 269
1973, 269
1976, 269–270
1980, 282
1984, 289
2012, 326
electricity, 171, 180, 200–201, 212, 228–230,
  264–265
Elgin, Lord, 129, 130
elites, 113, 205
Elizabeth II, Queen, 240, 285
emigration to the United States, 158, 161, 162
Émond, Bernard, 347
England (United Kingdom). *See also specific
  events and individuals*
 Constitutional Act (1791), 98, 99, 106
 disengagement from Canada, 139
 North American colonies in 1860, 141
 reform government of 1848, 129
 Upper Canada and Lower Canada, 98–99
English language. *See* language
Equality Party, 298
équipe du tonnerre, 4, 220–221
Eskimos (Inuit), 13, 265
"étapiste" strategy, 269, 290
Europeans, 10–12
Executive Council, 99, 115, 117, 124
exploration, 9–11, 14–17, 49–51
Expo 67, 243

• F •

Fabre, Édouard-Raymond, 122
Fabre, Hector, 162, 198
fabriques, 66, 101
family allowances, 202
famine of 1757–1758, 77
farmers. *See* agriculture and farmers
Farnsworth, Matthias, 56
Favreau, Guy, 237
federal government (central government).
  See also constitutional issues
 centralization, 201–202, 210
 constitution of 1867, 143–144
 Quebec government as subordinate, 153

Fédération des Femmes du Québec (FFQ), 233
Fédération Nationale Saint-Jean-Baptiste
    (FNSJB), 165
feminists, 165, 170, 198, 260, 299, 322
Fenians, 140
Filion, Gérard, 215, 228
filles du roy, 46–48
Filmon, Gary, 299
Fils de la Liberté, 145
firearms, 14, 23, 37
First Continental Congress, 93
First Nations (Aboriginals; indigenous peoples).
    See also specific tribes and events
  agreement of 1975, 265
  alliance with (1609–1610), 23–24
  culture shock upon Europeans' arrival, 12
  domiciled, 62
  earliest inhabitants, 12
  indigenous groups in Quebec, 13–14
  Jesuits, 34
  liquor trade with, 39
  mixed marriages, 62
  recognition of, 291
  sexual mores, 27, 28
  slaves, 62
  tortures and acts of cruelty, 24
  Treaty of Montreal (1701), 54
fishing, 18, 29, 265
Five Nations of the Iroquois Confederacy, 13, 54
flag, Quebec, 210
Fleurdelisé, 210
Fondaction, 288
Forbin-Janson, Monseigneur de, 132
foreign investment, 171, 177
forestry, 29
Fort Beauséjour, 74, 75
Fort Cataraqui, 51, 52
Fort Gaspareaux, 74, 75
founding of Quebec, 21–23
Fournier, Sarto, 214
framework programs, 242
France. _See also specific events_
  agreement with Quebec government
      (1965), 237
  colonization in North America, 20–23
  exploration, 14–17
  sovereignty policy (1995), 309
Francis I, King, 14, 16, 346
francization, certificate of, 267, 275
Franco-Ontarians, 166, 251
Francophone Summit, 292
free trade, 140, 297, 303, 319
Free Trade Agreement (1988), 297
freedom of the press, 105

French and Indian War (1754–1763), 73, 75–84
French and Indian Wars (1689–1763), 52
French Canadians, 151, 236. _See also_ Canadiens
French immigrants, attracting, 162
French language. _See_ language
"French Party," 89
French Revolution, 102–104
French West India Company, 46
Front d'Action Politique (FRAP), 258
Front de Libération du Québec (FLQ), 238, 240,
    256–259
Frontenac, Louis de Buade de, 49, 52–54, 62, 64
Fulton-Favreau amending formula, 237
fur trade, 18–19, 27, 36–37, 47, 51, 88

● **G** ●

Gagnon, Aurore, 173
Garon, Jean, 277
Gélinas, Gratien, 334–335
Gendron Commission, 255, 266
Genêt, Edmond-Charles, 103
"Gens du pays," 338
George II, King, 76
George III, King, 83, 88, 90, 92, 94, 97
Gérin-Lajoie, Marie, 165
Gérin-Lajoie, Paul, 220, 224, 237
Germany, 167, 179, 191, 192, 195–197
Giffard, Robert, 33
Gobeil, Paul, 292, 293
Godbout, Adélard, 184, 191–197, 199–202, 209,
    224, 229
Gomery, John, 321
Gomery Commission, 321
Gosford, Lord, 118, 120–122
Gouin, Lomer, 166, 169
Gouin, Paul, 183, 184
government and administration. _See also_ federal
      government
  budgetary matters, 101, 114, 116, 119, 124, 153
  constitution of 1867, 143, 144
  Constitutional Act, 98–99
  education policy, 154–155
  finances (1830s), 115
  local, 144
  under Louis XIV, 44–45
  reform government of 1848, 129–131
  Royal Proclamation (1763), 86
government assistance, 186, 222, 226, 233, 267
governors, 44, 98–99
Gravé du Pont, François, 22
Gravier, Charles, 95
Great Charter of Education, 224

Great Coalition of 1864, 142
Great Depression, 175–181, 193
Gregory XVI, Pope, 120
Groulx, Abbé Lionel, 172, 181, 185, 201, 214, 215
Groupe Réflexion Québec, 305
guerre des éteignoirs, 128
Guimond, Olivier, 335
Guyart, Marie (Marie de l'Incarnation), 36, 38, 45

• H •

Haldimand, Sir Frederick, 87, 95
Hamel, Philippe, 183–185
Hamilton, Alexander, 93
Hampton, Wade, 108
Harper, Elijah, 301
Harper, Stephen, 326
Haviland, William, 82
health and diseases, 12–13, 67, 116, 160, 165
healthcare, 226–227, 313
Hébert, Louis, 29–30
Henry III, King, 19
Henry IV, King, 18, 20, 22, 24, 31
Hérouxville, 323
high schools, comprehensive, 225–226
Hitler, Adolf, 191, 193, 195
Hochelaga (Montreal), 13, 16, 21, 346
horsemeat, famine of 1757-1758, 77
hospital insurance, 226–227
Houda-Pepin, Fatima, 322
Houde, Camillien, 182, 195, 214, 268
Houde, Marie-Anne, 173
Hudson Bay, 51, 58
Hudson's Bay Company, 49, 50, 58, 88, 341
Huguenots, 18, 31, 34
Hungarian refugees, 207
Huronia, 27, 37, 49
Hurons, 13, 23, 27, 28, 34, 36, 37, 62, 350
hydroelectricity, 171, 200–201, 228–230, 264–265, 351
Hydro-Québec, 212, 230, 261, 264, 313, 351
hygiene conditions, 67, 160, 226, 277

• I •

ice storm (1998), 313
icons used in this book, 5–6
Ile d'Orléans, 16, 35, 348
Ile Royale (Cape Breton), 74, 78, 84
Ile Sainte-Hélène, 26, 186
immigrants, 174. See also settlers
   accommodation policy, 322
   administrative agreement (1978), 278
   attracting French immigrants, 162
   cholera epidemic (1832), 116
   Constitution Act of 1982, 293
   earliest inhabitants, 12
   18th century, 60
   Hungarian refugees, 207
   postwar, 204
   refugees, 277
   1764–1776, 89–90
   1660s–1670s, 46, 48
   welcoming (1960s), 253
imperialism, 164, 167, 169
income tax, 202, 209, 211
indemnity for inhabitants of Lower Canada, 129, 130
indentured workers, 22, 33, 48, 59, 60
independence. See also autonomy; nationalists
   of Canada, 123–124, 165
   of Quebec (independentists), 166, 169, 235, 238–241, 243, 245, 256, 257, 259, 269, 274, 280, 305, 307–310, 315, 316, 339. See also secession of Quebec; separatists; specific events, political leaders, and organizations
industrialization, 158–159
Innu (Montagnais), 13, 21, 23, 32–34, 36
Institut Canadien, 134–136, 147
intendant, 44, 45
Intolerable Acts, 92–93
Inuit (Eskimos), 13, 265
Iraq war, demonstration against (2003), 319
Iroquois (Iroquoians), 13, 15, 23, 36–39, 43–45, 51–54. See also specific tribes
iron, 66
isolationists, 192, 195
Italian community, 174, 254, 255

• J •

James Bay, 264–266
James Bay and Northern Quebec Agreement (1975), 265
Jautard, Valentin, 87
"Je me souviens" motto, 274
Jesuits, 34–35, 37, 43, 44, 62, 133, 350
Jews, 114, 174, 180, 317
John Paul II, Pope, 290, 347
John XXIII, Pope, 223
Johnson, Daniel, 230, 241–245, 251–254
Johnson, Pierre Marc, 291, 296
joual, 223, 334–335, 339
judges and judicial institutions, 87–88, 285, 293

Jumonville, Joseph Coulon de Villiers de, 74–75
June 12 agreement, 308

• K •

Kirke brothers, 32, 33
Kirouac, Conrad, 186
kirpans, 322–323
Kyoto Protocol, 313, 319, 326

• L •

la Dauversière, Jérôme Le Royer de, 35
la Galissonnière, Roland-Michel Barrin de, 68
La Gazette de Montréal, 87, 118, 195
La Grande River, 264
La Hontan, Baron de, 52, 69
La neuvaine (film), 347
La Rochelle, siege of, 31, 32, 34
La Salle, Robert Cavelier de, 50
La Vérendrye, Pierre Gaultier de, 65
Laberge, Louis, 261, 288
Labor-Progressive Party, 207
Labour Relations Act, 193
Labrador, 90, 197
Lac à l'Épaule, meeting at (1962), 229
Lachine massacre (1689), 52
Lachine Rapids, 16
Lacroix, Édouard, 183
Laferrière, Dany, 277
Laflèche, Louis-François, 154
LaFontaine, Adèle, 126
LaFontaine, Louis-Hippolyte, 120, 125–130, 134, 135, 145
Lake Champlain, 23
Lake George, 23, 77
Lake Huron, 27
Lake Ontario, 27
Lake Superior, 28, 49
Lalemant, Charles, 34, 35
Laliberté, Guy, 336
LaMarsh, Judy, 234
Lanctôt, Médéric, 147
Landry, Bernard, 307, 318
Langevin, Hector-Louis, 143, 147
language
  Act of Union of 1840, 124
  bilingualism, 167, 235, 237, 255, 267
  Bill 22, 267, 269
  Bill 63, 255
  Bill 101, 275, 276, 285
  Bourassa, 166
  constitution of 1867, 144

  Constitutional Act, 99–101
  Frère Untel (Brother Anonymous), 223
  joual, 223, 334–335, 339
  LaFontaine, 127–128
  Laurin's white paper, 274–275
  New France, 47, 84
  schools, 164, 166, 252, 254–255, 267, 275, 285, 315
  Québécois identity, 236
  Regulation 17, 166–167
  Saint-Léonard crisis, 252–253, 255, 266
  Supreme Court ruling (1988), 298
  swear words, 340–341
  Tremblay, 334
Lapalme, Georges-Émile, 215, 218–220
Lapointe, Ernest, 180, 192, 193
Laporte, Pierre, 220, 257–259
Lartigue, Jean-Jacques, 120, 133
Laurendeau, André, 193, 218, 237, 330
Laurendeau-Dunton Commission, 237
Laurier, Wilfrid, 155–156, 158, 163–166, 169, 170
Laurin, Camille, 273–275, 291
Laval, François de, 39, 44, 66, 347
L'Avenir (newspaper), 134, 146
Le Canadien, 105–106, 108, 118, 119
Le Devoir (newspaper), 166, 168, 214, 215
Le Sage, Siméon, 162
Leclerc, Félix, 291
Lefrançois, Charles, 106
the left, 261–262, 320, 326
Léger, Paul-Émile, 209
Legislative Assembly
  Lower Canada, 99, 113
    choosing a speaker of (1792), 100
    language used in, 100–101
    92 resolutions and Russell Resolutions (1830s), 116–120, 337–338
    Parti Canadien reform program, 105
    union plan (1822), 110
  Quebec, 148, 153
Legislative Council, 99, 113–115, 117, 143, 148
Lesage, Jean, 219–222, 225–231, 234, 236–238, 240, 317
Letellier de Saint-Just, Luc, 156
Lévesque, Father Georges-Henri, 211, 216
Lévesque, René, 221, 228–230, 238, 240, 245, 250, 252, 256, 259, 263, 269–274, 276, 280, 282–284, 286, 290–292, 296, 300, 306, 308, 312
  constitutional repatriation, 286
  first sovereignist government, 271
  in France (1977), 273
  1976 election, 269–271
  Parti Québécois, 250, 252
  sovereignty-association issue, 250–252

Lévis, Chevalier de, 76, 77, 79–82
LG-2 dam, 264–266
L'homme rapaillé (Miron), 339
Liberals (Liberal Party), 142, 158, 181, 183, 198,
     239, 250, 256, 291, 298, 302, 303, 305, 319,
     321, 325. *See also* elections; *specific leaders
     and issues*
  autonomy of Quebec, 155, 157, 158
  1896-1936, 163, 165, 169, 170
  1873 scandal and 1874 election, 155
  during Great Depression, 176, 178, 180, 181
  1950s, 215
  1960s, 219–221
  rise of (1880s), 156
  sponsorship scandal, 321
  World War II, 192, 193, 196
Ligue Nationaliste, 166
Ligue pour la Défense du Canada, 196, 214
liquor trade with Aboriginal peoples, 39
Lorimier, Chevalier de, 123
Louis XIII, King, 25, 31, 42
Louis XIV (the Sun King), 42–44, 51, 52, 58, 62
Louis XV, King, 68, 95
Louis XVI, King, 102
Louisbourg, 59, 68, 74, 78
Louisiana, 50, 51, 74
Lower Canada, 98, 99, 101, 103, 104, 106–113. *See
     also specific leaders and events*
  declaration of independence (1838), 123–124
  rebellions of 1837–1838, 112
  union with Upper Canada, 110, 111
Loyalists, 93, 96–98, 103, 119–121
Lucide manifesto (2005), 320
lumber. *See* wood

• M •

Macdonald, John A., 142, 145, 147, 155, 157, 158
McGill, James, 88
McGill, Peter, 117–118
McGill University, 174
McKenna, Frank, 299
Mackenzie King, William Lyon, 192, 194, 196,
     197, 201
Mackenzie-Papineau Battalion, 180
Magdalen Islands, 348–349
Magnalia Christi Americana, 56
Maisonneuve, Paul de Chomedey de, 35, 38
Mance, Jeanne, 35, 38
Manic-5, 351
manifesto of 1840, 126–127
manufacturing sector, 171
Maoists, 261–262

"maple spring," 326
maple syrup, 342–343
Marchand, Jean, 239
Maria Theresa, 68
Marie de l'Incarnation, 36, 38, 45
Marie de Médicis, Queen, 25
Marie-Victorin, Brother, 186
Maritime colonies, 143, 146
Marois, Pauline, 326
Marquette, Father Jacques, 50
marriage, 17-18th centuries, 48, 61, 62, 69
Martin, Paul, 321
Martineau, Gérald, 218, 220
Mary Queen of the World Cathedral, 136
Massachusetts, 56, 92, 93
Mazarin, Cardinal Jules, 42
Meech Lake Accord (1987), 293, 295–301, 303,
     304, 315
Meilleur, Jean-Baptiste, 128
merchants. *See also* fur trade
  early colonial period, 19, 27, 30, 39, 43
  18th century, 89, 91, 101, 104, 106, 107
  19th century, 117–118, 121, 129
Mercier, Honoré, 151, 157, 158, 161, 199
Mesplet, Fleury, 87
Metcalfe, Charles, 128
Métis, 65, 151, 157, 158
Mézière, Henri, 103
Michaud, Yves, 317
middle class, 176
Mi'kmaq, 13, 15, 48, 348
Military Service Act (1917), 168
miners, Asbestos, 208–209
mining, 29, 171
ministerial responsibility, 127
Miquelon Island, 84, 348
Miron, Gaston, 339
Mitterrand, François, 292
Moffatt, George, 117–118
Mohawk Warrior Society, 300
Mohawks, 13, 23, 24, 35, 37, 38, 45, 300
Molson, John, Jr., 109
Molson, John, Sr., 109
monarchy, constitution of 1867, 143
monopolies, 19, 27, 63
Montagnais (Innu), 13, 21, 23, 32–34, 36
Montcalm, Louis-Joseph de, 76–78, 80
Montgolfier, Étienne, 88
Montgomery, Richard, 94
Montmagny, Charles Huault de, 35, 36
Montreal
  American Revolution, 94
  Champ-de-Mars demonstration (1885), 157
  defense of (1650–1653), 38

fall of (1760), 82
French and Indian War (1754–1763), 77
late 19th century, 160–161
1950s, 214
Parliament set on fire (1849), 130
riot of 1832, 115
War of 1812, 108
Montreal, Treaty of (1701), 54
Montreal Board of Trade, 109, 161
Montreal Canadiens, 344
The Montreal Gazette, 87, 118, 195
Montreal Island, 35, 37, 57, 254
Montreal Light, Heat & Power, 171, 201, 212
Montréalistes, 35, 37–39
Mont-Royal, 35
morality in politics, 213–214
Morin, Augustin-Norbert, 116, 118, 120
Morin, Claude, 222
Morin, Jacques-Yvan, 296
Mount Royal, 16, 160, 346
Mount Royal Park, 346
Mouvement Laïque de Langue Française,
    222, 225
Mouvement Québec Français, 298
Movement Souveraineté-Association (MSA),
    250–252
Mowat, Oliver, 157
MSA (Movement Souveraineté-Association),
    250–252
Mulroney, Brian, 289, 292, 295, 297, 299–301, 304
multiculturalism, 285
Murray, James, 82, 86–89, 95
Muslims, 322, 323

● *N* ●

Nadeau, Jean-Marie, 219
Nantes, Edict of, 18
Napoleon Bonaparte, 104, 107, 108
National Electricity Syndicate, 185
National Policy, 159
National Resources Mobilization Act, 194
nationalists (nationalism), 165, 166, 172, 245, 252
    divided (1950s–1960s), 214
    economic, 183
    economic and political dimensions, 200
    neonationalists, 215
    patriotic organizations (1900s), 166
    during World War II, 194–196, 199
natural resources, 29, 228–229, 325. *See also*
    hydroelectricity; mining; wood
Nazism, 180
Neilson, John, 115, 152

Nelligan, Émile, 333
Nelson, Robert, 122, 123
Nelson, Wolfred, 122
neoliberalism, 279, 292, 305, 319, 320, 326
neonationalists, 215
New Brunswick, 75, 141, 148
New Deal, 176, 177
New Democratic Party (NDP), 326
New England
    1702-1713 clashes, 56–58
    War of the Austrian Succession (1744), 68
New France. *See also* colonization; settlers;
    specific topics
    administrative reforms under Louis XIV, 44–45
    Anglo-Americans as adversaries (17th
        century), 74
    appeal for the English, 73–74
    beginnings, 25
    besieged (1717–1744), 59
    departure of Canadiens (1759–1760), 83
    end of (1763), 84
    guerrilla warfare in New England
        (1703–1704), 56
    military occupation (1759–1760), 83
    Treaty of Utrecht (1713), 58–59
    weakening of (1710s), 55–56
New World, what Europeans found, 11–12
New York, 56, 95
Newfoundland, 15, 18, 23, 51, 58, 96, 141, 148,
    284, 301
newspapers, 87
Nicholson, William, 57
92 resolutions (1834), 116–118, 337–338
Noël, Jacques, 19
North West Company, 88, 341
Notre-Dame-de-la-Victoire (Notre-Dame-
    des-Victoires), 54, 58
Nova Scotia, 58, 74, 75, 84, 141
nuclear power, 264

● *O* ●

O'Callaghan, Edmund, 115
October Crisis (1970), 256–259
"Ode to the Revolution," 102
Official Languages Act (1969), 254–255
Ohio Valley, 86, 90, 91
Ojibwa, 13
Oka crisis (1990), 300
Olier, Jean-Jacques, 35
Olympic Games (1976), 268
O'Neill, Father Louis, 213
Ontario, 142, 144, 148

Option Citoyenne, 322
Orangemen, 129
Ottawa River, 27, 38
Ouimet, Gédéon, 154, 155
Our Northern Neighbour (film), 206–207

• P •

Pacte de Famille, 83
Padlock Law, 186, 206
Panet, Jean-Antoine, 100
paper money, 63, 83
paper products, 171
Papineau, Louis-Joseph, 111–118, 120–123
    1834 elections, 117
    92 resolutions (1834), 116–120
    annexation to the United States, 134–135
    arrest warrant (1837), 122
    emancipation of the Jews, 114
    insurrection of November 1838, 122–123
    LaFontaine, 126
    personal background, 112–113
    trip to London (1823), 113
Parent, Étienne, 118, 121, 126
Parent Commission, 224, 232
Paris, Treaty of (1763), 95
Paris, Treaty of (1783), 96
Parish Schools Act, 101
Parizeau, Jacques, 222, 230, 272, 287, 291, 296,
    300, 302, 305–310, 317, 324
parliament
    Canadian, 98–99. *See also* Legislative Assembly
        constitution of 1867, 144
        Dorion, 146
        ransacked and set on fire (1849), 130
        representation by population ("rep by pop"),
        138–139
    English, 98
    Quebec, 148
Parti Canadien
    economic downturn of 1830s, 116–117
    1832 election, 114
    emergence of, 104–105
    insurrection of November 1838, 122–123
    LaFontaine, 125–126
    Lord Durham's proposals (1839), 124
    92 resolutions (1834), 116–118, 337–338
    Papineau as leader, 111, 113–122
    Patriote movement, 119–123
    reform program, 105
    schools, 101
Parti National, 158
Parti National Social Chrétien, 180

Parti Pris magazine, 238
Parti Québécois (PQ), 250, 255, 256, 258,
    261–264, 266, 268–277, 279–282, 285–287,
    290–292, 296, 300, 302, 308, 310, 312, 317,
    318, 321, 324–326. *See also specific leaders,
    events, and issues*
    "étapiste" (step-by-step) strategy, 269, 290
    founding, 252
    implosion of, 290–291
    1976 election, 269–273
    1994 election, 305–306
    reasonable accommodation crisis, 324–325
    referendum (1995), 305–310, 314
    reforms, 276–277
Patriotes, 119–123
patronage, 155, 181, 184, 185, 215, 220, 257
Patry, André, 237
Payette, Lise, 281
Pays d'en haut, 27
Pearson, Lester B., 237
Péladeau, Pierre, 309
Pelletier, Gérard, 239, 259
Pepin, Marcel, 260, 261
Percé Rock, 349–350
Perrault, Joseph-François, 101
Pétain, Philippe, 194
Pétuns, 13
Phips, William, 53–54
Pitt, William, 76, 78
Pius IX, Pope, 135, 153
Pius XII, Pope, 208, 209
Plains of Abraham, 345
    battle of (1759), 80
Plan A, 314–315
Plan B, 315–316
Plan Nord, 325
Plante, Pax, 214
Plessis, Joseph-Octave, 104, 106
Plouffe family, 339–340
Pointe-Lévy, 79, 94
Polish treasures, protecting, 207
political parties. *See also specific parties*
    contributions to, 276–277
    1850s and 1860s, 138
Pontbriand, Henri-Marie Dubreil de, 88
population
    1820, 109
    1871, 148
    1901–1931, 163, 164
    1941–1961, 204, 217
    Montreal and Quebec City (1861–1901), 160
    pro-birth policy under Talon, 48
Portneuf, 79
Port-Royal, 22, 34, 53, 57, 58, 68

Portugal, exploration by, 9
Prevost, George, 107
Price, William, 109
priests, 39, 66, 87, 88, 102, 106, 132
  recruiting in France, 133–134
Prieur, Claude, 235
Prince Edward Island, 96, 141
prisoners from New England, 62
privatization of public corporations, 293
Programme de Restauration Sociale, 182
programmistes, 154
Progressive Conservative Party, 288, 289,
  305, 321
prohibition, 174
prosperity, 170–171, 193, 204
Protestants (Protestantism)
  Company of One Hundred Associates, 32
  Edict of Nantes, 18
  Roman Catholic Church, 34
  Test Oath, 87
Province of Canada
  Act of Union of 1840, 124
  constitution of 1867, 144
  political instability (1850s and 1860s), 137–139
Province of Quebec. *See* Quebec Province
Prussia, 68, 76
public assistance, 186, 222, 226, 233, 267
Public Assistance Act (1921), 173
public health, 67, 116, 160, 165
public works, 178, 186
publishers, 201
pulp and paper, 171

• *Q* •

Quebec (Quebec City). *See also* Quebec
    Province
  American Revolution, 94
  bombardment of (1759), 79
  French and Indian War (1754–1763), 73, 74,
    78–84
  origin of the word, 17
  riots of 1918, 169
  siege of, 78, 81, 82
  surrender of (1760), 81
Quebec Act (1774), 90–91, 93, 97, 98
Quebec Citadel, 349
Quebec Conference (1864), 143–145, 147
Quebec Federation of Labour (QFL), 260, 261,
  265, 287, 288
The Quebec Gazette, 87, 99–100, 102
Quebec Liquor Commission, 174
The Quebec Mercury, 104

Quebec model, 317–320, 322
Quebec Province, 86
  birth of (1867), 148
  Constitution Act of 1982, 285, 286
  delegations in foreign countries, 198, 236–237
  emergence of a modern state, 173
  petition of 1773, 90
  Quebec Act (1774), 90–91
  renamed Lower Canada, 98
Québec Solidaire, 320–322, 326
Quebec Stock Savings Plan (QSSP), 287
Québec-Canada: A New Deal, 280
Quiet Revolution (1959–1962), 217–230, 241

• *R* •

radicalization, 259–261
Radisson, Pierre-Esprit, 49–50
railways, 140–142, 145, 146, 153, 155, 156,
  161, 162
Ralliement National, 240, 252
Ramezay, Jean-Baptiste-Nicolas-Roch de, 81
Rassemblement pour l'Indépendance Nationale
    (RIN), 239–241, 244, 252
Raymond, Maxime, 192
reasonable accommodation crisis, 322–325
rebellions of 1837-1838, 112
recession, 1981, 286–287
reciprocity treaty (1854), 140
Récollets, 28–30, 34
Redpath, John, 109
referendum (1995), 305–310, 314, 317
Referendum Act (1978), 280–283
Reform Bill of 1832, 112
Reform Party, 305
refugees, 207, 277
Refus global, 206
Régie des Rentes du Québec, 234, 235
Regulation 17, 166–167
Relations (Jesuit writings), 34–36, 38
religion, 66–67, 322–323. *See also* Protestants;
    Roman Catholic Church
  freedom of, 82, 84, 86
  revival of the 1840s, 131–132
  schools, 101
repatriation of the constitution, 236, 238,
  283–286, 297, 314, 339
resolutionaries, 117
retirement plan, 234, 312
Richard, Maurice ("the Rocket"), 329–330
Richardson, John, 100
Richelieu, Cardinal, 31–35, 62
Richelieu River, 59, 77, 82

Riel, Louis, 157–158
RIN (Rassemblement pour l'Indépendance
    Nationale), 239–241, 244, 252
riots
  1918, 169
  1955, 329–330
Roberval, Seigneur de, 16, 17
Rocheblave, Philippe de, 100
Rocher, Guy, 274
Rochon, Jean, 313
Roman Catholic Church, 34, 66, 67, 86. *See also*
    Catholics; priests
  Catholic Program, 154
  censorship of books and ideas, 135
  church-state relations, 153
  Duplessis, 186, 187
  French language, 166
  Patriotes movement (1830s), 120–121
  Pope John Paul II's visit (1984), 290
  Quebec Act (1774), 90
  schools and education policy, 101, 144,
      154, 225
  the state and, in 1960s, 222–223
  19th century, 133, 135–136, 138
  Treaty of Paris (1763), 86
  unions, 172
Roosevelt, Franklin Delano, 197
Rowell-Sirois Commission, 178, 202
Roy, Gabrielle, 177
Royal Proclamation (1763), 86
Rumilly, Robert, 215
Russell, John, 118–119
Ryan, Claude, 276, 281, 283, 285, 291
Ryan, Madeleine, 281

• S •

Sable Island, 20
Saguenay, Kingdom of, 15–16
Saguenay Fjord, 346–347
Saguenay River, 20, 21, 346, 347
Saguenay-Lac-Saint-Jean region, 88, 109, 159
St. James Street (Montreal), confrontation on
    (1837), 121–122
St. Lawrence River, Champlain, 21
St. Lawrence Valley
  early colonial history, 16–19, 21–24, 34, 37
  French and Indian War (1754–1763), 74, 75, 83
  planned invasion of (1710), 57
  population growth, 61–63
Saint-Antoine, 79

Saint-Benoît, 122
Saint-Charles, 121, 122
Saint-Domingue (Haiti), 84
Sainte-Anne-de-Beaupré, 347
Sainte-Croix, 79
Sainte-Croix Island, 22
Sainte-Foy, Battle of (1760), 81
Saint-Eustache, 122
Saint-Jean, Idola, 198
Saint-Jean-Baptiste Day, 337–338
Saint-Jean-Baptiste societies, 251
Saint-Laurent, Louis, 211
Saint-Léonard, 254–255
Saint-Léonard crisis, 252–253, 255, 266
Saint-Martin, Albert, 172
Saint-Maurice Forges, 66
Saint-Michel, Julien, 179
Saint-Nicolas, 79
Saint-Ours, 119
Saint-Pierre Island, 84, 348
Saint-Vallier, Monseigneur de, 53
Salaberry, Charles-Michel de, 108
Salvas, Élie, 220
Salvas Commission, 220
samedi de la matraque, 240
Saskatchewan, 164, 226
Sauvé, Arthur, 182
Sauvé, Paul, 218, 219
Schenectady, 53
school boards, 225, 315
school tax (1840s), 128
schools. *See* education and schools
Scots, 88, 342
Scott, Frank R., 186
scurvy, 16
secession of Quebec, 269, 306, 315, 316
Second Continental Congress, 93
Second Vatican Council (1962–1965), 223
"See, judge, act!", 181
Séguin, Philippe, 309
seigneurial system, 30, 46, 90, 98, 109, 131
Séminaire de Québec, 66, 104, 225
Senécal, Louis-Adélard, 156–157
Senecas, 13, 52
Senghor, Léopold Sedar, 292
separatists, 169, 181, 239, 240, 253, 270, 321.
    See also independence, of Quebec
set carré, 342
settlers. *See also* Canadiens; New France
  attracting, 28–31, 33
  Charles I and privateers, 32
  Communauté des Habitants, 37

defense of Montreal (1650–1653), 38
English-speaking, 88, 89
indentured workers, 22, 33, 48, 59, 60
Iroquois offensive of 1651, 37–38
sexual mores, Aboriginals', 27, 28
ships, 65–66
Sifton, Clifford, 165
signs, commercial and public, 275, 298
Ski-Doo snowmobiles, 343
slaves, 62
"social union" agreement (1999), 316
Société Générale de Financement (SGF), 228
Société Notre-Dame de Montréal, 35
Solidaires, 320–322
Solidarity Fund, 288
South Africa, 164
Sovereign Council, 44–45, 86
sovereignty (sovereignists), 269, 271–273, 281,
    286, 295–297, 302, 304–306, 308–310, 316,
    317, 322, 325, 326. *See also* Parti Québécois
Bélanger-Campeau Report, 302
Bloc Québécois, 304, 305, 308, 310, 321, 326
Plan A, 314–315
Plan B, 315–316
referendum (1995), 305–310
sovereignty-association, 250–252, 263, 269, 271,
    279–282
Spain
    discovery of America, 11
    in 1930s, 179, 180
    War of the Spanish Succession (1702–1713),
        55–56
speaker of the Assembly, 100
special status for Quebec, 236, 251, 253
sponsorship scandal, 321
square dancing, 342
Stadacona, 13, 15–17, 21, 48
strikes, 208–209, 216, 260
sugar shacks, 342–343
Sulpicians, 35, 66, 136, 145
Summit of the Francophonie, 292
Superior Council of Education, 224, 242
Sûreté du Québec, 300
swear words, 340–341

• *T* •

Taché, Étienne-Paschal, 143
Tadoussac, 20–22, 32, 53, 186, 347
Talon, Jean, 41, 46–48, 65
Tardivel, Jules-Paul, 154
Taschereau, Antoine, 184

Taschereau, Gabriel Elzéar, 100
Taschereau, Jean-Thomas, 106, 107
Taschereau, Louis-Alexandre, 171, 178, 180, 181,
    183, 184, 201
taxes, 91–92, 128, 202, 209, 211, 318
Taylor, Charles, 324
technocrats, 222, 241
Témiscamingue region, 13, 162
Terrebonne, 127
Test Oath, 87, 88, 90
Thúy, Kim, 277
timber. *See* wood
tobacco, 21, 119, 160
Tracy, Prouville de, 45
trade. *See also* fur trade; merchants
    free, 140, 297, 303, 319
    liquor trade with Aboriginal peoples, 39
trade unions. *See* unions
traditionalists, 205, 215, 227
Treaty of Aix-la-Chapelle (1748), 68
Treaty of Montreal (1701), 54
Treaty of Paris (1763), 84, 95
Treaty of Paris (1783), 96
Treaty of Saint-Germain-en-Laye (1632), 33
Treaty of Utrecht (1713), 55, 58–59
Tremblay, Michel, 333–334
Trois-Rivières, 33, 38, 43, 65, 81, 83, 132
Trudeau, Pierre Elliott, 215–216, 239, 251–255,
    258, 263, 270, 272, 273, 292, 305, 321
    Bill 101, 276
    confrontation with Johnson, 251–252
    constitutional issues, 283–286
    elected Liberal Party leader (1968), 253
    language policy, 254–255
    Meech Lake Accord (1987), 296–298
    1980 election, 282
    referendum campaign, 282
    retirement from politics, 289
trusts, 180, 183

• *U* •

U-boats, 196
ultramontanes, 135, 153–154, 157, 199–200
unemployment, 175–178, 186, 193, 286
unemployment insurance, 201
Union des Forces Progressistes, 321–322
Union Nationale, 184–186, 192, 193, 200, 204,
    205, 208, 212–215, 218–221, 230, 231,
    238–243, 251–256, 269, 270. *See also specific
    leaders and events*
union plan (1822), 110

unions, 172, 186, 193, 234, 260–262, 266, 286–288, 312
United Kingdom. *See* England
United States
  American Revolution, 85, 91–96
  annexation to, 134–135, 138
  emigration to, 158
  free trade with, 297
  reciprocity treaty (1854), 140
  rumors of American invasion (1861–1865), 139–140
  War of 1812, 107–108
Université du Québec, 242
universities, federal financing of, 210–211
Untel, Frère (Brother Anonymous), 223
Upper Canada, 98, 106–111, 121, 127
Utrecht, Treaty of (1713), 55, 58–59

• V •

Vallières, Pierre, 258
Vancouver Island, 141
Vatican II (1962–1965), 222–223
Vaudreuil, Pierre Rigaud de, 56, 57, 63, 64, 76–78, 82
Vautrin, Irénée, 184
Vergennes, Comte de (Charles Gravier), 95
Vetch, Samuel, 57
Vietnamese immigrants, 277
Vigneault, Gilles, 338
Villeneuve, Cardinal Jean-Marie-Rodrigue, 187, 195, 199
The Vindicator (newspaper), 115, 122
Virginians, 74, 75
Voltaire, 84
Voltigeurs, 108
voting rights, women's, 130, 165, 198–199
Voyages en Nouvelle-France, (Champlain), 33

• W •

Walker, Hovenden, 57, 58
War Measures Act, 167, 169, 259
War of 1812, 107–108
War of the Austrian Succession (1744–1748), 68
War of the Spanish Succession (1702–1713), 55–58

Washington, George, 74, 75, 93, 94
welfare state, 221–223, 241, 292
Wells, Clyde, 299, 301
Wells, Maine, 56
Wendake, 350
wheat production, 64, 109
William III, king of England, 52
Winthrop, John, 53
Wolfe, James, 78–81, 345
women
  civil code of 1866, 144–145
  famine of 1757–1758, 77
  feminists, 165, 170, 198, 260, 299, 322
  filles du roy, 46–48
  loss of voting rights, 130
  marriage, 17–18th centuries, 48, 61, 62, 69
  Muslim, 322, 323
  pensions for needy mothers, 185
  piety, 67
  Polytechnique massacre (1989), 299
  pro-birth policy of 1660s, 48
  religious orders, 134
  1660s–1670s, 46
  struggle for equality (1960s), 232–233
  voting rights, 130, 165, 198–199
wood (lumber; timber), 29, 65, 104, 109, 159, 171, 176
workers, 160. *See also* strikes; unions
  Action Libérale Nationale, 183
  early retirement plan, 312
  indentured, 22, 33, 48, 59, 60
  Lanctôt, 147
  miners of Asbestos, 208–209
  1901-1931, 172
  unemployment, 175–178, 186, 193, 286
  women, 165
workforce agreement (1997), 315
World War I, conscription crisis, 167–169
World War II, 191–197, 202, 203, 349

• Y •

YMCA, 323
young people, 181, 218, 238, 241, 242, 249, 287, 325, 326
"Yvette" gaffe, 281

About the Author

Éric Bédard was born in 1969. He holds a doctorate in history from McGill University and a degree from the Institut d'Études Politiques de Paris. He is a professor at TÉLUQ, the distance learning institute of the Université du Québec. His previous works include *Recours aux sources: essais sur notre rapport au passé (Use of Sources: Essays on Our Relationship with the Past)*, published by Boréal in 2011 and winner of the Prix Richard-Arès, and *Les Réformistes: une génération canadienne-française au milieu du XIXe siècle (The Reformers: A French-Canadian Generation in the Mid-19th Century)*, published by Boréal in 2009 and winner of the Prix Clio-Québec and the Prix de la Présidence de l'Assemblée Nationale du Québec. Professor Bédard writes a weekly history column that appears each Sunday in *Le Journal de Montréal* and *Le Journal de Québec*.

Dedication

I would like to dedicate this book to Marc Frenette and Denis Jetté, two people who have had a huge influence on me.

My uncle Marc Frenette was my first history teacher. His patience is legendary, and he is a fantastic storyteller with a phenomenal memory. Throughout my life, his generosity toward me has been tremendous. I owe him and his wife, Huguette, my father's sister, a great deal.

Denis Jetté, a teacher at the Collège des Eudistes, also provided enormous inspiration. His course on Quebec history in the fourth year of high school was a *tour de force!* His keen knowledge of the great events and leading figures in our history, his sense of narrative and synthesis, and his natural authority greatly impressed the teenager I was then.

In families and in schools, people like these instill a passion for history. Quebec is greatly in their debt.

Author's Acknowledgments

I would like, first and foremost, to thank the team at my French publisher, Les Éditions First, that guided me throughout this joyous adventure. A big thank-you to Jean-Joseph Julaud, the author of *L'histoire de France pour les Nuls (French History For Dummies),* for his friendly invitation; to Benjamin Arranger, the head of publishing, for his close collaboration and his rigor; and to Vincent Barbare, the firm's top executive, for his contagious enthusiasm. These "cousins" in France had long been looking for a Quebec historian to write *History of Quebec For Dummies*.

I wish to thank Wiley Canada for making this book available to all Canadians and to English speakers around the world who take an interest in the history of Quebec and seek to better understand the aspirations of the Quebec people. A special thank you to Production Editor Pauline Ricablanca for her diligence and to the team at John Aylen Communications for the translation.

Writing this book often required relying on the work of colleagues. Some of them had the great kindness to review certain chapters. I thank Gervais Carpin, Gilles Gallichan, Xavier Gélinas, Georges Aubin, and Frédéric Bastien for looking over my work. I also thank David Camirand, who was especially helpful in the preparation of the "Groups of Ten."

I thank my wife, Nadja, and my children, Nora and Arthur, who showed infinite patience during the summer of 2012. Their encouragement and support proved essential. Thank you to my mother, Jeannine, for her generosity, her good humor, and her unshakable faith in each of her three children. And thank you to my father, Alexandre, a decent, optimistic, and wise man.

Thank you to all those friends who urged me to take on this project. Special thanks to Myriam D'Arcy, who generously agreed to review each chapter and for her faith in this book, and to Mathieu Bock-Côté, Gilles Laporte, and Charles-Philippe Courtois.

Publisher's Acknowledgments

Assistant Acquisitions Editor: Anam Ahmed

Production Editor: Pauline Ricablanca

Copy Editor: Elizabeth Kuball

Editorial Assistant: Kathy Deady

Translators: John Aylen Communications—
Eric Hamovitch, Bob Chodos, and
Susan Joanis

Cartographer: De Visu

Cover Image Credit: © iStockphoto.com /
Maridav

Project Coordinator: Kristie Rees

Layout and Graphics: Jennifer Creasey,
Ron Wise

Proofreaders: Lindsay Amones, Susan Moritz,
Lisa Young Stiers

Indexer: Riverside Indexes, Inc.